PYRAMID RISING

THE GREAT PYRAMID RECONSTRUCTED

PYRAMID RISING

THE GREAT PYRAMID RECONSTRUCTED

RANDY L. GRIFFITH AND M.K. WELSCH

EVENING STAR PUBLISHING

Virginia Beach, Virginia

Evening Star Publishing
eveningstarpublishing@gmail.com
www.eveningstarpublishing.com

Book and interior design by The Book Cover Whisperer: openbookdesign.biz
Illustrations by R.L. Griffith

Publisher's Cataloging-In-Publication Data

(Prepared by The Donohue Group, Inc.)

Names: Griffith, Randy L., author, illustrator. | Welsch, M. K., author.

Title: Pyramid rising : the Great Pyramid reconstructed / Randy L. Griffith and M.K. Welsch.

Description: Virginia Beach, Virginia : Evening Star Publishing, [2022]

Identifiers: ISBN 9781737723103 (paperback) | ISBN 9781737723110 (ebook)

Subjects: LCSH: Great Pyramid (Egypt)--Design and construction--Pictorial works. | LCGFT: Illustrated works.

Classification: LCC DT63 .G75 2022 (print) | LCC DT63 (ebook) | DDC 726.10932--dc23

1st printing, January, 2022

Library of Congress Control Number: 2021919902

978-1-7377231-0-3 Paperback
978-1-7377231-1-0 eBook

Printed in the U.S.A.

In memory of June

*This book is dedicated to
the people of Egypt with
appreciation for preserving
a priceless treasure—and
sharing its wonders
with the world.*

"Many hidden truths
are often unobserved,
not invisible."

— Matthew A. Petti

CONTENTS

LIST OF FIGURES

ACKNOWLEDGMENTS

IT TAKES MANY GENERATIONS to make a pyramid rise — and many midwives to help give birth to a book about the process, especially one as complex as a study of the Great Pyramid of Giza. We owe an enormous debt of gratitude to a lot of people for their assistance during the years-long effort to make *Pyramid Rising* a reality. Some are no longer with us, but their contributions will never be forgotten.

First, it is important to express our deep appreciation for the work of the 20th-century psychic Edgar Cayce, whose readings have left an indelible mark on the world. His insights about the origins of humanity and ancient sacred sites across the globe were the catalysts that led us to dig deeper into the subject of the Great Pyramid. Our thanks, too, to the Association for Research and Enlightenment (ARE) in Virginia Beach, Virginia, which preserves and disseminates the wisdom found in the Cayce material to people everywhere seeking to better understand the great mysteries of life.

This book would not have seen the light of day without the inspiration and unflagging encouragement of the Egypt Group at the ARE: Elizabeth Waitekus, Camille McLean, Jo Ella Todd, Dan Urton, Lori Alaniva, Gail Sines, Alison Ray, Cathy Mann, Julia Edwards, and our two "members in spirit," Ann Clapp and June Bro.

We also want to extend our deep appreciation to the many friends and colleagues who, from the beginning, expressed their support in countless ways, large and small. To Kevin Todeschi, who thought enough of the Griffith theory to request an article about it for *Venture Inward* magazine, and to Don Carroll, who wrote the article. Our thanks, too, to Jim Sewards who, when he learned about the theory and heard about the book, decided to help further the cause with the gift of a new computer, which took Randy's research to the next level.

In addition, we were privileged to have access to a collection of incredible photographs due to the generosity of the individuals who own the copyrights. John Van Auken graciously allowed us to reproduce several pictures from his numerous visits to Egypt. Dr. Roland Enmarch, senior lecturer in Egyptology at the University of Liverpool, gave us permission to include his photo of the post holes at the ancient quarry at Hatnub — an early indication of the possible use of pulleys. And Dr. Randall J. Strossen, president of IronMind Enterprises, Inc., provided his company's dramatic image of a worker in a harness pulling an airplane — a 21st-century example of how much weight a group of men in harnesses tethered to a pull-rope might have been able to move.

Our eagle-eyed copyeditor, Ruth E. Thaler-Carter, deserves kudos and thanks for ensuring that the pieces of an unpolished manuscript were stitched together into a cohesive whole and that the text was grammatically correct from start to finish. We also had the privilege of working with an extraordinarily talented book designer, Christine, the Book Cover Whisperer. Our thanks to her for both creating a breathtaking cover with more impact than we ever could have imagined and turning thousands of words of text into an artful graphic presentation.

Saving the best for last, we will forever be grateful for the constant, loving support of our families. Conceiving and writing a work as detailed as *Pyramid Rising* was a daunting task spanning far too many years. But through it all, it was knowing we had our cheering squads behind us every step of the way that kept us going. Thanks to James, Jana, Kali, and John for always being there, lighting up Randy's life, and to every member of the Welsch family — my steady source of inspiration and help. Your love and encouragement made all the difference. We could not have done it without you.

PREFACE

THE SEEDS THAT GREW into this book were planted decades ago. In 1996, an ironworker named Randy Griffith was riding on a scissor lift inside a building under construction when the lift fell over. The serious accident kept him bedridden for months. There was an unusual upside to the lengthy recuperation process, however: Randy began reading about metaphysics and spirituality, including delving into the work of renowned 20th-century psychic Edgar Cayce.

With a lot of time on his hands and based on some of the advice Cayce gave, the former ironworker decided to start meditating regularly. Much to his surprise, quieting down and going within opened the door to a whole new world and way of thinking. It also sparked an avid interest in exploring some of the great mysteries of the universe. The trail eventually led him to undertake deep research on what is arguably the most investigated monument in history: the Great Pyramid of Giza. His incredible journey of discovery was the genesis of this book; a journey that continues to this day.

Having worked around construction sites his entire adult life, Randy — like thousands of people before him — was intrigued by the question of how a supposedly primitive culture inhabiting the Earth thousands of years ago was able to fabricate such an astonishingly large and elegant edifice. One path of inquiry soon led to another and then another, until he was hooked on finding out more about how the Great Pyramid was actually built. Spending hours reading about the subject, including analyzing several of the more esoteric texts, such as the *Egyptian Book of the Dead*, he kept asking himself a simple question: If an ironworker were told to build this structure, how would they go about it?

To wit, ironworkers regularly use cranes on the job site to lift the materials they want to raise higher. Wouldn't the ancient Egyptians have relied on some kind of crane-like object to pile up the stones for the 200+ layers of their pyramid, too? Furthermore, could it be possible that some of the images and symbols painted on tomb walls or found among the hieroglyphs in ancient texts represent pulleys? With those insights, the possibility of using the height and angle of the pyramid's air shafts as potential lifting mechanisms entered the realm of possibility. And a new theory was born.

Randy has spent the years since his accident researching and studying every aspect of the Great Pyramid to determine a plausible yet creative explanation for how the construction process might have unfolded. After more than two decades of work, his research and modeling of various scenarios finally reached the point where the pieces had fallen into place and it was time to release the broad outlines of his theory to the general public. *Pyramid Rising* is the result of that effort to elucidate what we are calling the Griffith theory.

The Griffith theory may appear to be new to the 21st century but in many ways, it is as old as the Great Pyramid itself, for it lets the pyramid speak — and builds on the foundation of what this baffling structure is trying to tell us. Taking into account the monument's many disparate components, the new theory, unlike many previous hypotheses, does not bypass the interior spaces, which historically have been left out of the conversation because they are difficult to explain. Rather, it offers a clear-cut explanation for all of the visible chambers and passageways, based in part on the functions they performed in the overall building process. This latest attempt to solve one of the riddles of the ages offers viable reasons for as many elements of the pyramid as possible — from the Subterranean Chamber to the missing capstone.

Because the Great Pyramid undeniably surpasses any structure we could ever hope to build, either then or today, some researchers firmly believe it must have been erected by entities possessing super-human intelligence and advanced technology, far exceeding the limited scope of our finest 21st-century inventions. They want to credit its construction to beings from outer space. We believe that laying the creation of the Great Pyramid at the feet of anyone other than the human race short-changes the boundless creativity and capacity of the human mind and spirit. The Cayce readings agree and describe the Great Pyramid as the product of a century of work by a highly evolved ancient Egyptian civilization some 10,500 years BCE — long before the date attributed to it by conventional archeology.

There is little doubt in our minds that human beings then — as now — were fully capable of not only generating inspiring works of art and literature able to lift consciousness to new heights, but also to solve the thorniest engineering problems in ways that we can only imagine today. What would a farmer living in the 18th century think if he suddenly stumbled upon a cellphone? That same level of awe and sense of "I'm looking at something utterly impossible" is how many regard the Great Pyramid of Giza. In both instances, the viewer tends to underestimate what the human family has been capable of accomplishing down through the long arc of history.

We make no claims that the manner in which pyramid construction proceeded is 100% accurate in every instance and particular as described in this book. At the same time, we believe the basic ideas underlying the new theory are sound, even if every detail is not perfect. Needless to say, the attempt to glean hidden knowledge by looking back many thousands of years through the dim light of the past presents enormous challenges for even the most storied researchers.

Our hope is that the Griffith theory will start a conversation and inspire countless other inventive and dedicated individuals — archeologists and Egyptologists, amateur pyramid investigators, academics, professional architects, and construction engineers — to work with these ideas and suggest ways to refine and strengthen the approach. Drawing upon the creativity of a worldwide network of Great Pyramid enthusiasts can only help all of us learn more about this extraordinary monument and better unlock the mysteries it may still hold.

One final note. Among the many complicating factors facing any author writing a book about the Great Pyramid of Giza is the abundance of excellent resources and points of reference already extant in the public arena. At the time of publication, Randy Griffith had not yet had the opportunity to visit Egypt and examine the Great Pyramid of Giza for himself. As a result, most of the dimensions and other data presented here were drawn from outside sources: books, pictures, videos, news articles, academic research papers, and related materials. Many fine professionals with the highest level of expertise (some of them considered giants in the field of pyramidology) have contributed greatly to the world's understanding of this subject. In some cases, a compilation of their findings on particular aspects of the Great Pyramid has been woven into the text in support of the Griffith theory.

To remain consistent, the vast majority of the measurements used throughout *Pyramid Rising* were drawn from a single source. While Egyptologists may disagree among themselves about whose numbers are correct; in most cases, the tiny, multi-decimal variations in the totals recorded for the length, breadth, and height of a block, room, or passageway were not material to the evidence at hand as the framework of the Griffith theory developed. Consequently, in general, we have chosen to use the numbers compiled in late 1800s by the renowned Egyptologist Sir William Matthew Flinders Petrie from start to finish, since numerous scholars and other knowledgeable researchers consider him to be the forefather of Great Pyramid calculations.

One additional piece of information is worth noting: The illustrations supporting the text are for explanatory purposes only and were not drawn to scale.

All of these millennia later, it is impossible to know with precision the sequence and timing of every event involved in the pyramid's construction. Consequently, in a few instances, we have taken creative license by presenting several potential options in an effort to offer the most plausible explanation for how the ancient Egyptians may have carried out their work. Our goal was to highlight the simplest and most direct route that would make the different elements of the construction operation fit together seamlessly. While we cannot claim with certainty that each and every step is spot-on, we fervently believe that the overarching parameters and principles underlying the Griffith theory are correct.

This book is the culmination of a very long process, one that continues to this day. Because until the enigmatic Great Pyramid of Giza divulges all of its secrets, the job will never be done.

M.K. Welsch

December 2021

CHAPTER 1

A MYSTERY FOR THE AGES

THE GREAT PYRAMID OF Giza, the most studied, measured, and celebrated structure on Earth, stands like a mountain on Egypt's desert sands, challenging us to unlock its secrets. A source of inspiration and awe, the pyramid evokes a feeling of mystery in all who encounter its presence. Yet even as we gaze in wonder at this architectural marvel, a sense of frustration persists, because for centuries, the Great Pyramid has mocked every attempt to satisfy our curiosity about its origins. We know that it exists, but no one can say with certainty how it came to be. The ever-elusive truth lies hidden in the mists of time.

Today, most students of the Great Pyramid tend to follow the well-worn path of mainstream archeology, which claims that a society wholly ignorant of the most elementary tenets of structural design was able to produce an edifice that not only rivals but exceeds the engineering prowess of the greatest buildings of the 21st century. Historians keep trying to reconcile the magnificence of a monument seemingly impossible to reproduce with traditional ideas about the low level of sophistication of the ancient Egyptian culture, when somehow, against all odds, this "primitive" people fashioned an extraordinary marker on the Earth, one still standing many millennia after it was built.

It strains credulity to believe that a structure reflecting the genius, proportion, and mathematical and astronomical precision of the Great Pyramid was constructed by a community incapable of understanding the wheel or the principle behind simple machines like the pulley.

To the contrary, the novel perspective outlined in this book — named the Griffith theory — is rooted in the conviction that the early Egyptians were ingenious master builders well versed in the principles of architecture, engineering, and heavy construction. The people alive at the time the Great Pyramid was rising from the Giza Plateau were quite capable of using industrial-type tools to their advantage. These ancient builders not only developed intricate systems to raise massive blocks of stone but also fit the pieces together flawlessly to create their Great Pyramid — a building unmatched in the history of the world.

A New Theory

Theories about how the Great Pyramid was constructed abound and circulate regularly in the public forum. Countless scholars, explorers, and scientists, many of them highly credentialed, have studied the pyramid in depth and proposed fascinating ideas about its origins, sparking ongoing discussion and debate. Pyramid enthusiasts searching for evidence have dissected every aspect of the building, from the sizes and angles of the chambers and shafts to the color of the stones and the seams in between them. Some people have investigated the pyramid's components as if they were studying the parts of an energy transmission station, while others have suggested possible links to aliens from outer space. Still, the central question remains unanswered: Who built the Great Pyramid of Giza and how did they do it?

By far, the majority of the prevailing theories about its origins describe the styles of ramp the builders must have used. Despite the challenges and limitations inherent in the one-giant-ramp hypothesis, which would have required work crews pulling millions of heavy blocks uphill against the force of gravity in record time, the single-ramp theory is difficult to dispel. But the ancient Egyptians were smart; smart enough not to construct their building twice, since an exterior ramp reaching the peak would have consumed more raw material than the pyramid itself. Equally daunting, once they approached the summit, the angle of the slope would have made it impossible to transport the giant loads up such a steep grade.

Similarly, an internal ramp corkscrewing around the perimeter of the structure inevitably would result in corners too tight for the huge blocks of limestone and granite inside the pyramid to navigate. Just as troubling, most of the theories now in vogue tend to ignore the fact that the interior of the Great Pyramid contains passageways and rooms, along with unexpected architectural features such as the colossal formation known as the Relieving Chambers. The cases these theoreticians make seldom pay much attention to the interior spaces or provide cogent explanations of how (or why) they were erected.

The Griffith theory takes a leap forward by precluding the need for massive ramps climbing upward at untenable angles, and proposes a novel approach to the pyramid's development. To wit, the new paradigm states that the Great Pyramid was built from the inside-out. The people of ancient Egypt constructed their impressive, more-than-400-foot-tall monument layer by layer by making use of the elements they had already put in place as the springboards for building higher.

The suppositions underlying the new theory evolved from one man's attempt to crawl inside the heads of the original builders and better understand their train of thought by viewing it through the lens of what we see in the pyramid today. When those early architects and engineers imagined the task before them, what did they understand would work? By employing a process of "reverse engineering" to deconstruct how the puzzle pieces fit together, patterns began to emerge and the bigger picture gradually came into focus.

The Griffith theory starts from the premise that nothing found inside the Great Pyramid is extraneous; each component had a purpose. Every shaft, angle, grooved wall, corridor, and quarried block showed up for a reason — to either aid in the construction process and/or relay some kind of message to the future.

For example, a key insight into the builders' methodology was the realization that the channels now referred to as air shafts are actually the remnants of four internal ramps. During most of their history, these passageways were large enough for regular-sized blocks to pass through them. Furthermore, their position on the north and south sides allowed engineers to quarter the primary work space. By assigning course construction to four separate work gangs, the buildout would progress faster and more efficiently than having a single distribution team tackle the entire multi-acre surface area. Only much later, as the number of levels increased and the stacks of courses grew taller than the top of each internal ramp, rendering that channel useless for raising more stones, did the construction crew shrink the size of the shafts with upside-down, U-shaped blocks to create the tight openings evident inside the King's and Queen's chambers today.

It is important to note that the theory presented in these pages diverges widely from the accepted scholarship in several other important ways. First, it places construction of the Great Pyramid within a much earlier timeframe — approximately 10,500 BCE — based in part on information found in the Edgar Cayce readings. The Cayce material paints a different portrait of the human story than the one normally taught in schools. Instead of viewing life on Earth as a straight linear progression, the readings describe the twists and turns of history as a cyclical process extending far back into the pre-recorded past, and traces humanity's intellectual and spiritual development through a series of peaks and valleys. Civilizations rose and fell, as did individuals' understanding of how the material world they inhabited worked. Construction of the Great Pyramid, which according to this source took at least a century to complete, occurred during one of the peaks, thousands of years before the date attributed to it in conventional history books.

GOBEKLI TEPE PILLAR
Carved pillar from Gobeckli Tepe.

No doubt a timeframe of 10,500 BCE stretches the imagination. Yet that date comports with the discovery of the stunning megalithic structures and sculptures found at Gobekli Tepe in southeastern Turkey. Approximately 12,000 years old, the Gobekli Tepe site, called the world's oldest temple, exudes a level of craftsmanship that defies description. The discovery of Gobekli Tepe sent shock waves through the archeological world and has upended long-standing ideas about the rise of civilizations across the globe. Under the new theory, the date of its establishment would make Gobekli Tepe a near-contemporary of the Great Pyramid, proving that the ability to produce megalithic monuments reflective of a high order of precision, complexity, and design must have been present on the Earth at that time.

SPHINX EROSION

According to some geologists, the Sphinx and its enclosure exhibit signs of water erosion, which may be the result of rainwater runoff during a more fertile period in Egypt's history.

Similarly, geological research into some of the erosional features found on the Giza Plateau has assigned a much earlier age than previously considered to the oldest portions or core-body of the Sphinx and its enclosure. The findings support a construction date before 5,000 BCE and well within a range extending as far back as 10,000 BCE — significantly older than the timeframe usually cited (ca. 2,500 BCE). While some New Age interpretations of this alternative view of history claim that the people living during that earlier epoch had access to more advanced forms of technology, the Griffith theory does not take a radical stance in terms of defining the equipment the ancient Egyptians may have used during construction. It describes a pyramid built by people with a basic knowledge of the most rudimentary tools: ropes, levers, knots, sleds, chisels, hammers, and pulleys.

In fact, the new approach places the humble pulley front and center in the birth of the Great Pyramid and reveals how this machine factored into critical design choices the builders made. One of the more obvious clues to their thinking and planning is the arrangement of the known chambers and passageways. Researchers have long wondered about the placement of the interior cavities because the layout is so unusual. Their relative positions beg the question: Why did the Egyptians erect all of them on a single axis? There must have been a reason behind the decision to build along a straight line, running north-south about 23 feet east of the pyramid's centerline, and never spread out east to west. The answer lay at the heart of the builders' construction strategy, a strategy dependent upon an extensive pulley system. Lining up the open spaces is what allowed that system to work.

The narrow slice of the Great Pyramid encompassing the few rooms and shafts discovered to date permitted ropes coming from the highest available level on either the north or south side and drop down the middle of the passage toward the bottom. By taking the lines and connecting them together in sequence, a work crew would have been able to string a rope descending from many stories overhead all the way down to the Subterranean Chamber. In short, a series of strategically placed pulleys working in unison — orchestrated top to bottom as a single mechanical device — produced a powerful, multifaceted pulling system. In time, this relatively simple technology was capable of elevating a sled or stone from the spot where it first arrived on-site up hundreds of feet to the summit.

The essential factor in successfully implementing a lifting system of this type was mounting rollers or pulleys at critical junctures where a change in elevation or the angle of a shaft occurred to either redirect the ropes or organize them for a pull. Equally important was determining the equipment needed at the center of the operation to assist in raising the loads. A geared apparatus lodged in the strange, corbelled niche in the east wall of the Queen's Chamber is one solution the Griffith theory proposes. and a giant wooden lift traveling up and down the Grand Gallery is another. Also adding heft to the lifting process was an enormous counterweight pulled along by an oversized wheel rotating in the Subterranean Chamber.

Perhaps most jarring to our current understanding of the Great Pyramid is the new theory's assertion, consistent with ideas put forth in the Edgar Cayce readings, that it was not built as a tomb. Up to now, archeologists have never found a mummified human body inside any major Egyptian pyramid, including this one. True, from time to time, they have unearthed the remains of deceased pharaohs from the distant past, but in general, those bodies were discovered in underground tombs in places such as the Valley of the Kings. The Griffith theory contends that the pyramid was never meant to be a burial chamber but was always conceived as a sacred space. When the work was done and the building dedicated, the Great Pyramid served as a Temple of Initiation.

It is no surprise, then, that the plot of land the ancient Egyptians ultimately chose for their staggering construction project incorporated a site on the Giza Plateau that had been sacred to their civilization for generations. And once the perfect spot was chosen, they were ready to build.

• Did Khufu Build •
the Great Pyramid?

The Griffith theory diverges widely from the accepted archeological record by placing the inception of the Great Pyramid of Giza at approximately 10,500 BCE. Consequently, the revised construction date makes it impossible to credit Khufu as the pharaoh responsible for erecting this monument. Instead, the new theory maintains that during Khufu's reign, he merely decided to refurbish what already existed and in so doing, left his mark on history.

Recent discoveries in Egypt of a diary and logbook written on ancient papyri have shed light on the daily activities of some of his laborers.

For example, a worker named Merer describes sailing blocks downriver from the quarries at Tura during the flood season to the artificial basins or canals at the foot of the pyramid site. (By Khufu's time, the Nile River had meandered many miles east of the Giza Plateau.) The highly polished blocks of limestone transported on board were probably the raw materials needed to repair or replace missing and broken pieces of the pyramid's blinding white cladding.

The Egyptians were master builders who planned meticulously and not only coordinated an extremely complicated project, but also kept it advancing relentlessly forward. That said, an edifice of the size and stature of the Great Pyramid would have taken far longer than 20 to 30 years to complete — the outer boundaries of Khufu's reign. Even assuming 24-hour work shifts, the logistics and effort involved to accomplish a feat of that magnitude is mind-boggling. Construction activity lasting at least 100 years reflects a much more realistic time-frame, which puts it out of reach of the Khufu period.

In attributing the original construction work to the Pharaoh Khufu, researchers say the pyramid was built as his tomb, which provides the incentive to claim that the job must have been started and finished during his lifetime, i.e., before the funeral. But the sarcophagus inside the King's Chamber is empty and the bare walls completely devoid of any of the ritualistic artwork that usually graced the tomb where a pharaoh was laid to rest. The Griffith theory contends that scholars have paid tribute to Khufu for the work of others and inaccurately named the Great Pyramid after him.

At the same time, Khufu undoubtedly had an outsized impact on the Great Pyramid if he were indeed responsible for patching up what may have been a mammoth building in a state of grave disrepair. Over-hauling the pyramid was no small task. Moreover, it seems logical that a pharaoh confronted with such a magnificent structure on his watch might want to restore it to its original luster, and in the process, possibly take credit for the entire enterprise. Given the evidence, the restoration hypothesis seems both reasonable and appropriate, for even in the 21st century, the experts charged with overseeing Egypt's antiquities continue to refurbish portions of the Great Pyramid as the need arises.

KHUFU

The only image of the Pharaoh Khufu discovered to date is a three-inch-tall ivory statuette in the Egyptian Museum in Cairo.

CHAPTER 2

SETTING THE FOUNDATION

THE GREAT PYRAMID OF Giza is constructed somewhat like a layer cake, with individually stacked levels that are composed of the different strata found in the limestone surrounding the Giza Plateau. Each layer is called a course. As originally designed and built, the structure had a total of 210 courses. Yet only 203 remain today, due to the fact that the blocks near the top, which comprised the final approximately 30 feet of the structure, and its capstone, are missing. The monolith's 13.6-acre-square base sits directly on the bedrock of the Giza Plateau. Significantly, when the ancient Egyptians first quarried the site, they had already determined with laser-like precision exactly where the apex of their pyramid was going to be. And each succeeding decision stemmed from that single detail.

• By the Stars •

According to archeologist Mark Lehner, Ph.D., a theory developed by the English Egyptologist I.E.S. Edwards explains how the ancient Egyptians may have oriented the sides of the pyramid on the landscape by using the stars and a circular, level wall that acted as an artificial horizon. "His method involved building a circular wall a few feet in diameter and tall enough to exclude all but the night sky from the view of a person standing inside … A person in the center of the circle facing north would select a star and mark its rising and setting points at the top of the wall. These points would be extended to the foot of the wall using a plumb line and joined to the centre of the circle. North was the bisection of the angle of the lines at the centre."[1]

On a more metaphysical basis, choosing the correct location for the pyramid was also associated with the surveyor goddess, Seshat, who was in charge of writing and measurement and referred to as the ruler of books. Believed to be the scribe or record-keeper, Seshat was considered an expert in the art of sighting the stars and planets. She was also recorded as having assisted the pharaoh in the "stretching of the cord" ceremony, which was part of the foundation rituals for laying out ground boundaries and determining the structural placement of temples and shrines. The ancient Egyptians gave her the epithet "Mistress of the House of Architects."

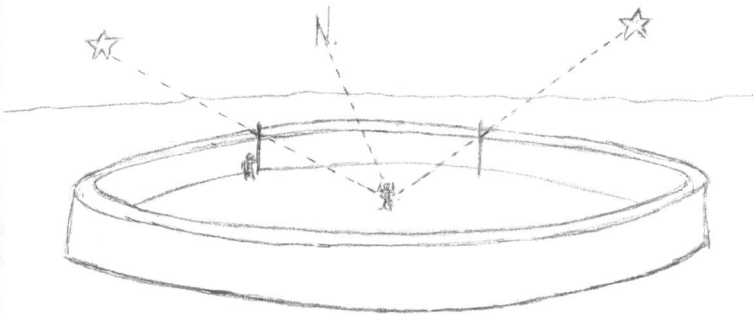

BY THE STARS

1. Mark Lehner, *The Complete Pyramids: Solving the Ancient Mysteries* (London: Thames & Hudson, 2008), 212

Like any savvy construction crew, the team of ancient builders responsible for erecting the Great Pyramid would have prepared the ground before beginning their work. Despite how it may appear at first glance from the outside, the land below the pyramid's foundation was never a totally smooth plane. They would have calculated the rises and drops in the layers of rock endemic to the plateau itself as part of the overall design.

The base of the pyramid also reveals an unexpected feature: It appears as if the monument is sitting on top of a wide dome protruding from the ground.

The Griffith theory speculates that this anomaly was the result of the builders' decision to construct the Great Pyramid over a smaller pyramid, which was probably a shrine dedicated to the god Osiris. The image of Osiris portrayed in sacred texts and on tomb walls depicts his throne atop a pyramid surrounded by water. Archeologists suspect that the Egyptians chose this particular site on the Giza Plateau because of its religious significance to their culture.

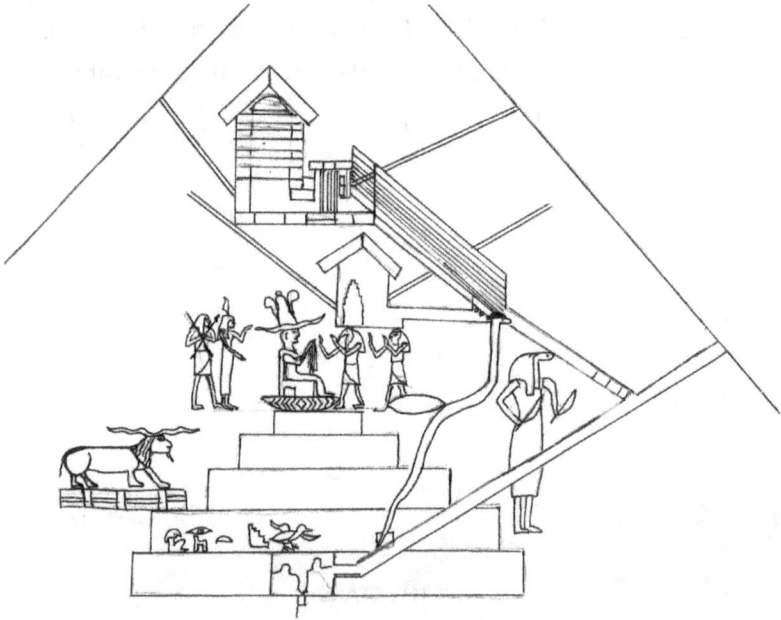

GREENFIELD PAPYRUS WITH OVERLAY

The image of Osiris on his throne at the center of this illustration is from the famous Greenfield Papyrus, housed in the British Museum. Curiously, the position of the serpent on the right and the way it bends and curves resembles the placement of the Well Shaft inside the Great Pyramid. Overlaying a schematic drawing of the Great Pyramid with the section of the Greenfield Papyrus shown here reveals a possible connection between the pyramid and the mythological throne of Osiris situated below it.

The hallowed memorial honoring Osiris, which rose as high as 45 feet tall, would have already been ancient by the time the Egyptians started to build, and may have covered a good portion of the multi-acre expanse beneath the Great Pyramid. Those early shrine builders would have created their memorial by carving the bedrock down into the shape of a crude mound resembling a squat step-pyramid with rough edges. No one knows what the exact dimensions or outline of this legendary structure might have been, since the steps eventually disappeared among the thousands of blocks of quarried limestone placed around it.

Because Egypt had more rainfall during this period of time, the construction site was green and lush, with the water table much higher than it is today. The Griffith theory posits that both the spot chosen for the Great Pyramid and overall design plans took into account the fact that the edifice would sit over what was then — more than 12,000 years ago — an underground lake fed by the Nile River at flood stage or a natural spring. If the strategy we believe the ancient architects pursued is correct, the relatively stubby step-pyramid located underground would have allowed the Egyptians to position their new building above that body of water on a site that had been sacred to them for thousands of years. From the moment of its conception, the Great Pyramid was destined to incorporate the magic and mystery of the god of death and resurrection into its very DNA.

Four Corners

Before the Egyptians could begin to go higher by building up, they had to establish the pyramid's corners and accurately chart the dimensions of the future monument. (The Great Pyramid is aligned to true north.) Taking into account the contours of the land, they laid down stones where the four corners would be by inserting large blocks of limestone deep into the bedrock as the first step toward making the foundation perfectly even all the way around.

In that same vein, workers laid giant limestone blocks on the ground in a straight line from corner to corner to delineate the outer perimeter of the pyramid's square, 13.6-acre base. The blocks comprising the row of border stones, which encircle the entire site, were huge — at least 10 feet long, 10 feet wide, and several feet thick — and sculpted on the bottom to conform to specific variations in the land. Leveling such enormous pieces of limestone was undoubtedly a very difficult task, but nonetheless an important one because as construction proceeds, the exterior walls for the pyramid's first course would rest atop these border stones, positioned just a few feet back from the outside edge.

In the past, the Great Pyramid's outer walls hid almost 99% of the surface of the huge blocks that surrounded the base. But since its Tura limestone façade is now missing, the row of blocks lined up at the bottom of the building is mostly visible today. Possibly set into place more than 12 millennia ago, the series of 10-foot-long limestone blocks ringing the Great Pyramid still serves as an impromptu walkway for tourists in the 21st century.

BASE BLOCKS

Example of the gigantic limestone blocks found at the base of the Great Pyramid.

Descending Passage

Perhaps the biggest step the construction team took in preparing to build the enormous pyramid that one day would soar above the Giza Plateau was to excavate a steep tunnel directly out of the bedrock. Positioned roughly parallel to the opening known as the Inspection or Well Shaft and lined with finished blocks of stone above ground, the Descending Passage runs north to south for almost 350 feet, declining at a 26-degree angle. Curiously, the north end of the long channel points directly to the position of the Pole Star during that period in history — an exceptional feat of engineering — and terminates at the entrance to a large horizontal room called the Subterranean Chamber, also dug out of the bedrock.

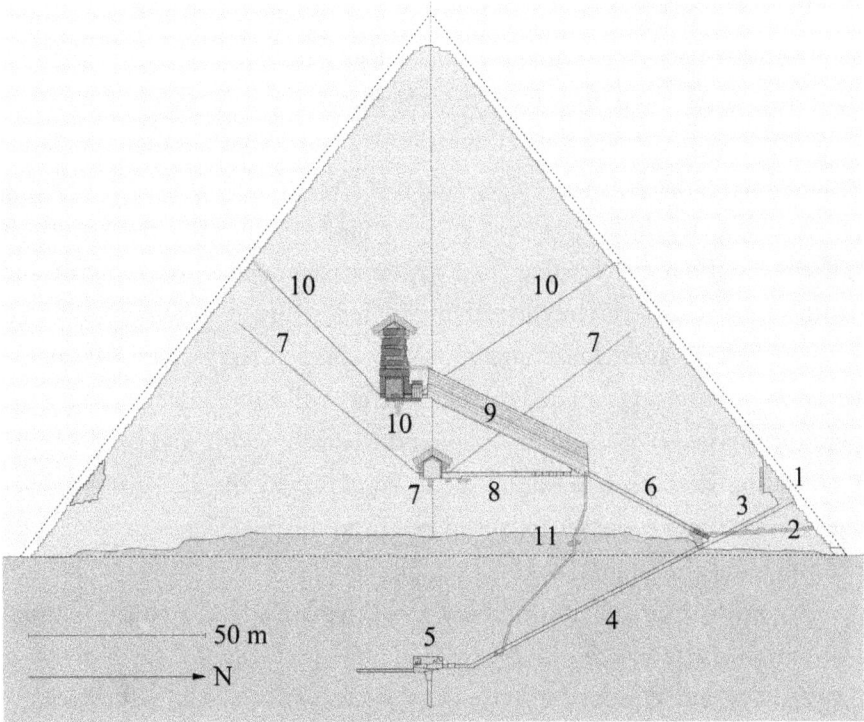

PYRAMID DIAGRAM WITH KEY

1. Original entrance to the Great Pyramid at Course 19.
2. Current visitor entrance created from a hole dug out by explorer Al-Ma'mun in the 9th century.
3. Upper end of the Descending Passage.
4. Segment of the Descending Passage excavated from the bedrock.
5. Subterranean Chamber.
6. First Ascending Passage.
7. Queen's Chamber and the air shafts on the north and south sides.
8. Horizontal Passage — also known as the Queen's Chamber Passage.
9. Grand Gallery.
10. King's Chamber with its northern and southern air shafts that pierce the outer walls.
11. Ancient mound on which the Great Pyramid is built.

Why did the Egyptians take the time and effort to chisel out a long, sloping passageway and human-made enclosure hidden deep below the surface? The purpose and function of these elements of the pyramid's design may have been twofold: metaphysical and mechanical. From the more technical standpoint, the Descending Passage filled an industrial purpose. While many previous theories about the Great Pyramid tend to ignore this passageway, it makes no sense to believe that the Egyptians expended all of that time and energy excavating a tunnel more than 300 feet long out of solid rock for no apparent reason. There must have been some compelling rationale behind the decision to create an extended corridor and cave-like room deep beneath the pyramid's base — especially an opening the length, width, and height of the Descending Passage. Unraveling the mystery of why the ancients did what they did becomes easier when considered from the perspective of solving an exceptionally challenging engineering problem.

According to the Griffith theory, the Egyptians developed the unusual underground arrangement as part of the infrastructure for a complex counterweight system designed to raise the sleds and stones required to actually build the Great Pyramid. In short, the cavities carved out of the bedrock were part of a strategic, highly organized, and efficient operation to construct the seemingly impossible. The underground openings provided both the angles and space the builders needed to multiply the available pulling power. By employing a substantial stone mass in the form of a counterweight rising and falling belowground, assisted by a rolling wheel and spool of rope circling a moving drum, the ancient Egyptians would have the capacity to elevate extraordinarily heavy blocks of stone hundreds of feet overhead. Further proof of the purpose and value of this innovative setup would become clear once the pyramid's courses began to rise.

Well Shaft

Supporting this novel interpretation of the pyramid's origins is a fairly narrow hole visible inside the pyramid in the west wall of the Grand Gallery, close to the entrance to the First Ascending Passage. Covered by a grate to keep inquisitive visitors out, the unexpected cavity marks the upper end of the channel Egyptologists have labeled the Inspection or Well Shaft.

SETTING THE FOUNDATION 17

As one might expect, the configuration of the lengthy channel changes as it descends into the darkness. Starting belowground, the lower portion of the shaft displays all of the hallmarks of a natural fissure. Such a wide crevice might be a remnant of an original water source, which the ancient engineers may have left intact to serve as an air duct and access point for workers laboring in the tunnels beneath the surface. While the real reason that the builders retained this aperture inside the perimeter of the Great Pyramid remains a mystery, scholars know that the craggy shaft connects directly to the Descending Passage just before that passageway straightens out as it approaches the Subterranean Chamber.

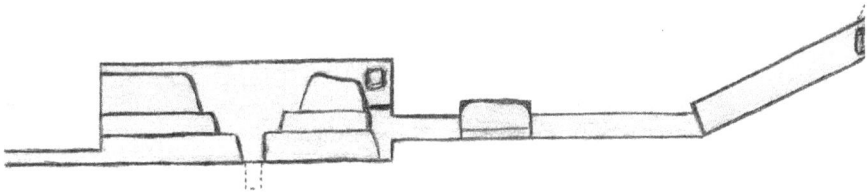

DESCENDING PASSAGE & SUBTERRANEAN CHAMBER

The point where the Descending Passage levels off leading to the entrance to the Subterranean Chamber with the opening to the Wells Shaft on the upper right.

Schematic drawings of the pyramid's interior sometimes portray the Well Shaft as essentially vertical when in reality, it meanders on its way up from the lower portion of the Descending Passage to the 25th course. The bottommost section of the long fissure in the rock is a twisted, tubular channel with bumpy walls because for the most part, the crevice was left in its original state.

The first few feet of the tunnel belowground travel west before turning slightly north and rising a short distance along a sharply angled slope of almost 60 degrees. After making a slight elbow turn, the incline decreases to about 45 degrees but keeps heading northward, more or less tracking a route parallel to the one the Descending Passage takes. The channel continues moving upward toward the spot called the Grotto, located at the same "latitude" as the intersection where the First Ascending Passage and Descending Passage meet. Still climbing, it pierces about 10 layers of courses before reaching the level where its appearance changes. The final segment of the Well Shaft rises at an almost 90-degree angle toward the Grand Gallery and ends at an opening in the floor by the west wall.

The section located directly above the Grotto is composed of blocks of limestone workers had chopped through to extend the Well Shaft upward above ground level. The assumption is that since there was no reason to bother finishing off a portion of the channel that few people would ever see, it was simply easier and more efficient to lay down the filler stones for each course and then break through those blocks and reopen the hole before moving on to construct the next level. Consequently, even though this part of the tunnel is surrounded by quarried blocks, the walls are rutted and uneven. Only when course construction reaches approximately the halfway point between the Grotto and the Grand Gallery did crews begin squaring off the topmost section of the Well Shaft with dressed blocks to make it conform to the finished look of the pyramid.

The Well Shaft would keep evolving as the layers of the pyramid develop until it finally arrives at Course 25. The Griffith theory asserts that the misshapen hole visible at floor level on the Grand Gallery's west side marks the upper end of an actual working tunnel. While the dressed blocks lining the south end of the narrow opening are intact, the ones on the north side are jagged and look as if someone had taken a hammer to them. (Early pyramid explorers trying to find a way into the hole must have chipped away at the north side.) The new theory maintains that from the time work on the Well Shaft was completed, the opening performed an essential service for the construction team. As production progressed, this opening became the primary access point for workers tasked with setting the rigging for an extensive underground pulley and counterweight system and making their way to and from the Subterranean Chamber.

As far as the Grotto is concerned, its meaning and purpose largely remain unknown, but evidence supports the notion that it represents the top of the step-pyramid carved out of the bedrock on which the Great Pyramid is built. Often overlooked is the fact that the step-pyramid underneath the Great Pyramid rises at least 45 feet higher than the base of the building that visitors encounter at ground level as they tour the area. For some reason, the Egyptians appear to have "bumped out" this segment of the Well Shaft, forming an unanticipated landing partway up the long cleft. The compact space includes a shallow depression in the rock (which may have at one time centuries ago held some water), along with a steep drop-off on the south side.

In addition, a large rectangular piece of granite sits in the Grotto on a ledge overlooking the drop-off into the fissure below. No one is certain how it got there. The stone may have been discarded or carried in early on as the Great Pyramid took shape around it. Was the lone piece of granite originally placed over the crevice in the rock to seal off the shaft and prevent people from climbing down into the hole? Or could the chunk of granite have previously served as some type of plug that the Egyptians pushed back and forth to help maintain the water levels in an underground lake? The anomalous stone block resting in the Well Shaft presents one of those baffling questions about the Great Pyramid that puzzle scholars to this day (including Griffith).

Underground Engine

Toward the lower end of the long Descending Passage, lined with finished limestone blocks at the top and smooth rock walls near the bottom, the corridor levels off. Then it contracts before terminating at the narrow entryway to a large (27' x 46') rectangular room. Referred to today as the Subterranean Chamber, the concealed space sits approximately 600 feet directly below what in time would be the apex of the Great Pyramid of Giza. The chamber's floor is a short step down from the doorway and its ceiling is more than 11 feet high.

A rather forbidding-looking pit sits near the center of the room. Because over the centuries, treasure hunters and other explorers repeatedly hollowed out and then filled in this hole, scholars are unable to determine exactly how big it was at the time of the pyramid's inception. Based on the current theory, however, a good guess is that it may only have been about 5 feet deep. The walls on three sides of the room are mostly flat, but the fourth or west wall (the wall to the right as you enter the chamber) remains unfinished. The undulations in the rough-hewn rock resemble a mountain with rolling hills lying just below it and a valley running between the north and south sides.

Taking into account the height of the room and clues the ancient builders left behind, the Subterranean Chamber most likely held the bottommost components of an elaborate pulley system. Under this scenario, the hole in the floor was put there to secure a large post mounted with a configuration at the top that allowed it to cradle — and stabilize — a fat, round wooden beam spanning almost the entire width of the room. The other end of the beam rested in the "valley" notched out of the unfinished west wall.

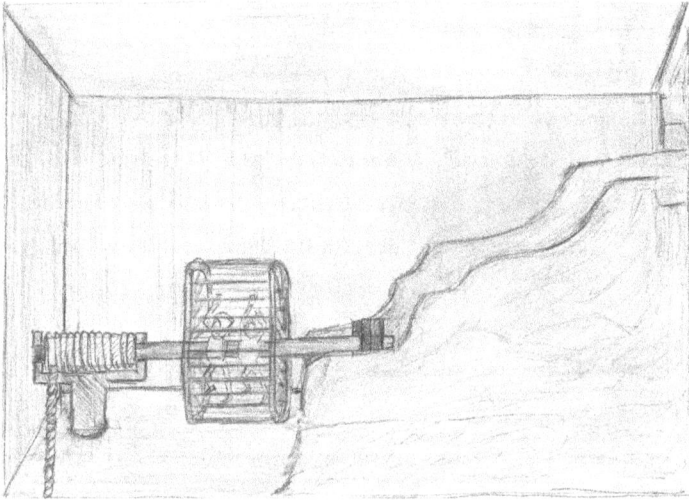

WHEEL IN SUBTERRANEAN CHAMBER

The ancient Egyptians fashioned a human-sized "hamster wheel" inside the Subterranean Chamber, capable of accommodating a couple of men. Ropes connected to a spindle turned by this wheel pulled the counterweight down the Descending Passage.

The function of the round pole was to act as a type of axle holding a large, open wheel — similar to the wheel found in a hamster cage but taller than a person — that the construction crew would turn either by standing inside it and/or making the wheel revolve via some other method. Each time the wheel rotated, it helped power an elaborate system of pulleys and counterweights crisscrossing the building site. Set up near the big, rotating wheel close to the chamber's east wall was a sizeable drum or spool of rope mounted higher than the floor to avoid dragging and positioned in a straight line with the doorway. As the giant wheel and spindle revolved one way or the other, the ropes and hefty counterweight connected to them would either be drawn up higher into the Descending Passage or pulled back as the lines grew taut, depending on what was needed at the time.

Curiously, by the back wall of the Subterranean Chamber at floor level is a square opening 2 and 1/2 feet wide leading to a finished shaft, which extends approximately 53 feet straight back behind the room before coming to a blind end. Egyptologists have not reached any conclusions about why the squared-off channel exists or the specific purpose it might have served.

While all of the aforementioned propositions about the Great Pyramid are part of an as-yet-unproven hypothesis, the logic behind them and other assorted pieces of the pyramid puzzle will start falling into place as the work moves forward beyond the foundation stage and construction gets fully underway.

• The Offset •

One of the most intriguing anomalies linked to the Great Pyramid is that its primary chambers are not located dead center inside the building. If it were possible to stand on the top of the pyramid today and look straight down through that gigantic mountain of stones, the view would reveal that the known cavities do not sit directly below the apex. While schematic drawings might make it appear as if the rooms are stacked on top of one another like separate sections of a single elevator shaft at the center of a building, all three are actually offset more than 23 feet east of the actual north-south centerline. On the other hand, there is great symmetry in the layout. For example, the vertical distance between the base of the pyramid and the floor of the Queen's Chamber is 70 feet, which is equivalent to the distance between the floors of the Queen's and King's Chambers. In addition, the peak on the gabled roof atop the Relieving Chambers sits 70 feet above the floor of the King's Chamber.

When the Egyptians originally laid out the site, they probably used a circular wall to create a false horizon, then looked to the stars, along with the sun, to help them establish the spot on the landscape where the center of their Great Pyramid would be as it rose from the Giza Plateau. The intersection where the north-south and east-west axes crossed also indicated the location of the future capstone, whose peak would sit almost 500 feet above the ground.

Based on their initial calculations, surveyors established a benchmark — 23' 11" east of the north-south centerline — as a point of reference for erecting the building's chambers and passageways. The new theory says that the decision to place major components of the pyramid off-center was purposeful. One reason was to create enough space to meet the fluctuating needs of a protracted construction process.

The benchmark was a way to determine dead center not only for the deep tunnel that crews were scheduled to dig out of the bedrock for the Descending Passage, but also for the Horizontal or Queen's Chamber Passage erected above that shaft on the 25th course. As the job progressed, the surveyor's mark would ascertain the location for the Grand Gallery and reconfirm that the angled passageway maintained the same distance from the site's centerline bottom to top as it developed over the years. The ability to indicate the precise midpoint of each shaft and room relative to the center of the pyramid as a whole was the key to setting the boundaries for all of the openings inside a massive monument built to exacting proportions.

The Griffith theory posits that the ancient Egyptians had invented any number of methods for double-checking the accuracy of their calculations to make certain that the positioning of the rooms and passageways stayed true as construction proceeded. For example, before they began to erect the Grand Gallery from the bottom (north) end, the team established a baseline by measuring the correct distance from the centerline and putting a benchmark on the floor. Workers may have driven a pin into the floor block, created a divot, scored a line, or drawn a streak with red ochre or some other hard-to-miss color. The idea was to keep advancing the bottommost benchmark further up the slope as the crews continued to build.

Computing the distance to the pyramid's original centerline would have been relatively straightforward for openings such as the Descending Passage, but when a wall or other impediment left the builders without a flat expanse for determining the distance from the centerline to recheck their work, they had to improvise and rely on other methods. Such was the situation that confronted engineers as they prepared to construct the lengthy Grand Gallery corridor. The problem the Egyptians faced was how to stay on track with the benchmark as work progressed on the 157-foot-long passageway.

The solution involved a worker standing at the bottom of the emerging ramp behind a tripod with a merkhet mounted on top. A merkhet is a horizontal wooden bar about 16 inches long with a plumb bob hanging from one end, which establishes a straight, vertical line to the ground. Used to mark where a particular star would rise above the horizon then sink below it later, the instrument also acted as a surveyor's tool.

To validate the boundaries, the worker at the base of the Grand Gallery positioned the plumb bob directly over the benchmark already inscribed in the floor. Their partner stood at the upper end of the incline at whatever height the flat surface above the ramp happened to be at the moment, clutching a long, skinny pole with a V-shaped notch on top for sighting purposes.

When it was time to build the next portion of the passageway and move the benchmark southward to ensure that the gallery's midpoint never deviated, the surveyor prepared to guide the rod in the co-worker's hand. Using a series of signals, the surveyor directed the co-worker to move it slightly left or right until the position of the notch was perfectly aligned with the sight guide. With everything justified, the person on the tripod shouted "Mark!" Once the correct spot was identified, a third team member, standing near the worker with the pole, added a brand-new mark verifying the center of the corridor at the current level. The alignment procedure would repeat itself many times before the gallery was completed.

Assuming the presence of a series of visible benchmarks on the floor up the middle of the gallery, the simplest way to confirm that its walls were positioned correctly relative to the centerline was to measure over from the two sides on a regular basis. After that, it was incumbent on the work gang to evaluate whether the latest calculation conformed to the benchmark — and course-correct, if necessary.

MERKHET

The ancient Egyptians used the merkhet to sight the stars and, similar to a modern surveyor's scope, establish precise boundary lines for the shafts and chambers found inside the Great Pyramid.

CHAPTER 3

LAYER BY LAYER

As SOON AS THE foundation was prepared and the underground portion of the Descending Passage completed, the second stage of pyramid construction could begin. This phase involved erecting the first 25 courses of the colossal structure. The Egyptians must have used sleds on wooden runners to pull a majority of the approximately 2.3 million stones used in the Great Pyramid from a nearby quarry on the Giza Plateau over to the construction site.

As a general rule, the limestone blocks quarried at Giza would have been used for the interior sections of the building more as "working" or filler stones, while the more-valuable white casing stones constituting the pyramid's exterior cladding — polished to the quality of an optical lens and designed to reflect the rays of the sun — came down the Nile River from Tura by ship. Those quarries lie to the south, on the eastern shore of the Nile, about 13 to 17 kilometers from the Giza Plateau. The precious material from Tura was probably offloaded at a dock somewhere near the Sphinx and then transferred onto sleds and pulled around to the north side of the building.

It is important to note once more that the climate and layout of the Giza Plateau around 10,500 BCE were not the same as they are today. If the landscape could have been viewed at that time using satellite imagery, the pictures would probably have revealed the Sphinx partially surrounded by water and a different configuration of buildings populating the area. Although it is difficult to imagine the Great Pyramid missing from the scene, the space it occupies was a wide plain that encompassed many natural features, as well as the ruins of an ancient sacred site.

While the 200+ courses that make up the Great Pyramid are not all equal in height, for the most part, each course was created out of limestone blocks equal in size and typically quarried from the same bed or layer of sedimentary rock. The seams in this type of stone vary from soft to hard, and workers at the quarry would routinely have accessed the harder, more durable veins for the blocks intended for the pyramid. The courses at the base of the structure boast the largest pieces of filler limestone found on any level of the building. (The humongous blocks used in other locations, such as the Relieving Chambers, are composed of granite.) No doubt this grouping was due to the fact that the blocks quarried for the lower courses could be hauled up an outside ramp and pulled directly onto the 13-acre platform still open to the sky. The bulky stones did not have to fit through any interior passageways before the builders maneuvered them into position.

GIZA PLATEAU
Aerial view of the layout of the Giza Plateau.

• The Pyramids and the Sun •

One way to explain the placement of three major pyramids on the Giza Plateau is to relate their sizes and locations to the position of the sun at certain times of the year. Under this hypothesis, the smallest pyramid represents the little or young sun linked in the hieroglyphic texts to the birth of the god Horus.

Based on Egypt's location and the curvature of the earth, Menkaure's pyramid characterizes the sun at 30 degrees south — the winter sun or solstice — which is at its farthest point away from the northern hemisphere and lowest point in the sky at noon. The center pyramid, named after the pharaoh Khafre, signifies the equator at the Equinox when the sun in this hemisphere is at its zenith directly overhead. The third pyramid — the Great Pyramid usually attributed to Khufu — denotes the sun at 30 degrees north and the summer solstice, when that star reaches its highest point at noon. From the perspective of our planet, this is the time of year when it appears as if the sun turns back to start moving in the opposite direction again.

PYRAMIDS AND THE SUN

In short, one of the reasons why the three pyramids are positioned the way they are on the landscape may reflect the Egyptians' view of the annual journey of the sun. Most intriguingly, the general concept of the pyramids marking time also comports with the idea of the three seasons that this ancient culture celebrated.

Ramps

From the outset, it was incumbent upon the Egyptians to find a way to move huge blocks of stone from ground level up hundreds of feet. As most pyramid theorists logically suggest, they employed a series of ramps to erect the bottommost courses of the structure. In this case, the stone inclines will only rise as high as the 25th course (approximately 70 feet), keeping the angle low enough so a reasonable number of workers would be able to haul up the weight of a loaded sled.

Furthermore, a smaller slope meant that the amount of raw material needed to construct the ramps in the first place was not prohibitive. Making use of the gradient found in the natural topography of the land, the builders would construct access ramps adjacent to the pyramid on the north, east, and west sides. The ramps did not start out full-sized, however, but evolved gradually. Beginning with the pyramid's first course and continuing with every level thereafter, more and more blocks were added, causing the ramps to grow taller in tandem with every layer the team completed.

The Griffith theory maintains that the west bank of the Nile River was much closer to the Sphinx and Giza Plateau during this period in history. In fact, that body of water acted as the primary shipping lane for not only the high-grade limestone the Egyptians floated downriver from Tura, but also the massive pieces of granite that stonecutters removed from Aswan, as well as countless other items needed to supply a multifaceted construction operation of the size and the scope of the Great Pyramid.

In general, the process of assembling the ramps that traversed the site began with workers following the underlying grade of the terrain and excavating an angled plane directly out of the bedrock by chipping away at the stone. As they removed the chunks of limestone from the ground and smoothed down what was left behind in the depression, crews steadily developed a sloped roadway. When the front end of the cuts drew closer to the outer edge of the pyramid, crews took additional limestone blocks quarried elsewhere on the plateau to start extending the incline above ground. Shards of rubble or other debris filled in the voids between the blocks of stone, and squat curbs erected along both sides of the ramp helped keep the raw materials in place — and the sleds passing up and down the incline inside the confines of the shallow channel.

The setups also included wooden beams inserted every few feet across the incline, flush with the surface on top. These intermittently placed insets were there to facilitate the sleds carrying heavy blocks in sliding uphill. The wooden slats made it easier for the workers lugging the cumbersome loads to move their cargo up to the particular level they were working on. Based on the overall dimensions of the Great Pyramid, the three ramps that eventually rose along its perimeter must have been at least 25 yards wide. Only a ramp that wide would provide enough space to be able to maneuver the freight coming up the incline and at the same time, maintain two-way passage for the loaded and unloaded sleds entering and exiting the work area.

For the most part, the Giza quarries lay to the south of the building site. Ramp development on that side of the plateau involved creating a series of fairly short thoroughfares to carry the chunks of rock extracted from the quarries toward the construction zone. Over time, a collection of angled roads circled the deep, open pits dotting the plateau where hundreds of workers were laboring to remove blocks of filler stone for the pyramid's interior. Several more road-ramps began at the edge of the river near the Sphinx, where the boats carrying the Tura limestone and assorted provisions docked.

In an intriguing side note, the causeway still evident behind the Sphinx today, which leads to Khafre's pyramid, may actually be a relic of one of these earlier ramps associated with transporting materials from the riverbank.

SPHINX AND CAUSEWAY

Remnants of an ancient causeway still exist behind the Sphinx, possibly part of the original ramp system constructed on the Giza Plateau.

The sprawling web of stone pathways zigzagging around the south end of the plateau, leading up from the quarries and water's edge, all converged at a point near the southwest corner of the construction site. There, they merged into the single ramp that was slowly rising along the west side of the building. The conjoined ramp hugging the west wall ran between the pyramid's southwest and northwest corners. Curiously, engineers had designed this incline to fan out as it approached the northwest corner, stretching perhaps 30–50 feet beyond the edge of the building. The extra space at that end was there to accommodate the sleds forced to make a sharp turn toward the east in a fairly confined area. In the future, the sleds loaded with blocks would turn this corner to reach the main construction entrance, which was on the pyramid's north side.

Once the ramp on the west side curved around the bend, it leveled off. Now, instead of using angled blocks to add more height to the slope, crews started stacking up rectangular pieces of limestone to erect a horizontal platform extending farther down the north wall. The initial layers of the new deck stretched at least 100 feet beyond the center of the wall before stopping. The midpoint was where the developing platform would soon intersect with the front end of the second major incline under construction: the ramp on the north side.

Moveable post-rollers* mounted at the corner where the westside ramp widened out also played a role in the operation. Positioned on the course currently under development, the post-rollers changed the direction of the ropes passing over them, which, in turn, assisted the teams handling the loaded sleds in swinging the unwieldy vehicles around the corner. The builders would continue to use the evolving western ramp, especially for deliveries from the Giza quarries, for many years to come. And decades later, when construction surpassed Course 25, this particular ramp and the wide, level platform wrapped around the northwest corner of the pyramid would serve as an enduring pathway for people and supplies entering and exiting the building.

*For purposes of this book, a post-roller is defined as a vertically mounted, grooved roller inserted into the floor or the ground that creates a leverage point that changes the direction of a rope to move a load.

Northern Ramp

The ramp that abutted the pyramid on the north side was also growing layer

HATNUB QUARRY
Photo: Roland Enmarch

In 2018, Egyptologist Dr. Roland Enmarch reported in an article for Newsweek magazine on a joint archeological mission to the ancient quarry site at Hatnub. The mission revealed the existence of a well-preserved haulage ramp flanked by sets of rock-cut stairs, which displayed evidence of post holes. The wooden posts at Hatnub are long gone, but the pattern of the holes alongside the ramp was sufficiently preserved to imagine the pulley system the Egyptians might have used to raise the heavy blocks of alabaster from the quarry. While the team of researchers dated their findings to the currently accepted timeframe for the Great Pyramid (roughly 4,500 years ago), their discovery supports the general idea of a device that the Griffith theory has labeled the post-roller.

by layer from the ground up. But instead of running parallel to the wall, this incline was constructed perpendicular to the side of the building, simila to the gangway for a ship. Considering the grade (26–30 degrees) from a geometric perspective, the ramp had to cover quite a distance to maintain a reasonable angle for the workers to pull up a load and still reach the height of the 25th course, which was approximately seven stories high. By the time the northern ramp was completed, it must have measured at least 1,400–2,000 feet from end to end.

This particular ramp differed from the one alongside the west wall in several distinct ways. While the lengthy incline was flanked by curbs, the surface on top was essentially divided into three sections. A smooth, wide plane composed of dressed limestone blocks to facilitate sliding lay at the center, bordered on both the right- and left-hand sides by sets of shallow stairs. These steps ran the length of the ramp, and in the future would play a central role in the Egyptians' ability to keep their workers in sync as they raised the substantial weights involved in erecting the Great Pyramid.

QUARRY WITH POSTS

Posts placed on either side of a ramp at the quarry would have assisted work crews in raising a load up the hill.

Throughout practically the entire era of pyramid construction, the stone ramp on the north side provided the most direct route to the main construction entrance, enabling crews and supplies to come and go efficiently. Moreover, the space immediately inside the expansive entrance on the north side would function as the primary storage/staging area for the tools, sleds, stones, and other materials required on-site on a daily basis.

Just as significant was the fact that the lower portion of the northern ramp — the far end where the incline started — extended all the way to the water's edge and a short distance into the river. Many years later, this proximity will make the docks on the north side the point of debarkation for the colossal blocks of granite used in the King's Chamber and Relieving Chambers. The pier at the north end was destined to serve as the principal landing stage for the largest barges the Egyptians employed, because crews could simply offload the oversized items from the ships and carry them straight up the northern ramp into the heart of the building.

The budding ramp on the east side of the pyramid protruded onto a spit of land that jutted into the Nile. What once had been a slim natural peninsula the ancient Egyptians must have built up over time and turned into a manmade jetty. Similar to the ramp on the north side, the front end of the eastern ramp abutted the wall, but it extended out at a slight northeast angle approximately 2,000 feet away from the pyramid's base, culminating in a dock that projected into the river. Here the barges transporting a constant supply of stones for the lower courses were unloaded and their cargo transferred onto sleds, which workers subsequently dragged up the eastside ramp toward the construction site. The Egyptians will dismantle this ramp once construction reaches Course 25, possibly taking it apart down to the level that archeologists currently identify as the remains of an ancient causeway on that side of the building. The ramp's limestone blocks subsequently became part of the filler used inside the pyramid.

In terms of shipping goods by water, the new theory further proposes that the unexplained ancient stone wall called the Wall of the Crow, discovered a few hundred yards south of the Sphinx, may have actually been a jetty. At 200 meters (656 feet) long, 10 meters (32.8 feet) high, and 10 meters thick at the base, it was unquestionably a significant structure. While a "hook" at the far end of the wall is lacking, the configuration retains many of the hallmarks of a breakwater. River currents can be strong and a jetty would have helped hold back the water flow to protect that stretch of the riverbank where the ships berthed to unload. The inference is that the portion of the Nile bounded at one end by the jetty known as the Wall of the Crow and at the other end by the pier linked to the eastern ramp may have functioned as an artificial bay.

Little by little, as the three ramps adjoining the pyramid became operational, the limestone blocks intended to fill out the initial layers of the pyramid streamed in from alternate sides. Having the process work properly was really a matter of ensuring that the upper end of the ramp in use for delivering the limestone was always equal in height to the top of the last course workers had completed. The horizontal plane formed by the blocks from the most recent course and the ramp's front edge created a flat, even surface, which allowed the builders to simply drag the newest set of blocks across the top of one finished level to construct the next one.

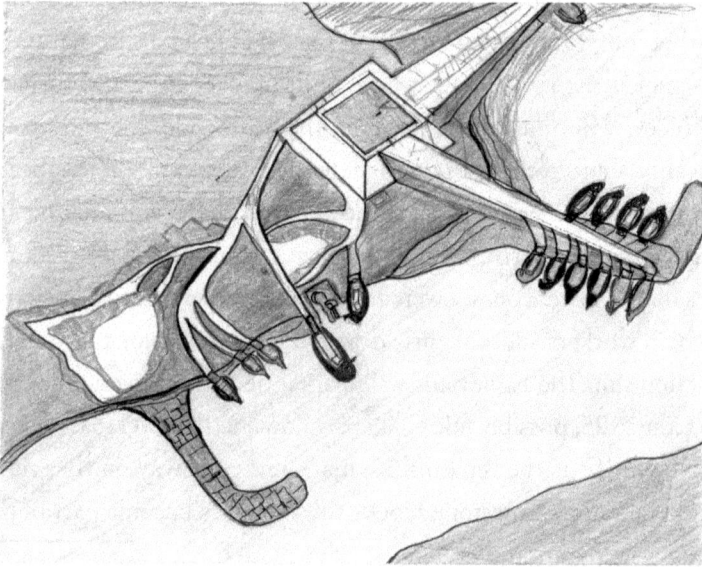

RAMPS ON THREE SIDES

A series of ramps that reached as high as the 25th course on the west, north, and east sides of the pyramid created the conduits for quarried stones, as well as the other equipment and supplies required on the work site.

Obviously, once the course currently under construction was complete, the ramp that the crew had been using would be too short to slide new blocks across the top of the filler stones they had just set into place. The solution to the problem was to engage a taller ramp — high enough to reach the upper edge of the latest course. Sometime during the process of erecting each level, the Egyptians must have been adding blocks to one of the other evolving ramps in preparation for it taking over the job of filling in the succeeding level. Back and forth from ramp to ramp, the process moved as the bottommost courses gradually came together. And because all three ramps were designed to rise only as high as Course 25, the angles never became too steep for the work gangs hauling in the stones to negotiate.

Rim to Center

As construction of the initial courses was set into motion, the workers put the heaviest pieces of the white casing stones — some of them as large as 10 feet by eight feet by five feet — in place first, forming the exterior walls for course number one. All of the blocks used on the outer walls of the Great Pyramid were fashioned out of the same highly polished limestone cut at an angle of 51° 50' and shipped downriver from Tura.

The monument's exterior looks different today because the Tura limestone originally covering the Great Pyramid has been missing for centuries. Over time, the locals pulled off individual casing stones to help rebuild Cairo after an earthquake and to use later for other construction projects. Fortunately, Egyptologists have been able to determine the approximate size of the angled blocks used on the lower levels from several pieces of the white limestone cladding recovered during the 1800s. That group must have been overlooked and left behind by the people pillaging the walls, because the blocks were found beneath a big pile of rubble.

The sequence the Egyptians followed to erect each course does not conform to current models purporting to explain how the Great Pyramid of Giza was built. In fact, the Griffith theory veers sharply away from generally accepted ideas about the approach the ancient builders took to their work. Observing the problem from a purely practical standpoint, engineers would have wanted to erect the structure in a manner that would protect the limestone on the façade from breakage while maintaining the angle and alignment of the outer walls, which, according to the best estimates, were accurate to within 1/100th of an inch.

The exterior walls had to remain perfectly aligned, which arguably presented one of the most challenging aspects of the entire construction project. Likewise, the team also wanted to avoid putting undue pressure on the face of the building. What did they do? They slid the outer casing stones into position around the perimeter first, then filled in behind them. Setting the blocks for the pyramid's façade in place before situating filler stones in back presented the most efficient and effective way to avoid damage. The process of trying to readjust the cumbersome blocks for the outer wall to an exact fit later might chip off chunks of the costly, precisely cut Tura limestone. Positioning the blocks for the façade in advance — course by course — also meant a simple straight edge held up against the outside wall would keep the 51° 50' angle true all the way to the top.

After depositing the blocks of Tura limestone for the pyramid's exterior, step two entailed packing the open expanse on the back side of the cladding with the less valuable pieces of standard, interior limestone. Pulling the filler stones on sleds over toward the walls, workers using long-handled levers and wedges unloaded the blocks and pushed them from behind into the spots where they belonged. Depositing row after row of filler, while occasionally incorporating roughly hewn stones and gypsum mortar into the mix, workers added to the course-in-progress as if they were laying down floor tiles, gradually working their way back toward the center of the building.

An ongoing succession of loaded and emptied sleds circulating around the site fueled the well-organized operation, as small teams moved back and forth to complete each new level. A reasonable estimate is that it took at least 12 months to finish a single course. The timing also depended in part on how much of the Tura limestone the builders were able to ship downriver each season.

Extending the Descending Passage

In their original design for the first 25 courses of the Great Pyramid, the Egyptians' plans included three shafts: the Well Shaft, First Ascending Passage, and continuation of the Descending Passage aboveground. To construct the upper extension of the steeply angled corridor known as the Descending Passage, excavated from the bedrock with smooth walls belowground and finished blocks lining the space near the top, the ancient builders made use of a device similar to what today is called a slip form. A slip form is an open wooden frame usually fashioned in the shape of a cube. In this case, the rigid rectangular structure was built close to the same dimensions as the opening to the underground portion of the passageway. The device was probably at least 15 feet long and a tiny bit narrower than the walls of the shaft. That way, the bottom half fit securely inside the channel and was held steady while the top half stuck out of the hole.

As work crews began assembling the pyramid's initial level aboveground, they placed the slip form partway into the tunnel, adding freshly cut blocks of stone around the sides before proceeding to fill in the remainder of that course. When employed correctly, a slip form not only kept everything square and at the proper 26-degree angle inside the passageway, it also ensured that the upper portion of the shaft remained aligned with the triangle of circumpolar stars — Deneb, Vega, and Altair — the Egyptians were using as the primary sightline to keep things plumb.

SUMMER TRIANGLE

The Egyptians employed the triad of stars known in the 21st century as the Summer Triangle to find true north. The stars comprising this trinity are all circumpolar, which means that they never set below the horizon. That ancient culture called them "imperishable."

Once course number one was complete and sporting a squared-off hole (3' 5" x 3' 11.5") for the Descending Passage, the team slipped the form forward at the proper angle and repeated the process on the next level, then up and up until they finally reached Course 19, the point at which the Descending Passage exits the pyramid, having combined the two sections — underground and aboveground — into a single shaft. In an amazing display of engineering prowess, a mere half-inch difference exists from floor to ceiling and just a quarter of an inch from side to side along the entire 350-foot channel.

First Ascending Passage

Built at the same 26-degree angle as the Descending Passage but only about half as long at 128 feet, the First Ascending Passage starts in the bedrock at the juncture where it connects with the Descending Passage and climbs all the way up to Course 25, culminating at what later would become the entrance to the Grand Gallery. For the most part, the builders would have created the almost four-foot-high tunnel in a similar fashion to the aboveground portion of the Descending Passage by leaving a hole in each course above the opening from the course below and filling in around it.

But unlike the smooth planes of the Descending Passage, the walls inside most of this channel are uneven. The interior of the shaft exposes a variety of finished limestone blocks in different shapes and sizes, fitted together at odd angles like the interlocking rocks in a stone fence. Similar to the arrangements found at other ancient sites such as Sacsayhuamán in Peru, the uneven seams may have prevented the blocks from sliding and thus fortified the passageway by making it more earthquake-proof. Per the Griffith theory, the single exception to this setup was a long section (34' 4") at the upper end of the First Ascending Passage near the current entrance to the Grand Gallery. There, the channel abruptly expanded to more than six feet wide and was lined with dressed limestone blocks.

This claim is based primarily on the fact that the specific measurement of 17' 2", which the Egyptians used regularly, must have held significance for them because it was integral to the setup of the entire passageway. In three spots along the First Ascending Passage, 17' 2" apart from each other, the builders had inserted huge blocks of finished stone with square holes cut at a 26-degree angle and removed from their centers. But where the highest girdle in the passageway should be, 17' 2" above the one further down the shaft, there is no girdle.

Rather, engineers deliberately left an approximately six-foot-wide fin-ished-off space whose length doubled the magic number 17' 2" at the upper end of the tunnel. This area remained unoccupied because it was where the Egyptians were slated to construct an enormous wooden lift to carry the raw materials and equipment for their building project up the Grand Gallery. The opening at the top of the First Ascending Passage was reduced to its current size much later, when work on the pyramid was winding down.

The massive girdles set inside the passageway may have served to sepa-rate individual sections of the tunnel, acting as buttresses to help keep the chunks of limestone from sliding downhill. Curiously, several more of these square stone "doughnuts" are lined up one right after the other in a tight row at the very bottom of the First Ascending Passage. The distance between the highest girdle in the lower group and the next one farther up the tunnel is also 17' 2". Although they reside in an angled corridor, all of the girdles were set upright, vertical to the horizontal plane.

FIRST ASCENDING PASSAGE

The First Ascending Passage looking up.

In addition, the upper three girdles inside the tunnel had been quarried out of single blocks of limestone, but the series of girdles at the bottom end were divided in half horizontally. The two-part configuration permitted a certain degree of movement, which would allow the two sections to separate a tad if and when that ever became necessary. Moreover, the square holes at the center of the girdles positioned in the lower part of the passageway taper in slightly on their east and west sides. The reason for this design detail would only become obvious decades into the future, when the work was almost done and the Egyptians were sealing up the pyramid.

Why were the stones in the First Ascending Passage left unfinished? Possibly because that passageway was not one of the channels through which finished blocks of limestone had to pass during the balance of the construction process. This particular shaft was merely a pathway for the ropes and pulleys that moved the building materials into place.

Mastaba

The initial 25-course segment of the Great Pyramid ascends approximately 70 feet above the pyramid's platform, rising on all four sides at an angle of 51° 50'. An intriguing detail is that when viewed from one side, the configuration of the first 25 layers mirrors the shape of an ancient Egyptian mastaba or tomb. Known as the "eternal house" or "house for eternity," a mastaba was originally fashioned out of mud bricks and had sloping walls and a flat roof. The grave itself consisted of a deep, underground burial chamber connected by a vertical shaft to the rooms above, which, in most cases, were equipped with a small offering chapel and false door. Access to the tomb was normally through the roof.

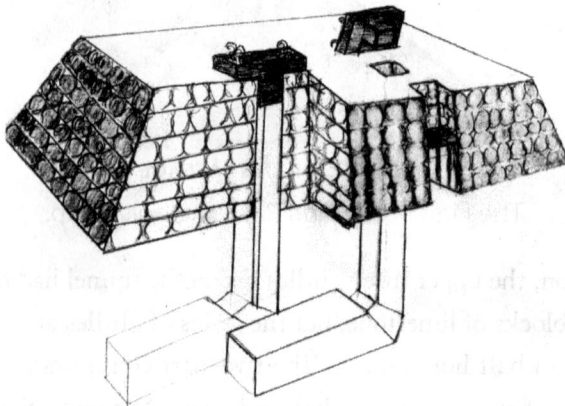

MASTABA
Cross-section of an ancient mastaba.

In the case of the Great Pyramid, the top of its 25-level internal mastaba was destined to become both the foundation for many critical features associated with the pyramid and the launching pad for a totally new phase of the construction process. Exactly why the Egyptians incorporated what appears to be a mastaba into their pyramid remains a mystery, one potentially fraught with meaning. As with other mastabas found across Egypt, perhaps one day we will find hidden chambers buried beneath this false tomb — along with the answers to many of our outstanding questions.

• Was the Djed a Pulley? •

The Griffith theory is based on the premise that the ancient Egyptians were master builders who not only had access to pulleys, but also used them throughout the course of constructing the Great Pyramid. An example of what scientists call a simple machine, the pulley helps multiply the force when attempting to lift a weight. For example, in terms of physical power, our muscles can supply only so much force, and a pulley effectively augments the power the human body is able to produce. Modern versions of the device usually consist of a wheel on a fixed axle, with a groove along the edges to guide a rope or cable. Not every pulley involves the same degree of complexity, however. A rope thrown over a tree limb to help lift a weight tied to the other end is also a pulley in its most rudimentary form.

Was the djed actually a pulley? Shown among the colorful images painted on the walls of ancient temples and tombs, the djed is a pillar-like object commonly interpreted as representing the spine or backbone of the god Osiris. In the hieroglyphs, it denotes the concept of stability. But beyond those somewhat metaphysical or symbolic interpretations may lie a much more practical reason for the djed. If the object were carved out of a piece of wood, the djed could potentially perform a function crucial to the building process. Turn the djed on its side and this "pillar" with the turned grooves at the top suddenly bears a striking resemblance to a pulley. Laid horizontally and greased on both ends to reduce the amount of friction if and when it rotated, the beam could be attached laterally between two wooden posts or stretched across the gap between a couple of stone blocks positioned side by side.

No one knows for certain what role the djed may have played in the daily life of the ancient Egyptians. What we do know from some of the pictographs they left behind is that the djed seems to have been an item that workers typically could handle on their own. While it may have been referred to as a pillar, the djed does not appear to be the correct size for holding up a building. Perhaps this object always filled a tangible purpose in addition to serving as a religious emblem. The djed may, in fact, provide the solution to a problem that has confounded Great Pyramid enthusiasts for generations: Did the Egyptians have pulleys? The answer to that question may have been staring us in the face all along.

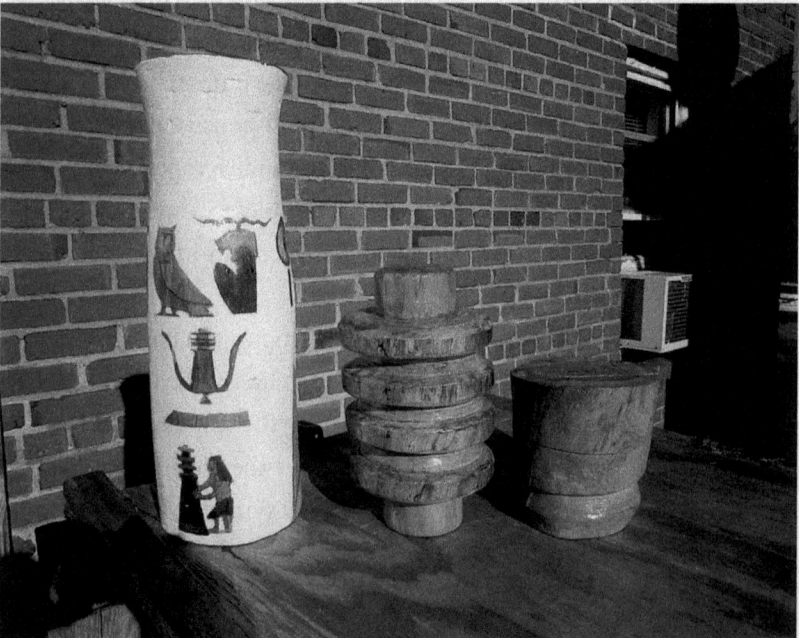

DJED PARTS

It is possible that the djed could be taken apart to extract the grooved roller from its stand.

DJED ON TOMB WALL
The djed depicted on a tomb wall.

CHAPTER 4

QUEEN'S CHAMBER

UNDERSTANDING THE NEXT STEP in the construction journey provides a glimpse into the sheer genius of the people responsible for bequeathing the Great Pyramid of Giza to posterity. Imagine looking across the 25th course before it was finished and later encased in stones, closing it off to the outside world — several unique features would stand out. The acres of open space included a rectangular hole where the squared-off opening for the First Ascending Passage came through the floor* as well as the opening for the Well Shaft.

It also held a set of blocks that marked off a particular area in the southeast quadrant. Offset approximately 23 feet east of the pyramid's north-south centerline, the section workers had set aside formed a depression about 33 inches deep and delineated the boundaries of the as-yet-unbuilt Queen's Chamber. In addition, this recess extended north another 18 feet from the northeast corner of the future room, defining the space where a corridor (3' 8" wide) would one day connect the chamber to the Horizontal Passage.

*Note: Unlike the First Ascending Passage, the upper portion of the Descending Passage never actually reaches the 25th course but comes to an end at Course 19. It stops at the outer wall on the north side of the building in the same general area where the Egyptians would one day place the main entrance to the Great Pyramid.

Considerable speculation exists among scholars about the meaning and purpose of the Queen's Chamber, especially the enigmatic stepped niche found in its east wall, situated to the left of what is now the doorway into that room. Five recesses 41 inches deep, positioned a few feet south of the center of the wall and corbelling upward as they climb toward the ceiling, comprise the niche. Looking at it straight on, its shape resembles the tiers of a giant wedding cake.

Why the pyramid builders took the time to create this odd bit of recessed space has baffled Egyptologists for centuries. Was it a spiritually significant symbol or some sort of inscrutable message left behind for the ages? Or did the intriguing configuration hold religious statues or icons? Due to the niche's position in the wall, it is unlikely that the primary purpose was to hold effigies, since an important figurine would not be visible upon entering the chamber. A visitor would have to walk to the center of the room and turn around to see it.

QUEEN'S CHAMBER - NICHED WALL

The stepped niche in the east wall of the Queen's Chamber, with the opening for the southern air shaft.

According to the Griffith theory, the rationale behind the existence of the shallow, corbelled alcove is comparatively straightforward and mundane: The recessed wall held one of the core elements of the gear and pulley system, which made it possible for the Egyptians to begin erecting the next 185 courses of the Great Pyramid. (The finished pyramid was 210 courses high, including the capstone.)

After they had completed the major part of Course 25 and demarcated the space for the Queen's Chamber on the floor, the most plausible path the builders followed in introducing the next phase of the operation was to erect the hollowed-out wall on the east side of the room. Fashioned out of polished, finely textured limestone in front and reinforced with blocks of filler from behind, the niched wall had to be in place first before succeeding steps could occur. Built to be extremely sturdy and hard-wearing, the free-standing wall would have to withstand enormous amounts of pressure for many years to come. The peculiar stepped niche, just short of 16 feet tall, was there to stabilize crucial components of an innovative "engine" the pyramid builders had developed to drive construction forward from the 25th course and beyond.

Machine in the Niche

Such a novel take on the chamber's unusual configuration and the Egyptians' unique construction methods is based on the premise that this ancient culture had already conceived of and regularly used simple machines and pulleys*, which they would employ during the course of their decades-long project. To that end, they had invented a machine specifically designed to assist them in hauling the heavy stones into the building. The tall wooden form engineers had fabricated housed an intricate system of gears of various sizes, with the largest cogs near the bottom of the mechanism and the smaller ones at the top. One end of the contraption sat inside the stepped niche in the east wall, while the rest of it jutted out into the room. This was the primary purpose of the recessed wall: to anchor the machine's wooden frame and keep it from wobbling as the ropes, gears, and rollers moved.

*Note: For purposes of this book, the term pulley refers to a device that changes the direction of a rope while a roller helps keep the rope off the surface of a stone.

QUEEN'S CHAMBER - MACHINE IN NICHE
Artist's rendering of the wooden machine mounted in the corbelled niche inside the Queen's Chamber.

Over time, with the pyramid slowly rising around them, the construction team would inevitably start losing more and more of the critical space necessary to conduct their work. The machine in the niche compensated for the fact that someday, the entire operation would reach a point where there simply would not be enough room to lug in the vast number of blocks required to build additional courses. On the other hand, cords circling around a drum moved by sets of gears would be able to double or triple the amount of force applied to moving a heavy object. Moreover, the strange device configured with the multi-sized cogs, which projected out from the recessed wall, was just one facet of a much larger integrated system that the Egyptians had developed to eliminate the need for big groups of workers crowding into tiny spaces, attempting to heave gigantic stones.

Pyramids within a Pyramid

At this stage of the game, only a single wall of the Queen's Chamber was standing and the 25th course remained under construction. Taking advantage of the still-wide-open space, the Egyptians made the ingenious decision to develop two internal step-pyramids — in the southeast and northeast quadrants — to assist them in their work. Over the years, as efforts continued and crews kept building their way back toward the center of the structure, the two interior pyramids would steadily be swallowed up by the larger pyramid, disappearing into and becoming part of the whole. That is why we see scant evidence of them today.

On the back wall of the Queen's Chamber, approximately eight feet from the corner where it meets the wall with the stepped niche and five feet up from the floor, lies a small eight-inch by eight-inch opening that Egyptologists have labeled an air shaft. The position of this shaft represents the approximate centerline of the first internal utility pyramid and what remains of the channel that ran up its front side. The second step-pyramid, begun in the northeast quadrant during the same period of time but finished much later, sat facing its twin in the southeast. The air shaft associated with pyramid number two, which also sits five feet above the floor and about eight feet west of the chamber's doorway, denotes the position of the center channel built into the front of the utility pyramid on the north side. A dimension

significant to the Egyptians (17' 2") — the width of the space reserved for
the Queen's Chamber north to south — separated the bottom edges of the
two pyramidal structures.

Herein lies the crux of the Griffith theory. It posits that the construction of a pair of internal step-pyramids — with pulleys mounted on top of
them — was the quintessential factor that enabled the ancient Egyptians to
construct the Great Pyramid of Giza. For all intents and purposes, they built
the massive structure from the inside out. Envisioned as the key elements
within a highly sophisticated industrial system involving counterweights and
pulleys, these internal pyramids will provide the requisite leverage to erect not
only hundreds of courses but also the distinctive chambers and passageways
found inside this most celebrated edifice in the world. Furthermore, as work
progressed and the number of levels increased, the builders would erect a
second pair of step-pyramids to support construction of the uppermost strata
of the towering monument. Once the original two were fully formed, both
Pyramid #1 in the south and Pyramid #2 on the north side ascended from
Course 25 to at least the 80th course.

Going High

Trying to analyze the specific procedures the Egyptians employed from our
vantage point in the 21st century only leads to speculation about how long
it may have taken them to assemble the first pair of working pyramids that
bolstered the development of the Great Pyramid. No doubt the many practical
constraints inherent in a construction project of such magnitude influenced
how the process unfolded.

Having no real obstacles in their way, the builders probably used sleds to
haul in the limestone for the utility pyramids' steps, directly from the outside
ramps. For the one in the south, the blocks would have come straight across
the top of Course 24 toward the area designated for the Queen's Chamber,
where crews stacked them in the space behind what later would become the
room's back wall. Similarly, workers hauled in the steps for the northern
utility pyramid by pulling the blocks up an exterior ramp and setting them
in place to the left or right of the open area designated for the construction
entrance. The limestone pieces used to create the stepped levels on both

pyramids varied in size, but each layer conformed to the dimensions of the course those blocks would become part of in the future.

The utility pyramids started out comparatively small, covering just a portion of the vast expanse within the southeast and northeast quadrants, which together covered only half of the total building site. The limestone layers did not extend out as far as the outside edges of the larger pyramid — with one noteworthy exception. From the beginning, the backs of the two internal pyramids reached all the way to the borders of the Great Pyramid on the north and south sides. As the working pyramids grew, their back ends were assimilated into and became part of its exterior walls. Crews had incorporated blocks of the highly polished, white Tura limestone used for the cladding into their construction. Both of the internal pyramids were designed with a 39-degree angle in the front while the slope of their steps east and west, and smooth back walls, remained consistent with the 51° 50' angle of the outer façade.

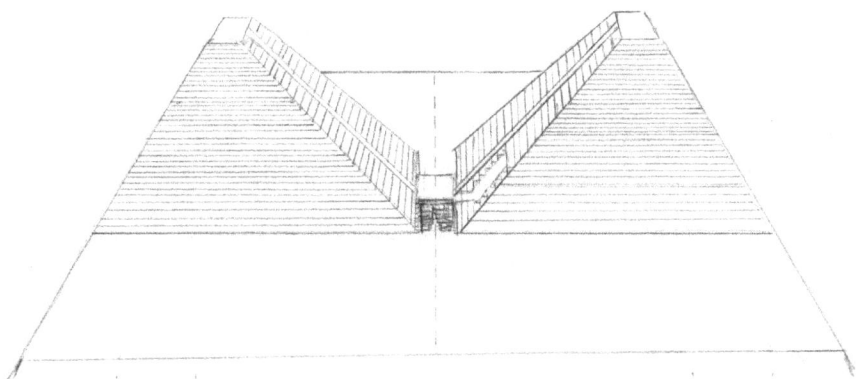

UTILITY PYRAMIDS FROM EAST

Artist's rendering of the first two utility pyramids, in the northeast and southeast quadrants, with the Queen's Chamber at the center.

The Griffith theory also submits that development in the southeast and northeast quadrants followed two distinct paths and timetables. Erecting the southern step-pyramid would have been a relatively uncomplicated procedure. Moreover, the builders probably pushed ahead to get that one finished as early as possible, because its height and position behind the machine in the niched wall was going to furnish the necessary elevation to start raising the blocks of stone slated for distribution across the site.

The utility pyramid in the northeast quadrant followed its own independent track and schedule. It sat near the top of the exterior ramp on the north side, a very busy spot that presented a potential chokepoint for the entire operation. The workers needed a staging area — someplace where they could take the limestone blocks arriving from the quarries off the sleds and prepare them for the next stage of their journey; store stones and equipment until requested for a specific job; and readily access other parts of the building site. To that end, a triangular-shaped piece of the northern utility pyramid immediately surrounding the construction entrance would remain unfinished and open to the outside for an extensive period of time. The Egyptians would only fill in the missing section many decades later as the Great Pyramid neared completion.

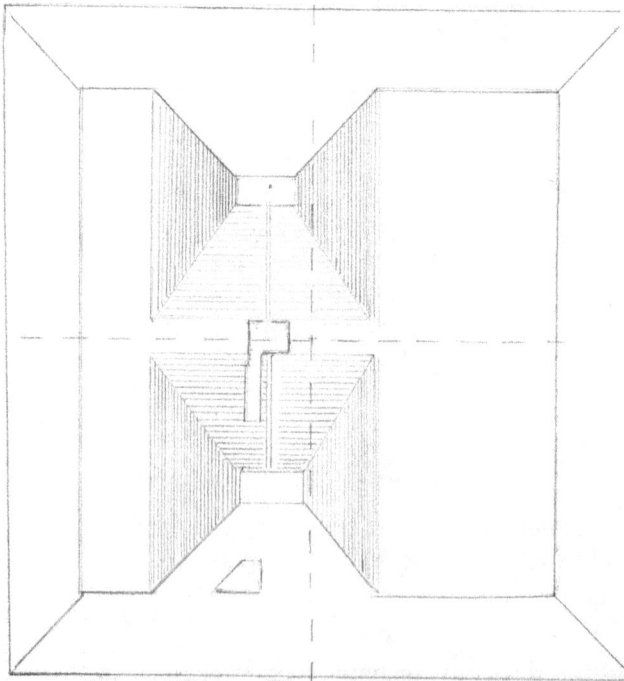

UTILITY PYRAMIDS FROM ABOVE

The northern and southern utility pyramids viewed from above. The small white square in the middle represents the Queen's Chamber, which sits more than 23 feet east of the Great Pyramid's north-south centerline.

Meanwhile, a good portion of the western half of the northern step-pyramid, including the lower portion of its center channel, did exist. The utility pyramid at the north end would not mirror the one on the south side for a while, yet the heights of the layers comprising both pyramids would match all the way up to their summits. The levels had to be the same size since the steps on both pyramids ultimately would be integrated into the same courses. By this time, work crews had constructed the second internal pyramid up to approximately the 30th course — just a few courses higher than the level where the entrance to the Grand Gallery was going to be someday.

Up the Channel

Other aspects of the Egyptians' building techniques are also worth highlighting. First, like all of the Great Pyramid's exterior walls, the white casing stones used to craft the back sides of the two internal pyramids were set into place first as the stepped levels came together. There was no difference in how workers approached this portion of the façade, which originally belonged to the utility pyramids, and every other layer they put together. Not surprisingly, the largest limestone blocks sat toward the base of the developing structures (and in the future, on one of the heaviest courses: Course 35); smaller stones were used on the higher levels as the utility pyramids grew.

How did the builders raise the heavy blocks of stone to compile the stepped layers? Each utility pyramid was designed with a smooth open channel almost four feet high and more than three feet wide (3' 11.5" x 3' 5") running straight up the center on the front side. It was the size of this channel that dictated the size of the upper blocks. Years later, when construction closed down, these same conduits would turn into the so-called air shafts that have confounded pyramid researchers forever. Curiously, although the air shafts in the Queen's Chamber are no longer open to the outdoors, ending approximately 20 feet short of the Great Pyramid's outer wall, the channel at the center of the southern utility pyramid was aligned with the position of the star Sirius at approximately 10,500 BCE and the one in the northeast quadrant with Ursa Minor.

Using the angled plane of the center channel as a ramp, workers pulled the stones up from one step to the next, forming the first few layers of the two working pyramids. In the process, they proceeded to extend the ramps, which were formed by a series of angled blocks built into the center-front of the two structures. The inclines would grow higher with every level they completed. Crews also laid thin slabs of a more durable material on top of the limestone ramps as they progressed, in anticipation of a constant stream of heavily laden sleds traveling up those two passageways for many years to come.

The challenge workers faced was an incline that soon would become too steep to keep hauling up the hefty pieces for the steps without more assistance. To solve the problem, the Egyptians mounted a critical mechanism on top of the flat, even surface at the highest point on both utility pyramids: a pulley stand. These stands were portable so the workers could elevate them as the work of building more stepped levels advanced and the structures continued to develop layer by layer toward their predetermined heights. Years later, when both pyramids were fully built, they would be almost 110 feet tall.

A set of bulky ropes draped over the tops of the pulleys allowed one end of the lines to descend down the center channels into the heart of the emergent building, while the other end dropped down the north and south walls to the groups of workers stationed below, ready to take the ropes in hand, attach them to a harness, and pull. With the pulleys on top of the evolving utility pyramids now operational and the latest phase of the project fully underway, the builders had made an enormous amount of progress. But that was only the beginning for Course 25.

Course 25

The 25th course was a pivot point in the construction process, an apt description reflecting the vital role this particular level was fated to play in the formation of the Great Pyramid of Giza. Course 25 was the level that delineated the room known as the Queen's Chamber, as well as the recessed section of the floor directly in front of the entrance to the chamber: the narrow hallway labeled the "panhandle" for these purposes.

Stones from the 25th course, which make up the bottom row of blocks in the Queen's Chamber walls, were previously placed on top of Course 24 to define the area set aside for the impending room. (Remember that the Egyptians were in the midst of constructing the last three walls in the

Queen's Chamber; the one with the corbelled niche was already standing.) Made of high-grade, polished limestone, the initial row of blocks outlining the rectangular space was a little more than 33 inches tall and completely surrounded the room with the exception of three spots. The builders left a 46.5-inch-wide gap for the entrance in the northeast corner and another break — 41 inches wide — directly beneath each of the center channels on the two utility pyramids. Access to both channels was left open.

In the future, a series of small sleds transporting single blocks would ride up the ramps built into the front sides of the two step-pyramids. For those vehicles to be able to make the transition from the floor and start up the incline, workers had to allow the base of each chute to remain accessible. Instead of the flat walls inside the chamber that visitors encounter today, work crews left openings on both sides of the room where the wall blocks from the first and second rows were missing. As the work pressed forward, they took a couple of blocks cut at an angle and placed them inside each cavity.

The lower ramp stone sat on the floor at the bottom of the chute where it backed into a rectangular piece of filler. The filler block positioned directly behind the angled block formed the base for a second piece of limestone, also cut at on the diagonal. The second slanted stone inserted into the opening extended the incline further. This temporary setup spanned the gap between the flat surface of the 24th course and the entry point to the utility pyramid's center channel on both sides of the room, producing a smooth, unobstructed plane for pulling up a loaded sled.

Decades later, when the Egyptians no longer needed the channels inside the Queen's Chamber to raise more stones, they removed the angled blocks sitting at the bottom of the two chutes. Teams would swap out those ramp stones for rectangular blocks and seal up the deep indentations where flat wall blocks were supposed to be. Workers would place a single squared-off block in the lowest row on either side and two more in the next row up.

For the blocks in the second row, the replacement stones sitting behind the blocks in the front wall would be precut along the top with an eight-inch-square groove (the air shaft) that no one was able to see. The blocks in the front position on both sides side also contained a channel on top of exactly the same size, but those grooves did not extend all the way through the stone.

Instead, they stopped about five inches short of the chamber's interior walls. Consequently, when work on the Queen's Chamber was originally completed, the eight-inch by eight-inch cavities on the room's north and south sides were completely hidden from view. Only centuries later, when pyramid explorers broke through part of the limestone walls, did they finally discover the openings for the two air shafts.

The replacement blocks lining the chamber's interior must have also been slightly beveled on at least two sides. When the time came to put the finishing touches on the Queen's Chamber, beveled edges would allow the crew to simply slide the chunks of limestone into the tight-fitting slots and sit flush with the rest of the wall. The sets of blocks the Egyptians ended up installing at the base of the utility pyramids' center channels in the future may be why the shafts on both sides of the room go straight back approximately eight feet before rising at an angle of 39 degrees.

Stone Passage

Perhaps the most important function Course 25 filled was serving as the inlet for the raw materials entering the building. What's more, this particular level would continue to operate as the primary conduit for moving blocks toward the center of the Great Pyramid for quite some time. Yet before that level could play its pivotal role long-term, the builders faced a problem. Packing the entire 25th course and subsequent levels with filler would unavoidably close off the access route they were using to haul in the quarried blocks. Before constructing any more courses, the Egyptians had to find a way to retain an open lane for the incoming stones.

Engineers planned to solve the problem by developing a permanent channel bridging the space between the construction entrance/staging area on the north side and the opposite end of the site. Instead of completely covering the top of Course 24 with tightly packed filler from Course 25, workers would leave an opening 46.5 inches wide between two rows of blocks stretching from the First Ascending Passage all the way across the floor to what is now the entrance to the Queen's Chamber. Egyptologists refer to this channel as the Horizontal or Queen's Chamber Passage.

Pyramid researchers have estimated the general size of the filler blocks used throughout most of the 25th course to be about 33 inches tall. Work on the new channel for the inbound building materials must have begun when the team chose a group of shorter blocks and fashioned a limestone pathway as a prelude to the Horizontal Passage. Starting approximately 18 feet away from the entrance to the Queen's Chamber, the line of stones extended a total of 108.9 feet toward the north end of the work site before stopping near the front edge of the hole where the First Ascending Passage came through the floor from below.

The row of blocks the work gang laid down extends almost the entire length of the Horizontal Passage tunnel as it exists today and forms its floor. These floor blocks, which according to geologist and researcher Dr. Robert M. Schoch stand 20.6" high (a royal cubit),[1] are the exact depth of the step-down into the hollow or panhandle in front of the doorway into the Queen's Chamber. The Egyptians have since added a smaller block below the step-down to keep tourists from falling.

With the trail of shorter limestone blocks in place, crews began to extend the first row of high-quality limestone wall blocks ringing the Queen's Chamber toward the Horizontal Passage. Commencing at the north end of 18-foot-long panhandle, which began at the chamber's door, they extended the series of wall blocks from the 25th course down both sides of the recently constructed stone track. The parallel lines of blocks flanking the pathway continued northward, framing the passageway to its end point, several feet in front of the First Ascending Passage.

Work gangs subsequently set a second row of blocks, equal in height to the first row and part of Course 26, around the three unfinished walls of the Queen's Chamber and on top of the blocks now edging the panhandle and Horizontal Passage. Taken together, the stacks of wall blocks from the 25th and 26th courses bordering the partially built chamber and the corridor extending from the entrance were five and one-half feet tall. Obviously, the interior of the Horizontal Passage today is much shorter than five feet because

. . . .

1. Robert M. Schoch, Ph.D. and Robert Aquinas McNally, *Pyramid Quest: Secrets of the Great Pyramid and the Dawn of Civilization,* (New York: Jeremy P. Tarcher/Penguin, 2005), 254

the blocks on the bottom make its floor more than a foot and a half higher than the floor of the panhandle.

The inclusion of mismatched stones on such an important level of the pyramid may have been rare, but during this era, Course 25 included a collection of multi-sized blocks. The Griffith theory's unique explanation for the phenomenon begins with a basic assumption: Every block sitting directly on top of Course 24 — no matter what its dimensions are — belongs to Course 25.

Granted, this hypothesis does not comport with generally accepted ideas about the heights of the 200+ layers found in the Great Pyramid. But one often-overlooked, yet relevant, fact applies to those conventional lists: Most, if not all, of the heights associated with the different courses making up the pyramid were derived from measurements taken solely from the exterior of the monument. Obviously, they fail to take into account any variations in the size of the blocks hidden behind the outermost walls.

Given the reality of the situation, the only way the builders would have been able to create a smooth pathway to haul in and transfer the raw materials was to install blocks the same size as the blocks lining the floor of the Horizontal Passage in a few additional areas. The space in front of the First Ascending Passage was one of those places. In addition, engineering protocols and common sense dictated that crews also had to cover the pie-shaped construction entrance at the top of the northern ramp with blocks that were 20.6 inches tall, thereby creating a clear track into the center of the building.

As soon as the cut stones delivered from the quarry arrived at the staging area at the top of the exterior ramp, they would be prepped and sent straight down the Horizontal Passage. Consequently, the ancient Egyptians wanted to eliminate any potential bumps in the road caused by variations in the heights of the blocks that the new pieces had to traverse. The goal was to create a flat, even surface for the stones to ride in on.

At some point in the distant future, when workers would finally be sealing up the construction entrance, they must have stripped away the first few rows of the shorter floor blocks several feet back from the edge of the north wall. They could have replaced those blocks with the white Tura limestone for the façade, along with a couple of rows of the normal 33-inch-tall filler stones from the 25th course positioned behind them. Work gangs closing down the staging area may also have overlaid what remained of the shorter floor blocks with a series of stones a little less than 13 inches high. The stacks of two would have compensated for the discrepancy in height from the regular-sized filler used for the rest of Course 25.

Any attempt to describe the exact sequence and timing of all the work the Egyptians undertook in assembling Course 25 would be difficult at best. The blocks for the stone pathway, plus the ones used in the bottommost row of the Queen's Chamber walls and down the sides of the Horizontal Passage, may have been put in place at the beginning — before any of the other elements gelled and crews started packing the leftover space with limestone filler.

The most reasonable scenario, however, has the Egyptians setting the casing stones and most of the filler blocks that belonged to Course 25 in place first, hauling the pieces across Course 24, and bringing them as close as possible to the perimeter of the areas reserved for the Queen's Chamber and Horizontal Passage. Then they tackled construction of the passageway's floor and the different walls. Or separate crews may have been laboring on individual sections at the same time. No one knows for sure.

One final yet striking detail about Course 25 is that it was also the level where the Egyptians began construction on a new set of walls at the north end of the Horizontal Passage, which in time, would become part of the Grand Gallery.

• Secret Passage? •

In 1986, a team of French scientists searching for hidden, treasure-filled rooms in the Great Pyramid drilled three small holes through the west wall of the Horizontal Passage leading to the Queen's Chamber. Gilles Dormion and Jean-Patrice Goidin, two architects who had postulated the existence of secret rooms based on their observations of architectural anomalies in the interior stonework, led the project. The plan was to observe and photograph the mysterious space with an endoscope. After boring a series of three small holes through more than eight feet of hard limestone, their drill eventually hit a peculiar type of sand,[*]

which indicated the presence of a previously unknown cavity. The work was suspended shortly thereafter, however. At one time, visitors could still see the remnants of the metal stoppers used to plug up the tiny holes the researchers had made in the west wall of that passageway. The Egyptian authorities have since capped them.

It may indeed be true that any number of secret chambers exist within the Great Pyramid of Giza. In this case, a construction team thousands of years ago might have built a second, parallel passageway on the west side of the Horizontal Passage, which they subsequently decided to fill up with sand. From a purely practical standpoint, if, as the Griffith theory suggests, a portion of the northeast utility pyramid remained unbuilt and was still accessible to the exterior ramp, then creating a second passageway and leaving it open for some period of time seems to be a reasonable proposition. Such a corridor would have allowed workers to freely move back and forth to the area around the Queen's Chamber relatively easily.

The presence of a hidden space behind the Horizontal Passage wall and the special type of sand the French team found there hold the promise of countless other secrets the ancient Egyptians may have left behind that we have yet to discover.

METAL PLUG - HORIZONTAL PASSAGE

A metal plug capping one of the holes in the Horizontal Passage's west wall.

*Note: The fine sand the research team found was later determined to be from the southern Sinai area and further analysis showed it to be 99% quartz, which does not tend to clump together when exposed to moisture, making it easier to remove. The locals refer to this material as "musical sand" due to the beautiful tones it produces when the dunes are tossed by the wind.

• Tools & Machinery •

The Griffith theory maintains that the Egyptians employed a vast array of tools and simple machines to build the Great Pyramid. From wooden post-rollers to multi-rope pulleys to triangular crew ladders, levers, and dolerite pivot stones set into circular indentations on the underside of a heavy block, these master builders produced the implements to meet their construction needs. While most objects made out of wood have long since deteriorated after many millennia, archeologists have discovered metal tools, including sculptors' chisels, from ancient Egypt. Paintings displayed across tomb walls have also offered glimpses into some of the devices our ancient ancestors may have used as part of their daily lives. Proof that the Egyptians not only developed effective machines and tools that were up to the task at hand, but also wielded them deftly, lies in the magnificent products of their work, with evidence such as the Great Pyramid of Giza.

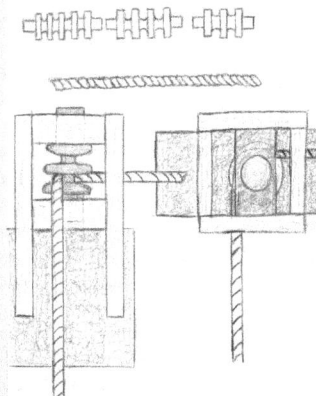

TOOLS 1

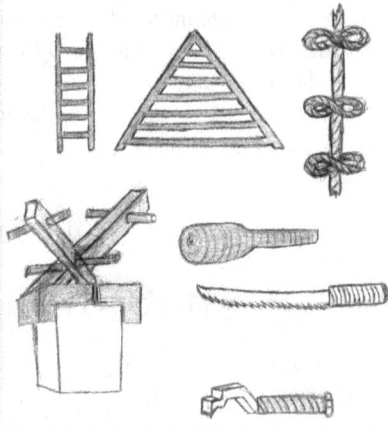

TOOLS 2

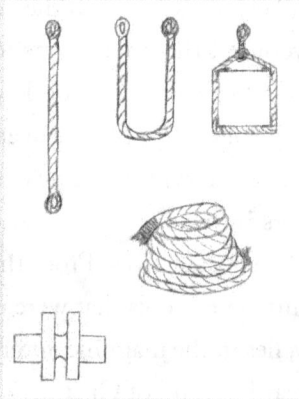

TOOLS 3

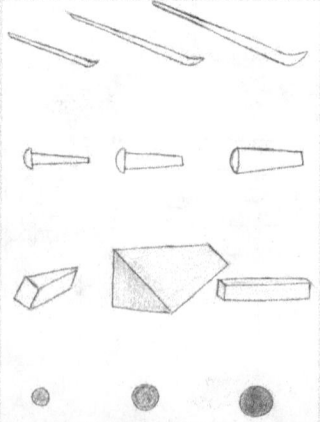

TOOLS 4

CHAPTER 5

FOUR QUADRANTS

WITH THE TWO WORKING pyramids ready to go and the machine in the Queen's Chamber operative, construction on the next set of courses beyond Course 25 could begin in earnest. It seems logical to assume that one strategy the builders may have employed in approaching their task was to create imaginary lines dividing the entire 13.6-acre site into four equal sections: northeast, northwest, southeast, and southwest. This methodology also respects the overall design of the Great Pyramid.

Looking down on the edifice from above at certain days and times of the year reveals an unusual feature of the Great Pyramid impossible to perceive from ground level with the naked eye: The pyramid's four walls from base to peak are indented along their centerlines, making the structure an eight-sided figure—one of the few pyramids with eight sides ever discovered in Egypt. Executed with an extraordinary degree of precision, the indentations split each of the exterior walls exactly in half.

Egyptologist Sir William Matthews Flinders Petrie had observed the phenomenon while he was measuring the pyramid in the 1880s, but an actual picture of the eight sides did not exist until 1940 when, by accident, a British Air Force pilot, General P. Groves, captured the startling image in a now-famous aerial photograph. Remarkably, on the spring and fall equinoxes, the concavity causes both the rising and setting sun to "flash" onto half of the wall for a brief period, illuminating one side of the indentation. While some pyramidologists maintain that the concavity was built into the courses solely underneath the exterior cladding, others believe the highly polished Tura limestone façade was also designed to have eight sides, especially since the way the sun reflected on the pyramid apparently held some significance for the ancient Egyptians.

EIGHT-SIDED PYRAMID

An aerial photograph taken in 1940 revealed the Great Pyramid's eight sides.

In light of this surprising feature, it would not be too far-fetched to believe that pyramid-building proceeded down a track, which at its roots supported construction of an eight-sided form.

One line of attack would be to assign four separate work gangs to the different quadrants, having them focus their efforts on and take primary responsibility for one-quarter of the building. As the teams of workers began filling in each course from the outer walls toward the core of the structure, the pyramid's north-south and east-west axes created an imaginary cut-off point where the different crews "met in the middle," so to speak — at the boundary demarcating the indentation.

Assembly Line

By this time, the construction process begins to crudely resemble an assembly line. The machine in the niche served as the chief mechanism for dragging stones toward the center of the building to service the different sections on the north and south sides. Workers took a series of limestone blocks offloaded from the exterior ramp and prepared them, one after the other, to slide across the 25th course toward the Queen's Chamber. Then, after setting them on small sleds, the individual stones proceeded to their final destinations.

Another innovative technique the Egyptians may have employed to transfer the blocks from the staging area to the other end of the site involved a simple device fashioned out of wood and rope. Taking short, rectangular boards several inches thick and a little taller and wider than the limestone blocks themselves, workers cut two long notches up from the bottom edge, several inches away from the right- and left-hand sides. The notches also stopped a short distance below the upper edge of the board. The cutouts permitted the piece of wood to slide down over a pair of heavy ropes and be anchored front and back by a couple of clamps spaced far enough apart to slip the board in between them. In addition, the series of clamps sat at specific intervals along the lengths of rope, which left enough room for a single block of stone to fit between the hanging pieces of wood.

Securing the boards in this manner would have prevented them from moving back and forth or collapsing when someone pulled on the lines and the chain of limestone lurched forward. The easiest way to load the quarried blocks into the device in the first place was to haul them onto the work platform at the construction entrance and set the individual chunks of stone in a straight line, like the beads of a necklace. Once all of the pieces were in order, crews set the wood-and-rope contraption over the top of the initial four blocks.

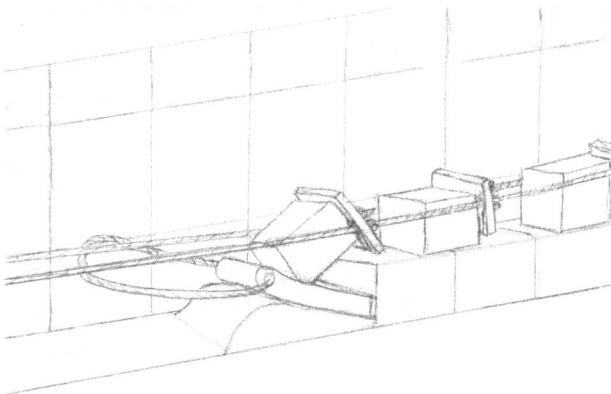

ROPE AND WOOD HARNESS

The builders used a harness made of rope and wooden boards to pull the blocks arriving from the quarry from the construction entrance toward the Queen's Chamber.

The ropes corralling the procession of stones stretched all the way across the building site in a double line to bring the blocks inside. At the south end, the lines circled around the rotating drum at the bottom of the geared mechanism lodged in the niched wall. This drum was specially designed to have a divider down the middle, which kept the rope on the right-hand side away from the one on the left and allowed the two to roll up separately yet stay in sync. At the opposite end of the site, near the construction entrance, the ropes were strung around a couple of post-rollers mounted in holes on the floor. As the gears in the machine turned, the spinning drum spooled up the rope and dragged the chain of blocks forward toward the Queen's Chamber. Later, the post-rollers on the north side would permit workers to pull the empty harness back toward the staging area, where the team would load it with more blocks.

Gears in Motion

The strange-looking wood-framed device associated with the corbelled niche in the Queen's Chamber was vital to the success of the operation. When a quartet of limestone blocks was ready to go, the machine began dragging the heavy procession forward toward a small group of workers standing in the depression at the south end of the Horizontal Passage. One by one, as the blocks reached the spot where the panhandle began, they dropped over the lip formed by the step-down and onto a sled situated on the floor (the top of the 24th course). Assessing the dimensions of the Queen's Chamber front to back, intriguingly, another space measuring 17' 2", four sleds tied together like the railroad cars on a train would have fit into that area. The size of the room is a good reason to speculate that the builders hauled in four blocks at a time.

The cogs from a stack of gears five levels high, progressively decreasing in size from bottom to top, interacted with the drum at the base of the mechanism. Due to the multiplication of force that the configuration of multi-sized gears provided, it required just a small group of workers standing behind the device — between it and the back wall of the Queen's Chamber — to operate the machine. A circle of rope twisted to incorporate a series of small openings, which mimicked the links on a bicycle chain catching the sprockets, caused the sequence of gears to turn. Then, with crews pulling hand over hand on the continuous loop of rope, the wood-and-rope harness and its chain of limestone blocks would skid across the floor.

NICHE DETERIORATION

The corbelled recess in the Queen's Chamber displayed a great deal of wear and tear before repairs. In addition, it is reported that when the chamber was first discovered, the walls were covered with salt as much as half an inch thick. Could the unexpected layer of salt have originated from the respiration or breaths of countless pyramid workers laboring inside the enclosed space over many decades?

Tall Enough for a Man

Schematic drawings of the Great Pyramid reveal a drop-off in the Horizontal Passage approximately 18 feet in front of the entrance to the Queen's Chamber. The purpose of this drop-off is one facet of the colossal monument that has perplexed scholars for a very long time. The Griffith theory posits that the recessed floor of the panhandle was integral to the overall design of the Queen's Chamber for one clear-cut and very practical reason: The Egyptians realized they had to preserve enough space to keep the vast number of limestone blocks arriving daily from the quarries continuously moving. Achieving that end meant having a sufficient number of people on hand inside the building to be able to receive and distribute the stones. But as soon as Course 27 was completed and the height and width of the Horizontal Passage leading to the Queen's Chamber were locked into place, the options for where overseers could place their workers would begin to shut down.

HORIZONTAL PASSAGE STEP-DOWN

The step-down from the Horizontal Passage to the panhandle, which leads to the entrance to the Queen's Chamber, was tall enough for someone to stand and wait for the blocks coming from the construction entrance.

The almost two-foot drop at the south end of Horizontal Passage tunnel provided ample room (more than five feet) for a person to stand in the panhandle next to the step-down and receive the incoming stones. The dimensions on the interior of the Horizontal Passage added another variable to the equation. The longest part of the passage north of the panhandle is only 46.5 inches wide east to west and 46.5 inches high. These proportions are significant because they dictated the upper limit of how large the stones used on succeeding levels could be — until the situation changed when construction eventually reached Course 30.

From the staging platform at the top of the exterior ramp, the chain of blocks traveled the relatively short distance across the gap in the northern step-pyramid. Proceeding down the more-than-100-foot-long lane between the side walls of the Horizontal Passage, the materials kept moving along by means of the rope-and-wood harness stretched tight across the 25th course. As the blocks approached the south end of the passageway one by one where the panhandle begins, they would drop onto a sled sitting in the hollowed-out

space on top of Course 24. The primary job of the workers staffing this intersection was to ensure that a sled was in position and the blocks dropping
over the ledge were loaded correctly.

As each stone dropped off the edge of the step-down, the wooden par-
tition in between them remained hanging overhead. Once the initial sled
had received a block, workers moved the wooden carrier out of the way by
pulling or pushing it across the floor of the Queen's Chamber and setting
it directly below the open center channel on one of the two step-pyramids.
When the next sled had its block, the team placed it behind the vehicle already in position and connected the front end of the second sled to the back
end of the first one. The process repeated itself until all four sleds were lined
up one after the other at the base of the center channel and hooked together.

• Egyptian Rope •

The ancient Egyptians left behind some fascinating clues that the rope
they used to build massive structures such as the Great Pyramid was
highly valued and held a place of honor in its own right within their
culture. The magical rope upon which construction depended was so
prized that the representation of a length of rope encircled the hieroglyphs spelling out the Pharaoh's name in a design now known as the
cartouche. A powerful protective symbol shaped like an elongated
oval, the cartouche represented everything the sun encircled and thus
signified the king's rule of the cosmos. Possibly due to the enormous
size of most of the ancient ropes, the one surrounding the cartouche was
not depicted with a knot. Rather, it was held together with a binding
strap wrapped around the two ends at the bottom, forming an elongated
shen — a symbol that represented eternal protection. A case could also
be made that the single braid the Pharaoh's children wore on the sides
of their heads resembled a small length of rope. Called the side lock
of youth or Horus lock, it identified the wearer as a legitimate heir
and indicated a divine attribute along with the special duties bound
up with that status.

Central to the new theory is the premise that the Great Pyramid would not have been built without this single indispensable tool: rope strong enough to withstand the heave and tug of many tons of weight without breaking. From tombs decorated with scenes of daily life and industry, we know something about the rope the pyramid builders were able to access. Certain drawings even depict how rope-making was done. According to scholars who have studied the images, the central technique employed in manufacturing the most basic type of rope involved "… twisting and counter-twisting fibres. In the first step, yarns or cords are created of bundles of individual fibres, each yarn being twisted in the same direction."[1] Then the rope-makers twisted these yarns around each other in the reverse direction. Apparently, layering the fibres in this way (opposite directions) created a tension that kept them together in the final rope shape. Researchers believe the twisted fiber rope to be the most common type of ancient rope. (Some of the ropes these ancient people used were purported to be as long as 2,400 feet.[2])

An example of a second more complicated type of rope produced — plaited rope — was known as the Pharaoh's rope. Considered sacred and used only with permission, it had greater tensile strength for dragging and lifting than its simpler cousin. Similar to its modern counterpart, plaited rope, which is sometimes called a square braid, was "made up of multiple yarns without a core section." By braiding twisted strands, the final product ends up being not as round as twisted rope but coarser to the touch and less prone to kinking. Depending on the material chosen, this style is quite flexible, which makes it easy to handle. Tomb walls display great variety in the "diameters and lengths, and in fibres" used in rope-making. In fact, "recent botanical studies of rope in the collection of the British Museum have identified dom palm, halfa, and papyrus. Other studies cite camel hair, flax, and leather rope."[1]

Perhaps the most valuable type of rope produced those many thousands of years ago would have been what today is termed the double braid, also known as the braid on braid, which consists of an inner braid filling in the central void inside an outer braid. Each braid consists of the same or different material. Often the fiber for the inner braid is chosen for its strength while the material used for the outer braid is selected for its resistance to abrasion. At the end of the day, it was imperative that the Egyptians fashion ropes equal to their monumental task. Because it took much more than just know-how, they needed the right equipment to be able to move more than two million gigantic blocks of stone.

1. Emily Teeter, "Techniques and Terminology of Rope-Making in Ancient Egypt," *Journal of Egyptian Archeology*, Vol. 73, 71–77

2. Martin Isler, *Sticks, Stones and Shadow: Building the Egyptian Pyramids* (Norman, OK: University of Oklahoma Press, 2001), 254

ROPE - PALM FIBER

In 2002, researchers studying the Great Pyramid found strange red markings inside the southern air shaft in the Queen's Chamber. What did these random smudges mean? Some have suggested they were hieroglyphs. But the Griffith theory posits that the smears were more likely the result of a twisted rope with wet paint on it slapping against the stones. One simple way for construction supervisors and their work crews to know when to either stop pulling or release a line was to mark the rope at the correct transition point with a color everyone could see. Once the color came into view and reached the pullers, it signaled the block or sled going up or down on the other side of the wall was in the correct position and the team should halt. What seems to have happened, according to the Griffith theory, is that a piece of the painted rope hit against the blocks before it was completely dry.

• Stanchions •

On at least two separate occasions in the early 1930s, Egyptologist Dr. Selim Hassan (1887–1961) was excavating near the Giza Plateau and discovered identical stones with a very peculiar shape. From the front, these objects hewn out of Aswan red basalt look like mushroom-shaped spindles with a hole bored through the lower portion or stem. A side view reveals three grooves on top, which appear as if they might have held ropes. After much deliberation, Dr. Hassan became convinced the pieces represented intact pulleys, which the Egyptians must have used to build their extraordinary monuments.

While the theory presented in this book agrees with Dr. Hassan that the use of the pulley was central to getting the Great Pyramid built, it parts ways with the archeologist in defining exactly how the stone objects he had unearthed were employed. Since the items uncovered near the pyramids were relatively short and small, they lacked the necessary bulk required to withstand the enormous amount of pressure spawned by the tremendous loads involved in constructing the pyramid. Consequently, they must have been created for a different but nonetheless related purpose.

The spindles were probably part of a series of temporary stanchions, which the Egyptians mounted in strategic locations along the Great Pyramid's outer walls. The grooves at the top existed to help direct the pull-ropes draping down from above to the workers below and prevent the thick lines from slapping against the fragile façade. In fact, select pieces of the outer casing stones may have had holes pre-cut into them — openings where the builders would have been able to place the stanchions and anchor them to the wall.

The rope-guides the ancient Egyptians developed may have also included a metal collar attached below the mushroom-shaped crown. The collar would have been connected on either side to a rectangular metal band resembling the handle on a basket, which stood several inches above the grooves carved into the top of the piece of basalt. The purpose of the metal guard was to prevent the ropes from falling off the stanchion and dropping onto the side of the building. Once construction of the Great Pyramid was completed, workers would have removed the stanchions and repaired the holes in the casing stones where they had been fastened.

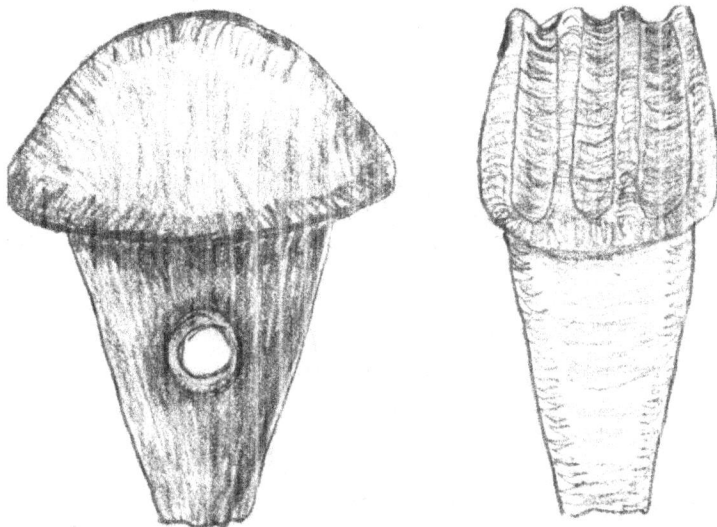

STANCHIONS

Red basalt figures shaped like mushrooms were discovered on the Giza Plateau.

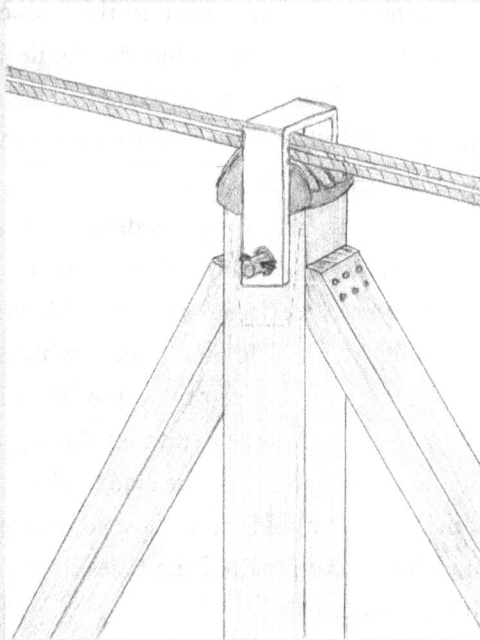

STANCHION FRAME

Mounted in frames, the spindle-like pieces of basalt were attached to the cladding on the pyramid's exterior walls.

Sleds

During the era when the Egyptians were transporting the stones for the Great Pyramid, the sleds they employed probably resembled small boats with curved bows and sterns, which would make it easier to move up a ramp or other gradient. In fact, some of the ancient Egyptian symbols and drawings scholars previously identified as boats may actually be representations of sleds. And similar to a boat, the crew handling the sled would be able to rock it up and down as they attempted to maneuver the vehicle around a space. A curved front end would also permit workers to seamlessly navigate the transition from a level plane to the start of an incline by eliminating the need to physically lift the sled over the gap between the two.

Perhaps most tellingly, when transporting materials on a sled with curved edges front and back and a rounded bottom, which usually holds the largest share of the weight, the center will more consistently maintain contact with the flat surface of the floor.

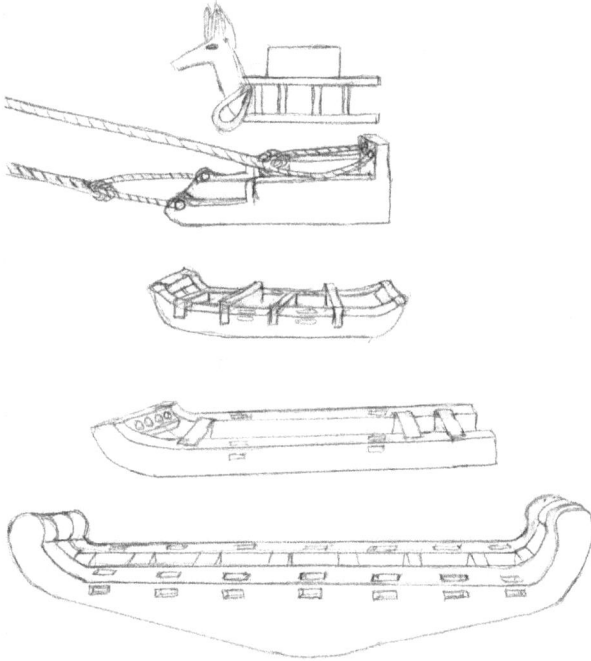

SLEDS · STYLES

The wooden sled was an essential piece of equipment throughout the construction process. These low-slung carriers came in multiple shapes and sizes, depending on the dimensions of a specific passageway and what the particular job required. The illustration at the top does not depict a real vehicle, but represents the hieroglyph for "sled" and includes the head of the god Anubis at the front end. Among other characteristics, Anubis was considered the pathfinder in the ancient Egyptian culture. The remaining four illustrations show different types of sleds, which the builders may have employed throughout the years to carry a variety of loads. For example, the one shown directly below Anubis was designed to transport blocks up the exterior wall as work on the pyramid neared the summit. The next three (illustrations 3, 4, and 5) were more standard-issue sleds, with the vehicle at the bottom built to move the very largest blocks found inside the Great Pyramid, including the enormous granite slabs for the Relieving Chambers

Depending on the specific requirements of the job, some sled styles included wooden runners, which would have helped reduce friction. The effort to minimize friction may also have been why the Egyptians never took the time to smooth out and finish off the floor of the Queen's Chamber, but retained its bumpy surface. Each limestone block rode on top of a U-shaped insert built into the sled, resulting in a small space underneath the stone, which left sufficient room to slip a cord or handle through the opening that would allow the hook on a large shadoof to pick it up.

At some point, as the blocks sat on their sleds, the team must have placed what in modern parlance is called a choker or sling around them. Chokers are regularly used to hoist weights during the operation of mechanical devices. Made out of a relatively short piece of rope with a small loop or eyelet braided into each end, the sling would have been threaded through the opening underneath the block to encircle it by pulling one eyelet through the other at the top of the stone. Employing the same principle as a choke-chain on a dog's collar, pulling on the end of the rope laced through the first loop tightened the choker and made it grow taut.

CHAPTER 6

STONES ASCENDING

THIS IS THE PERIOD in the construction process when the wisdom behind the development of two internal pyramids adjacent to the Queen's Chamber reveals itself. The unbroken sequence of stones arriving at the chamber every day was intended to fill in layer after layer of the Great Pyramid: north, south, east, and west. But first, those stones had to be raised higher to reach their allotted destinations. What we know for certain is that a train of four sleds joined together carrying individual blocks of solid limestone, some weighing as much as 2,000 pounds, would have been exceptionally heavy.

When a string of loaded sleds parked alternately at the base of one of the utility pyramids was ready to go, it was time to start erecting more courses. An overview of the procedure has the Egyptians attaching at least four extremely long ropes to the chain of sleds sitting on the floor of the Queen's Chamber. After traveling up the center channel and through the set of pulleys mounted atop the step-pyramid, the ropes continued down the exterior of the building on the north and south sides.

Proceeding down the length of the outside wall, the lines passed over a few more rollers mounted on wooden stands, which stood about eight feet tall, set into the Tura limestone façade. The series of rollers affixed to the wall permitted the ropes to move freely up or down, but at the same time, kept them in check and away from the fragile cladding. To further protect the white casing stones from the huge ropes slapping against the façade, workers would have strung the lines over some temporary stone stanchions inserted into the side of the building on their way down to the bottom. (See sidebar about stanchions.)

The ropes kept going, threading through another set of pulleys at ground level that were fitted out with locks and measures. The final set of pulleys on the south side was mounted between two or more tall stone blocks anchored deep in the ground at the base of the outer wall. Situating the pulleys at ground level not only helped control the lengthy pull-ropes but also produced a more efficient angle for tugging on the lines and keeping them rigid. On the north side, the pulley stands with the locks and measures were installed at the outer edge of the 50-foot-wide platform adjacent to the north wall, overlooking the stairways on the east and west sides of the ramp. Still the ropes carried on, extending far enough beyond the final sets of pulleys for a sizeable group of workers stationed outdoors on both sides to grab the lines and attach them to their harnesses.

In addition, the Egyptians had sculpted the topsoil on the south side of the pyramid into a series of wide yet extremely shallow — almost flat — stair-steps that were fairly long from front to back. Similar to the permanent steps built into the stone ramp at the north end, the stairway dug out of the ground not only assisted the pullers in navigating the angle of the slope but also helped the long lines of hundreds of people who were standing shoulder to shoulder heaving the ropes, to stay in sync.

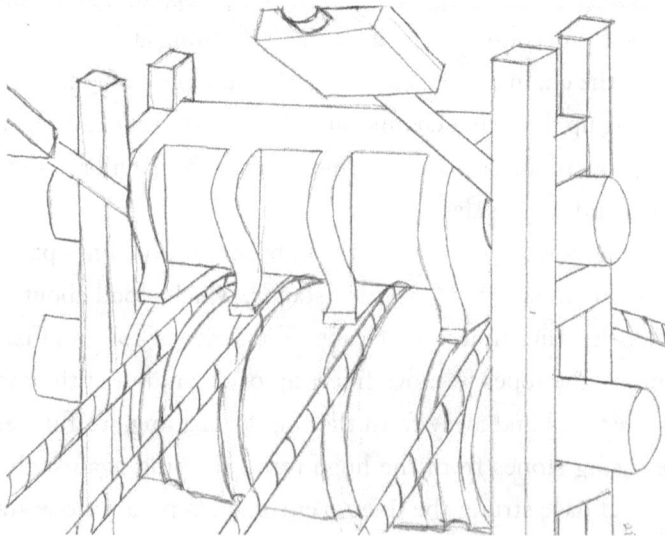

PULLEY BRAKE

The Egyptians were able to control the huge pull-ropes by employing the braking mechanisms built into their pulleys.

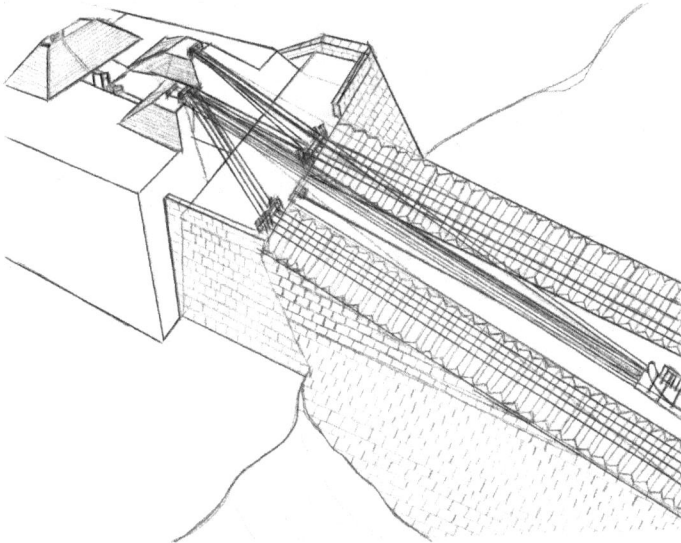

NORTHERN RAMP AND PLATFORM

The northern ramp and platform were at the core of the construction process.

Assembling the larger pyramid course by course now began to follow a regular routine. After both the polished white casing stones from Tura and the filler blocks arrived at the panhandle and were dropped onto sleds, workers moved the loaded vehicles into the Queen's Chamber. Arranging the sleds at the base of the center channel built into one of the step-pyramids, workers strung the four vehicles together. Then each chunk of limestone was wrapped with a choker and possibly marked in some way to indicate exactly where it was supposed to go.

This assertion is based on the fact that researchers have found odd markings on some of the blocks inside the Great Pyramid. The marks may have been made at the quarry and/or put there sometime later in the process, perhaps when they arrived at the staging area at the top of the exterior ramp or after they entered the Queen's Chamber. It is easy to believe the Egyptians were as meticulous about cutting and assigning individual pieces of stone to specific areas of the building as they were about every other mathematical and architectural detail involved in their epic project.

Using a simple communications system to signal the assemblage of workers posted outdoors handling the ropes, the order was given to pull. Swiftly the train of loaded sleds started climbing up the center channel until the initial sled reached the appropriate step on the utility pyramid where another team of workers was waiting. (As construction proceeds, the steps of the two internal pyramids would serve as temporary work platforms for the different courses.) Once the first one in line reached the level where the crew was stationed, a shadoof lifted the block off its carrier and set it down on another sled situated nearby. Then the original sled in the four-car train was dragged a little higher to move it out of the way, which allowed the second one coming up the channel to slide into position and have its block removed. The procedure repeated itself until all four sleds in the chain were empty.

• Synchronizing the Pull •

In a construction operation of the intricacy and scale of the Great Pyramid, with its endless array of moving parts, timing was everything. Knowing what must happen and when was central to the success of the multifaceted project. Simply put, it was vital that every element involved in the decades-long effort stay in sync. This principle applied especially to the coordination of the hundreds of workers posted outdoors behind the two utility pyramids — on the other side of a huge wall — who were assigned to pull the ropes.

Most of the weights these workers had to lift were so extreme that the loads required at least four ropes dropping down the wall from the pulleys on top of the internal step-pyramids to the teams waiting below. Harmonizing the pullers' movements, and, in turn, the movement of the sleds carting the stones up the center channels, was no small feat. It demanded an incredible amount of precision. Such extraordinary circumstances resulted in the Egyptians developing a unique system to organize a time-sensitive and very challenging process for maximum efficiency and power—by synchronizing every footstep forward and back.

One method to ensure the progress of the pull stayed uniform and steady — and the strain on individual sections of the rope did not fluctuate wildly — was to have the workers wear harnesses they could connect to the lines. Fastened to the back of the padded vest was a leather "tail" with an attachment at the other end to insert into a loop woven into the pull-rope. The position of a harness waist- or chest-high meant a laborer walking forward would be able to put their full weight against the burden.

The succession of pullers dressed in harnesses extended down at least one-quarter of the length of the enormous ropes, with row after row of workers (perhaps as many as 1,200) standing eight abreast — two to a loop — as far as the eye could see. Such a setup would have allowed the overseers to keep the pull even as the huge mass of laborers walked forward, step by step, heaving the load and advancing as a single unit to the beat of a drum.

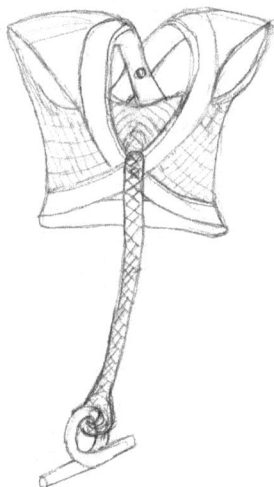

PULLER'S HARNESS

The workers on the pull-ropes wore harnesses that allowed them to put their full body weight against the load at the other end. The harness was critical piece of equipment since it was impossible for the pullers to hold the thick ropes in their hands, and that much weight digging into their shoulders would have caused bodily harm.

MAN PULLING AIRPLANE

©Randall J. Strossen | IronMind Enterprises, Inc.

Employing a harness is a proven method for moving substantial weights, as was evidenced by Hafthor Julius Bjornsson (Iceland) who won the Plane Pull at the 2016 World's Strongest Man contest in Kasane, Botswana. The plane weighed 88,000 lbs. (40,000 kg) and the course was 82 feet (25 m) long. No athlete completed the full distance within the one-minute time limit, but Bjornsson won with a pull of 81.7 feet (24.9 m). Such a feat lends credence to the idea that a cohort of workers outfitted with harnesses and pulling in sync would be able to move a multi-ton object with relative ease.

Shadoof

To pluck a block of stone from its sled, the Egyptians employed a device called the shadoof: a long rod or pole balanced on a vertical beam that acts like a fulcrum. The pictures displayed in textbooks and painted on the walls of ancient buildings typically show a simple version of this tool used by someone standing at the river's edge drawing water with a bucket tied to a pole that has a weight attached to the other end.

In the case of the Great Pyramid, the wooden beams used for the base of the shadoof were thick and tall, and the tip of the horizontal pole would have had a rope with a sizeable metal hook dangling from one end. At the opposite end was the counterweight — a stone or other heavy object roughly equal in weight to the block workers wanted to lift. Using the hook, they would attach the choker encircling the piece of limestone in the sled to the hook and push down on the counterweight to raise the block higher than the sides of the step-pyramid's center channel. By pivoting the pole on its beam, the crew was able to swing the block around and place it on another sled sitting on the same step, where a second work gang waited to transport it across the floor.

SHADOOF

A shadoof is a hand-operated device that employs the principle of the counterweight to hoist a load.

After the shadoof had unloaded the series of blocks, the pull-ropes would go slack to let the sleds slide back down to the bottom of the center channel. The line of sleds was likely weighted in some way to overcome the heft of the pull-ropes, or the empty train had a rope tied to the back end and was pulled down the shaft by hand from inside the Queen's Chamber. Once workers had unhooked the quartet of vehicles from the climbing ropes and each other, all four were set aside in anticipation of another round of stones. Pushing them out of the way made room for the next series of loaded sleds to move forward, one by one, to the base of a step-pyramid and form a chain. Judging from the size of the space, the prevailing assumption is that the Egyptians used the same eight or more sleds over and over again until they finally wore out and needed to be replaced.

Meanwhile, further up the steps of the utility pyramid, the building process continued to advance as small teams started pulling the newly loaded sleds away from the transfer point to their assigned quadrants. Once the vehicles reached their final destinations, workers removed the blocks and pushed them into place toward the exterior walls. Moving inward from the outer edge, team members assigned to a specific zone were responsible for positioning the polished white limestone for the outside wall, as well as all of the blocks precisely cut to fit the interior angle where the back of the Tura limestone wall met the floor — based on the height of that particular course.

Starting at the corners, workers inserted the blocks for the façade at each end before proceeding to line up the other pieces along the edge of the wall. Installing the corner blocks first was primarily a safety measure to ensure a proper fit. Reaching the corners in a row of cladding and discovering a gap in the middle or an overhang would generate problems. It was simply easier to tailor the size of the casing stones situated further down the wall — in between the corners — if for some reason, the original measurements were inaccurate, resulting in a slit between two blocks or a piece of limestone that was too long to slip into the allotted space.

Shoving block after block of filler toward the outer edges, the workers in each quadrant moved one way, covering the space from the corner toward the utility pyramids on the north and south sides, and the other way, toward the east-west axis at the center of the pyramid. (The Egyptians had already covered the back side of the utility pyramids in white Tura limestone when they originally erected those two structures.) Moving roughly in a semi-circle, crews added row after row of the standard, lower-grade limestone behind the line of filler blocks bumped up against the exterior wall, slowly working their way back from the perimeter of the building toward the center of the site, where the key elements of the Great Pyramid are located.

Roofing the Horizontal Passage

As construction of the courses was beefing up, rows of blocks from Courses 25 and 26 still surrounded three sides of the Queen's Chamber and framed both the panhandle and stone pathway leading toward the First Ascending Passage. Crews would set filler stones behind all of those walls as they completed the two courses.

Once the filler blocks were in place and the parameters of both levels fixed, the Egyptians set up a temporary stone ramp at the north end of the building, close to the entry into the Horizontal Passage. As work proceeded, workers would continue to add rectangular blocks to the base of this short-term ramp, as well as angled stones at the front end, gradually increasing the height and length of the slope. The purpose of the comparatively small incline was to allow the crew to drag in some of the larger blocks, which had to be in place before the Horizontal Passage had its ceiling. When fully enclosed, the tunnel's dimensions would be too constricted for the bulkier pieces of limestone to pass through. In truth, some of the blocks in question were the substantial slabs bound for the passageway's roof itself.

Assisted by the machine in the niche, crews hauled in the bulky stones for the Horizontal Passage's ceiling on sleds by pulling them through the gap in the northeast step-pyramid and over to the bottom of the recently installed temporary ramp. Then, using ropes, log rollers, and brute strength, work gangs moved each slab up from the level at which it had entered the building to the top of Course 26. Sliding the ceiling blocks south one at a time in the direction of the Queen's Chamber, small teams maneuvered the slabs into position by setting them side-by-side over the open channel. Accordingly, the limestone forming the passageway's roof became part of Course 27. It is impossible to determine exactly how wide the "lintel stones" in the ceiling are end to end, but a good guess is that they extend at least to the outer edges of the wall blocks from Course 26 lining both sides of the Horizontal Passage.

Taking advantage of the temporary ramp again, the builders heaved up the next row of wall blocks for the Queen's Chamber, which also belonged to Course 27. In this case, workers dragged the pieces of the higher-grade, polished limestone up the short incline and over to the chamber, setting them atop the blocks from Course 26 that surrounded the room on three sides. By introducing additional blocks to extend the temporary ramp and build it higher, the Egyptians may have gone even further by sliding the wall blocks for Courses 28 and 29 down the Horizontal Passage's new roof and adding the next two rows to the chamber's walls.

Per the Griffith theory, the builders also transported one more ungainly yet critical block during this same period of time while the temporary ramp was still in place. Also quarried out of polished limestone, the strange-looking block was squared off on the bottom but sported a 26-degree angle along its upper edge with a large notch cut into the front side. The construction team deposited the special stone on top of the recently installed roof blocks over the entrance to the Horizontal Passage. And with its installation, the ancient builders set the stage for their next big area of focus: the Grand Gallery.

The Griffith theory further postulates that several more sizeable pieces of limestone, such as the wall blocks intended for the lower third of the Grand Gallery, probably came up the temporary ramp before it was removed. The presumption is that as soon as construction in this general area was completed, the ramp was dismantled and its stones used elsewhere. On the other hand, the smaller blocks that crews were using to fill out the remainder of Course 27 had entered the building in the usual manner. After pulling the filler stones south through the Horizontal Passage and loading them onto individual sleds, both the exterior casing stones and the filler blocks for the interior were pulled up the open center channel on one of the utility pyramids and handed over to the work gangs assigned to pack the latest course.

A Century of Work

Layer by layer, assembling each level of the Great Pyramid followed the same general pattern. Workers would bring stones into the building and send them on to the Queen's Chamber before moving the blocks up to the designated course. Focusing on a single course at a time, teams assigned to the four quadrants working their way back toward the center of the building typically completed work on an entire level before moving on to the next one. Under these conditions, Edgar Cayce's claim that it took the Egyptians approximately 100 years to build the Great Pyramid gains credence.

The pyramid's mammoth base covers a total of 13.6 acres. If one acre equals 43,560 square feet, then 13.6 acres would have required workers to cut, dress, and move enough stones to pack a 592,416-square-foot area on the first course alone. (Scholars estimate the total number of stones used in the Great Pyramid to be approximately 2.3 million.) While the quantity of blocks required to complete each course would become incrementally smaller as construction advanced, filling in a couple hundred courses, as well as creating all of the interior rooms such as the Grand Gallery and King's Chamber must have consumed enormous amounts of time and energy.

The sheer volume of material needed to erect the Great Pyramid along with the immense number of people and moving parts involved in an operation of such magnitude and complexity to quarry, transport, and lift so many stones meant the builders were probably only able to finish, at most, a mere two courses per year. This calculation comports with the Cayce readings, which state that the colossal monument took at least a century to complete. Erecting a total of 210 levels — the original height of the Great Pyramid — at two courses per year comes out to a number very close to 100 years.

[CHAPTER 7]

A GREAT LIFT

IN CONCERT WITH THE extensive amount of development linked to Course 25, including creating the horizontal tunnel leading up to the Queen's Chamber, the Egyptians were also in the midst of launching the next phase of construction, which in due time would literally enable them to finish the Great Pyramid. They began to build the Grand Gallery.

To gain some perspective on the orientation of the various pieces in play, it is useful to remember one fundamental yet often-overlooked fact: The steeply angled corridor known as the Grand Gallery, which may appear in photographs and drawings to be detached from other elements of the pyramid, actually sits directly above the Horizontal Passage and Descending Passage. In schematic drawings, these shafts running north-south often resemble different sides of the same triangle. Yet visitors in the 21st century climbing up the Grand Gallery to the Antechamber are, in reality, walking over the two channels located courses below.

The distance between the entrance to the Horizontal Passage and the upper rim of the First Ascending Passage on the 25th course is approximately 16.5 feet, and it is within this space that the Grand Gallery officially begins. Old illustrations plus the current appearance of an opening on the west side of the gallery near the floor, which represents the top of the Well Shaft, provide a glimpse into how the ancient Egyptians may have pieced together the gallery walls. Judging by the relative positions of the blocks surrounding the small cutout on the west side, it appears that engineers took a distinct approach to developing the bottom end of the corridor versus the top.

Even though the blocks making up the lower portion of the Grand Gallery sit on a level surface and not on a slanted floor, the team still had to construct an angled ramp and walls. The most plausible scenario has them hauling in the first three segments of the side walls from the exterior ramp through the gap in the northern step-pyramid. Before those sections arrived, however, workers had deposited a series of shorter blocks along both sides of the al- most–17-foot-long hallway in front of the First Ascending Passage. Although difficult to ascertain now, the base blocks were flat on the bottom and angled at 26 degrees on top. Set in a straight line, the set of stones formed a smooth incline along the east and west sides of the developing gallery corridor. The high end of the slope sat next to the entrance to the Horizontal Passage, with the rise dropping as the chunks of limestone proceeded north, then stopped at the opening to the First Ascending Passage.

WELL SHAFT · UPPER END

The upper end of the Well Shaft terminates in the west wall of the Grand Gallery. The blocks on the north side of the opening were damaged sometime in the past.

When the rectangular wall slabs to enclose the lower portion of the gallery arrived, crews arranged the hefty pieces one by one in a row atop the two inclines, which made the north end of each panel lean slightly downward. Workers would have installed the northernmost blocks left and right first, then shoved the other two against the initial one in line, letting gravity help them slide the individual panels downhill. In addition, because the mouth of the First Ascending Passage at that time was wider than it is today, the filler stones from Courses 26 and 27 bordering the entrance served as stopper blocks that obstructed the tilted wall panels and kept them from falling forward. Consequently, the north face of the lowest panel on both sides was beveled. Cutting the front end at an angle eliminated the gap that occurred naturally when a slab on an incline came in contact with the barricade's vertical surface. The slanted front edge permitted the wall block to rest solidly against the flat plane.

Due to the way the slabs are positioned, their dimensions are somewhat deceptive. The trio of polished limestone wall blocks east and west are probably all the same height, but the second and third panels farther up the hill appear to be taller because they are standing on a higher base. The six modest panels defining the first set of gallery walls were the genesis of what one day would be a dramatic and breathtakingly beautiful corridor. In addition, this simple setup established the gradient not only for the ramp that in time would span the length of the passageway end to end, but also for its lofty corbelled walls.

Based on the configuration of the blocks surrounding the opening in the gallery's west wall where the Well Shaft comes through from below, along with several other structural components, the north end of the newly assembled gallery space contained some unique features. Crews were ready to build a couple more walls in front of the two they had just erected, but the second pair would only reach as high as the upper edge of the notched block positioned above the door to the Horizontal Passage. Using a collection of squared-off pieces of filler limestone about 12 inches thick and flat-bottomed blocks shaved to a 26-degree angle on top, workers began fashioning the interior walls for what is now the short hallway between the Horizontal Passage and the entrance to the First Ascending Passage. Since the latest set of walls was supposed to decline, becoming shorter as it approached the front edge of the ascending passageway, the number of blocks in the stacks piled up on each side would decrease accordingly.

Starting at the south end by the Horizontal Passage, the team set the stones for the bottom row in straight lines, placing them against the base blocks that supported the wall panels east and west. The initial row was composed entirely of rectangular blocks except for the stones on either side at the end closest to the First Ascending Passage. The very last piece in line was slanted on top. Due to the reduced size of this pair of walls, which would only grow as tall as the notched block over the doorway at their highest point, workers were able to use small temporary ramps (rectangular blocks cut in half on the diagonal) to assist them in elevating the next group of blocks and add a couple more rows. As the workers built up, they always installed an angled block in the topmost position on the stack.

Eventually, crews had assembled a stack at least three blocks high on either side of the Horizontal Passage doorway. By then, the upper edge of the pair of interior walls had become a continuous 26-degree incline that extended north to the ascending passageway. With the job at the lower end of the corridor completed, crews had laid the foundation for the next item on the agenda for the Grand Gallery: a lengthy ramp climbing up the middle of the space.

QUEEN'S CHAMBER PASSAGEWAY

A series of squared-off cavities line the hallway leading up to the Horizontal Passage.

One additional important detail should not be overlooked: The blocks in the uppermost row of the sloped walls inside the hallway had fairly deep, rectangular recesses carved into the front (the side facing the center of the gallery). Still visible today, the rectangular cavities were cut downward through the upper edge of the block on top, which means that originally, the crevices in the limestone were open-ended. While a couple of the slots are bigger than the others, all 10 of them sit square to the level plane of the pyramid.

It may also be true that the largest recesses were cut out of a single block to provide greater stability, while the rest of the holes were produced from pairs of blocks placed side by side. In those instances, stonecutters either on-site or at the quarry notched out half of the cavity from the north face of one block to create the rectangular recess, and the other half from the south face of a second piece of stone, shaping the two edges to fit snugly together. The purpose behind this series of indentations in the walls will be discussed later.

Studying the first few rows of wall blocks up and down the entire Grand Gallery, it is hard to imagine that the builders did not craft every one of its most prominent features in an identical fashion. Yet it seems that the Egyptians had conceived of the lower portion of the corridor — the area north of the door into the Horizontal Passage — differently from the approximately 140 feet of the gallery that rise above it.

For example, the panels making up the bottom row in the walls at the gallery's upper end appear to be self-contained units cut in the shape of a capital "L."* Conversely, the wall panels in the lower part of the corridor, which at first glance appear to be L-shaped, derive from two separate blocks. The vertical portion of the letter is represented by the wall slab itself, while the ramp stones installed on top of the sloping walls in the short hallway form the horizontal portion of each L. But the team was not ready to deal with those ramp stones just yet.

Notably, the Grand Gallery as a whole would remain without most of its towering walls for many years to come. During the initial era of construction, only the first three sections of the walls at the bottom end were standing — a mere 16- to 17-feet tall at their highest point. Why? The Egyptians were in the midst of creating the infrastructure for a scaled-up operation, which would soon provide the means to transport inordinately heavy blocks of stone such as the mammoth slabs of granite used in the King's Chamber.

*Note: A question remains about whether the wall panels in the upper portion of the Grand Gallery were cut as single units or the builders created an L shape using two separate blocks. For purposes of this book, they are considered single panels cut in the shape of a capital L.

Fabricating a Lift

Found at the lower, north end of the developing corridor, the initial three-paneled section of the gallery's walls was integral to the success of an expanding operation. Together, the blocks in the side walls plus the short pair of walls standing in front of them would anchor a removable bridge spanning the space between the First Ascending Passage and the Grand Gallery. Furthermore, the ingenious system the Egyptians developed at the lower end of the gallery would, in short order, allow them to transport an astonishing number of blocks to their final destinations.

The Griffith theory offers a good reason for its earlier statement that the First Ascending Passage widened out to almost seven feet (6' 10") immediately before the entrance to the Grand Gallery and why the first approximately 34 feet of this passageway — unlike the rest of the tunnel — was covered with dressed limestone blocks. The uppermost portion of the First Ascending Passage is where the Egyptians planned to erect a massive wooden lift to transport the sleds, blocks, and assorted building materials for their enormous project, including the largest chunks of rock found inside the Great Pyramid. Built to fill an area that started at the edge of the floor at the base of the gallery, and stretching the length of the finished, upper end of the First Ascending Passage, the wooden lift was sizeable and sturdy. Furthermore, the vehicle would prove to be the linchpin in a cutting-edge pulley and counterweight system responsible for raising ridiculously heavy loads.

The Egyptians had begun marshalling all of the necessary resources to manufacture such a lift much earlier in the construction process. Preparations got underway when work crews began to establish space for the huge vehicle by creating a hollow measuring more than six feet wide and 34' 4" long in the topmost section of the First Ascending Passage. Leaving out some of the filler stones meant the hole where the missing blocks were supposed to go gradually turned into a deep, rectangular depression positioned between the highest stone girdle installed in the ascending passageway and the bottom of the Grand Gallery.

As the builders were developing their big pit at one end of the ascending passageway, they not only finished off the opening with flat walls and a smooth stone floor; they also added a ledge on either side to extend the future ramp descending from the lower end of the gallery by another 34+ feet. The wall blocks used in this section of the tunnel were different from the plain slabs that crews had deposited when they began constructing the gallery's walls or the L-shaped panels they planned to insert further up the hill — south of the entrance to the Horizontal Passage.

The panels covering the walls of the ascending passageway were L-shaped and also quarried as single units, but unlike the ones that the team would install later in a majority of the gallery, they were not tilted at 26 degrees. Instead, the series of blocks inside the First Ascending Passage sat upright, level with the horizontal plane. Only the upper edge of the horizontal portion of each capital L was slanted at 26 degrees in anticipation of supporting a set of ramp stones. Interestingly, when the new lift is fully operational, it would include a pair of slim, wooden "wings" attached to the sides. Designed to ride atop the ramp stones during the slow trip up the long corridor, the wings would help keep the heavily laden vehicle balanced and steady.

Little by little, as course after course came together and the sides of the pit grew taller, but before the fissure became too deep to navigate easily, workers carried in timbers to begin developing the substructure for the giant lift inside the squared-off space. Connecting joists, struts, boards, and rollers, the unusual vehicle kept growing as the hole it sat in continued to rise around it. By the time the lift was completely assembled, it would be more than 30 feet long, with supports underneath that stretched almost 18 feet downward.

The front edge of the wooden deck (the platform on which the sleds and stones would ride) sat even with the horizontal surface of the floor on the 25th course at the entrance to the Grand Gallery. Decades later, when the pyramid neared completion and the bulky lift was no longer needed, the team would dismantle its beams and braces, and remove all of the wooden pieces before reducing the size of the opening at the upper end of the channel to its current dimensions and sealing off the First Ascending Passage.

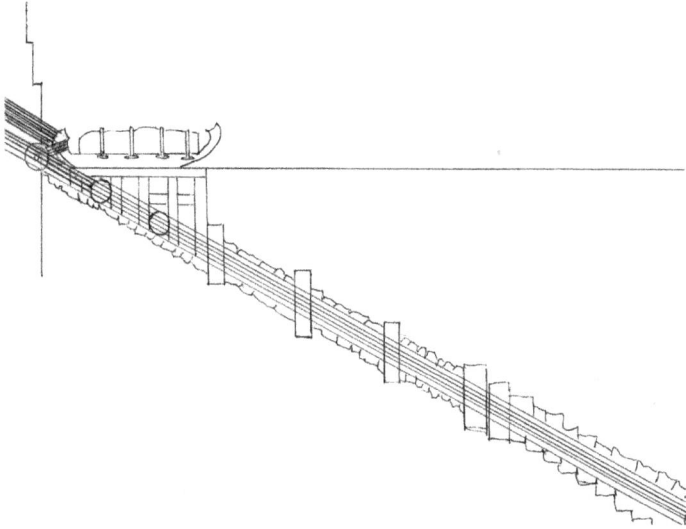

LIFT IN FIRST ASCENDING PASSAGE

The great lift sat at the top of the First Ascending Passage in the area between the highest stone girdle found inside the tunnel and the floor of the Grand Gallery at Course 25.

• The Great Lift •

Constructed of wood and more than 30 feet long and a little less than seven feet wide, the lift the ancient Egyptians designed to raise the heaviest stones in the Great Pyramid was both inventive and effective. The open-ended mechanism not only had the structural integrity to carry loads weighing as much as 70 tons; its construction also made room for the ropes and pulleys that permitted the process of elevation to work. On the underside of the lift was a series of wooden rollers positioned east to west between short boards, leaving sufficient space between the small planks to allow the wheels to shift slightly back and forth. Cut narrow enough to fit between the ramp stones along the sides of the well in the floor, which runs down the center of the gallery, the rollers rode on top of that limestone base as the carrier moved up and down the incline.

A pair of "wings" (two long boards) was fastened to the sides to help balance the vehicle as it ascended the Grand Gallery. The wings were there to stabilize the device by never letting the deck tip over too far. They also suggest one possible answer to the mystery surrounding the sequence of right-angled recesses found in the floor and walls of the gallery corridor. The rectangular depressions in the floor probably held ball bearings — rounded stones that protruded slightly above the horizontal cavity. Their placement allowed the lift's wings to ride on top of the circular objects, making it easier for the enormous vehicle to climb by alleviating some of the drag.

For safety reasons, the top of each roller ball would have barely cleared the upper edge of its rectangular hole. It was important that the curvature not rise up too far. That way, if one of the stones cracked or broke in two, the lift would only tip or fall a short distance and not put either the workers or an entire load in jeopardy. In addition, the vertical portion of the recess in the side wall probably held grease or some other type of emollient feeding into the cavities with the rounded stones to keep them lubricated.

The Griffith theory also offers a plausible explanation for the variations that researchers have observed among the horizontal cavities in the gallery ramp. Might some of the rectangular holes have housed the stone ball bearings while others were left empty? The empty slots would have permitted the builders to place chunks of stone or wood into the openings at different points in the process of raising the lift as a safety measure. As the lift passed a predetermined mark, workers would drop a block or wooden form into the void to help prevent the vehicle carrying tons of weight from rolling backward like a runaway semi-trailer on a mountain road.

A second method of stabilization was the relatively shallow straight-line groove (six inches tall and three-quarters of an inch deep) scored into the walls on both sides of the Grand Gallery at the third corbel — approximately 15 feet up from the floor. The purpose of these

indentations is puzzling until the operation of the lift is taken into account. Projecting out from the back end on both sides must have been
some kind of arm that held a flat disc, able to spin around a dowel or
axle. Made out of stone, metal, or wood and sized to fit neatly inside the
small channels cut into the walls, these discs or wheels were adjusted
to the same angle as the furrow. As the lift moved up and down the
hill, the discs rolled along inside the groove to assist in steadying the
gigantic vehicle and prevent it from tipping.

When fully operational, massive blocks or individual loads of smaller
stones would ride on top of the lift's platform, sometimes on sleds, and
be raised higher by the power of the sophisticated pulley and counterweight system crisscrossing the Great Pyramid construction site.
In the end, the inspired setup the ancient Egyptians had developed
would prove equal to the task of making even the heaviest pieces of
limestone and granite rise.

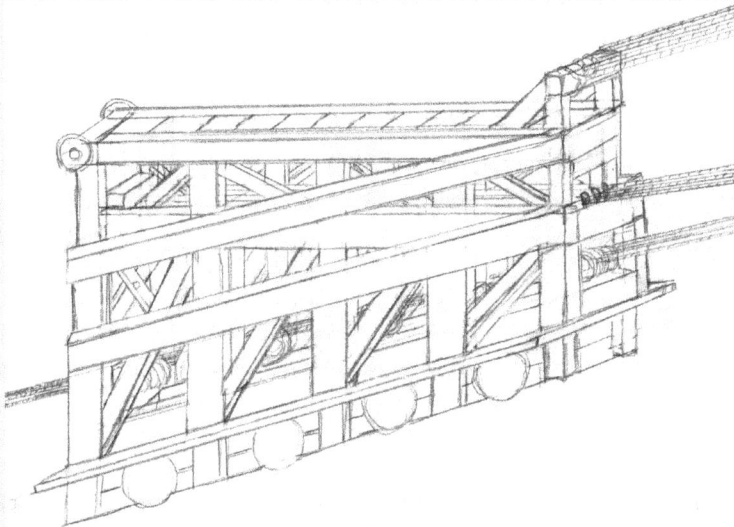

GREAT LIFT

The great lift.

Holes in the Walls

Equally significant in the scope of the team's preparations were the baffling rectangular cavities inset into the walls along the hallway in front of the Horizontal Passage. The reality was that a gap existed between the front edge of the new lift parked at the top of the First Ascending Passage and the large angular stone installed above the entrance to the tunnel leading to the Queen's Chamber. This break presented a problem because the lift could not move forward without some sort of track to ride on.

The Egyptians' solution was to construct a detachable bridge connecting the disjointed parts of the ramp. Soon the squared-off recesses in the hallway's short walls would hold five solid wooden beams harvested from a mature forest somewhere in the region. (Could the wood have come from the famed cedars of Lebanon?) Spanning the width of the small corridor, the timbers would act as supports or girders for the base of a unique wooden structure erected to link the two channels — the First Ascending Passage and the Grand Gallery — together.

Since it would be virtually impossible to bend or slide the cumbersome lengths of wood into holes sitting directly across from each other, the prevailing assumption is that the girders were the reason why the recesses along the sides of the hallway were left open on top. Although today the indentations appear to be enclosed, four-sided "cubbyholes," they were in fact created from separate pieces of stone. Fashioning the cavities so the top and bottom halves came apart would have allowed workers to simply drop the heavy beams straight down into the slots on either side, and then add another block to frame the top of the recess afterward. Likewise, splitting the top from the bottom gave crews an easy way to remove or replace the struts as necessary. While the Egyptians no doubt attempted to build a bridge strong enough to withstand enormous amounts of pressure, even the most painstakingly designed wooden structures will not last forever, especially when tasked with handling such tremendous loads.

The beams themselves were cut square at the bottom to ensure an exact fit inside the rectangular cavities, but slanted on top to match the 26-degree angle of the incline for the ramp. When the time comes to start extending the floor of the Grand Gallery, which served as the track for the enormous lift, the builders will place the upper half of the opening — the ramp stones — directly over the thick timbers.

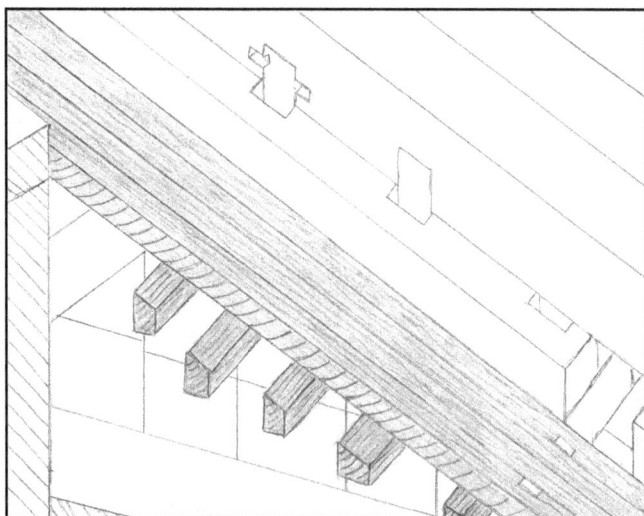

BRIDGE FOR THE LIFT

To close up the gap in the lift track, the Egyptians built a wooden bridge that connected the notched block above the entrance to the Horizontal Passage to the upper end of the First Ascending Passage.

Right-Angled Recesses

Besides the rectangular openings cradling the wooden beams, the bottom end of the Grand Gallery — similar to the rest of the 157-foot-long corridor — includes another set of baffling recesses on both sides at the corner, where the ramp stones meet the walls. Each right-angled recess is 10 to 12 inches deep. Higher up the corridor, the indentations were hollowed out of the L-shaped wall blocks as a single hole. Although the depressions found at the lower end seem to match all of the others, they were actually developed from two separate blocks. Stonecutters had carved the horizontal part of the depression into the ramp stone itself while they hollowed the vertical portion out of the wall panel.

Contrary to what the optics might lead us to believe, the sequence of right-angled depressions inside the gallery sit level to the horizontal plane of the Great Pyramid. As a result, the north and south sides of the indentations are not parallel to the seams between the wall panels because those blocks rest at an angle of 26 degrees. As the Grand Gallery expands further south, the Egyptians will include a total of 55 similarly shaped cavities in the floor and side walls, evenly spaced approximately 5.5 feet along the entire length of the corridor. One exception is the second L-shaped recess in the gallery's west wall, which does not exist, because that spot is where the opening to the Well Shaft comes through the floor.

RIGHT-ANGLED RECESSES

A historic photo shows the right-angled recesses evident along both sides of the ramp inside the Grand Gallery.

One odd characteristic of the right-angled depressions that has long puzzled researchers relates to the depth of the holes along the ramp track. The dimensions seem to vary somewhat and their interiors do not match in every instance. Evidence suggests the builders used two types of cavities along the incline, alternating between horizontal holes that were perfectly flat on the bottom and others that were slanted at a 26-degree angle inside. As the series of recesses climbs upward, the two styles interchange so a flat hole is followed by an angled one.

Another counterintuitive detail involves the relative positions of the cavities. The builders did not pair them up so that the two styles matched as they ascended the gallery. Instead, they placed a straight-bottomed hole directly across from an angled one on the opposite side — and vice versa. This arrangement results in a crisscross pattern of the different styles up and down the ramp.

Some of the confusion and debate about the unorthodox appearance of the indentations may simply be due to changes wrought by the passage of time as debris built up and filled in the crevices. It may also be that the different styles evolved because the holes served different purposes.

While to date, Egyptologists have not settled the many outstanding questions about the right-angled recesses embedded in the gallery's walls, including the ostensible variations among them, the Griffith theory submits that these cavities served a critical function within the larger construction process. Further, the logic behind the strange-looking depressions in the Grand Gallery would become evident soon — when the giant lift was ready to deploy.

Bridging the Gap

Closing up the short distance between the First Ascending Passage and the Grand Gallery was central to construction moving forward. As soon as the blocks and timbers within the bottommost section of the gallery were in place, crews deposited two or three ramp stones on top of the inner set of walls flanking the short hallway. While the blocks for the ramp were rectangular, they rode at a 26-degree angle due to the sloping walls underneath them.

The team was ready to make use of the beams spanning the gap as part of the infrastructure for the removable wooden bridge. Built from thick boards and supported by the hefty joists to brace it up, the temporary bridge was set against the ramp stones on the right- and left-hand sides of the open area in front of the Horizontal Passage, capping the space in between. The deck's slanted plane and smooth surface were critical components of the infrastructure that would let the team raise the lift.

Now the purpose behind the angled stone with the notch sitting over the entrance to the Horizontal Passage becomes more obvious. When the Egyptians decided to build a bridge to eliminate the breach between the ascending passageway and the gallery, they deliberately configured it to rest against the notch in that large block. Why? The cutback in the stone would prevent the boards in the new connector from shifting back and forth. In short, the reason for the notch was to keep the bridge's wooden deck in place.

Similarly, researchers have discovered a small bump or lip in the floor block straddling the entrance to the First Ascending Passage. In the same fashion as the notch over the doorway, the small protrusion in the floor performed a very useful function. The bump marks the spot where the north end of the temporary bridge came to rest. The minor outcropping provided stability because it prevented the wooden slats from slipping downward. Erecting the platform-bridge over the empty space in front of the tunnel leading to the Queen's Chamber completed the first segment of the track for the lift.

This simple overpass would allow the track's 26-degree angle to continue without interruption or obstruction all the way from the lower end of the gallery corridor to the point where it met the lift at the top of the First Ascending Passage.

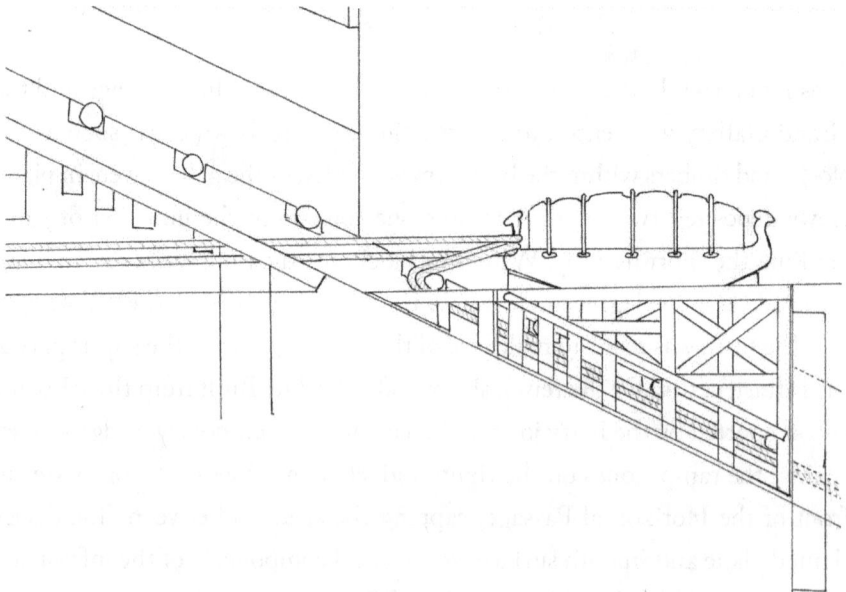

LIFT TRACK

Due to the temporary wooden bridge spanning the gap at the bottom of the Grand Gallery, the lift would have an uninterrupted pathway from the First Ascending Passage into the gallery corridor — and eventually to the top of the ramp.

Before launching into a more global discussion of the Grand Gallery and the larger pulley system, it is important to call attention to one corresponding detail. Until the new wooden bridge was installed, obstructing most of the entryway into the Horizontal Passage, construction on Course 27 and beyond — up to approximately the 30th course — had continued unabated. Blocks of stone were streaming regularly into the construction site through that passageway and into the Queen's Chamber, then carried up to the higher levels course by course.

As the courses above the Horizontal Passage developed, workers would continue to insert squared-off blocks in the space directly over its roof — in between the top of that tunnel and the as-yet unbuilt portion of the Grand Gallery. At the same time, course by course, workers were in the process of laying the groundwork for the remainder of the gallery's sloped floor. The goal was to develop an incline rising at a 26-degree angle that started at the notched block and extended southward the length of the corridor. Consequently, as the project progressed, every time work gangs assembled a layer and reached the area on a particular level that would reside beneath the gallery, they fabricated part of the base for the future ramp. Judiciously selecting the correct filler stones, the team made sure to integrate blocks that were angled on top into the course-in-progress to produce a slanted floor. In this way, they slowly developed the sloped plane from which the upper (south) end of the Grand Gallery would emerge in the future.

It is important to remember that construction of the initial segment of the gallery ramp had been underway for some time with the placement of the giant notched block, the wooden bridge, and the set of ramp stones inserted at the lower end of the corridor. And it would keep growing as crews started heaving L-shaped wall panels into position further up the incline east and west. But the longest portion of the 157-foot-long channel would only become a reality in the years ahead, as additional courses within the Great Pyramid come together.

CHAPTER 8

DOWN AND UP

ACCORDING TO THE GRIFFITH theory, pulleys were central to the process of pyramid construction from the start. Pulleys were mounted on top of the utility pyramids north and south to assist in elevating the blocks for the multi-sized courses and exterior Tura limestone walls. Additional pulleys stood at the edge of the platform at the top of the northern ramp and in between giant blocks of stone implanted in the ground behind the southern step-pyramid to direct the pull-ropes toward the workers responsible for lifting the colossal loads.

But at this stage, that setup, which had served Egyptians so well, would be switching over to head in a slightly different direction. In the revamped operation, crews installed a second pulley atop the southern pyramid, positioned toward the east end of its upper step. With this new equipment, the ends of the ropes leading from the pulleys in the southeast quadrant, which formerly dangled from the top of the utility pyramid into the Queen's Chamber and were attached to a line of sleds, would drop down into the Grand Gallery instead. In addition, a second more complicated and highly integrated system of ropes and pulleys was coming online. Running all the way from the Subterranean Chamber through the descending and ascending passageways and into the Grand Gallery, the ingenious arrangement would soon make the previously unattainable goal of erecting the Great Pyramid a reality.

This is the period when the ancient engineers began to alter their building methods to handle the extreme weights and oversized blocks that were impossible to push or pull by manpower alone. Now the motive behind the extraordinary amount of time and effort the Egyptians had expended upfront to excavate a vast underground network of tunnels finally becomes clear. The purpose behind such a complicated infrastructure, which included a Subterranean Chamber hidden 100 feet below the pyramid platform, sloping tunnels carved directly out of the bedrock, and the Well Shaft intersecting the entire arrangement, was to create an industrial lifting machine. Workers would weave a far-reaching, multifaceted web of ropes and pulleys across the sprawling construction site. To do the system justice and bring the full picture of its many linkages and component parts into sharper focus, it is useful to begin the description at the nethermost point in the Great Pyramid.

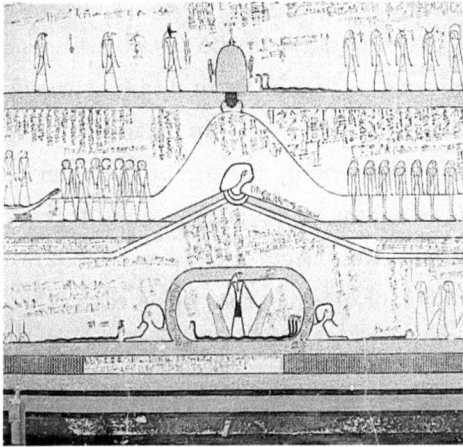

SCARAB-PULLEY

A fascinating image on a wall in the tomb of Thutmosis III depicts an upside-down scarab holding a rope and groups of workers standing on either side with the lines in their hands, looking as if they were waiting to pull. Adding to the intrigue, the scarab was drawn above a pyramidal-shaped object. Among its other meanings, could the painting be a symbolic representation of a pulley?

Counterweight

Architects originally designed the site with two critical spaces concealed deep below the surface of the Giza Plateau. Decades earlier, crews burrowing into the bedrock had dug out the cave-like room and lengthy channel known as the Subterranean Chamber and Descending Passage respectively. While some pyramid researchers have questioned why any sane people, much less a culture as savvy as the ancient Egyptians, would take the time to excavate two such purportedly useless cavities, their arduous dig occurred with a single objective in mind: According to the Griffith theory, the underground tunnels and hidden chambers were developed to accommodate the one indispensable tool capable of powering their project forward to its astonishing conclusion. The builders made room for a counterweight.

The use of a counterweight is no surprise in light of one of the core values inherent in the ancient Egyptian culture: the principle known as *ma'at*, which represented harmony and balance. The idea of balance was a central aspect of life and deeply held conviction in their society. In fact, the concept of *ma'at* was later personified as a goddess of the same name. From the Egyptians' perspective, the universe had an order to it, and it was *Ma'at* who allowed life on earth to function as it should — in balance.

The basic principle underlying the use of a counterweight is simple. By definition, a counterweight is an equivalent opposite, balancing weight that equalizes a load. When two objects of equal weight, power, or influence are acting in opposition to one another, they offset each other and are said to be in counterbalance. Similar to a seesaw with two people of approximately the same size seated at opposite ends, a counterweight reduces the amount of energy needed to raise the object on the other side. In general, counterweights make lifting a load more efficient, which saves energy and is less taxing on the lifting machine. In the case of the Great Pyramid, the "machine" doing the lifting was hundreds of laborers.

The pyramid builders knew that someday, they would have to raise colossal pieces of limestone and granite blocks weighing as much as 70 tons. Consequently, it was incumbent upon them to develop a counterweight as close as possible to the weight of those inordinately heavy blocks to help offset the corresponding loads. Obviously, from the estimated 125-ton obelisks that the ancient Egyptians produced, including an unfinished one still lying in a quarry at Aswan, their society had the knowledge and wherewithal to move such humongous slabs of stone. They were resourceful master engineers.

The Griffith theory postulates that the primary counterweight used in building the Great Pyramid was composed of granite and located in the Descending Passage, which is more than double the length of the Grand Gallery but built at the same angle — 26 degrees — as the gallery ramp. Furthermore, the Egyptians probably placed the counterweight inside that passageway sooner rather than later. Since the builders had erected a sprawling platform

25 courses high against the pyramid's north wall, that structure would have blocked the opening at the top of the Descending Passage where it pierced the side of the building at Course 19, cutting off access to the tunnel. As a result, the team must have lowered the counterweight into its shaft as soon as construction had reached the exterior wall at that level, before the northern platform grew as high as the 25th course. Tying off the heavy stone, they let the counterweight float inside its channel until the time came to hook it up to the lift.

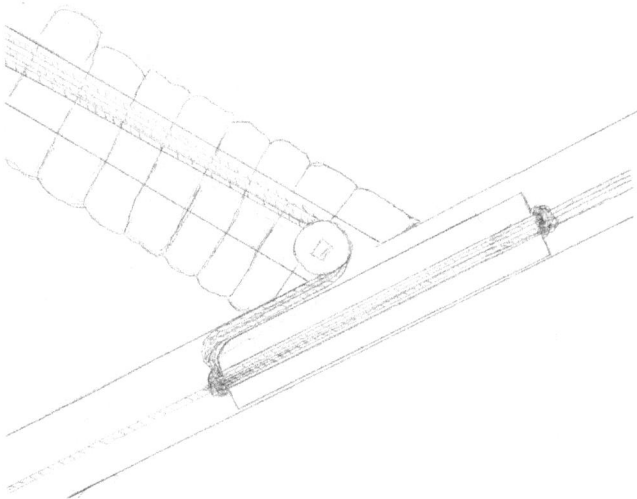

COUNTERWEIGHT AT FIRST ASCENDING PASSAGE

When not in use, the counterweight was parked inside the Descending Passage, right below opening to the First Ascending Passage. Some of the ropes from the counterweight went over a roller mounted at the bottom of the ascending passageway and continued up the tunnel to the Grand Gallery.

The device consisted of a very large stone that fit snugly inside the Descending Passage on the east and west sides, but was a few inches shorter than the ceiling. The block's dimensions were exact, leaving just enough room around the edges for the apparatus to rise freely and fall as it moved up and down the open shaft. Stone masons had chiseled out a small channel to contain the anchor rope looped around the block. Several inches deep, about seven or eight inches wide, and centered between the edges, the incised groove encircled the piece of granite longways. The furrow was there to prevent the line tucked inside it from sliding off the stone's slippery surface. It was also deep enough to avoid undue wear and tear on the thick rope because it wouldn't stick out like a lump and rub against the tunnel walls.

A few more lines were tied to the belt, ringing the slab as part of the overall counterweight system. One of them originated in the Subterranean Chamber, climbed up the Descending Passage, and was hooked onto the bottom (south) end of the block. A separate pair of ropes, also attached at the bottom end, traveled across the block in between its upper face and the ceiling, then made a left turn over the pulley mounted at the opening into the First Ascending Passage. Due to the angles involved, workers had rounded off the sharp edge at the southwest corner of the rectangular piece of granite to avoid fraying the lines on their upward journey. The set of ropes used to reset the counterweight, which stretched north toward the opening in the exterior wall at Course 19, were fastened to the top.

Because the Descending Passage does not show evidence of gashes or other marks indicating a pattern of wear and tear from repeated dragging, the Egyptians must have made some sort of accommodation to the bottom of the passageway to help reduce the friction caused by sliding stone on stone. When not in use, the bulky block was stationed immediately below the spot where the First Ascending Passage and Descending Passage meet. If the counterweight had been sitting any higher in the tunnel, it would have interfered with the ropes that were scheduled to travel up the ascending passageway toward the Grand Gallery.

It is true that the counterweight the Egyptians had manufactured could not possibly have equaled the weight of the heaviest stones they had to raise — 70-ton blocks plus the mass of a giant lift, but pulleys would have added enough auxiliary force to the effort to make their building strategy viable. Without a counterweight to assist with the construction, however, it would have required many hundreds of workers crowding into confined spaces, trying to pull gigantic loads up steep angles and around sharp corners virtually impossible to navigate.

Conversely, by employing a pulley and a counterweight system, the Egyptians' capacity to raise the staggeringly heavy blocks of stone found inside the Great Pyramid of Giza entered the realm of possibility.

Rigging

As mentioned in Chapter Two, the workers in the Subterranean Chamber performed one of the project's most elementary — and central — functions: They made the pyramid's pulley and counterweight system work. Laborers standing in a large open wheel, similar to the running wheels found in a hamster cage, propelled a key part of the operation. The giant wheel was connected to a big spool of rope positioned directly behind the entrance to the chamber. As the workers in the wheel made the circle turn one way or the other, the revolutions caused the rope to either wind or unwind around the spool. What purpose did this rope serve?

It traveled out the door and up the shaft of the Descending Passage and was fastened to the lower end of the counterweight. A work gang had attached it to the anchor line held inside the block's deep groove.

The rope leaving the Subterranean Chamber did not run straight up the tunnel because at the bottom of the Descending Passage, 29 feet in front of the chamber's doorway, is a slight elbow turn where the shaft's 26-degree incline levels off. To steer the rope through this space, engineers mounted a pulley in front of the doorway and placed another one at the crook of the elbow. One sensible way to lock both pulleys into place, stabilize their movement, and avoid excessive wobbling was to attach a wooden frame to the walls of the short tunnel by the entrance, then fasten the rollers to the frame. Passing underneath the two pulleys redirected the rope that had been running horizontally as it exited the room up the underground channel, heading toward the counterweight.

The workers assigned to the Subterranean Chamber had one explicit job to perform: They were responsible for pulling the giant counterweight down the Descending Passage. That process, in turn, assisted the mammoth lift in moving up the Grand Gallery to the level currently under construction where a team stood by to unload the cargo.

Due to the amount of friction and the tunnel's comparatively low 26-degree grade, the Descending Passage was not really steep enough for the counterweight to travel downhill on its own. (And the builders would never have wanted it to freefall in any event.)

At the appropriate moment, the people standing in the revolving "cage" used the force of their own body weight on the wheel to rewind the rope. Coiling the line around the spool near the doorway slowly pulled the heavy counterweight down the passageway. Other crew members assigned to the chamber were probably stationed next to the big spool by the entrance to help guide the uncoiled rope as it was rewinding. Just like a fisher pole's line, they wanted it to be evenly distributed across the reel for the next time it was needed.

SUBTERRANEAN CHAMBER EQUIPMENT

The layout in the Subterranean Chamber showing the take-up spool and giant wheel.

At the other end — coming from the high side of the counterweight — were the two ropes that led outdoors. Mimicking the setup used with the utility pyramids, the lines reached all the way to the top of Course 19 at the north end of the building in the area where the main entrance to the Great Pyramid is today. A pulley mounted at that spot changed the direction of the lines, guiding the ropes into a small tubular channel built underneath the platform on the north side of the building. Developed when the northern ramp was under construction, the pipeline beneath the platform carried the lines tied to the counterweight farther north and gradually conveyed them upward toward the top of the deck. When the ropes reached the intersection where the horizontal platform met the angle of the northern ramp, they surfaced through a small opening at the edge of the platform on the ramp's centerline. A low roller installed in that hole subsequently turned the lines downward in the direction of the river.

And just as they had raised the loaded sleds from the Queen's Chamber up the center channels of the two utility pyramids, a group of workers charged with raising the heavy granite stone back up the Descending Passage stood on the northern ramp, waiting to pull whenever the signal was given. Hauling the block up the shaft toward the First Ascending Passage after the great lift had shed its load, they closed the proverbial loop by resetting the counterweight.

An overarching goal of the teams managing the operation at both ends of the ropes was to prevent the counterweight from drifting by holding it tightly inside its channel. Accomplishing such a feat meant the team had to ensure that the lines fastened at the base and top of the substantial piece of granite stayed taut at all times.

As the crew in the Subterranean Chamber turning the wheel pulled the stone down the slope, the crew outdoors walked forward at about the same pace, then quickly tied off the ropes, locking them down as soon as the block had dropped as far as it was supposed to go. When it was time to prepare for the next load, the pullers standing at the center of the northern ramp began tugging on the lines to equalize the tension. Once the ropes were arranged, they released the lock, then heaved the counterweight back up the Descending Passage to return it to the start position.

A general rule of thumb governing situations of this type — that involve the use of a flexible material such as a cord to handle a significant burden — is never to let the line go slack. Slackness makes the object harder to control. It requires much more lifting power (in this case, brute strength) to first remove the slack in the line, then lift the weight from a dead stop when it's time to move the load again. Keeping tension on the rope also helps prevent moisture from seeping into the lines and possibly stretching them.

Controlling the counterweight was one of those instances when the Egyptians may have applied colors to signify the position of the stone and the progress made in raising or lowering it. By painting certain sections along a length of the rope different hues, the workers outside managing the pull-ropes would be able to see when the lines were about to reach a predetermined mark, indicating that they would soon have to stop pulling or releasing the rope. Similarly, an overseer positioned on the platform near the pulleys at the top of the ramp, for example, watching the colors go by, would know when the counterweight was getting close to the spot where it was either as low as it should go inside the tunnel or had arrived back at the start position — and could order the crew to halt.

• Footholds •

Based on where the counterweight rested inside the Descending Passage (blocking access to the Subterranean Chamber), a logical question might be: How were the people assigned to turn the giant wheel able to reach the lower chamber? A little-known fact about the Great Pyramid is that portions of the Well Shaft, also known as the Inspection Shaft, show evidence of rough manmade indentations in the walls that curiously look a lot like footholds.

No one knows exactly when the small hollows were carved into the walls, but the Griffith theory proposes that they were indeed footholds, which would have allowed workers to climb up and down the shaft to make their way in and out of the Subterranean Chamber. While the chute itself is quite long, its diameter is only about two feet wide, which would have made it relatively easy — and safe — for crew members to place their feet in the toe holes and brace themselves against the rock wall in back.

Pathway to the Gallery

The Egyptians' already complicated network of ropes spreads out even further with the inclusion of the Grand Gallery. A total of six lines, including the anchor rope, connected to the counterweight. The two at the upper end continued up the Descending Passage toward the north wall and the workers stationed outside the building assigned to the reset operation. A third length of rope trailing from the low end dropped down the passageway and traveled over the rollers near the bottom of the channel, which directed it toward the giant take-up spool in the Subterranean Chamber.

The team had also affixed two more ropes to the counterweight's back end. This set proceeded up and over a pulley installed at the juncture in the bedrock where the Descending Passage and First Ascending Passage intersect. (The bottom end of the ascending passageway sits directly above the Descending Passage.) A heavy wooden pulley mounted in that spot, extending from one side of the shaft to the other like a curtain rod, spanned the width of First Ascending Passage. As the pair of ropes passed over this roller, it redirected them uphill through the shaft.

The set of ropes continued on, negotiating a path through the First Ascending Passage, then traversing the wooden substructure beneath the lift with the lines wending their way in and out of the open spaces between the struts that supported the deck. After emerging from the lift's underbelly, the ropes kept climbing toward another pulley positioned about midway up the Grand Gallery ramp.

It made sense to place a pulley farther up the ramp because the floor on either side already had a series of horizontal holes cut into the top and capable of holding a pair of moveable uprights. Workers could easily mount a roller between those two posts. Circling around the pulley inside the gallery, both lines reversed course and dropped back down the incline toward the lift, where they were attached to the vehicle's front end.

At least four more ropes from the pulleys positioned on top of the southern utility pyramid — now strung down the center of the Grand Gallery — also came into play during the preparations for raising the lift. With the Great

Step and Antechamber not yet built, nothing impeded the lines coming from the south, which had a clear run directly from the top of the step-pyramid to the lift below. While one end of the ropes was attached to the lift, the other end was in the hands of the pullers standing outdoors on the south side who had fastened it to their harnesses. Working in unison with the counterweight, the group stationed on the ground were able to multiply the available pulling power for lifting even the heaviest blocks of stone.

30th Course

By the time the builders had bridged the gap at the lower end of the Grand Gallery and linked that corridor to the upper end of the First Ascending Passage, construction had turned another critical corner. The Egyptians' ability to handle the tremendous blocks ordained for their construction project would increase dramatically once they began to employ the gigantic lift. The lift will make it possible for them to transport the bulk of the materials for the remainder of the pyramid up the unfinished Grand Gallery.

At this stage, crews had completed the lower levels of the Great Pyramid to approximately the 30th course, which also included hauling in a collection of L-shaped blocks to extend the gallery's side walls a little farther up the evolving corridor.

It is worth noting that the machine in the niche remained operational despite the fact that the wooden bridge in front of the Horizontal Passage hindered access to the Queen's Chamber. The entrance into that passageway still existed, but the three small openings built into the bridge were too tight and narrow to handle any blocks. (Blocks such as those installed for the gallery walls were much too large to have passed through the Horizontal Passage anyway.) Only the ropes going to and from the chamber and individual members of the crew fit through the tiny doors.

Luckily the crews could still count on the wood-framed mechanism with the winch located inside the Queen's Chamber to help pull the sleds and stones arriving from the quarries closer to the area where they were working and onto the lift. To that end, the builders would maintain the device in the niched wall far into the future. Much later, when the Queen's Chamber was finally under roof and completely closed off from above, the team controlling the machine in the niche would still be able to crawl through the Horizontal Passage and make their way into the room — just like the tourists do today.

To extend the Grand Gallery's walls further up the ramp, the construction team had already lugged in and set aside the initial group of limestone panels for the walls in the section immediately south of the entrance to the Horizontal Passage. The blocks were probably carried up to at least the top of the 27th course much earlier, while crews still had access to the temporary stone ramp set up near the north end of that passageway. Similar to all the other panels lining the gallery's sloping walls, the series of blocks forming the bottom row slanted downward at a 26-degree angle.

After dragging the new wall panels over and setting them in place, work gangs deposited a second row of rectangular blocks (3' x 4' x 8') directly on top of the base blocks in the new section, which made the side walls almost 11 feet high. Why didn't the blocks on top slide down the incline and drop off the tilted edge of the L? Engineers had started construction of the side walls from the bottom of the gallery. As a result, the stones positioned at the lower end served as a barricade, which obstructed the blocks further up the corridor and prevented them from tumbling downhill. Remarkably, the Grand Gallery is the only place in the entire pyramid where such a prominent set of blocks rides at an angle.

Corbels

It is when the construction crew places succeeding rows of rectangular blocks on top of the ones in the bottom two rows of the wall that the first of the gallery's corbels begin to emerge. Soon after the initial set of squared-off blocks was placed on top of their L-shaped bases, workers set down three more rows of stones above them, each three feet tall. The Griffith theory breaks with the conventional thinking that every corbel block was cut three inches longer than the one underneath it. Instead, the new theory states that the slabs were all the same size and workers merely pushed each piece forward to overhang the block in the row below it by three inches. (The corbels also lean in approximately five degrees toward the center of the gallery.)

This hypothesis is based in part on the belief that the ancient Egyptians were eminently practical and efficient. It is far easier to cut every slab the same size at the quarry and adjust their placement on-site rather than deal with a multiplicity of pieces of different shapes and dimensions. Without the ability to measure the blocks end to end, no one really knows how far the corbels extend behind the gallery's east and west walls. What is clear is that they were long enough to stay put and not tip forward when offset by a few inches.

During the process of assembling some of the previous courses, crews stacked up blocks at the lower (north) end of the Grand Gallery. Those stacks held back the blocks in the side walls and prevented them from falling off the incline onto the floor. The Griffith theory proposes that these "stopper" blocks, which today are hidden behind other stones, were not aligned edge to edge with the blocks in the walls. Although it is impossible to establish the precise point where the slabs of polished limestone in the side walls came to rest, they probably hit the stopper blocks somewhere near the middle of the stone. This meant that before the Grand Gallery was finished, the portion of each stopper block closest to the center of the corridor was not obscured because nothing stood in the way to conceal that half. Only years later, when workers erected the corbelled wall around the entrance to the First Ascending Passage in front of them, would the columns of stopper blocks east and west completely disappear from view.

From here on, the team will continue to insert wall panels and blocks up both sides of the gallery ramp in conjunction with the progress made on the individual courses. As the number of layers in the pyramid slowly increased, the sides of the corridor grew longer north to south. At the same time, extending the gallery's walls was a carefully planned endeavor in which the builders took great pains to avoid overshooting the height of the last course they had filled in. The Egyptians had designed their lift to facilitate moving sizeable pieces of stone with maximum efficiency. Consequently, it was essential that the wall panels never get in the way of the mechanism's platform as it stopped to offload. The lift was always supposed to meet the top of the most recent course constructed to form a flat plane with the floor at the level where crews required fresh blocks.

The logistics involved in the operation writ large meant that the sides of the Grand Gallery were far from complete and would remain that way for a very long time. From the floor up, the unfinished walls lining the corridor rose only as high as the third corbel — the block where the shallow channel or stability groove for the lift was cut into the stone. Keeping in mind the entire construction site was still exposed to the outdoors, it is worth noting that ensuing sections would remain the same height (up to the third corbel) for decades to come. Likewise, the addition of new wall panels will ultimately take the side walls no further south than the top of the 49th course.

Why? The gallery is a little less than seven feet across at its widest point. If the builders had kept going, the area at the upper end of the ramp would have shrunk and become too narrow, which for all intents and purposes would have made it impossible to complete the Great Pyramid. Before putting the final touches on the Grand Gallery, the Egyptians had to retain ample open space for the very largest slabs of granite to arrive at the King's Chamber.

Roofing the Queen's Chamber

The bulky slabs of high-quality, polished limestone used in the ceiling of the Queen's Chamber were probably some of the very first blocks transported on the lift once it was put into service. While the vehicle was originally designed with the idea of handling the most extreme weights in mind, before building the King's Chamber, the lift would have carried a majority of the construction materials for Courses 30 through 49. As soon as the building process went beyond that point, the lift would still be in use, but core facets of the operation would shift again with the introduction of two more internal pyramids.

Up to now, most of the limestone blocks entering the building site followed a route that took them through the Horizontal Passage dragged along by the machine in the stepped niche, then up the center channels of the two utility pyramids — elevated by the power of laborers pulling on the ropes attached to the loaded sleds. But the wooden bridge linking the Grand Gallery to the First Ascending Passage had essentially put the Horizontal Passage out of commission as far as dragging stones through that tunnel was concerned. Even so, sufficient room remained for ropes connected to the machine in the Queen's Chamber to fit through the doorway. As a consequence, the mechanism was still pulling the blocks and sleds arriving from the exterior ramp toward the primary work area and the lift.

Over time, crews would raise the stones targeted for different sections of the Great Pyramid by stacking piles of regular-sized blocks on top of the giant lift, then transferring them to smaller sleds stationed on the specific course under construction.

In other cases, work gangs would haul in larger pieces of stone already loaded on sleds sized to fit on top of the lift's deck and/or set the heaviest and bulkiest blocks directly onto the platform itself and, if necessary, tie them down for the ride.

The blocks quarried for the Queen's Chamber roof, which reaches as high as the 35th course, were large, but as far as we can tell without knowing the precisely how thick the slabs are, they are not gigantic. Six limestone blocks (3' 6" wide) cover the room on each side, creating a double pitched roof with a 30-degree angle, almost 19 feet long east to west and more than 20 feet tall from floor to peak. Egyptologists have conjectured that the ceiling was vaulted to help carry the load over the cavity, as well as shoulder some of the burden from the rest of the Great Pyramid. The chamber's four walls are composed of blocks 33 inches tall, and both the north and south sides are six blocks high. The blocks at the east and west ends below the gabled roof make those two sides narrower but a couple of rows taller near the peak. Furthermore, the highest row of wall blocks around the upper edge of the room was slanted on top, possibly to help maintain the equilibrium of the roof slabs and hold them in place.

The Griffith theory submits that the Egyptians began using the lift when construction reached approximately Course 30. One by one, the work gangs would maneuver the sleds carrying the blocks quarried for the ceiling in the Queen's Chamber up the outside ramp. Then, taking advantage of the machine in the niche, they drew the loaded sled into the vicinity of the lift before positioning it on the deck. By making use of both the counterweight and the pullers on the ground, the lift moved up the corridor until it was even with the top of the 30th course. There, the sled carrying the slab was removed and dragged across the floor toward the small "valley" where the Queen's Chamber sat. The reference to a valley denotes the shallow trenches running alongside the chamber's north and south walls. The builders had developed them by leaving out some of the filler stones from the course adjacent to the upper row.

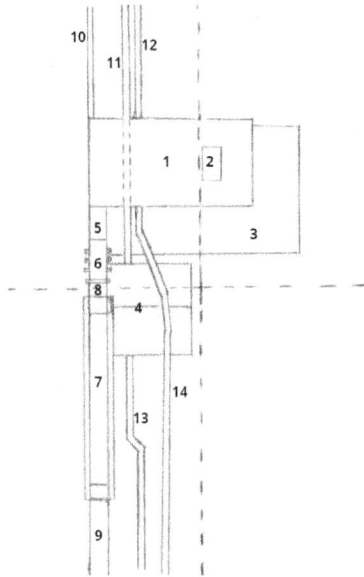

CORE OF PYRAMID

1. King's Chamber

2. Sarcophagus

3. Subterranean Chamber

4. Queen's Chamber
   [Note: The dark line through the middle represents the peak of the gabled roof.]

5. Royal Passage

6. Antechamber

7. Grand Gallery

8. Great Step

9. Horizontal/Queen's Chamber Passage
   [Note: The Horizontal Passage sits directly below the Grand Gallery. The portion of the tunnel visible in this diagram is the short hallway between it and the First Ascending Passage (not shown).]

10. Dead-end shaft on the south side of the Subterranean Chamber

11. Queen's Chamber southern air shaft

12. King's Chamber southern air shaft

13. Queen's Chamber northern air shaft

14. King's Chamber northern air shaft

One way to transfer the hefty slabs and construct the roof was to haul the first sled across the floor toward the east end of the Queen's Chamber. There was no trench at that end because the build-up of course blocks on the east and west ends reached as high as the top of the chamber itself. After removing the roof slab from its carrier and positioning it next to the north wall, workers rested the block against the wall's slanted rim. Then they maneuvered the piece of stone into place by pulling it west down the edge of the wall along the north side of the room. Once the slab reached the far end, the crew slipped it into the trench, which temporarily held it steady.

Soon a second block — following the same general route but transported along the beveled edge of the south wall — was placed opposite the first piece, lowered into the trench, and tipped forward. To control an outsized slab that is set on an angle such as those used in the roof of the Queen's Chamber, typically the objective is to try to handle the block so that it remains a bit off center.

In this instance, overbalancing the stone toward the outside to maintain a greater share of the weight near the bottom decreased the chances that it would fall headlong into the room as the team attempted to tip it forward over the top of the wall. The trenches that the work gangs had developed on the north and south sides were deep enough to slip the lower end of the ceiling block into the ditch. Crews would subsequently lean the slab inward at a 30-degree angle toward its mate on the other side of the room to form a peak.

One after the other, the ceiling blocks traveled from east to west until a 12-piece roof covered the open space. (In an interesting side note, the Egyptians may have also erected scaffolding inside the Queen's Chamber before construction getting underway to help them control the ceiling blocks and pair them up. With no cover on the room yet, workers could have lowered the wooden beams for the scaffolding into the room from above.)

As soon as the tips of the limestone pieces on both sides of the chamber were shoved together, work gangs packed filler blocks in the trench around the bottom of each ceiling slab. The weight of those stones bearing down on the base not only increased the pressure on the slab but pushed it even harder into the piece facing it, which helped stabilize the roof and lock it into place.

• Leveling Courses •

Regardless of how it may appear in some photographs, the 200+ courses comprising the Great Pyramid of Giza were not all the same size. The ancient Egyptians used blocks of varying heights as they built their way up, and as with most aspects of this architectural marvel, did so for a reason. The Griffith theory contends that at specific intervals during the construction process, the builders inserted individual courses expressly designed as part of an engineering strategy to ensure the building was still level — before proceeding to the next stage of their work. Placed at calculated points among the huge stacks of blocks that produced the Great Pyramid, these specialized layers were the leveling courses.

Observing the pyramid from the outside where most of the official course measurements were calculated from exposed blocks on the exterior walls obscures the truth. Many of the stones filling up the rest of the space within the perimeter of the building were probably rough-cut and on occasion, little more than rubble. There is no reason to believe that the people who constructed the Great Pyramid expended inordinate amounts of time and energy on dressing every block that would end up hidden deep inside the interior of the structure.

Furthermore, even though the pieces used for filler were generally flat on the top and bottom, bumps and undulations on one course would no doubt have created an uneven surface for the next course installed on top of it. While the effect of small irregularities on a single course might be minimal, the cumulative effect of misshapen or broken blocks could potentially be enormous in the long term. An assortment of dips and ripples lying underneath any number of courses might push all of the succeeding layers out of line.

In an attempt to remedy the situation and maintain a perfectly flat surface for construction, and ensure that the upper portion of the pyramid was not crooked, the architects strategically inserted leveling courses intermittently throughout the structure. These layers acted as stabilizers to help even out the entire pyramid. A leveling course was usually much larger and heavier than the courses immediately above and below it. In fact, judging from the heights of the courses as a group, and especially those near the top of the pyramid, it appears as if the Egyptians would construct a leveling course, then decrease the size of the subsequent courses. They kept installing smaller layers until it was time to drop another leveling course into the design. The heavier courses made it more difficult for the sections underneath them to shift around.

In many ways, the leveling courses also injected a pause into the construction activity as the monument continued to grow. Establishing a fresh base for building higher allowed engineers to confirm whether all four corners were straight and exact, the surface of the latest course was smooth and completely level from one side to the other, and the evolving pyramid was still square and uniformly aligned across the site. Crews could then make the necessary adjustments before resuming work on the enormous operation. It seems the greater size of many of the leveling courses may have also helped distribute the load across the 13-acre expanse to prevent weak spots that might be crushed more easily under many tons of additional weight.

Course 25 — the roof of the symbolic mastaba — was a key leveling course, as was Course 35, standing at more than 49 inches high, the largest course found above the Queen's Chamber. It is important to note that adding such an extraordinarily thick, heavy layer was particularly important at this juncture to even out the underlying courses before erecting the King's Chamber.

CHAPTER 9

FIT FOR A KING

WHILE THE FINISHING TOUCHES on the Queen's Chamber were in motion, another major buildout had begun. By the time the layers reached the height of the 49th course, the Egyptians had started erecting a second, higher utility pyramid over the first one in the southeast quadrant in the area behind the chamber. Likewise, construction had also begun on another step-pyramid in the northeast quadrant that would stand next to the original interior pyramid on that side.

The second utility pyramid at the north end was offset slightly from the first one because the Egyptians had to retain a sufficient amount of open space in the primary work area, which they are going to establish on Course 49, to be able to accommodate the very largest blocks inside the Great Pyramid. Remember, too, that the original step-pyramid on the north side was still missing a significant pie-shaped section from its lower half, which left an area on the 25th course wide open to receive the building materials entering the site from the exterior ramps.

Eventually, the new structures in the southeast and northeast — assembled above and beside the first two utility pyramids — would ascend to Courses 101 and 98, respectively. And that great height would provide the means for the Egyptians to construct the final half of their colossal monument. In a curious twist, the latest pair of interior pyramids did not precisely match the original two but were built at slightly different angles. The incline on the center channel running up the front of the southern pyramid was 45 degrees — too steep to walk — while the one at the north end sported a center channel with a 32-degree incline.

In addition, unlike the previous set of utility pyramids, engineers de-signed the upper step-pyramid on the north side with a center shaft almost

30 feet wide to accommodate the enormous blocks of stone they planned to use in upcoming sections of the pyramid, some of them slated to be at least 28 feet long. Before too much time passed, it would also be the northern step-pyramid that dominated the entire construction operation, since in the future, the ropes coming from the utility pyramid on the south side would essentially have gone out of service as far as raising blocks was concerned. Those ropes would instead operate a second, supplementary counterweight that would interconnect with the lines at the north end.

Since construction had now surpassed the 35th course, crews were in the process of readjusting the ropes hooked onto the underground counterweight, which came through the First Ascending Passage, to allow the lift to go higher. Dismantling the pulley stand mounted mid-way up the Grand Gallery ramp, workers took the uprights and inserted them into the last two floor holes at the upper end of the corridor. As in the past, the lines circled around the repositioned pulley before looping back down the ramp and connecting to the front of the lift. Meanwhile, the ropes originating on the south side of the site from the top of the latest step-pyramid behind the Queen's Chamber functioned as they always had, passing over the roller in the gallery before attaching to the lift.

The method involved in depositing the blocks to erect the latest two utility pyramids followed the same general strategy that the Egyptians had employed in constructing the initial pair on the 25th course — except in this instance, the limestone blocks came up the gallery ramp on the lift, rather than traversing the floor to the Queen's Chamber before being pulled up the center channels. By the time the construction team began hauling stones on the lift for step-pyramids #3 and #4, the vast majority of the original two internal pyramids had been buried beneath them, absorbed into prior courses.

Birth of an Air Shaft

The Griffith theory maintains that during this era, when construction reached Course 35 and the southern pulleys were redirected to permit their ropes to drop down the center of the Grand Gallery, the air shafts in the Queen's Chamber as we know them today were born. The situation had changed and the normal route up one of the center channels on the original set of utility pyramids was no longer viable for elevating blocks. A slew of modifications, including the loss of the Horizontal Passage as a conduit into the Queen's Chamber and the giant lift now acting as the main transporter, had for all intents and purposes rendered those channels moot.

The challenge engineers had faced in the past was twofold. To keep building, it was imperative that they maintain a shaft up the center of each step-pyramid large enough for the sleds and blocks traveling from the Queen's Chamber to slide through. But leaving the channel's slanted surface exposed would have made it impossible to build higher since workers needed a flat, solid surface upon which to construct subsequent courses to make certain that the Great Pyramid remained level. Obviously, circumstances demanded some sort of cover on top of the chute. As a result, the team had been laying the foundation for the future air shafts as the courses evolved by roofing over the inclines running up the front of the two step-pyramids level by level, gradually turning them into tunnels.

The solution came from the quarries, where stonecutters had fashioned a series of header blocks in a standard size for the two passageways. Wide enough to span the open channels, the rectangular chunks of limestone formed a roof over the gap built into every layer of the step-pyramid.

While five of the header stone's six faces were flat, the underside was slanted at a 39-degree angle, tracking the slope of the ramp built into the front of each structure. The ceiling inside the tunnel had to retain the same angle as the floor or its dimensions would vary as the ramp climbed upward. Only the east and west edges along the bottom of the block remained flat, which allowed the piece of limestone to rest solidly on the ledges flanking the channel.

Due to the fact that the steps or levels on the utility pyramids were different heights but the header blocks set above the channels were identical in size, the Egyptians must have compensated for the variations in height from course to course. To address the shorter courses, the team most likely placed short filler blocks on either side of the channel before installing a header stone over the gap. The idea was to prepare the base for the next course before the job proceeded by doing what was necessary to make the surface level with the horizontal plane. By the time construction reached Course 30, the open-air ramps built into the interior pyramids south and north had turned into enclosed shafts.

It was at this point, after the two original utility pyramids had for the most part been integrated into the finished courses, that the plan to shrink down their center channels even further kicked into high gear. The strategy the ancient builders deployed would systematically reduce the size of both passageways by a considerable amount, eliminating the internal ramps engineers had depended on to construct a majority of the courses in the Great Pyramid. The first step in the transformation process was restoring the blocks in the walls of the Queen's Chamber where the channels began.

The lower end on the pair of chutes was created from three blocks. Crews had set a piece of stone that was angled on top, on the floor inside the space where they had originally left a gap in the wall. A rectangular filler block was positioned behind it. Then they extended the brief incline by placing a second slanted block cut at the same 39-degree angle above the squared-off piece in the bottom row. During the prolonged period when the first two internal ramps were operational, the walls in the Queen's Chamber had contained a pair of indentations — a single block of limestone wide — on the north and south sides.

The restoration procedure involved pulling out the angled blocks sitting on the floor at the base of each channel, along with the ramp stone in the second row that had extended the incline, and replacing them with rectangular blocks. Workers would also insert one more block in the walls. Switching out the angled blocks for rectangular pieces had resulted in a hole in the second row on each side where the block in front was now missing. Inserting the final set of squared-off blocks of limestone into these cavities closed up the walls.

But the chamber still did not look like it does today. The rectangular replacement blocks in the second row — the one in front and the block right behind it — had eight-inch by eight-inch grooves precut through them for the air shafts to come. Together, the cutouts formed an uninterrupted groove across the top of the blocks.

Strangely, though, these "pipelines" inside the walls were not visible at that time. The openings stopped several inches short of the interior walls on both sides of the chamber.

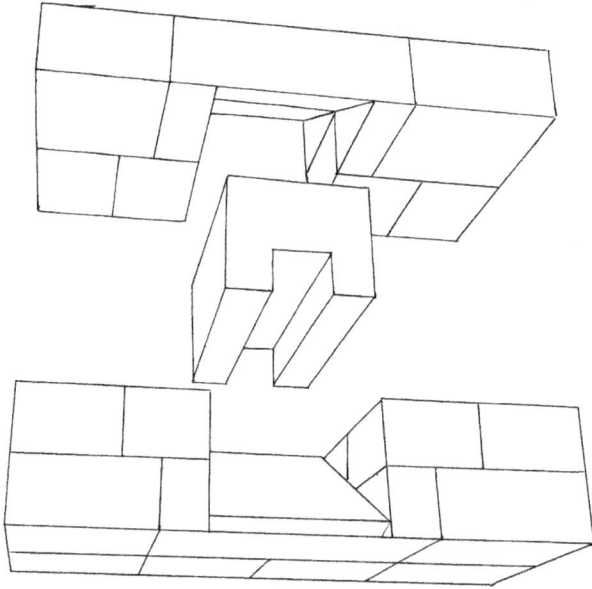

AIR SHAFT INSERT · DIAGRAM

An analysis of the air shafts in the Great Pyramid reveals that altogether, they contain four distinct components. In this case, the first element was the angled ramp stones that comprised the center channel itself. Second was a thin slab of a more durable stone that covered the limestone blocks at the bottom. Installing a layer of harder material made sense, given the wear and tear the floors in these passageways experienced on a regular basis as thousands of heavy sleds were dragged up the inclines. Set on top of the stone liner was the notched-out piece called the insert block. Since the rectangular inserts were flat on the bottom, they leaned downhill at a 39-degree angle. As a result, the leading edge on the first one in line at the base of the tunnel was beveled to eliminate the gap between it and the vertical plane that the insert abutted. The fourth and final component — already in place — was the header block, which was angled on the underside. The builders had set it over the top of the internal ramp as the courses developed to bring the sloped center channel back to level with the horizontal and thereby create the foundation for building higher.

With the lower ends of the chutes now closed off, the builders were ready to place prefabricated insert blocks into what used to be the utility pyramids' center channels to shrink them down. Designed to fit securely inside the

tunnels, which previously had been large and accessible enough to accommodate full-sized blocks and sleds, the inserts created a consistent eight-inch
by eight-inch opening through the entire shaft. Cut with a rectangular notch
along the bottom, the inserts resembled an upside-down, square-cornered
"U" or — viewed from the front — a flat wall with a rectangular, mouse-size
doorway at the bottom.

According to the Griffith theory, the Egyptians would have quarried the
series of inserts from one long block. After laying a slab of limestone on the
ground, stonecutters carved a rectangular notch along the top of the stone,
straight down the centerline end to end. Only then would workers slice the
lengthy block into approximately four-foot-long segments, knowing that
when the inserts were sitting front to back inside the tunnel, they were going
to fit together perfectly. In addition, the team may have used red ochre to
paint one of the faces on each block to indicate which side was supposed to
be at the low end as it dropped down the angled shaft. These markings may
be why pyramid explorers have found tiny red edges here and there inside
some of the air shafts.

Workers stationed on the uppermost course would take the insert blocks
one by one and send them down to the bottom of the close-fitting tunnels.
The series of inserts crafted to retain an opening through the humongous
pile of stones inside the Great Pyramid may have been a way for the builders
to maintain temporary airways for the people laboring in the chambers and
passages below. No one knows for sure. The small aperture formed by a line
of notched-out blocks extending up the two passageways not only shrank
the northern and southern center channels by a substantial amount but also
turned them into the air shafts we recognize today.

Barrier Stone

Another item associated with the air shafts was what the new theory calls
the barrier stone. While workers were packing individual courses with filler,
they probably set removable blocks in front of the openings into the center
channels to cover them up temporarily and prevent trash or other objects from
falling into the empty chutes as they labored overhead. Since by this time, the
pull-ropes dropped into the Grand Gallery instead of down the two center

channels, nothing obstructed entry into the sloped shafts. Later, when crews were close to completing the level currently under construction, they must have removed the barrier stone safeguarding the hole to deposit the header block on top of the chute and roof it over, creating a tunnel. When the work gang moved on and started constructing the subsequent course, they would place the barrier stone in front of the open passageway again to re-secure the hole.

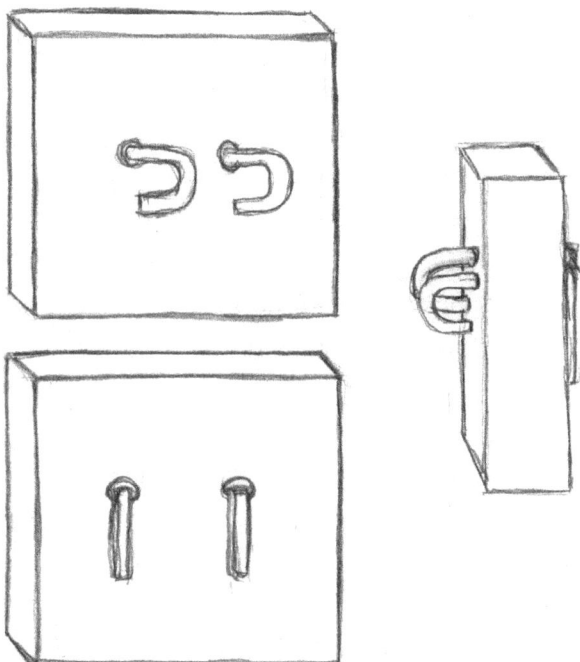

BARRIER STONE

The Egyptians may have used a barrier stone to close off the center-channel tunnels during construction to eliminate the possibility of foreign objects falling down the shafts.

The idea of the Egyptians employing a compact stone barrier, either for safety or other reasons, comports with the larger narrative about the Great Pyramid and what modern researchers involved in the Upuaut Project detected in 1993 when they were exploring the southern air shaft in the Queen's Chamber with a miniature robotic rover. Approximately 20 feet from the upper end of the narrow tunnel on the south side, investigators discovered a block of stone obstructing the passageway, which they labeled a door. This block was striking in that it had two strips of metal that looked like copper attached to the face of the stone as seen from below. Years later, a team directing another rover drilled a tiny hole through the block with the metal slivers to allow a camera to take a peek at the other side. The pictures revealed a second blockage some eight inches away. The undressed piece of limestone situated a short distance beyond the small door marks the spot where the southern air shaft in the Queen's Chamber comes to an abrupt end.

What if the copper rods the camera observed are actually the reverse side of handles embedded in the front of a barrier stone? It seems logical that engineers would have affixed some type of handle to a portable stone and the metal pieces visible on the opposite side were part of the design. The compact nature of the bent-down strips of copper meant the metal strips at the back lay flat against the surface of the stone, which kept them out of the way as workers moved the device up and down. A set of handles would have made it much easier for the people managing the process to both set the portable block over the cavity and lift it up again when the time came to deposit the barrier stone on the next course.

Under this scenario, the reason for the short gap between the door with the copper strips and what the camera saw beyond the upper end of the shaft may be less complicated than previously imagined. Considering what a work crew might have done once they had dropped the final insert into the channel — the limestone block that the camera revealed behind the door may not have been part of the shaft at all. It could merely be a piece of filler stone from the next course up. With work on that small section of the pyramid nearing completion, the workers probably left the barrier stone in place to close off the hole by setting it against the last U-shaped piece in line, maybe even hoping that it might be discovered someday.

While the shafts ascending from both sides of Queen's Chamber do not appear to have ever reached as far as the outer walls of the Great Pyramid, during this period of time, with the building site still exposed to elements, these openings would have permitted a little fresh air to reach the people working below. The fact that the air shafts end at a spot within the interior of the pyramid leaves open to speculation the possibility that they may very well terminate at the entrance to a secret chamber(s), still hidden today somewhere inside the massive structure.

• Secret Cavities •

When the ancient Egyptians were finishing off the first set of air shafts in the Great Pyramid on the north and south sides of the Queen's Chamber, they replaced the angled stones at the base of the center channels with rectangular wall blocks. But unlike the U-shaped inserts found further up the tunnels, in the beginning, there was no evidence that the replacement pieces had any sort of rectangular holes cut through them for an actual shaft. Only much later did researchers discover that the wall blocks in the second row on both sides of the room were notched out along the top. But those notches stopped about five inches short of the face of the stone in front. Once they were installed, the flat surfaces on the pair of blocks with the hidden holes made the interior walls north and south appear smooth and unmarred.

GREAT PYRAMID IN THE 1800s
The Giza Plateau in the 1800s when Waynman Dixon was exploring Egypt.

For this reason, the air shafts in the Queen's Chamber remained hidden until 1872, when British engineer Waynman Dixon was exploring the Great Pyramid and began to wonder why there were air shafts in the King's Chamber but none in the chamber below it. After determining the position of the two cavities in the King's Chamber and measuring off approximately the same distance from the corners and floor in the Queen's Chamber, he noticed a small crack in one of the wall blocks and decided to examine it further. Breaking through the first five inches of stone near the crack, Dixon discovered the southern air shaft and later the shaft on the opposite (north) wall, too.

Up and Up

When work on the newest pair of step-pyramids was completed, the job of filling in the next round of courses was ready to move forward. And once the buildout finally reached Course 49, it began to play a crucial role in advancing the construction process. The Egyptians had targeted this level specifically — the level one course below the floor of the King's Chamber — to establish their primary work space. Engineers purposely set aside an open area approximately 40 feet by 40 feet to serve as the landing site for workers and materials in the succeeding months and years. The small portion of the 49th course located immediately west of the lift had to remain empty because that was where the lift would debark the necessary supplies to finish the Great Pyramid.

In truth, the great lift was at the heart of the buildout writ large, and the open space the team had maintained on the west side at the upper end of the gallery was a key factor in its deployment. The traversable space on Course 49 was designed as a transit station — the interim stop — that allowed workers to transfer, rig, or elevate the sleds, blocks, ropes, and other raw materials essential to their operations. Due to the lift's significance in transporting and unloading critical equipment and provisions, the builders had made some adjustments at the south end of the gallery ramp.

The goal was to bridge the gap on the west side — between the lift and the edge of the floor — to establish a contiguous, even surface in a very busy spot. Using blocks that were slanted on the bottom but flat on top, the team replaced the first 34 feet or so of the ramp alongside the vehicle. Setting the series of blocks in the "ditch" produced after workers had removed the top layer of ramp stones from the target area would achieve a few objectives. It eliminated the break between the lift's wooden deck and Course 49 while widening the floor on that level by another four feet or more. And the new blocks slotted into the shallow trench, which made it level to the horizontal plane, would join the lift to the main workspace whenever it parked at the upper end of the corridor to unload cargo.

Many decades would pass before the incline in that small section of the ramp was restored — only when the Egyptians were finally ready to wall in the remainder of the Grand Gallery.

The number of layers in the Great Pyramid were going to keep growing through a process nearly identical to the one the builders had used on prior levels. The white casing stones and filler blocks for the next series of courses would arrive on the 49th course on individual sleds, four at a time. Since the center channel on the latest step-pyramid sat more than 30 feet away from the gallery and lift platform, the layout left a sufficient amount of space to maneuver the building materials. But it also meant that the workers transferring the loaded sleds were forced to pull them west by hand to line them up in a row at the base of the center channel, directly below the pulley mounted many courses overhead.

For current purposes, the Egyptians had revived the setup and routine used so successfully to raise the sleds transporting blocks up the channels leading from the Queen's Chamber. Workers would hook the vehicles together with the back end of the sled in front fastened to the front end of the one behind it to form a chain. Once the four-car train loaded with the limestone was ready to go, the crew would attach it to the pull-ropes, which stretched all the way up to the pulley on top of the upper utility pyramid and down the outside wall.

Proceeding down the side of the building, the lines passed over several rollers mounted on tall stands inserted into the cladding. When the lengthy ropes approached the bottom, they laced through the lock and pulley system installed on the outer edge of the northern platform before reaching the team of workers assigned to pull. As the cohort of laborers pulled, just as they had some thousands of times before, the procession of sleds carting the blocks moved up the passageway to the course presently under construction. Here, a separate team operating a shadoof transferred the stone from the first sled in line onto another sled, permitting the gang working on that level to drag it over to the zone they were filling in.

Then the pull-team posted on the northern ramp drew the short train further up the channel, which put the second sled in position for the shadoof to unload. The process continued until all four carriers were empty and slack in the rope allowed the train to slide back down the incline. Blocks and sleds kept moving in and out in an uninterrupted cycle. While one sled-train traveled up the center channel toward the shadoof, the lift was heading down to Course 25 to retrieve another load. Then, after depositing four more sleds with blocks in the workspace at the top of the ramp, the lift carried the now-empty vehicles from the previous group down to the bottom of the gallery to receive another set of stones.

If it were possible to look down from above onto the latest pair of utility pyramids, their relative positions would reveal an obvious challenge the builders had to overcome. In the past, it had been comparatively easy to direct the blocks on the lower courses arriving from the Queen's Chamber to the different quadrants. For the most part, workers were able to shuffle the limestone around to all four sectors of the larger pyramid with little or nothing standing in their way. Now the partially built Grand Gallery with its lower walls three corbels high was there, plunked down like a river valley in the middle of the space, dividing east from west at the north end of the site.

At first, workers had to convey the blocks designated for the northeast portion of the current course toward the south to skirt the ropes dangling from the southern utility pyramid before circumnavigating all the way around to the other side of Grand Gallery — that is, until the levels in the Great Pyramid reached the height of the third corbel. Once the elevation of the courses grows tall enough to be even with the unfinished walls in the gallery, the builders would install a wooden platform (removable bridge) over the chasm to create a more direct route for transporting the quarried stones across to the other side. Workers may have removed the temporary bridge when the lift went up or down, restoring it as necessary.

• Tafla •

In the most basic terms, friction is the resistance that one surface or object encounters when moving over another. In other words, friction is what makes it difficult for one surface to slide past the other. In the case of the Great Pyramid, the problem of how to overcome the tremendous amount of friction caused by stone moving against stone presented a constant challenge. The Egyptians had access to many different types of lubricants, primarily used outside the building, that may have helped to make their job easier: water, certain oils, and even a type of sand characterized by tiny grains with rounded edges worn down by the sifting motion of dunes tossed about in the desert winds. When scattered underneath an object, this sand forms a slippery surface able to assist in rolling an object forward or backward.

Yet none of these lubricants were likely to work as well as the natural buff-colored desert clay found around the Giza plateau and known as *tafla*. Used as plaster and mortar in ramps and embankments, tafla may have played an important role in aiding the Egyptians in moving the massive blocks of stone found inside the Great Pyramid. "Egyptologist Mark Lehner, director of Ancient Egypt Research Associates (AERA) says that thin tafla clay layers have been seen under multi-ton blocks either left in place at the wall of a temple or other monument, or where workers left the blocks en route, and not yet in their intended place in a building."[1]

When wet, this lime-rich mud or marl becomes quite slippery. It requires only a thin layer of the moist clay spread between two blocks of stone or in between a stone and a ramp, for example, to create a surface slick enough to push or pull a heavy load with relative ease. Dr. Lehner and his team experienced the phenomenon for themselves when they were involved in a WGBH-TV NOVA program and created "a hauling track of wood beams, sand, and limestone debris, and then coated it with a thin layer of calcareous desert clay, called *tafla* in Arabic. We had workers pull a two-ton limestone block on a wooden sledge, while one worker wetted the clay by sprinkling or pouring water in front of the runners of the sledge (he was crouched and moving backward as the sledge progressed). The slick clay acted as a lubricant and greatly facilitated pulling the block."[1]

A famous image from the tomb of a nobleman named Djehutihotep shows workers hauling a mammoth statue on a sledge with one worker standing at the front end, wetting down the area immediately ahead of the vehicle as it moves forward[2]. The workers with the pull-ropes may actually have been walking to the side — on dry sand or clay — while the statue itself rode along a path of wet tafla spread directly under the sled.

1. Mark Lehner, The Complete Pyramids: Solving the Ancient Mysteries (London: Thames & Hudson, Ltd., 1997), 203

2. Sudeshna Chowdhury, "Ancient Egyptians used wet sand to drag pyramid stones, say scientists," Christian Science Monitor, May 2, 2014, http://www. csmonitor.com/Science/2014/0502/Ancient-Egyptians-used-wet-sand-to-drag-massive-pyramid-stones-say-scientists

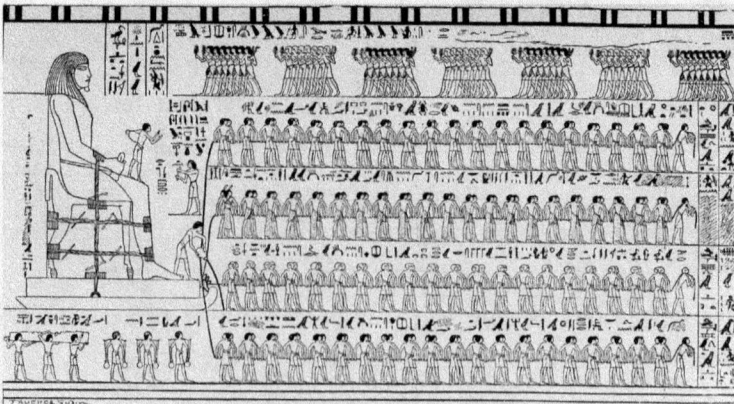

TOMB OF DJEHUTIHOTEP · WALL RELIEF

A wall relief from the tomb of Djehutihotep at el-Bersheh depicts an army of laborers moving a statue of the nobleman estimated to weigh approximately 58 tons.

King's Chamber

With all of the conditions ready, the builders were able to turn their attention to the most important room discovered inside the Great Pyramid of Giza to date: the King's Chamber. Step-pyramids on the north and south sides soared above the open space on the 49th course that had been set aside for this chamber. Besides being the springboard for the next phase of the greater construction operation, Course 49 formed the foundation for both the King's Chamber and the Antechamber leading up to it.

An intriguing but often-overlooked fact about the King's Chamber is that its walls sit five inches below the floor. Egyptologists surmise that the ancient Egyptians may have constructed the room in this manner as a hedge against potential catastrophe if and when an earthquake ever struck the Giza Plateau. Separating the floor from the walls would have permitted the structure some "give." No matter what the true motivation was behind their decision, in the end, it dictated which blocks the builders set in place first.

After unloading the first pile of stones for the walls, workers transferred them over to an area of the floor already marked off for the King's Chamber. One by one, they placed the blocks directly on top of Course 49 according to the outline by positioning the individual pieces to have the front ends create a rectangle in the dimensions of the room as it has existed throughout history. The initial group of blocks bordering the edges was quarried out of limestone 31 inches high. But because they sit lower than the chamber's floor, the first row is hidden beneath succeeding rows of granite so visitors are generally unaware of any limestone in the walls.

Soon a sequence of dressed granite blocks — 47 inches high — for the next row in the wall traveled up the ramp on the lift and was set atop the limestone edging. The granite blocks for the second row were all the same height with the exception of the four pieces that will flank the air shafts, located about waist high on the north and south sides of the chamber. When quarrying those pieces (two for each wall), stonecutters had made a horizontal notch along the upper left edge on one block and the upper right edge on another.

Placed side by side, the space missing between the two blocks formed a rectangular channel through the pair, front to back. In reality, the air shafts in the King's and Queen's chambers are not rectangular holes cut through the middle of solid blocks. Rather, the upper edge of each cavity is formed by the bottom edge of the block placed directly above the notched-out piece. Later, the builders would position two more sets of identically shaped blocks, but composed of limestone, behind the granite set at the front on both sides of the room to extend the rectangular openings in the King's Chamber by another four feet.

KING'S CHAMBER AIR SHAFT · NORTH WALL

The vertical seam underneath the air shaft in the King's Chamber is evidence that the opening was fabricated from two notched-out blocks set side by side. The piece of granite placed on top forms the upper edge of the hole.

The ring of blocks two rows high delineating the boundaries of the King's Chamber also included an opening at the northeast corner for a doorway into the space. Interestingly, the east wall actually extended north a short distance (about four feet) beyond the gap for the entrance. This extension foretold the development of the low passageway that one day would lead into the King's Chamber. Before long, the builders would place two huge granite blocks on top of the room's north wall, which would reach over the top of the entryway and enclose this little "hallway," forming a tunnel just tall enough for someone to creep through on their hands and knees. The Griffith theory refers to the constricted opening between Antechamber and King's Chamber as the Royal Passage.

Besides the opening set aside for the entrance, one additional section of the granite rectangle was missing. Workers had left a second gap in the north wall by the northwest corner. Later on, materials for the floor will enter the space through this access point. As with other key elements of the Great Pyramid, the area outlined by the first two rows of wall blocks also reflects the mysterious number: 17' 2". The Egyptians had doubled that number to arrive at one of the room's dimensions (34' 4") — the length of the King's Chamber east to west.

It was at this juncture that workers dragged in the polished granite blocks for the floor. After transporting the collection of floor blocks in assorted loads on the lift, they hauled them over to the opening at the northwest corner and into the unfinished room. Similar to laying tiles for a new kitchen floor, the construction team started at the far end of the room-in-progress and worked their way back toward the gap in the wall, placing the blocks directly on top of the 49th course. In this instance, the starting point was the area next to the chamber's entrance, which received its floor first. Then, moving east to west, workers set block after block into position, covering the entire space with granite until they reached the opening by the northwest corner, where they were able to exit the room with the job done.

Because the stones quarried for the floor were 36 inches tall but the initial row of wall blocks defining the chamber's dimensions was only 31 inches high, the floor sat five inches above the bottom row of limestone wall blocks. A three-foot-high floor also meant that the granite pieces now spread across the room were five inches taller than the lower edge of the wall blocks in the second row, also made of granite. The Egyptians' building technique and the differences in the heights of the various stones are the reason why the walls inside the King's Chamber sit below its floor.

Sarcophagus

With the space now ready and access through the opening at the northwest corner still available, it was time to carry in the most significant — and mystifying — article found inside the Great Pyramid of Giza: the sarcophagus. This object holds the distinction of being the only item specifically fabricated for the Great Pyramid ever discovered inside the building.

Without a cover, the outside of the sarcophagus measures more than seven feet long, three feet wide, and three feet high. Each of its four sides is approximately six inches thick and the stone base about seven inches deep. Carved out of a single block of Aswan granite (which may be distinct from the type of granite used elsewhere in the chamber's floor and walls), the coffer appears as if it were hollowed out, much like a carpenter might hollow out a wooden block with an auger. (Students of pyramidology have proposed this theory based on evidence of some spiral markings discovered on the inner walls of the granite coffer.)

Curiously, a small ridge or lip along the inside edge near the top of the sarcophagus hints at the possibility that the granite container may once have had a lid. To date, no one has discovered its cap, but based on the precision with which the Egyptians developed every other aspect of the Great Pyramid, the question remains: Why would they carve such an obvious ridge into the central icon of their extraordinary monument without it fulfilling any purpose?

To place the heavy sarcophagus inside the room, the team constructed a temporary stone ramp bridging the space between Course 49 — the level at which it arrived — and the upper edge of the 36-inch-high floor blocks lined up behind the opening at the northwest corner. After carrying the sarcophagus up on the lift on a low sled that was a few inches shorter east to west than the base of the coffer, a group of workers lugged the unwieldy object over to the access point.

Since the piece was hollowed out, it was considerably lighter than an intact granite block would have been. Then the crew hoisted the stone box up the small incline and over to the spot designated as its final resting place. Using levers placed below the small overhangs on either side, the work gang jacked up the edges and shoved four wooden blocks underneath the corners, creating enough space to pull out the sled. Once the wooden carrier was gone, the workers used their pry bars again to remove the blocks of wood supporting the base and carefully lower the sarcophagus to the floor.

Positioned lengthwise, almost dead center between the chamber's north and south walls, the sarcophagus lies near the room's west end. While it is impossible to tell whether the baffling granite box has been moved over the centuries, we do know that once all four walls were fully built, the only way in or out of the room would have been too low and narrow for anyone to be able to remove it from the space. It seems that the destiny of the sarcophagus was to stay right where it was, inside the King's Chamber for countless millennia.

SARCOPHAGUS
The sarcophagus inside the King's Chamber.

Leaving nothing to chance, the Egyptians designed the placement of the coffer so it was located in the west, the horizon that this ancient culture associated not only with the setting sun but with death. This single detail is striking because all of the rooms constructed inside the pyramid up to that time (Subterranean Chamber, Queen's Chamber, and unfinished King's Chamber) were built along a vertical line offset more than 23 feet east of the pyramid's north-south centerline. The fact that the architects decided to make the King's Chamber more than 34 feet long *east to west* was not only intentional but extremely significant. It meant the room crossed the midpoint of the building, which put the last approximately 11 feet of the interior space on the other side of the centerline. The width of the King's Chamber permitted them to actually situate the sarcophagus in the western half of the Great Pyramid — a remarkable outcome by any standard.

10 Feet Long

What probably occurred next were the preparations for transporting the two largest blocks introduced to that point above the base of the Great Pyramid — many decades after construction began. The builders will add twin pieces of granite, which are each more than 10 feet long, seven and one-half feet wide, and four feet thick, to the King's Chamber, positioning them back-to-back directly above the entryway to serve as a type of lintel.

We know through measurements taken from inside the King's Chamber that the two enormous pieces of granite above the entrance are at least 10 feet long. Yet these header blocks may actually extend some distance beyond the east wall of the Royal Passage, which would make them longer than 10 feet. A good guess is that the concealed ends on both blocks may reach at least to the far edge of the wall blocks lining the Royal Passage on the east side and might even continue further. Since it is impossible to see behind the wall, we can only estimate how big the two giant blocks really are.

Before taking the next step and hauling in such extraordinarily heavy pieces, the builders would have created a temporary stone ramp in the open area on Course 49 to accommodate the massive size of the two upcoming blocks. The new ramp must have been at least a dozen feet long or longer end to end, encompassing an area from the west end of the Royal Passage to midway down the north side of the King's Chamber. At least 78 inches high, the incline met the upper edge of the second row of blocks in the chamber's wall. In addition, for safety reasons and to assist them in handling the huge stones, workers probably set some scaffolding or smaller limestone blocks inside the empty space representing the Royal Passage to temporarily fill in that gap.

How did the Egyptians manage to transport such gigantic chunks of granite? As far-fetched as it may sound, the arrangement they used to convey the lengthy blocks was akin to the way someone might carry a mattress through a tight doorway.

The most logical setup places the granite on the lift lengthwise north to south lying on its narrowest side, which is about four feet wide. That meant the top of the stone soared almost eight feet above the lift's platform. The block had to be in this particular position or the edges would have hung over the sides of the lift and made the load too large to fit through the Grand Gallery, which was less than six feet across at the lower end, taking into account the reduction in width caused by the set of walls three corbels high. Work gangs would have tied down the piece of granite with ropes and/or affixed the giant block to the lift with wooden planks.

The tricky part came after the lift reached Course 49 and the huge weight had to be offloaded. Before moving the burdensome block of stone, workers had attached a curved wooden frame to one of the 10-foot-long sides, which bowed out like an overturned bowl sitting on a plate. Knowing the slab would have a tendency to teeter-totter and was much too heavy to control if momentum took over as they attempted to lay it on the floor, the builders had created the wooden bulge to help cushion the blow. Instead of slamming down hard onto the 49th course, the block would rock on its makeshift sled.

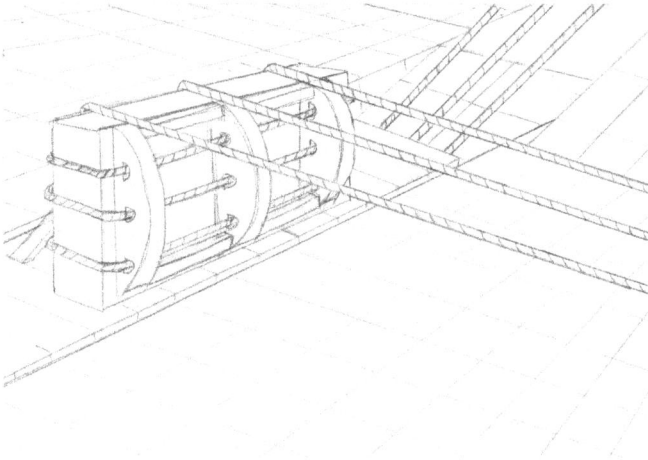

FRAME - 10-FOOT LINTEL STONE

The Egyptians built a special wooden frame to hold the ten-foot-long granite blocks for the headers that sit above the doorway into the King's Chamber. The side that bowed out allowed workers to remove the piece from the lift and rotate it without losing control of the extremely heavy stone slab.

When it was time to slide the giant piece of granite off the lift platform, workers started pulling it toward the bottom of the temporary ramp then carefully laid the slab down on the side sporting the convex frame. Because its curvature decreased the drag, they were able to slowly spin the block around, rotating the stone until the longest 10-foot-plus side was parallel to the north wall of the King's Chamber. Meanwhile, a separate crew had attached wooden supports to the other side of the room's north wall that was two rows high.

The series of beams and planks, which stood taller than the upper edge of the interior wall, began at the doorway to the chamber and continued west another 10 feet or so. The wooden uprights served as a stopgap measure to prevent the lintel block from slipping off the edge and tumbling into the room as crews tried to move it into place.

Then, using rollers, hooks, and the pulleys and ropes atop the southern step-pyramid, the team hoisted the first lintel block up the temporary ramp, stood the stone on its narrow edge, and began maneuvering it into position. Setting the rectangular piece of granite on the chamber's north wall, they slid the slab across the top of the opening for the Royal Passage and pulled it slightly forward (south) until the block sat flush with the interior wall. Viewed from inside the King's Chamber, this initial slab is the header stone that rests horizontally above the entrance.

LINTEL OVER DOORWAY
The southern header block above the Royal Passage viewed from inside the King's Chamber.

Notably, the second giant block the Egyptians hauled in displayed four vertical grooves, a little more than three inches wide and two inches deep, carved into one side of the 10-foot-long surface. Spaced several inches apart from each other, these indentations run from the top to the bottom of the stone and span an area 41 inches across east to west. Once it was pulled into position and set upright, the portion of block number two with the series of precut grooves formed the back wall of the Antechamber.

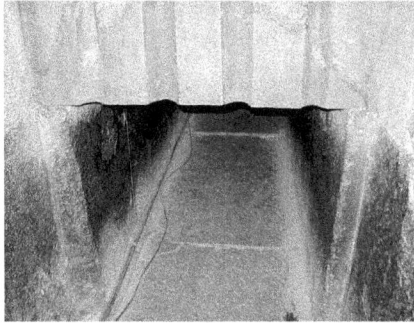

ANTECHAMBER BACK WALL

The back wall of the Antechamber was formed by a giant piece of granite that had vertical grooves carved into one of its faces. The lintel stone with the shallow channels sits over the Royal Passage on the north side.

While the second piece of granite came up the Grand Gallery on the lift in the same manner as the first one before its bowed frame was laid on the floor at the bottom of the temporary ramp, several additional factors influenced how the setup proceeded. First, workers had to make sure that the grooves carved only on one side, which covered a circumscribed portion of the block's longest face, would be exposed (facing north). In addition, the cutouts not only had to point in the proper direction but also end up situated directly above the Royal Passage. Adding to the challenge, the team had to contend with the giant block of stone already installed above that crawl space, which partially obstructed the pathway for the ropes suspended from the top of the southern step-pyramid.

To solve their engineering problem, the Egyptians must have moved the second block as far as it could go toward the west end of the temporary ramp and repositioned the pulleys on the utility pyramid's summit further west, too. Such an adjustment was possible because the work platforms created by the uppermost steps on each of the utility pyramids were deep, and the space was wide enough to both accommodate two pulley stands and allow workers to walk back and forth. A shift in the angle of the ropes dropping from above may have helped the team below in heaving the huge slab upright, on top of the chamber's unfinished north wall. Then, using another set of pulleys altogether, the people working the pull-ropes on the south side of the building dragged the second block toward the east end of the Royal Passage until the pair of lintel blocks stood back-to-back and the edges of the new piece of granite were even with the one parked behind it

These two giant blocks, which were essential to the future formation of the Antechamber, had enclosed the Royal Passage and created the tunnel less than four feet tall that tourists in the 21st century still scramble through. Once both slabs were firmly in place, crew members were able to dismantle the temporary ramp.

The King's Chamber was nowhere near finished at this point, but the rest of it would have to wait until construction had turned the next corner, making it possible for the team to elevate both the granite for the remainder of its walls and roof, as well as the massive blocks targeted for the Relieving Chambers that tower overhead. To proceed, the pyramid builders designed a separate room on the north side of the Royal Passage to house the nerve center for a highly sophisticated pulley and counterweight system unmatched in the ancient world. The Egyptians were ready to build the Antechamber.

CHAPTER 10

ANTECHAMBER

DESPITE EVERYTHING WE BELIEVE we understand about the mysterious space called the Antechamber it continues to captivate pyramid aficionados from around the world. Referred to as the mechanical heart of the Great Pyramid, the Antechamber is a kind of Rubik's cube that seemingly defies solution. Yet according to the Griffith theory, a deeper examination of this room will disclose its central purpose. Understanding the Antechamber is really a matter of seeing what is right before our eyes. At the same time, the process of discovery may never truly end, because this fascinating chamber holds the promise of revealing many more secrets to come.

At this point in time, the broad outlines of the King's Chamber were in place and a pair of huge granite blocks almost eight feet tall rested atop the crawl space known as the Royal Passage. The grooved section of the lintel block on the north side was, in fact, the first official wall of the Antechamber. As far as its other walls were concerned, the two framing the room east and west began to take shape next. However, the Egyptians would not erect the fourth and final wall at the front (north) end of the room — the wall that separates the Antechamber from the Grand Gallery — until construction had advanced considerably and the Great Pyramid was approximately two-thirds done.

Unlike the original wall with the vertical grooves at the south end of the Antechamber, its side walls were not built from single slabs of granite but composed of a series of granite blocks of different shapes and sizes. In addition, the Antechamber's side walls are two layers deep. A set of "outer" walls more than 12 feet tall touch the ceiling and stand behind a much shorter pair. The height of the shorter, inner wall on the east side is eight feet, seven inches and the one on the west side is nine feet, four inches.

Because the lower walls are only 12 inches deep, they form narrow shelves in front of the two taller walls erected behind them. Furthermore, both inner walls contain a sequence of four rectangular grooves down the front. Set five inches apart from each other, the first indentation at the south end on both sides is almost 17 inches wide north to south while the width of the next two is 21 and one-half inches. All three start at the shelf's upper edge and stop almost four inches below the floor. But the wider, fourth groove at the north end of the chamber extends only halfway down each wall. Curiously, the top of the 12-inch-wide shelf on the east side of the Antechamber is flat while the ledge on the west side is scooped out as if its front edge were scalloped into three semi-circles. The purpose of these dips or half-moons will become apparent later.

ANTECHAMBER - SCALLOPED WALL
The Antechamber's west wall has a scalloped edge formed by a series of semi-circular channels that extend from the front to the back of the 12-inch-deep shelf.

Pieced Together

The most practical approach to constructing the Antechamber was to build the bottom rows for the double-layered walls east and west first by setting those blocks directly onto Course 49. The way the chamber appears to be assembled indicates that the sizes of the blocks installed in the first and second rows of the taller, outer walls varied. In addition, the bottommost rows were not composed of granite. The assumption is that the Egyptians seldom chose granite blocks in places that would be totally hidden behind other walls. Although out of sight now, the limestone blocks hauled in for the initial rows were probably 31 inches tall. Adding the next row to the outer walls on each side entailed putting 47-inch blocks on top of the 31-inch-high stones, which together made the first two row in both walls 78 inches high.

On the east side of the Antechamber, the line of blocks in the first couple of rows comprising the outer wall started one foot east of the doorway underneath the giant grooved lintel stone above the Royal Passage. The reason the row of blocks started 12 inches away from the edge of the door was to leave space for the inner wall. The line of blocks also extended north more than nine feet, stopping at a mark that indicated where the front edge of the evolving Antechamber was going to be someday. After workers had arranged the first and second rows of blocks on the east side, they laid limestone filler behind the wall-in-progress.

Stacks of workaday blocks 78-inches tall and several rows deep were placed behind the new set of wall blocks, covering the general area between the east end of the huge lintel stone and the north end of the future room. Because it is impossible to gauge the precise length east to west of the lintel blocks situated over the Royal Passage, we can only approximate the width of the space that workers overlaid with filler. What we do know is that the accumulation of filler stones on the east side resulted in a flat work deck adjacent to the short wall.

Likewise, the bottommost rows in the outer wall on the Antechamber's west side began at the north wall of the King's Chamber, about a foot away from the doorway and, mirroring the east side, stretched another nine feet, eight inches north. The filler blocks, which workers subsequently set behind the developing wall, covered an area almost 30 feet wide. The deck on the west side also extended to the front (north) end of the short wall the team had just installed.

When all of the preliminary work on the Antechamber's two outer walls was done, the combination of the base blocks two rows high plus the filler blocks packed behind them created good-sized work platforms 78 inches tall on both sides of the narrow space.

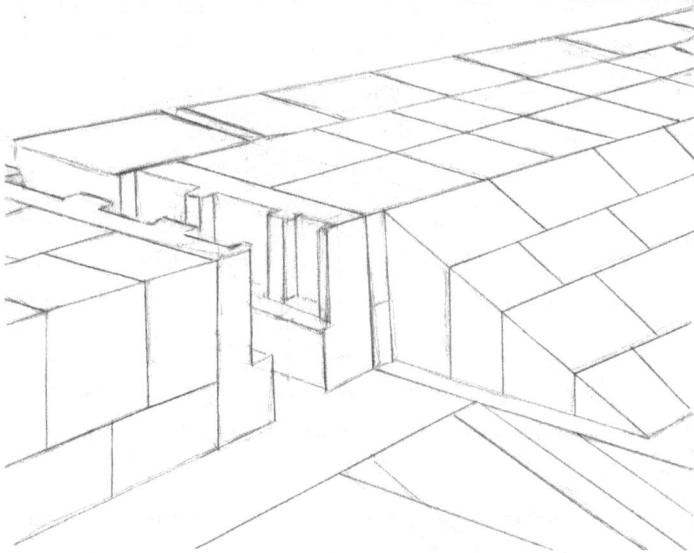

ANTECHAMBER · WORK DECKS AND RAMP

A temporary ramp was erected on Course 49 along with work platforms on both sides of the developing Antechamber.

Inner Walls

Since the inner set of walls inside the Antechamber is only 12 inches thick, the blocks used to assemble them were not as bulky as the pieces of granite the builders will insert later to complete the outer walls. As a result, the weight of any given piece quarried for the shorter pair of walls, labeled the "shelves," was no doubt lighter than the blocks set behind them.

Accordingly, the Egyptians' plans to assemble the first two rows of the two inner walls took its own unique path. The bottommost rows for the two shelf walls were installed as a series of blocks — each 78 inches tall — but with distinct widths side to side. Set directly on top of the 49th course, flush with the entrance to the Royal Passage leading into the King's Chamber, the upper edges east and west on the first row of inner-wall blocks are even with the top of that doorway. Equally significant, the blocks on both sides had rectangular indentations carved into the front surface. These channels, which were precisely aligned to sit straight across from each other inside the constricted room, served as the grooves for the portcullis stones.

The lowest row in the shelf wall on the east side consists of three blocks. Two of them are granite while the third one, at the north end, is limestone. Moving south to north, the first block in the sequence contains the southernmost portcullis groove plus half of the next groove, which is divided between the initial block and the block beside it. The second block includes the other half of that indentation plus the third portcullis groove. The width of the final block in the row, composed of limestone, is narrower than the previous two. Despite the variations in their widths, all three blocks in the first row of the east wall are 12 inches deep, 78 inches high — and sit directly on Course 49.

The configuration of the first row of blocks in the shelf wall on the west side does not conform to the setup on the east side because almost three-quarters of this wall was crafted out of a single piece of granite 78 inches tall. In the case of the 12-inch-deep west wall, all three portcullis grooves were carved into that one slab. The second and only other block in the first row, situated at the north end and made out of a relatively narrow piece of limestone, is also 78 inches tall.

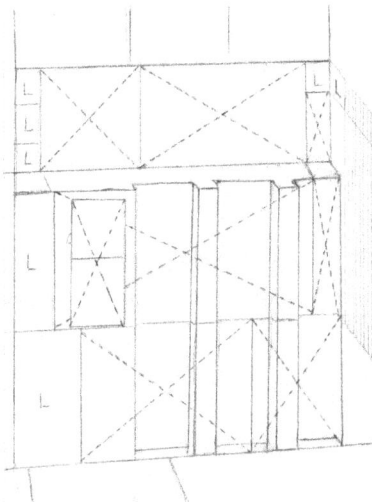

ANTECHAMBER · EAST WALL

The Antechamber's east wall, showing the individual blocks and the shelf.

The Griffith theory includes another intriguing proposition: that there is a special feature hidden below the wall blocks bordering the entrance to the Royal Passage. The hypothesis states that the builders had cut the blocks next to the doorway to the King's Chamber in the shape of a capital L with a lip at the bottom of each piece, approximately five inches wide and 31 inches high. Both the southernmost block in the first row of the inner wall on the east side and the inordinately long block forming most of the first row on the west side, contain such a lip concealed beneath the floor. The purpose for this unusual configuration will become evident once the Antechamber is completed.

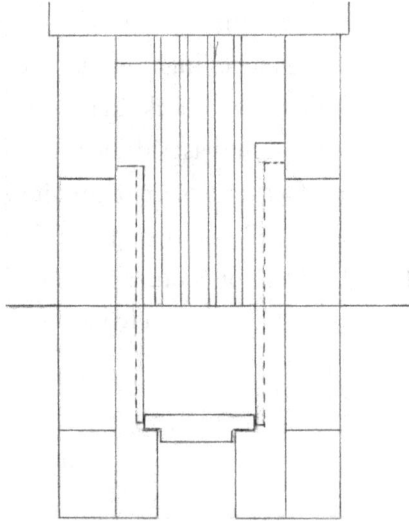

L-SHAPED BLOCKS AT ENTRANCE

According to the Griffith theory, the wall blocks in the Antechamber on either side of the entrance to the King's Chamber are L-shaped to support a floor block that can be removed.

The Egyptians soon followed up their work of assembling the lowest portions of the Antechamber's side walls by gathering a group of granite blocks on Course 49 and constructing its floor. These floor slabs, which ran down the center of the space between the unfinished walls that now delineated the boundaries of the chamber, also extended partway underneath the Royal Passage at the room's south end. One floor block actually straddles that tunnel, with about two-thirds of the stone lying within the Antechamber and the final foot or so inside the short passageway.

At the north end, the granite floor stopped at the spot where the builders would one day place the 36-inch-high limestone block known as the Great

Step. Similar to the setup in the King's Chamber, the floor blocks in the Antechamber rise higher than the bottom edge of the walls, causing the grooves cut into the granite on either side to extend almost four inches below the floor. These are the hollows that visitors notice between the floor and the walls as they pass through the Antechamber today.

Constructing a Portcullis

Before the side walls grew any higher, the granite pieces for the portcullis arrived. The new theory suggests that the primary reason the Egyptians constructed the two shelf walls in discrete sections rather than using larger blocks of granite was to accommodate the heavy stones used for the portcullis. A reasonable guess is that the three blocks in the mechanism, crafted to ride up and down inside the square-cut grooves in the walls, weighed several tons each. Due to their density, the chore of trying to slide the hefty blocks into the individual channels as the final step *after* the side walls were fully built would have been much more difficult than it had to be.

The Egyptians positioning the portcullis blocks at the inception of construction — before assembling the upper portions of the Antechamber's walls — afforded a clearcut advantage. Instead of having to hoist the heavy granite blocks some distance overhead in an attempt to slip them into the grooves from above, crews could set the indentations around the slabs as they finished the remainder of the Antechamber. Piecing the walls together from the bottom up made the process infinitely easier because at the end of the day, workers would not have to lift the stones for the portcullis any higher than the first row of the inner walls.

Just as they had attacked prior engineering challenges, the builders solved the problem of transferring the weighty portcullis blocks to their stations by developing a temporary ramp. The ramp, 78 inches high, extended east to west across the front of the Antechamber to the far end of the recently constructed work platform on the west side. Crews may have also laid down planks of wood by setting them along the upper edges of the short walls that now defined the evolving room. The purpose of the wood was to cover up the gaps from the indentations precut into the inner wall blocks. The boards extended down both sides, reaching as far as the last set of rectangular grooves at the south end. The two openings at that end were not topped with the wooden planks but were left open.

The temporary ramp at the north end permitted the construction team to haul in the slabs for the portcullis one at a time, using the ropes from the southern utility pyramid, and deposit them at the top of the incline. Each block was approximately 47 inches high, 46 inches wide and 16–21 inches thick, judging from the width of the three grooves in the side walls. (The fourth pair of indentations at the north end of the Antechamber did not extend all the way to the floor and served a different purpose.) Then, after pulling, dragging, or walking the initial portcullis stone down the planks set along the upper edge of the side walls and steadying the block, the crew inserted it between the southernmost set of indentations and gently slid the piece of granite down to the floor.

Workers probably spread small logs or some other type of material inside the Antechamber to create a little space underneath the bulky stone, which would allow them to not only detach its choker but also protect the floor from scratches. The team could have removed the protective sheathing when the portcullis blocks were finally raised or left it in place throughout the remainder of the construction process. Given the near-pristine state of the granite in the Antechamber's floor, the second scenario seems more likely.

With the initial portcullis block in place, crews pulled the wooden planks back beyond the next set of indentations a little more than two feet away, and prepared to install the second one. The process of inserting the slabs one by one continued until all three were in their channels. It is worth mentioning that even after the blocks were successfully settled into their slots, the team left the temporary ramp in place. The incline would continue to serve the workers dragging up the next group of wall blocks, as well as make it easier for the different crews to climb on top of the growing walls.

Another interesting feature of the portcullis blocks was the accessories they wore. The blocks must have been clad in some type of hardware, which allowed the builders to raise them up. Since the inner walls were still so short — just a single row high — the tops of all three portcullis blocks protruded above the upper edge of the wall and thus were accessible for affixing articles to the stone. Later on, when the portcullis blocks are completely enclosed in their channels, it would have been extremely difficult, if not impossible, to fasten anything to them. Only if the lift were ever shut down and a slab removed for repairs would workers be able to add or adjust the hardware.

One viable technique involved drilling holes three inches in diameter front to back, near the upper edge of the portcullis block. Preparing one end of the stone first, crew members took a short piece of wood that had a circular hole cut through the center of it and two "legs" fastened at each end, and long enough to reach the holes drilled into the stone. Then they attached the supports to the slab, using pins made out of copper or some other type of metal.

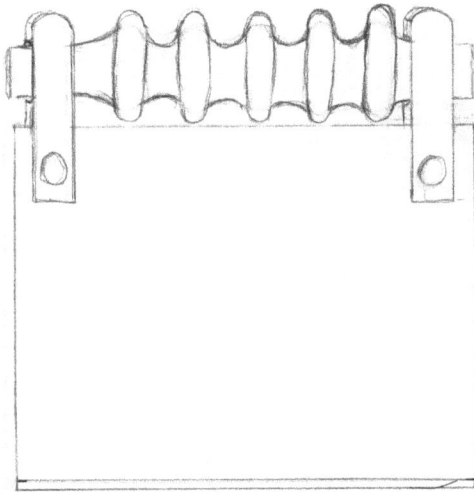

PORTCULLIS BLOCK HARDWARE

The ancient pyramid builders attached specially designed hardware to the tops of the three portcullis blocks. Ropes wending their way through the Antechamber and around the rollers made the blocks rise and fall.

When upright, the wooden device stood taller than the piece of granite because the hole at the center of the board was there to support one end of a large roller designed to sit a few inches above the block. At least 16 inches in diameter, the roller resembled a baker's rolling pin due to the narrow handles found at either end. Starting with the bracket already pinned to the stone, the team inserted the handle through the wooden holder on that side. Once the initial handle was fitted into its slot, workers pushed the other one through the opening in a second bracket, which they then secured to the opposite end of the stone.

The outcome was two short supports pinned to the portcullis stone holding a fat, round beam between them. Similar to other pulleys, each of the rollers attached to the top of the portcullis blocks had turned grooves worked into the wood. When it was time to employ the portcullis system inside the Antechamber, these grooves would help guide the ropes passing over them. The machinery in the chamber was part of a skillfully executed procedure to safely move the lift and its ginormous loads up the ramp in the Grand Gallery.

Building Blocks

This moment marks a minor turning point for the Egyptians who needed to finish the Antechamber before any more work on the King's Chamber was able to proceed. The granite blocks quarried for the walls and upper stories of that chamber were simply too big and heavy to transport otherwise.

After carrying the collection of blocks for the Antechamber on the lift by bringing them up the gallery in shifts without the use of sleds, the team assigned to complete the growing room set the individual pieces of granite and limestone onto Course 49. Then they dragged the blocks toward the west, setting the stones for the remainder of the walls and the roof at the bottom of the temporary ramp. Shortly thereafter, workers using the pulleys mounted on top of the southern step-pyramid began sliding the wall blocks up the short incline one by one. The crews stationed on the work platforms adjacent to the narrow space at the center of the Antechamber were the people tasked with depositing the latest collection of blocks onto the unfinished, double-layered walls by adding more rows to each side.

The size and proximity of the two enormous pieces of granite positioned above the Royal Passage offered the builders another attractive option for finishing the Antechamber. The Egyptians planned to erect a huge mechanical arm on top of that eight-foot-wide surface. Based on the same principle as a shadoof, such a machine could help elevate the wall blocks. Moreover, using a "crane" to pick up a stone and briefly suspend it in the air would give workers the opportunity to carefully maneuver the blocks into position from below. Unlike the usual shadoofs depicted on river banks that the local villagers might use to fill up buckets of water, this device functioned as part of a massive industrial operation and was much larger in scale.

Made from heavy pieces of timber, the apparatus consisted of a thick crossbar resting atop two low A-frames similar to a child's swing set positioned at either end. Balanced perpendicularly across the horizontal piece of the scaffold was an exceptionally long, round wooden post with a substantial hook dangling from one end. Connected to the opposite end of the post, behind the north wall inside the King's Chamber, was the counterweight. The ballast was most likely a stone block(s) enclosed in a wooden frame. Since the gap in the wall near the chamber's northwest corner was still accessible, workers must have carried in the materials for the counterweight through that aperture.

By making use of the ropes coming down from the southern utility pyramid and the temporary ramp out front, plus the mechanical arm rotating overhead, the construction team was able to pluck a stone from the work platform and move it into the correct position. Meticulously, piece by piece, the Egyptians would continue to build up the sides of the emerging Antechamber until its outer walls grew to more than 12 feet tall and they were ready to enclose the room with a roof.

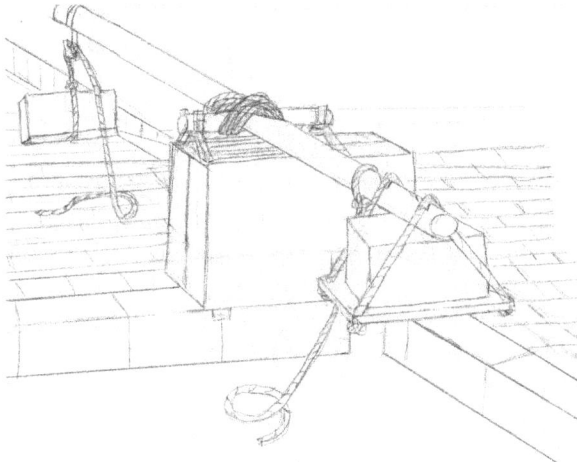

LIFTING MACHINE

The ancient Egyptians used a modified, industrial-sized shadoof set up on top of the massive granite lintel blocks above the Royal Passage to help them elevate the materials for the Antechamber.

Patchwork of Stone

A peculiar characteristic of the set of inner walls under construction were the unique shapes and sizes of the various blocks. Diverging from the basic design elements applied to most of the other chambers found inside the Great Pyramid, the builders did not duplicate the layout of the stones on the Antechamber's right- and left-hand sides. The blocks in the inner walls don't match — on purpose.

The innermost wall on the east side of the room includes just two rows of blocks, with the second or upper row forming the top of the 12-inch-deep shelf. (The bottom rows on both sides were already in place.) In a curious twist, the shelf at the east end of the room is nine inches lower than the one on the west side with the scalloped edges. Later on, by taking into account the discrepancy in the heights of the two ledges and reconfiguring the east side, the dips included in the west wall would make it possible to place a roller into one of those half-circles and have it lie flat as it crosses the chamber between the two shelves.

While the second row in the inner wall on the east side has a total of three blocks that are each 12 inches thick, their other measurements differ markedly from the stones sitting below them in row number one. Looking south to north, the initial piece of granite in the second row nearest the King's Chamber is 62 inches tall and fairly slim. This block encompasses only one-half of the upper part of the groove for the portcullis block at that end of the room. The other half of the same indentation is carved out of the middle wall block, which is also 62 inches tall but significantly wider. Besides including half of the southernmost portcullis groove, the span of the middle wall block also contains the upper halves of the other two portcullis channels in the east wall. The edges of all three of these indentations match up perfectly with the grooves beneath them in the first row.

What's more, a fourth groove (21.5 inches wide and three inches deep) was also cut into the surface of the center block in the second row, very close to the shelf's north end. Because that portion of the middle block extends beyond the northernmost groove in the first row, this particular indentation does not have a bottom half to match up with and was never intended to hold a portcullis stone. Rather, the cutout was a clever way to create a small ledge on top of the lower row of wall blocks to support the Granite Leaf at some future date. The third and final block in the upper row of the inside wall on the east side is a slender chunk of limestone. Similar to the two previous stones in that row it, too, is 12 inches thick and 62 inches high.

The one-foot-deep shelf wall on the west side is also only two rows high with a total of three blocks comprising the upper row. The biggest difference between this inner wall and the one on the other side of the Antechamber is that the top edge of all three channels fashioned to hold the portcullis blocks have half-circles cut into them. The lip at the top of the western shelf looks almost as if it had been scooped out.

A tall, skinny granite block 71 inches high, positioned at the south end next to the King's Chamber, starts the second row on the west side. This initial piece sports one-half of the groove for the southernmost portcullis block and thus includes one-quarter of a circle at the top. The middle block in the second row is the same height and depth as the skinny block but wider from side to side. It contains the other half of the first indentation topped by a quarter-circle in addition to the upper halves of the other two portcullis grooves, which both display semi-circles on top. Similar to what occurred on the east side, the wide piece in the middle of the west wall has a fourth channel running down the front, detached from any type of indentation in the first row. In due time, this cutaway will support the west end of the Granite Leaf.

Now the Egyptians began to take a new tack in approaching the job of completing the Antechamber. The three portcullis blocks lined up one after the other resting in their slots presented an opportunity: Those blocks could serve as the substructure for a temporary floor or work platform inside the space, giving the team a place to stand or set up ladders in the space between the unfinished walls. Every bit of elevation gained might help them maneuver the higher pieces into position.

To the Ceiling

In the 1830s, Italian Egyptologist Giovanni Battista Caviglia chopped and dynamited his way through some of the limestone filler behind the Ante-chamber's west wall. (The large hole he dug out has been closed to tourists for many years.) Even with what his crude cavity exposed, however, no one really knows the precise measurements of every block in the more than 12-foot-high walls behind the shelves inside the Antechamber. We know that they touch the ceiling, but most of their masonry is completely hidden from view.

What does become obvious to anyone standing in the middle of the Antechamber and looking straight at the side walls is the placement of the uppermost blocks. The pieces of granite directly below the ceiling must be more than five feet tall because they start below the shelves on both sides of the room. This conclusion is not unexpected, given the Egyptians' proclivity for detail. Making sure the bottom edge of the upper row of blocks in the back walls sat lower than the ledges situated in front of them gave the shelves a finished look.

Hub of the Pyramid

The Antechamber was still a work in progress. The room was without a roof and its other internal components, including the imposing Granite Leaf by the entrance, did not exist yet. But before the builders could close off the space from above with a ceiling or lock the Granite Leaf into place, they had to prepare the chamber for the core functions it was meant to perform.

Employing simple materials, the ancient engineers had conceived of and developed an intricate rope and pulley system with one central objective in mind: to elevate loads that, for all intents and purposes, appeared impossible to raise. In devising their ingenious mechanism inside the Antechamber, they would also find a way to make the heavy portcullis blocks rise and fall without ever touching the floor. The rationale behind creating the portcullis in the first place was to maintain constant tension on the ropes attached to the great lift, which soon would transport granite blocks whose weight was almost beyond the scope of the imagination.

The Egyptians had designed the constricted vestibule known as the Antechamber to hold a series of pulleys mounted across the room. This is why the space is so narrow: because it enclosed the tightly held components of a compact machine with multiple moving parts. The shelf on the west side already had half-circles cut into the top of the wall channels developed for the three portcullis blocks. These semi-circles were suitable for holding one end of a round wooden post with four turned grooves. But because the shelf wall on the east side was flat, the builders had to retrofit that ledge to accommodate the other end of the thick rollers fabricated to span the room.

To level the height wall to wall, carpenters had carved a semi-circular channel down the center of a block of wood that was several inches thick and about a foot wide front to back (the depth of the shelf). Then they divided the furrow in two, creating two sides of a half-pipe. Each right-angled piece had been hollowed out to produce a quarter-circle along one side. When matched up with the quarter-circle facing it, the two halves created a dip or bowl where the east end of a roller was able to rest.

Once workers had set all three rollers into place, a single plank the same size front to back but flat on top — and thick enough to have three half-pipes chiseled out of the bottom — was set over the rollers to enclose them. Looking directly at the wooden contraption without any rollers in it was a little like looking at the stocks that held prisoners in the town squares of colonial America. Likewise, the west side of the Antechamber had its own solid wooden plank with three semi-circular channels hallowed out on the underside. This piece of wood covered the beams resting inside the dips on top of the granite shelf.

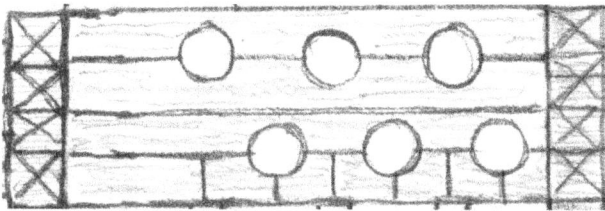

ANTECHAMBER · WOODEN STOCKS
The east wall of the Antechamber was outfitted with a wooden frame, which held two sets of rollers spanning the narrow room.

The team was not done yet. The idea was to install a second series of rollers above the original set to position three more across the room. In this instance workers put the wedges to support the new trio directly on top of the substantial framework that already existed on both sides, overlaying the lower set of rollers. The final touch was to add another thick board with three semicircular channels carved out of the bottom over the latest groupings east and west. When the final piece was in place, the wooden configurations containing a total of six rollers reached as high as the back walls.

It is quite possible that the builders chose to fashion the bottom portion of each row on the east side in quarter-circle segments, instead of using one long chunk of wood, in case it ever became necessary to replace a roller. The multileveled apparatus appointed to hold the pulleys would be more likely to stay securely in place if the construction crew only had to remove one section of it to pull out the problem piece. Using smaller, detachable wedges generally made the task easier because the workers could handle a single roller at a time rather than deal with the entire collection all at once.

Raising the Roof

With three portcullis blocks topped with rollers sitting at floor level and six more pulleys stacked in between the walls, the Antechamber was ready for its ceiling. The roof is significant for a number of reasons. First, the weight of the granite slabs installed overhead was critical to making the mechanism housed inside the room operate properly. The dense stones in the ceiling pressing down on the wooden stocks that encased the upper rollers would prevent them from wobbling or shifting around too much as the ropes weaving through the chamber traveled from pulley to pulley.

Three blocks of granite, estimated to be about four feet north to south and at least eight feet long east to west, cover the Antechamber and form its ceiling.

Not surprisingly, the size and weight of the roof slabs and soon to be installed Granite Leaf compelled the builders to make a few adjustments before they began. Workers constructed a temporary stone ramp on top of the platform composed of filler blocks located behind the Antechamber's west wall.

Built parallel to the north wall of the King's Chamber and sloping downward from east to west, the ramp was a little more than four feet wide — large enough for a roof slab — and as much as 15 feet long. The east end of the incline reached the upper edge of the Antechamber's outer west wall where it ended in a small landing spacious enough for a few workers to stand on. In terms of the gradient, since this particular ramp sat on top of a layer of filler stones, its starting point was already 78 inches above the floor on

Course 49. That meant the angle only had to climb another six feet or so to reach the top of the Antechamber's tallest wall.

The area behind the room's east wall did not require a separate ramp, but it did demand a sizeable work platform to accommodate the needs of the crew stationed there. Due to their vantage point, workers on the east side would be tasked with raising the stones for the roof and the Granite Leaf up to the top of the newly built ramp on the west side when the various components were ready. That effort required a sufficient amount of space suitable for pulling. Given this responsibility within the larger construction operation, workers continued to add blocks to the layers of filler stones to the deck on the east side behind the Antechamber's outer wall as they were assembling that part of the room. Crews both fortified the deck and built it higher — until their work platform was even with the top of a wall that was more than 12 feet tall.

Slab by slab, workers would transfer the blocks for the Granite Leaf and the chamber's ceiling from the lift, moving them up the 78-inch-high temporary ramp on the 49th course and over to the new incline that ran east-west hugging the north wall of the King's Chamber. After a block had journeyed from Course 49 up to the filler-stone work deck, then was moved west to sit at the base of the latest ramp, it was in a position to climb the slope. First, the westside work gang lassoed it around the bottom and tied the rope off at the top.

Using wooden ladders or some sort of scaffolding, the group of laborers on the east side scrambled up on top of the tall platform. They stood ready to clutch the line looped around the granite, attach it to their harnesses, and trudge eastward, heaving the stone up the incline on the opposite side. Ropes from the pulley atop southern step-pyramid were also available to assist the workers in dragging the pieces forward. And with the mechanical arm or shadoof-like crane installed over the Royal Passage still functional, that machine may have been put into service to help raise the heavy pieces and set them into place. Very carefully, the pull-team would draw each block upward onto the landing where the ramp met the top of the Antechamber wall.

The builders must have started the process with the block that comprised the bottom half of the Granite Leaf first. The particular set of circumstances inside the Antechamber presented a unique challenge to this particular job.

Because the leaf was narrow enough to slip into the room without touching the sides, workers were not able to set the slab across the gap and balance it for any length of time on the upper edges of the two walls. Instead, after the bottom half of the leaf reached the landing, the crew posted on the west side would take over and lower it into place from above. They dropped the piece of granite straight down into the grooves in the shelf walls at the north end of the Antechamber.

The northernmost indentations on the inner set of walls did not extend all the way to the floor, which left the bottom half of the Granite Leaf resting on a couple of small ledges located on either side of the room. Since nothing rested beneath the center portion of the stone, it was possible to crawl underneath it. That being the case, the team did not have to worry about removing the rope slung around the underside since they could easily undo the line and yank it back up to the top of the chamber.

By contrast, the other half of the Granite Leaf sits on top of the lower piece. As a result, before the westside crew lowered the top half into place, they positioned a set of wooden wedges along the upper edge of the lower block to retain some space for extracting the rope. Following the same procedure that they had employed before, the small team lowered the upper half into the grooves from their position overhead, removed the line, then pounded on the wedges to work them out from in between the two stones.

Up next was the Antechamber's first roof slab. The distance between the room's side walls is not huge, so it would have been fairly easy to move the ceiling block trekking up the western ramp to the landing and over to the wall on the other side of the room. The team probably erected a temporary bridge to span the gap inside the room, and simply hauled the block across that gulf as they prepared to slide it into the appropriate spot.

Starting near the south end and using the upper edge of the walls like the rails on a train track, the crews posted on each side acting in unison slid the block toward the front of the Antechamber. The hole in the roof where the initial block was supposed to go sat directly over the area that the Granite Leaf, which the work gang had just lowered into position, now occupied. (See sidebar about the Granite Leaf.) It is also worth noting that when the Egyptians pushed the first ceiling slab into place, it projected out a short distance beyond what was then the northern boundary of the Antechamber. This overhang would disappear in the future once the limestone blocks at the north end of the room were installed.

Moving on, workers drew up the second ceiling block and, placing it across the gap, slid the granite northward until it sat next to block number one. The slab at the south end went in last. To complete the job, the team pushed all three pieces together hard against the back wall.

Finally, it is important to add that because the ceiling is more than 12 feet high and the Antechamber's back wall is almost a foot shorter than that, the layout left a hole at the south end of the room. Added together, the height of the Royal Passage by the entrance to the King's Chamber plus the lintel blocks resting above the passage is approximately 11 feet, three inches. The difference between that number and the height of the Antechamber (12' 5") meant an opening at least 14 inches tall existed between the chamber's back wall and its ceiling.

This aperture would prove to be vital to the ongoing success of the project because it would provide enough space for the thick ropes linked to critical pulleys to enter and exit the room.

Plugging up the slit today is a stone insert whose texture and color obviously do not match the block beneath it. The mismatched piece masking the hole offers more evidence of the care that the ancient Egyptians took in putting the finishing touches on their pyramid. While the team used limestone to seal up the gap in the back wall as they concluded work on the Antechamber, they also took the time to cut indentations into its surface so the odd chunk of limestone would sync up with the grooves in the granite wall below it.

By now, the pyramid builders had established three walls and a ceiling for the Antechamber, but the fourth and final wall was still missing. And it would stay that way for a very long time. Only many decades later would the builders close up the front of the room by stacking up blocks of limestone to create the squat doorway (41" x 41") that 21st century tourists can only enter by bending down. Why was closing off the room such a protracted process? The north end of the Antechamber had to remain open and accessible for as long as possible to provide an unobstructed pathway for the ropes raising the great lift that would deliver the raw materials for the balance of the Great Pyramid.

Turning North

Wrapping up construction on the core of the Antechamber represented another crossroad in the building process. Once again, most of the critical functions involved in the project as a whole were shifting over to the north side of the construction site and a step-pyramid whose broad center channel was specially designed to accommodate the very largest blocks of stone. Engineers had developed a clever strategy, which included the type of shaft that would make the goal of elevating impossibly heavy loads achievable.

Studying the Great Pyramid's component parts, it is easy to lose sight of the immense length and breadth of the building's footprint. Suffice it to say the step-pyramids erected within its borders were enormous structures in their own right. Reflecting the scope and scale of the massive undertaking, the upper utility pyramid on the north side would not only act as the primary conduit for hundreds of thousands of blocks far into the future, but also handle the Egyptians' fluctuating construction needs for generations to come.

Unlike previous center channels designed to pull up sleds and blocks, the passageway on the northern utility pyramid associated with the King's Chamber — rising from the 49th to the 98th course — had not been fashioned with the sides of the passageway perfectly parallel. Picture the setup as closer to the shape of an upside-down, half-opened fan. The edge along the west side of the channel ran straight up the hill, stopping several courses short of the top of the step-pyramid and the platform where the pulley stands were mounted. But toward the bottom end of the incline, the channel became wider because that side of the "fan" arced toward the east.

In addition, the boundary wall on the west side was fairly high since it had grown taller as the courses alongside it were evolving. Conversely, only a short rim or hump similar to a small curb defined the east side of the shaft, which swept up at an angle from Course 49 as it headed toward the pulleys high above. The curb's low mound was there primarily to help corral the sleds and prevent them from wandering off course.

The unorthodox northern center channel was sufficient to meeting the needs of this new phase of construction, which included transporting the multi-ton blocks of granite intended for the Relieving Chambers. One of the passageway's most important features was that it maintained access to the work area near the lift. The open space on Course 49 was critical not only for carrying the sleds with their massive loads into the heart of the building, but also for preparing them to ascend hundreds of feet up to the courses where the blocks belonged. With the west wall positioned as far away as possible from the lift when it was parked at the top of the gallery ramp, the team had ample space to offload a sled before slowly pivoting it to make sure the vehicle was facing in the right direction for the ride up the slope. Equally important, the northern center channel was wide enough to tow the huge sledges up the steep incline at a slight angle by carefully veering them upward on a gradual northwest trajectory.

This was also the period when the pulleys atop the southern step-pyramid towering above the contours of the King's Chamber lost their usefulness for hauling in blocks because the Antechamber stood in the way. As a consequence, the Egyptians would soon begin using the channel built into the front of the upper utility pyramid on the south side to house an extra counterweight. Per the new theory, the Egyptian's decision to put a second counterweight into service makes a lot of sense given the fact that the plan to elevate 70-ton pieces of granite loomed on the horizon.

The extra counterweight on the south side would never be as big or heavy as the giant block of granite sitting in the Descending Passage. At 45 degrees, the shaft on the utility pyramid was much steeper than that underground passageway — too extreme to walk — and not nearly as long. The size of the center channel at the south end was more akin to the size of the shafts on the original pair of interior pyramids associated with the Queen's Chamber, now mostly buried beneath stacks of courses. But in the end, a substantial chunk of limestone able to travel up and down the southern shaft would help counterbalance some of the extraordinarily heavy loads the builders had coming their way.

Up, then Down

At least 95 percent of the upper utility pyramid on the north side was stepped, but engineers had also inserted a relatively narrow band of smooth, angled blocks on the back side of the center channel's west wall, which essentially functioned as a secondary ramp. Why? They needed a wall to delineate the center channel and keep the sleds in their lanes, but they also had to develop a method for delivering the stones, including massive blocks of dense granite, to the different courses as the courses evolved. The two parallel ramps were designed to work in tandem, but obviously a loaded sled could not jump over the west wall and onto the incline leading to the targeted course by itself.

The solution was to readjust the vehicles carting the stones. When the heaviest sleds progressed up the northern channel at a slow angle and finally stopped at a point higher than the upper end of the west wall, a work gang would swing the lower end a little further west. Manipulating the sled in this manner, they aligned it with the top of the narrow ramp located on the other side of the wall. A minor reorientation put the load in a good position for its downward journey toward the level where the block was supposed to go. Then, as soon as the pullers outdoors got the signal, they began lowering the weighty sledge down the second incline, halting only when it reached the top of the course that crews had just filled in. A separate team took over from there, moving the vehicle and its cargo across the latest course to the zone currently under construction before unloading it.

Having such a capacious center channel afforded the Egyptians one additional benefit as well. Even as a work crew readied the next load to climb up the center shaft in one direction, enough space remained for a second gang to be able to return their empty sled by lowering it down the channel — hugging the inside of the west wall — until it arrived at the main work area on Course 49 many courses below.

• The Granite Leaf •

Standing like a solitary sentry guarding the interior of the Antechamber, the strange block divided into two sections called the Granite Leaf has mystified Egyptologists for thousands of years. The Granite Leaf, which rests in its own groove at the north end of the chamber, confronts a visitor with its sheer mass and curious positioning. Why did the Egyptians put it there? What was its purpose?

The more than four-foot-tall stone was actually quarried as a single block approximately 51 inches high, 40 inches wide, and 16 inches thick, then split horizontally across the middle. The break may not be precisely at the center of the piece, since it is impossible to know exactly how tall the block was when the builders deposited it in the Antechamber. Damaged sometime in the past, the top edge of the upper section is disfigured and irregular. The north face of the upper stone also has a "boss" sticking out from the front surface. (This usage of the word defines a boss as the stud on the center of a shield.) The small mound with the rounded edges was not attached to the stone after it was quarried; rather, the block was cut back and evened out around the protrusion, leaving the bump behind. Approximately five inches wide and one inch high, the boss sits in the lower right quadrant of the upper portion of the Granite Leaf near the vertical centerline — at least five inches higher than the bottom edge on that half of the block.

The Griffith theory's general reasoning about the Granite Leaf provides an explicit explanation for the many anomalies that seem to surround this particular block of stone, which continues to puzzle pyramid scholars to this day. The new theory suggests that this extraordinary object was part of an inventive system the Egyptians had conceived to allow them to lift up one of the floor blocks in the Antechamber. Moreover, the special piece of granite embedded in the floor may cover the entrance to an undiscovered chamber hidden deep within the Great Pyramid.

All things considered, there is little doubt that the two halves of the Granite Leaf were lowered into the Antechamber from above and slipped into the slots they currently occupy. What may also be true is that the top half of the block had holes drilled through it front to back near the upper edge that were large enough for a rope to be threaded through. Such holes may have made the stone weaker in that general area, which contributed to it having a tendency to break and may account for the rough edge on top. In the new scenario, the Granite Leaf as a whole served as a type of counterweight and the upper portion of that counterweight was elevated by ropes looped through those openings.

Outfitting the Antechamber to make the counterbalancing mechanism work required the Egyptians to reconfigure the room's original pulley system to elevate the Granite Leaf. By the time the Great Pyramid was nearing completion, the portcullis blocks and pulleys crossing the room between the two shelf walls would already have been dismantled and carried away. That was when the builders used the cleared-out space to mount a separate, more portable contraption to hold the rollers involved in moving the Granite Leaf. One of the original pulleys hung directly above the leaf, and ropes curved around that roller would eventually raise and lower both halves of the stone.

Because the original granite block was so heavy before being cut in half, being able to lift it would have required a large group of workers trying to squeeze into the narrow Antechamber. The tight space is probably why the Egyptians divided the Granite Leaf in two: to decrease its weight. Instead of demanding the combined efforts of a host of workers impossible to fit into that tiny area, just a handful of people would be able to position themselves at the center of the Antechamber and pull on the ropes.

After developing a set of reconfigured wooden frames for the shelves on both sides of the room, crews installed a couple of thick, round rollers in between the side walls as high as they could go. The new posts with the grooves were situated by the ceiling at the south end of the space near the King's Chamber. The job of the pulleys at the back of the room was to redirect the ropes coming from the top of the Granite Leaf down toward the floor.

Similarly, the boss protruding from the front side of the block's upper half seems to have been developed so a crew member using some sort of pole or lever would be able to push up on the bump to help separate the two pieces as the lifting process was getting underway. After throwing the ropes lashed to the top piece over the pulley positioned directly overhead, the workers would tug in unison. Once the upper portion of the stone rose as high as it could go, the team tied it off. Then they slung ropes underneath the lower stone and lifted that piece up against the top half before tying both pieces together. The weight of the entire block was now hanging overhead. As a unit, the two halves would have been substantial enough to counterbalance the weight of the floor block at the other end.

The ropes continued toward the back of the room then passed over the high-set pulleys at the south end and dropped down to the floor. Here, the lines were attached to a wooden tool similar to brick tongs or a bracket capable of clamping onto and lifting a heavy stone when the handles are squeezed together. Placed into the hollows in between the grooves in the side walls, which extend lower than the floor, the tongs grabbed the east and west sides of the block straddling the Antechamber and the entrance to the Royal Passage. (To date, this spot appears to be the only place in the entire pyramid where someone would be able to pick up a stone in this manner.) The Griffith theory hypothesizes that the detachable piece of granite found in the floor sits on the rim of the L-shaped wall blocks installed on both sides of the entrance to the King's Chamber.

The portable floor block is probably a mere 12 inches thick, similar to the width of the shelf walls east and west. Taking into consideration the fact that the repositioned Granite Leaf was not able to rise very high before hitting the roller overhead, the floor block at the opposite end could not be too thick. However, due to its length (more than seven feet long) and the fact that the block is composed of granite, the squat, T-shaped piece of stone would still be incredibly heavy — another possible reason why the Egyptians made it slimmer than all of the other floor blocks: Workers had to be able to pick it up.

The piece of granite also had to be short enough from top to bottom to easily clear the hole it was sitting in. Due to the relatively shallow depth of this stone, the crew would be able lift up the block and float it over the top of the slot in the floor to expose the entrance to the hidden chamber.

Counterbalanced, the floor block would rise as workers at the other end of the rope used brute strength and the weight of their own bodies to pull down on the Granite Leaf, steadily lowering it. As the conjoined stones went down, the piece of granite in the floor went up. Work crews may have also shoved boards underneath the Granite Leaf to relieve some of the tension on the ropes once the floor block had moved. As soon as they raised it high enough to clear its cavity, the group of workers at the south end gently pushed the block toward the inside of the Royal Passage, perhaps rolling it along a series of short wooden dowels.

In addition, the builders may have prepared a pre-fitted wooden lid for the hole the crew had exposed in the floor, which they could quickly slide into place to prevent either the floor block — or a worker — from accidentally falling into the cavity. Damage, since repaired, on the granite blocks framing the doorway to the King's Chamber may have been intentional to provide clearance for the handles on the brick tongs.

Intriguingly, in 1977, SRI International (once known as the Stanford Research Institute of California) conducted a brief acoustical survey on the interior of the Great Pyramid.[1] Spending a single night using acoustic soundings, the researchers gathered data on the King's Chamber and Antechamber leading up to it. Despite several problems with "clutter" from multiple waves emanating from the blocks in the pyramid's core, the survey appeared to reveal an anomalous echo 7.25 meters beneath the floor — about halfway between the King's and Queen's Chambers. Among other things, SRI's report suggested that the echo could represent a possible void left behind during a change in the original construction plans or even a large crack. With only two sets of data gathered over a single night, making a final determination was problematic. But the question remains: Is there something down there?

1. Source: www.touregypt.net.

GRANITE LEAF - BOSS

The boss on the upper half of the Granite Leaf.

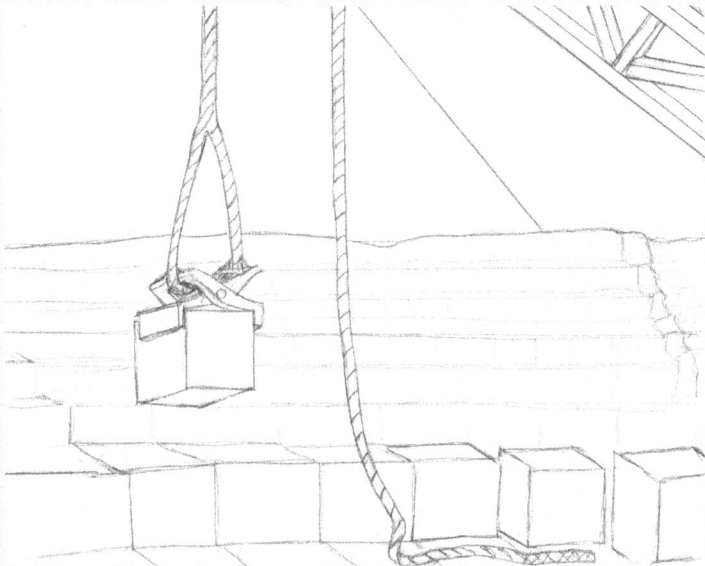

BRICK TONGS AT QUARRY

Brick tongs are a regular part of the equipment used at quarries and in construction projects to move blocks of stone.

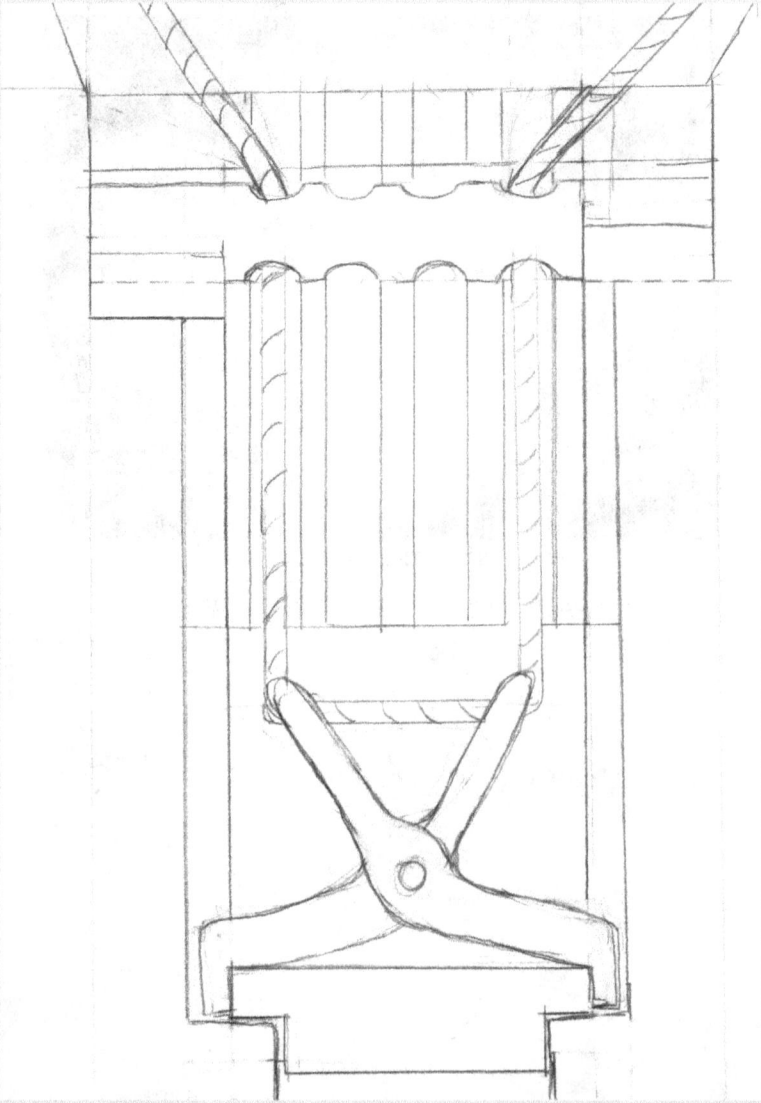

FLOOR BLOCK REMOVAL

According to the Griffith theory, the floor block at the south end of the Antechamber straddling the entrance to the King's Chamber is removable. Using the Granite Leaf as a counterweight, the Egyptians were able to lift up the piece of granite with brick tongs, slide it southward, and temporarily store the block inside the Royal Passage — exposing the opening to a hidden shaft.

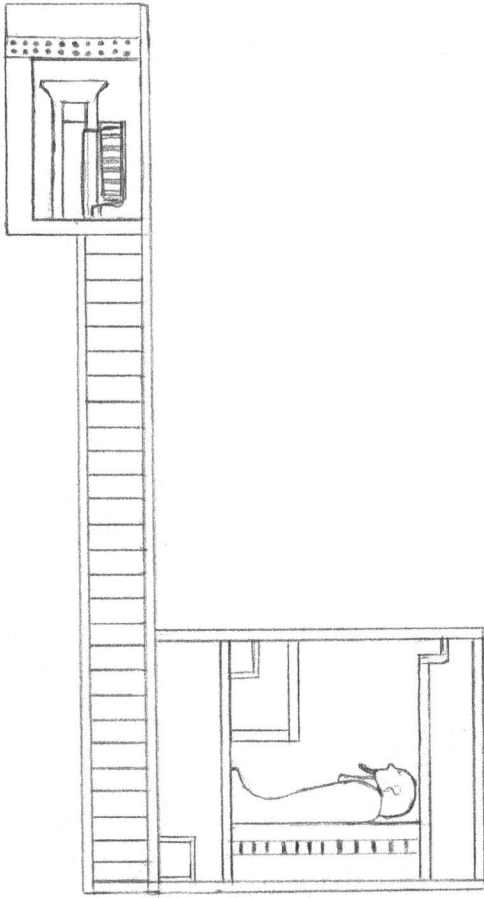

HIDDEN CHAMBER - BOOK OF THE DEAD

One of the images in the *Egyptian Book of the Dead* depicts a room where people seem to be in the midst of preparing a mummy for the afterlife. A second room resembling a burial chamber is displayed below it, along with a ladder or stairwell connecting the two. Could the pictograph also be a representation of a secret passage beneath the Antechamber? If the Griffith theory is correct, there is an undiscovered chamber, which can be opened up by the Granite Leaf, below the floor. To enter this hidden room, a person would pass through the hole at the top, then climb down a vertical passageway to access the tomb-like vault below — a process very similar to entering an ancient mastaba.

• Serekhs and the Antechamber •

Unraveling the deep mystery surrounding the Antechamber involves understanding both its function during the process of constructing the Great Pyramid and the symbolism incorporated into the physical properties of the chamber itself. Certain features unique to this room indicate that there is far more to the Antechamber than meets the eye.

One of the most telling markers is the representation of a serekh in the east and west walls. The word serekh derives from the Egyptian term for "façade." In ancient times, the high wall that surrounded a building expressed a specific architectural style. Incorporating a series of relatively narrow rectangular indentations inset vertically into the walls, the design denoted the king's palace. In addition to the palace, any number of temples and tombs were set apart by this type of enclosure. The overall look of the exterior walls was deceptive, however, because the vertical indentations tricked the eye into believing there were multiple openings to the interior of the building. But in fact, they were false doors. There was only one entrance and it was usually well hidden among the numerous recesses.

The serekh was also displayed as an ornamental symbol combining a view of the palace façade, indicated by some vertical lines, with a rectangular extension at the top. The Egyptians used the written sign for the serekh — drawn, carved, or painted on an object — as a royal crest to accentuate and honor the name of the pharaoh. Artists placed the hieroglyphs forming the king's name inside the rectangular space above the vertical lines. In addition, they often topped the figure of the serekh with a depiction of the falcon linked to the god Horus, thus evoking the celestial patron of the named king. The completed pictogram signified the pharaoh's Horus name. (Over time, the Egyptians also adopted the cartouche as a royal crest, using a representation of plaited rope to encircle the king's name.)

The Antechamber's connections to the serekh are hard to miss. Viewed straight on, the chamber's east wall bears a striking resemblance to the symbol of a serekh. The flat section at the top comes down to an offset where the ledge is located, then continues toward the recesses carved into the granite below (the palace walls). One might say the east wall is a mirror image of the figure that means serekh, thus linking it to the king.

In addition, if one were able to stand at the north end of the room and have an unobstructed view of the east wall, its shape would reveal an astonishing similarity to the crown worn by the goddess Isis. Most images of Isis show her from the side. The silhouette of her headdress from that angle calls to mind the outline of the Antechamber wall. Intriguingly, when observed from the front, her crown exhibits many of the basic hallmarks of a serekh (see picture of Isis below). The layout of the inside wall imitating the general notion of a serekh, as well as its association with the figure of the goddess Isis, leads to the conclusion that the Egyptians may have left us a message hidden in plain sight. All of the elements involved point to the same idea — throne — merely displayed from several different perspectives.

On the opposite (west) wall, the offset or ledge is not a flat shelf but rather, carved into the shape of three semi-circles, which sit higher than the shelf on the east side. One cannot help but notice that this bowl-shaped design is the same one used in depictions of the ancient Egyptian goddess Nephthys, who wears a headdress resembling a basket or bowl. That shape, too, represents the idea of the throne room. Notably, this wall also contains a flat section at the top and vertical indentations carved into the blocks below, implying an association with the serekh (palace walls). The half-circles scooped out of the front of the ledge on the west side, linking that part of the Antechamber to Nephthys, evokes the goddess who was the sister of Isis and whose name means "Lady of the [Temple] Enclosure."

Isis was typically paired with her sister in depictions of funerary rites. Together, the two served as the protectors of the mummy and the door to the underworld where the god Osiris resides. The significant role these two goddesses played as guardians of the unseen elements, along with their association with the idea of a serekh and its false door, leads to the belief that it was not by chance that the ancient Egyptians invoked their presence inside the enigmatic Antechamber. Could the secret they guard be an opening to the underworld we have yet to discover — directing us to the site of Osiris's throne?

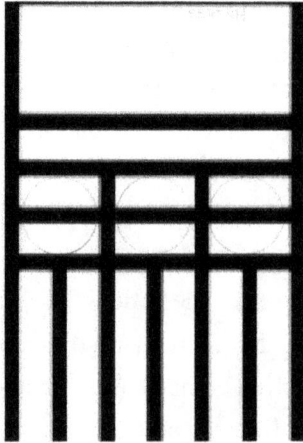

SEREKH OUTLINE
A general outline of a serekh.

DISH FRAGMENT
This dish fragment dedicated to the goddess Hathor of Dendera shows a serekh with a rectangular extension containing symbols at the top.

DJOSER PALACE FAÇADE

The façade at Djoser displays a series of vertical indentations meant to obscure the actual doorway into the palace enclosure.

ISIS HEADDRESS

Most representations of the goddess Isis, a major deity linked to rites for the dead, show her from the side, which does not provide the full picture of her headdress. In this painting she is depicted from a slightly different angle with the throne on top of her head facing more toward the front. From this perspective her headdress clearly resembles the outlines of a serekh.

CHAPTER 11

A GREAT STEP FORWARD

To say that the Egyptians were clever builders would be a gross under-statement, as evidenced by the configuration of the Antechamber and its constituent parts. The pulley system alone was an engineering marvel. These ancient people were geniuses whose skill in pyramid construction remains unmatched in the history of the world.

GREAT STEP IN DISREPAIR

The Great Step was badly worn down and in a general state of disrepair in the past.

By this point, the temporary ramp sitting in front of the Antechamber was gone and the builders were ready to begin outfitting the room with ropes to make the internal components work. Not to be overlooked was one more critical feature: the Great Step, which also was set into place during this period of time. Quarried out of a solid piece of limestone 36 inches high, more than six feet wide and approximately five feet long north to south, the Great Step sits at the upper end of the Grand Gallery, between the gallery ramp and the Antechamber. When first discovered by early pyramid surveyors, the front edge of the block had been worn away, leaving a deep depression in the soft stone. The Egyptians have since repaired the step so that visitors in modern times climb over a squared-off chunk of limestone before entering the Antechamber. The top of the Great Step also has two rectangular holes about five inches deep near the back edge on the right- and left-hand sides.

The most reasonable explanation for the presence of the two cavities on top of the block is that they held a pulley stand, which assisted in towing the lift up the Grand Gallery. Work crews may have built a brand-new stand or merely transferred the same pair of uprights previously inserted partway up the ramp to the south end of the corridor. Somewhere along the way, crews had dismantled the two pulleys used earlier, and their replacement was this new stand wedged inside the holes bored into the step. But the rigging was essentially configured in the same manner as before. The lines emerging from the First Ascending Passage traveled up the gallery to the far end and looped around the new roller mounted atop the Great Step before dropping back down the incline and connecting to the front of the lift.

Pulley Path

Having established the basic infrastructure for the Antechamber, activating its mechanics could begin in earnest. Workers had to snake ropes in, out, and around the multifaceted interior to deliver both operational control and maximum lift. Besides the rollers attached to the portcullis blocks and a total of six round beams spanning the room, the Egyptians had installed three more pulleys outside the chamber. They put a wooden stand holding a pair of pulleys on top of the granite lintel over the Royal Passage — several feet behind the rectangular hole in the back wall. This particular pulley frame had a single roller with four turned grooves on top and an identical roller mounted below it. Workers had positioned the double-roller pulley stand on the lintel stone, leaving enough space between it and the opening at the back of the Antechamber to place a third roller in a short stand on the edge of the room's south wall.

Four ropes extended down from the pulleys mounted at the top of the original northern utility pyramid associated with the Queen's Chamber, since the uppermost steps on that internal pyramid had never been entirely buried beneath new courses. Traversing the building site, the lines crossed over the pulley stand mounted outside the Antechamber's back wall. The grooved roller on top caused the ropes to turn downward, which directed them toward the lower pulley on the two-roller stand. Passing underneath the bottom roller pointed the ropes dropping from above, toward the inside of the room. Continuing on, the lines traveled over the top of roller number three that was sitting on the front edge of the hole on the south side of the room. The final pulley guided the ropes downward inside the indentations — two and one-half inches deep — precut into the back wall. From there, the lines proceeded into the heart of the Antechamber. The width and depth of the indentations in the back wall are a good indication of how thick the Egyptians' ropes must have been.

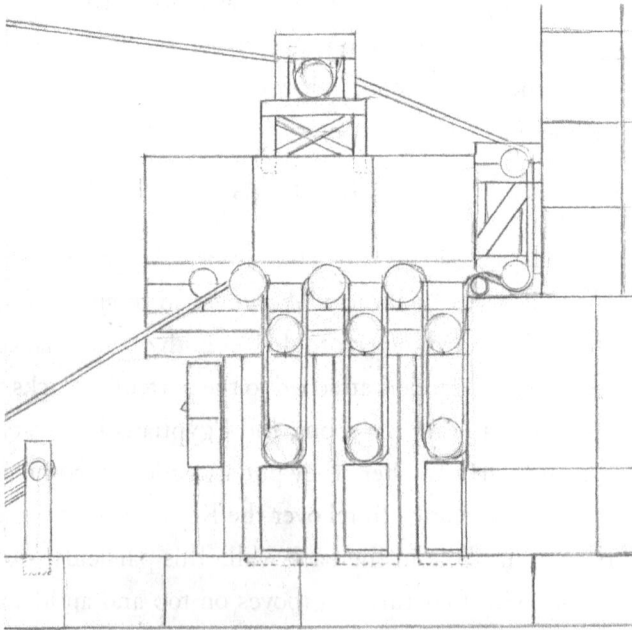

ANTECHAMBER RIGGING - EAST WALL

Illustration of the rigging inside the Antechamber, looking at the east wall from the west.

The lines kept going. Separated from one another by the channels in the wall, they continued under the grooved roller on top of the first portcullis block and up and around the uppermost roller next to the ceiling at the south end. Coiling over that roller and turning back down, the lines looped under the roller attached to the middle portcullis stone, up and over the next pulley in line at the very top of the room, then down and around the third portcullis roller. The final turn in the ropes took them up toward the ceiling again, curving over the very last pulley by the ceiling at the north end of the room and out the front of the Antechamber. After wending their way through the narrow chamber from beginning to end and dropping down the ramp in the Grand Gallery, all four ropes were attached to the lift. A set of inordinately heavy ropes traveling that route and slapping into the front edge of the Great Step may be why the limestone had worn away over time.

It is useful to call attention to one more unusual fact: The middle set of pulleys resting in the half circles on the shelf walls, which spanned the Antechamber, existed solely to help direct the ropes-in-motion. This series of rollers is referred to as the middle set due to their position in between the three pulleys next to the ceiling and the ones attached to the tops of the portcullis blocks. Since their primary function was to simply maintain the alignment of the ropes while the device as a whole was operating, this particular subset of rollers was never involved in the actual lifting process unless for some reason they were employed during a repair.

Taut Line

Contrary to the prevailing assumption that the Egyptians had designed the Antechamber's portcullis to bar potential thieves from entering the King's Chamber, its purpose was much more down to earth from an engineering standpoint. (Intruders would have been able to slip over the top of the blocks when the stones were lowered in any event.) The portcullis was a critical component of the strategy the builders had developed to handle the colossal loads scheduled for the next stage of their epic project.

The blocks that comprised the portcullis have been missing for centuries. The Griffith theory maintains that when the portcullis's job was done, workers removed the slabs of granite from their channels, possibly by chipping away at portions of the blocks. Eventually, they got rid of the debris when it was time to start sealing up the Great Pyramid. There is conjecture that some early explorers may have found fragments of the portcullis blocks when they discovered a piece of granite on the Giza Plateau with perfectly round holes drilled through it. Other finds over the years unearthed granite chunks inside the Well Shaft at the bottom of the Descending Passage. Could those broken pieces be remnants of the portcullis stones?

Whatever the case may be, it appears that at one time or another, the ancient Egyptians discarded some of their rubble by throwing it down the lower interior tunnels, knowing those passageways would no longer be needed once construction was done.

It is impossible to say with certainty where the three heavy portcullis blocks ended up, but the mechanism as a whole filled an indispensable role among the wide array of building activities associated with the Great Pyramid. The unusual three-part apparatus kept tension on the ropes. One of the worst things someone can do when trying to lift an outsized weight is to let the line go slack. A loose rope normally means the people charged with raising the object must walk forward each time and grab onto the line to resume pulling. Worse, the pullers have to remove every bit of slack first and tighten up the rope to begin tugging on it. Only then can the actual job of lifting really commence.

Contrary to a limp rope, a rigid line is also a reliable way to keep moisture from invading the fibers, which prevents the cord from stretching or succumbing to fungus and rot. In summary, preserving a taut line is generally the most efficient and effective method for handling a lift. A sagging rope not only wastes energy, it presents formidable challenges, especially when workers have to struggle to jolt a substantial load forward from a dead stop.

In the case of the extreme weights the hulking lift platform climbing up the Grand Gallery had to carry, it was essential to keep the ropes taut for one more tremendously important reason. Whenever the lift started to move, the tension in the ropes would build up against the end carrying all of the weight. This tension created a potential breaking point due to the force required to overcome inertia and start moving the now stationary load again. If the lines running between the Antechamber and the lift were ever allowed to droop and suddenly the workers on the pull-ropes yanked on them in an attempt to move the huge mass that was the loaded vehicle forward, it could spell disaster. The extreme amount of stress on the ropes, which had built up against the enormous weight at one end, might cause the lines to snap.

To circumvent this potential problem, the Egyptians had done two things. First, they instituted procedures both inside and outside of the building to immobilize and lock down the lines whenever any single pull had concluded. Secondarily, they had developed their novel portcullis system to regulate the pressure on the ropes. The portcullis blocks rising and falling provided some intermediate play by repeatedly refocusing the stress away from the weakest point in the system.

The situation had changed markedly when engineers had brought the hefty portcullis blocks into the construction project. The slabs of granite sitting in the three channels inside the Antechamber essentially hung in mid-air a few inches off the floor, never really touching bottom. This assertion is based on the fact that the edges around the base of the chamber are still sharp, with few signs of chipping.

Starting at the south end, the portcullis stones shifted one by one as needed to adjust the tension on the ropes. As soon as the initial block moved up and climbed almost as high as the top of the shelf walls on either side, it stopped, which allowed the second block to take over. Similarly, the third block picked up where the middle one left off when stone number two had reached its upper limit. In this way, the stress or energy was gradually dispersed among all three blocks as they continuously rose and fell to alleviate undue pressure on the lines, which, for the most part, was concentrated in a single spot at the front of the lift.

If there were ever a time when all three stones had attained peak levels by ascending as high as they could possibly go and stopping, it would indicate that the system had reached maximum capacity in terms of the pull. Otherwise, the movement among the trio of portcullis stones was staggered while they continued shifting up and down in succession, depending on the direction the lift was going and the activity required to sustain the correct amount of tension.

The Egyptians' ability to adjust the tautness of the lines and prevent them from sagging — and at the same time, regulate the stress on the ropes — made the goal of raising 70-ton blocks of granite attainable.

A Chamber Rises

With the mechanics installed inside the Antechamber, a new era in pyramid construction had opened up. Rigging now crisscrossed the busy construction site. Ropes strung from the pulleys set on the highest step of the original utility pyramid on the north side hung down to Course 49 to assist with adjusting the very largest sleds. In addition to that set of ropes, plus the ones circulating around the interior of the Antechamber and down the gallery ramp, many other lines were suspended above the building.

At least two ropes were attached to the extra counterweight in the center channel of the southern step-pyramid. They traveled over a pulley at the top of that shaft before stretching all the way across to the opposite end of the site. Reaching the northern utility pyramid linked to the King's Chamber, the lines passed over a roller mounted on its summit. After looping around that pulley, the clutch of ropes coming from the south end continued down the northern center channel to the work space on Course 49. From there, the supplementary counterweight would be available to assist the workers handling the blocks and sleds offloaded from the lift.

The team had also fastened four more ropes to the latest counterweight on the south side. But instead of following the same route as the initial two, this set went up and over a pulley installed on top of the southern utility pyramid and dangled down the back wall. From this position, the ropes were available to reset the supplementary counterweight whenever a pull concluded. Upon a command, the workers stationed on the ground would tug on the ropes and heave the heavy stone back up the center channel to its start position. To be sure, the smaller counterweight did have real limits compared to the one in the Descending Passage. Still, it was an asset able to assist in the lifting process overall.

At the north end of the construction site, the team had installed an entirely separate set of pulleys above the center channel with the lines leading outdoors — just like all of the other ropes arrayed over the top of the upper step-pyramid. The latest group of ropes, which descended down the utility pyramid's back side in anticipation of elevating the materials for additional courses, proceeded over several rollers mounted on stands inserted into the cladding before dropping to the bottom. There, they threaded through the pulleys and locks mounted at the front edge of the northern platform at Course 25. In an echo of the past, a large group of workers assigned to handle the ropes cascading down from above stood by, ready to raise the grueling loads up the wide northern channel to the level under construction.

Each of the component parts north and south was designed to work in concert with every other facet of the lifting operation. Like interlocking gears or the cogs in a well-oiled machine, all of the assorted elements worked together seamlessly to function as a single unit during the course of a pull. For example, as the mass of workers on the northern ramp attached to the lines started heaving themselves forward, the southern counterweight progressed down the shaft, augmenting the available force. And as the block on the south side dropped lower in the channel, its weight helped elevate the inordinately heavy pieces of limestone and granite trekking up the incline on the north side.

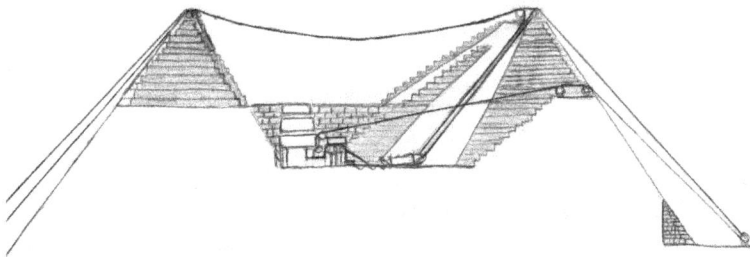

RIGGING · UTILITY PYRAMIDS

The extensive rigging associated with the utility pyramids involved a complex system of pulleys and counterweights at work across the building site.

Granite Walls

With a system established to sharply increase the amount of weight that the lift inside the Grand Gallery was able to manage, the builders now had the means to erect the remainder of the walls in the King's Chamber, along with its ceiling and Relieving Chambers. Meanwhile, construction on the pyramid's courses continued to advance as blocks of the white Tura cladding for the façade and ordinary filler blocks for the interior rode up the gallery ramp on sleds parked on the lift, aided by the pulleys inside the Antechamber and elsewhere. After unloading and separating the different types of stones once they reached Course 49, crews dragged the sleds carrying individual blocks for the level they were currently assembling toward the west and the expansive center channel on the northern step-pyramid. Hooking four of the vehicles together, workers attached the chain to the ropes suspended from the pulleys at the top. And with that, a regular routine kicked into motion.

Pullers on the north side of the building stepping down the exterior ramp at an even pace hauled the loaded sleds up to the course under construction. Using a shadoof, the workers stationed on that level removed the block and placed it on a second sled positioned nearby. Then the work gangs assigned to the various quadrants transported their stones north, south, east, and west, and began steadily filling in the course-in-progress. As usual, starting at the outer wall of the Great Pyramid, they set the polished casing stones in place first. As the gangs packed row after row of filler blocks behind the exterior walls, the teams slowly worked their way back toward the center of the building and the outline of the King's Chamber. The process took the better part of a year to complete.

Only after crews had filled in the majority of a particular course and reached the boundary line of the evolving King's Chamber would the bulky pieces of granite quarried for specific sections of its walls arrive on the lift. Granite is so tremendously heavy — a square foot of granite a mere three-quarters of an inch thick weighs almost 13 pounds — that the construction team made a concerted effort to avoid picking it up at all costs. The dense piece of stone for the wall that had sailed downriver from Aswan traveled into the building on its own extra-large sledge. And there it would remain until the builders were ready to slip the block into place.

While the load may have been heavier than usual, the basic construction techniques remained the same. After the lift stopped at the top of the gallery ramp, workers offloaded the special sled transporting the granite and spun it so the nose was facing northwest for the trip up the wide passage on the utility pyramid. Retaining the ability to transport such a great weight across a stone floor was one reason the sleds transporting the granite blocks bore a resemblance to a small boat, which comes to a gently rounded point at the bottom. The underside of the "boat" was designed to reduce the amount of drag beneath the load and allow workers to rock or pivot the sled in multiple directions.

In an odd twist, the Egyptians' commitment to the principle of never physically lifting a piece of stone, especially the enormously heavy blocks of granite, dictated the height of the limestone filler surrounding the King's Chamber. That general rule also provides the most plausible explanation for how the chamber's walls came to be. The blocks in every row on all four sides of the King's Chamber are exactly the same height: 47 inches. For the process of wall-building to succeed, engineers had to make the filler stones abutting the room-in-progress several inches shorter than the granite wall blocks themselves.

The minor difference in height between the upper edge of a wall block already in place and the filler stones beside it took into account the depth of the wooden sled transporting the next block of granite for the chamber. Since the top of the filler stone was lower than the upper edge of the wall block installed in the previous row, the thickness of the wood in the sled when it was pushed up against the existing piece of granite created a flat surface — level with the top of the wall. An even plane permitted the work gang to simply slide the new block straight across from the sled onto the unfinished wall and align the interior edge with the block(s) already situated in the row below.

The builders would have laid in the granite blocks for all four walls on a single level before moving on to erect the next layer of the Great Pyramid. A good guess is that the team started with the chamber's shorter east wall before tackling the one on the south side, followed by the walls to the west and north. After depositing each wall block, workers moved the hulking sled that had held the stone onto the lift, which carried it back down the gallery to Course 25 to await more granite as soon as the next course was ready to receive it.

The walls in the King's Chamber are unusual in their own right. While the blocks on all four sides of the room are the same height (47 inches), their widths can vary as measured left to right. Most of the blocks are also offset from the ones beneath them. The Egyptians did not position the blocks in the walls with the vertical joints stacked up in a straight line because that configuration would have substantially impaired the chamber's structural integrity. Yet they did not create a true running bond, either. As defined in masonry, a bond is the patterned arrangement of brick or stone in a wall where the mason laps the bricks over each other to prevent the vertical joints from falling apart. With a running bond, the vertical joints are evenly spaced to break exactly in the middle of the bricks positioned directly above and below it.

Furthermore, in several places around the room, it appears as if the builders may have constructed the walls with an upper block serving almost as a lintel with respect to the piece of stone underneath it. That type of horizontal structural support spanning an opening would take the pressure off the lower block. One possible example of this configuration is evident near the northwest corner of the King's Chamber. Examining the second block in from the corner at floor level on the west side of the room, it looks as if it might be possible to remove that block without destroying the wall. A few other placements, similar in nature, are also evident elsewhere around the chamber.

Do these blocks actually serve as lintels? And, if so, were the header stones built into the walls so the Egyptians conceivably would be able to remove the granite blocks below them for some unexplained reason? Moreover, if any of the wall blocks in the King's Chamber truly are removable, there is a good chance that they are also slightly beveled on all four sides. That way, the face visible from the front would fit snugly into the finished wall while the sides retained some give, allowing the stone to slide in and out of its slot more easily. Conforming to the high standards displayed throughout the rest of the Great Pyramid, without the use of any mortar in the joints, the granite walls in the King's Chamber are sealed so tightly that it is impossible to slide a razor blade or piece of paper in between them.

Topped Off

The highest blocks topping off the walls of the King's Chamber were slipped into place when construction finally reached the fifth row. The granite pieces quarried for the uppermost row differ from the ones further down the wall in one key way, however. While the blocks in the last row are identical in height to all of the other wall blocks, most of the stone slabs ringing the room at the roofline are much longer end to end. Engineers may have included a row of lengthy horizontal beams on top to help tie the walls together.

As with the other blocks in the chamber's walls, trying to guess exactly how wide these blocks are from front to back is problematic. In general, a logical estimate is to assume that most if not all of the wall blocks surrounding the space extend approximately four feet behind the walls — based on the depth of the granite block at the base of the air shaft on the north side of the room. We can measure the depth of that block through the rectangular opening in the wall.

With the walls now complete, the room was ready for its flat ceiling. The Griffith theory posits that before the process of erecting a roof for the King's Chamber began, the Egyptians constructed wooden scaffolding inside the mostly empty chamber, which was bare except for the sarcophagus, to assist them in handling the unwieldy granite roof slabs. The blocks in the ceiling are relatively narrow, measuring only four feet across east to west, but longer than the width of the chamber north to south — a distance of 17 feet, two inches. We can only imagine how far the "tail" of each ceiling block extends beyond the walls on either side. What is obvious is that a total of nine granite blocks cover the room, making the interior of the King's Chamber more than 19 feet high from floor to ceiling.

How were the builders able to haul in and distribute such sizeable granite slabs to enclose the chamber? Work gangs would have completed the courses surrounding it up to the final row of wall blocks and brought the sled bearing the first piece for the ceiling around to the west end of the exposed room. As expected, the wood forming the sled's base sat flush with the top of the wall. Researchers investigating the first Relieving Chamber above the King's Chamber have observed that the slabs used in the ceiling were only dressed and polished on three sides: the bottom, which was visible from inside the room, and the east west faces, which would have allowed the ceiling slabs to sit squarely against the blocks positioned on either side of them. Apart from any decorative purposes, the decision to polish the bottom seems logical given the fact that the construction team planned to slide the pieces for the ceiling into place along the upper edges of the north and south walls.

The Egyptians had concocted an elegant solution to the problem of roofing over the King's Chamber. Spreading the scantest amount of an emollient in between the top of the highest row of polished wall blocks and the polished granite on the underside of the ceiling slab would be akin to placing a drop of oil between a couple of mirrors. The two surfaces will glide against each other. Thus, by using some sort of lubricant to create a slippery plane, workers either pushed or pulled the first ceiling block toward the east end of the chamber along the rails formed by the tops of the walls and set it into place. Slab by slab, the roof began to grow — east to west — until eventually it covered the length of the room.

[CHAPTER 12]

STONES OF TITANS

If the Great Pyramid were merely a solid mass of millions of individual stones piled up roughly in the shape of a mountain, that feat alone would mark an astonishing achievement in human history. But the soaring edifice also contains a number of interior passageways and chambers with the possibility of more concealed rooms and hollow spaces yet to be discovered. Chief among the openings known to date is the King's Chamber with its mystifying coffer — and the colossal configuration called the Relieving Chambers that rises 70 feet above it. While a great deal of conjecture exists around this imposing, multilayered structure, Egyptologists have not been able to determine the specific purpose it fulfilled.

Many scholars allege that the builders erected the Relieving Chambers to help the King's Chamber withstand the humongous weight of the millions of blocks of stone stacked overhead. To that end, the motive behind its construction was to increase the stability of the open cavity inside the "mountain" by alleviating some of the stress that might crack the ceiling or cause the chamber to crumble. It is important to remember that the limestone peak at the apex of the five levels in the Relieving Chambers tops out at about Course 90. Almost another whole pyramid — at least 120 more courses — is above it.

Other architects and engineers disagree that the function of the Relieving Chambers was to discharge pressure by spreading out the weight pushing down on the cavity below. They question why the Egyptians would build so many chambers when a single gable over the flat ceiling in the King's Chamber would have served just as well in distributing a portion of the weight to the walls. In that same vein, why wouldn't the Queen's Chamber, situated much lower in the pyramid and carrying a far greater load, need similar protection?

Engineer Rudolf Gantenbrink, whose robotic crawler explored the air shafts in the Queen's Chamber as part of the Upuaut Project in 1993, believes the term "relieving chambers" to be a misnomer.[1] From an engineering standpoint, he has suggested that without the five chambers overhead, the roof beams on the King's Chamber, which deflect about 50 percent of the load into the horizontal, would have pushed against the south end of the Grand Gallery. To alleviate that problem, the builders were compelled to lift the roof above the static structure of the gallery. Other engineers have supported Gantenbrink's view. Whatever the underlying cause or reason for their existence, the Relieving Chambers contain the heaviest stones found anywhere inside the Great Pyramid.

1. http://www.pyramidofman.com/chambers.htm

Blocks and Voids

The ancient Egyptians faced countless challenges along the way in building their pyramid, but the difficult task of constructing the Relieving Chambers may have presented the biggest trial of all. A total of 43 blocks makes up the floors and ceilings inside the massive structure, and estimates are that most of them weigh as much as 70 tons each. As with other elements of the pyramid, the Relieving Chambers would only rise as the levels of the Great Pyramid increased and the layers of filler stones surrounding the King's Chamber continued to grow, giving crews access to the higher courses for their work.

Studying a sketch by an artist who imagined having an unobstructed view of the Relieving Chambers from the east side looking west reveals a strange-looking configuration whose silhouette from that perspective resembles a tower. Composed of five stone levels stacked up like the rungs of a ladder, with empty spaces in between them, the outline also bears a curious resemblance to a djed. Any attempt to ascertain a full picture of these chambers from that vantage point is deceptive, however.

If the edifice were freestanding and not totally encased in stone, the view from the front (north) side would look very different from the relatively narrow pylon shown in a side view, which portrays the five openings between the layers as if they were visible from the interior of the Great Pyramid. The enormous granite formation runs the entire length of the King's Chamber east to west (34' 4"), and the blocks comprising its base, which form the floor of the bottommost cavity, are the same nine granite slabs found in the ceiling of that room.

The imaginary drawing also shows the blocks of granite, which make up the rungs of the "ladder," marginally decreasing in length north to south as they climb toward the peak, causing the tower to look narrower at the top than it does at the bottom. In truth, although explorers in the 1800s dynamited their way into the Relieving Chambers and researchers have since documented the dimensions of many of the blocks, it is virtually impossible to discern the precise measurements of every piece of granite the builders installed or the structure writ large.

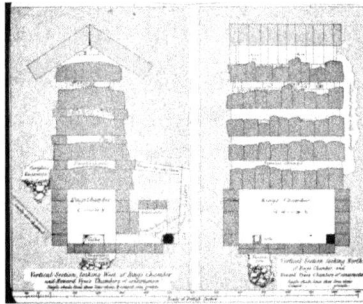

RELIEVING CHAMBERS FROM EAST & NORTH
Artist's renderings of the Relieving Chambers as viewed from the east and north.

Defying the Odds

Any attempt to deconstruct and chronicle the process of assembling the Re-lieving Chambers from a 21st-century perspective cannot possibly do justice to the time and effort required to build those five cavities more than 12,000 years ago. The work took decades to complete, yet the same techniques the Egyptians had employed to build the walls and roof of the King's Chamber made it feasible for them to erect the structure that towers seven stories above that room. The process began with work gangs filling in the next few courses of the Great Pyramid one by one. Proceeding from the outside edge of the building toward the center, they added limestone filler up to the perimeter of the King's Chamber and the area where the first set of blocks for the Relieving Chambers was scheduled to go.

Another critical element of the building process was the narrow strip of courses along the wall of the King's Chamber on the north side. Despite the presence of both the primary work area and lower end of the broad center channel on Course 49, engineers still had to generate some altitude right next to the chamber because workers had to be able to get high enough to drag the loaded sleds over to that construction zone. While the stack of course blocks built up over many years to cover the space only spread as far as the front edge of the Antechamber, it had supported the team in erecting the room's north wall. And the rows of filler had continued growing taller as the walls developed, until eventually the pile of stones turned into a work platform for the Relieving Chambers on the north side. At the same time, the strip of limestone blocks would never extend further north since it was imperative to preserve enough open space on the 49th course to maintain access to the lift.

The general pattern of constructing the walls for an interior room by surrounding the targeted area with filler stones up to the boundary lines had served the Egyptians well. In fact, the only reason they were able to assemble the granite walls and roof for the King's Chamber was because filler blocks ran right up to the edge of the chamber on all four sides as the courses developed. The horizontal surface formed by the blocks set directly behind the walls, plus the depth of the wooden sleds carrying the granite, had created a flat plane for sliding the heavy slabs into position. Likewise, only when the filler was in place on a subsequent level and available to receive the next row of wall blocks would workers transport another piece of granite up the gallery ramp and over to the emerging room. This unique approach, which was both efficient and quite successful, remained fundamentally the same during the process of assembling the Relieving Chambers.

The enormous job the builders had undertaken to fabricate the five mysterious chambers would last many years because the surface area workers had to pack with filler stones was so vast. Taking into account the fact that the width of the King's Chamber east to west is a meager 34 feet plus a few inches, compared to the Great Pyramid itself, which is approximately 755 feet wide at the base, it no doubt took a year or more to complete just a couple of courses. Granted, the levels would become incrementally smaller as the number of layers increased and the pyramid began to taper off on its way to the summit, but that reduction was not significant enough at this point to affect the progress and timing of the construction operation.

Sailing Downstream

Undoubtedly the biggest problem the construction team faced was creating a successful strategy for transporting and managing the oversized chunks of granite intended for the Relieving Chambers. It is difficult to imagine how these ancient builders even entertained the idea of not only extracting but transferring 70-ton blocks up to the 25th course and into the core of the Great Pyramid. Suffice it to say, implementing such a game plan was both a daring move and an incredibly taxing chore.

The material came downstream to the Giza Plateau on barges after an extended journey north from Aswan some 500 miles away. Not surprisingly, the determinative factor influencing the timing and progression of the build-out was the natural rhythms of the Nile. If the river during that bygone age was anything like it is today, the water level fluctuated wildly depending on the season and when the annual flooding occurred. Due to the exceptional weight of the blocks destined for the Relieving Chambers, the Egyptians would have only been able to float the granite downriver on barges during those few months when the Nile River was at flood stage. Otherwise, the ship's draw would have been too deep and the water level too shallow around the docks and ramps to discharge the load.

One might hazard a guess that the Egyptians transported as many blocks as possible — the eight or nine needed to install either the floor or ceiling for a single cavity — during that limited time frame, which lasted about three months. Simultaneously, the white limestone from Tura continued to arrive at the docks near the Sphinx. By shipping one full set of the granite blocks each season, the builders would be able to store them in the interim until a specific stone was needed. No doubt the most practical and accessible storage area was toward the east end of the 50-foot-wide platform running along the north side of the pyramid at the top of the exterior ramp. By stowing the loaded sleds temporarily in this unused space, the granite would be readily available when the time came to start moving the massive blocks into the building and up the Grand Gallery.

Luckily the northern ramp leading to the construction entrance offered a straight shot into the interior of the pyramid, which meant the mega-blocks the Egyptians were transporting did not have to turn any corners to get inside. Another advantage of this particular ramp was the helpful design. Built on a spit of land that jutted into the river, the tip of the long slope actually began several feet underwater at the far end of the small peninsula. As a result, barges were able to pull directly into the docking area projected into the riverbed and deliver their loads onto the solid surface of the manmade rise. Once the ramp approached the height of the 25th course, it leveled off and converted into the platform in front of the construction entrance. The flat surface at the top of the ramp was in reality a continuation of the same approximately 50-foot-wide deck, which started at the northwest corner of the building and extended down the wall a good distance past the main doorway.

The northern ramp was customized to routinely accommodate the hundreds of workers and special equipment involved in moving mammoth loads. Besides the smooth, wide surface that covered the center of the incline, there were short steps along both sides for workers to climb up and down as they pulled one way or the other. In addition, at the intersection of the ramp with the horizontal landing, crews had inserted several low rollers inside the "seam" where the two angles met. The apparatus resembled a pipe cut in half lengthwise, cradling a stone dowel, with only a small portion of the curved edge peeking up from below. The function of the rounded top was to redirect the ropes so that instead of the lines tied to a load retaining the same upward trajectory and ultimately ascending into thin air, the ropes would level off and begin to run horizontally, allowing a sledge to traverse the platform.

The Griffith theory suggests that the largest granite slabs — approximately five feet wide, six feet thick, and more than 28 feet long — came down the river resting on sturdy boat-sleds most likely crafted from solid pieces of wood. Designed to be slightly rounded on the underside, the sleds had curved bows and sterns because a curved edge made it easier for the vehicle carting the stone to start up an incline. The gently rounded underbelly also helped decrease the drag.

On the other hand, the contours of the wooden sled meant it may have had a tendency to sink into the ground, if and when it ever had to cross soft soil or desert sand along the route. The boat-sled transporting the chunk of granite had holes drilled through the right- and left-hand sides, and ropes inserted through those openings are what the pullers would use to heave the carrier up to the top of the northern center channel after it arrived on Course 49.

Because the primary sled did not sit level, crews had pulled it onto the top of a second sled as they loaded it onto the barge. The one on the bottom was flat and shaped more like a long toboggan with runners on both sides. Workers may have also put dunnage beneath the bi-level sledge as they pulled it onto the boat to provide a little space underneath the freight for maneuvering purposes. Besides tying down the granite block itself, the workers shoved wooden wedges front, back, and under the sides of the boat-sled positioned on top to prevent it from rocking or tipping over as the "toboggan" shifted forward.

Picture a barge at least 100 feet long and 30 feet wide engineered so the bow operated like the front of an oversized Higgins Boat, the amphibious landing craft used during World War II to disembark troops and supplies on D-Day. The ship's crew was able to lower a gate at the front end and turn it into a short ramp for loading and unloading cargo. Attached to the barge's port and starboard sides were the legs of a tall A-frame made from a wooden crossbeam held between two giant beams on either side, which were at least a foot thick and approximately 28 feet tall. The side beams had circular holes drilled through them near the base, which fit around pins affixed to the interior walls of the ship, and those fasteners permitted the sailors to either stand up the frame vertically or lay it down over the deck. While the basic structure of the sturdy scaffold was fixed, the A-frame itself was adjustable in terms of its function, doubling as both a crane for dragging cargo forward to pull it on or off the barge, as well as a mast for hoisting the sails when the vessel was underway.

A second A-frame just as high stood parallel to the one on the barge a short distance (20-30 feet) up the northern ramp. Its legs were spread far enough apart to virtually span the width of the center section of the incline east to west. Similar to the frame on the barge, the one close to the water's edge was also mounted on wooden pins that allowed it to rotate. From an upright, vertical position, the wooden scaffolding was able to bend forward or backward almost 45 degrees. To halt the rotation at the proper angle, workers probably attached some type of adjustable bar or other safety mechanism to the device to prevent it from falling all the way to the ground.

Once the barge had docked, the two A-frames — on ship and on land — were connected together at the top by fixed-length ropes, which allowed them to operate in unison.

BARGE WITH A-FRAME
Ancient Egyptian barge carrying an A-frame.

The frame installed on the barge had a total of four ropes firmly fastened to the corners on the side facing the center of the river. After leaning the apparatus down slightly toward the stern, workers tied this set of lines to the back of the sledge. The crew had also connected four more ropes to the same side of the wooden beams: two on the east leg and two on the west leg. The second group was not attached to the sled but stretched all the way to the stern where the hook built into the back end of the ship held a horizontal pulley. Similar to other rollers, the one mounted onboard had four turned grooves to separate and align the ropes that passed over it.

The pulley at the back of the barge also filled another critical function: keeping the lines taut. The job of the workers handling the ropes circling the roller at the back end was to make sure that once the frame started to lean down toward the deck when it was time to debark the cargo — and the sled began moving forward — the lines remained rigid to prevent the wooden device from falling too far. This was also the pulley that the team will use to reset the frame overhead once it is disconnected from the load.

The massive wooden A-frame fronting the water's edge was similarly festooned with ropes. At least eight were permanently connected to the legs, four to a girder, on the side facing the river. After stringing those lines onto the barge, the team attached them to the front of the sled, possibly using some sort of hook. The overall setup mimicked the one on the barge because workers had also fastened eight more ropes to the uphill side of the frame, four to a leg. Those lines were the ones the longshoremen unloading the ship would use to lean the frame southward as they headed down the staircases flanking the ramp.

Since the A-frame's crossbeam rose as high as 40 feet, crews had installed pulleys 60 to 80 feet above the bottom of the steps on the east and west sides. Ropes coming from the legs of the land-based A-frame circled those pulleys and were attached to the pullers' harnesses, which allowed the workers to walk downhill, heaving the giant scaffold in the direction of the pyramid. The availability of the land-based ropes immediately doubled the team's overall pulling capacity because the two devices — one standing on the barge floating in the water and the other installed up the ramp on the riverbank — would function as a single machine.

Rigging the Pull

Nudging the granite off the barge and actually moving it onto the building site presented a challenge as daunting as trying to climb Mt. Everest. The Egyptians had to formulate an approach that would succeed, an effort that demanded enormous amounts of ingenuity and planning. The crews tasked with pulling loads weighing more than 90 tons up an incline at least 1,400 feet long were dealing with a rise of 170+ feet.

But shuttling around the severely laden sledge was not out of the realm of possibility — assuming these ancient people had the benefit of a system of strategically placed ropes and pulleys.

As usual, the shrewd and indomitable Egyptians had made exhaustive preparations. And in the end, the groundwork they had laid would pay off handsomely. Proof of their ability to meet the epic challenge lies in the five Relieving Chambers that exist at the center of the Great Pyramid.

Preparations for the arduous pull kept workers busy at both ends of the lengthy ramp. Achieving the ultimate goal hinged on engineering the most efficient method for moving the enormous granite blocks from the water's edge — as much as a half-mile away — up to the top of the Giza Plateau and into the pyramid. The setup for the upcoming pull involved not only rerouting many of the ropes but also figuring out a way to use the counterweight in the Descending Passage for at least a portion of the operation. The good news was that since the team could only transport a limited number of the giant stones on an annual basis during the comparatively short flood season, work crews would have to readjust the rigging and return the equipment to its original position just once per year.

The monumental weights involved in the Relieving Chambers' project demanded every bit of pulling power the Egyptians could muster. Consequently, they made use of every available pulley. To redirect the exceptionally long and bulky ropes, which regularly required an entire team of workers to handle, the builders took their cue from the way sailors might manage the lines on a naval vessel.

Normally it would be impossible for one man or even a small group of workers to pick up and throw a piece of heavy, plaited rope onshore to moor a ship. But if they spliced a line that had a much narrower circumference onto the thicker piece and tied a metal weight to one end, the crew would be able to throw the weight back and forth to each other, as well as hurl it the short distance onto the dock, causing the bulkier rope to follow behind. Then the people waiting onshore would be able to seize the skinnier rope and, pulling hand over hand, direct the more substantial line wherever they wanted it to go. This practice was essentially no different for the ancient builders who were switching out the ropes crisscrossing the interior of the pyramid. Lengths of narrow, everyday rope weighted at one end and attached to a line as thick as a man's arm, assisted them in reconfiguring the complicated pulley system.

Restringing the four ropes mounted atop the original utility pyramid on the north side of the Queen's Chamber, workers carried one end of the lines down to the bottom of the ramp and attached them to the east side of the sledge sitting on the barge. (While the majority of the step-pyramid associated with the Queen's Chamber had been absorbed into prior levels, course blocks had not overtaken its summit, which rose as high as the 70th course.) The other end of those same ropes curved over the roller on top of the utility pyramid and dropped down to the pullers assigned to the staircase along the ramp's east side.

Toward the west end of the same utility pyramid, another extremely long set of ropes (2,400 feet or more end to end) extended down from a second, newly installed pulley. Similar to the four ropes coming from the pulley situated toward the east, this group also stretched all the way down to the barge docked at the riverbank, many hundreds of feet below. Pulling the lines forward, workers posted on the ship affixed the latest set of ropes to the west side of the sled carrying the granite. High above them, at the opposite end of the lines, the clutch of ropes curved around the pulley at the top and, after turning back, proceeded toward the stair-steps along the west side of the ramp and the group of haulers waiting to pull.

The beauty of this setup was that the workers attempting to move the massive blocks were able to start pulling from their position at the upper end of the ramp and walk downhill. In contrast to most of the prevailing ideas about how the Great Pyramid was constructed, the Griffith theory does not place the laborers building the massive structure in front of the stones — working against gravity — to pull their enormous burdens up impossibly steep slopes. Rather, in cases such as this, it sees the oversized load as ascending the slope as the pullers make their way down the incline step by step. Striding forward in a synchronized fashion, they put all of their weight against the harnesses strapped around their bodies.

Estimates of the number of people required to elevate specific amounts of weight indicate that more than 1,200 workers may have taken part in the pull — a total of 600 or more people on each side of the ramp. If this rudimentary assessment is correct, the sum would result in at least 75 workers handling each of the eight ropes that extended down from the pulleys atop the Queen's Chamber utility pyramid. It was also true that similar to the bar or strap hooked onto an animal harnessed to a yoke, the length of rope workers access at any given time will only be as long as necessary to drag the sled toward the top of the ramp.

The teams on the pull-ropes would stand eight across in pairs of two down the sets of stairs, with each pair hooked onto a single loop spliced into the rope. This army of pullers, which occupied 75 or more of the steps along both sides of the ramp, had to work as a unit and move in cadence for a synchronized pull. Allowing three feet of space for every team member plus a little extra legroom for freer movement, the staircases must have been about 30 feet wide. Furthermore, engineers would have gauged the depth of the steps to allow a sufficient amount of space level to level between the rows of eight pullers, recognizing that a team member leaning forward with their full body weight must not interfere with the person walking in front of him.

The full complement of workers would cover less than one-fifth of the entire length of the northern ramp. Yet the operation will never run out of pullers, because once the initial groups east and west reached the bottom, they skirted around their teammates and took up new positions at the rear of the rope-line. Conversely, the work gangs on the riverbank assigned to tilt the land-based A-frame will have a short-lived task. That crew would clear off the staircases by the time the second group of pullers descending from the top of the ramp arrives.

At the same time, a reshuffling of the ropes inside the ascending and descending passageways was also underway. Workers had taken the two lines fastened to the middle of the counterweight, which usually traveled up the First Ascending Passage and into the Grand Gallery, and detached them from the stone. Then they wound those lines around a bar or hook mounted near the opening to the passageway, stashing the ends out of the way to prevent them from becoming entangled with the counterweight or impeding its movement. The idea was to put the heavy counterweight to work during the final portion of the pull. For the first time, the team prepared to raise it up the Descending Passage past the entrance to the First Ascending Passage all the way to the top of the channel — an extra 90 feet.

Long before any of these changes occurred, when the main ramp and the platform against the north wall were under construction, the seeds for the reconfiguration had been sown. Without that deck, the ropes connected to the upper end of the counterweight would have surfaced from inside the Great Pyramid at Course 19. But because the outside platform rose as high as Course 25, that structure blocked the hole in the exterior wall at the lower level. This was the purpose of the small tunnel built underneath the deck: to create a pathway for the ropes tied to the counterweight and allow them to exit the building. As mentioned previously, the lines snaked beneath the platform and gradually rose at an angle toward the top until they emerged through an opening directly in front of the construction entrance at the intersection, where the upper edge of the ramp on the north side met the platform.

CHAPTER 13

A HARD CLIMB

Now THAT THE EQUIPMENT was in place and the coordinate systems rigged, the moment the Egyptians had been waiting for had finally arrived. The building blocks for the Relieving Chambers were practically on the pyramid's doorstep. It was only a matter of transporting the enormous stones up the slope to bring them inside.

The initial step in the process of moving a granite slab ashore was to use the two A-frames to pull the double-decker sled off the barge. The first set of ropes fastened to the frame mounted on the ship's deck was hooked onto the back of the sled. Premade eyelets were likely woven into the ends of the rope to connect the two objects. A team stationed at the back of the barge controlled the other set of lines, which passed over the pulley at the stern. While the hardest part of their job would not really shift into high gear until it was time to reset the apparatus, this crew played a pivotal role in the debarkation process. Letting a little slack into the ropes, the workers on the boat slowly pulled the A-frame forward to lean it down toward the center of the river. Concurrently, the group of pullers on the riverbank who had taken up positions along the steps on the uphill side of the land-based frame let slack into the lines to lower their scaffold in the direction of the ship.

When the signal came, the crews midway up the ramp who controlled the lines from the pulleys temporarily mounted on the two staircases, began moving down the steps, raising the A-frame on the riverbank to a vertical position again. Once the device shifted, the motion tightened the connector ropes linking the two frames together. As a result, the frame on the boat started to stand up, too. In concert with all of the activity occurring at the bottom of the ramp and to aid the process further, the pullers in their harnesses stationed at the top of the two staircases started to walk downhill. As they heaved on the ropes connected to the sledge, which circled the pulleys on top of the step-pyramid overlooking the scene, a cohort of workers some 1,200 strong added their muscle to the task of inching the mammoth load forward.

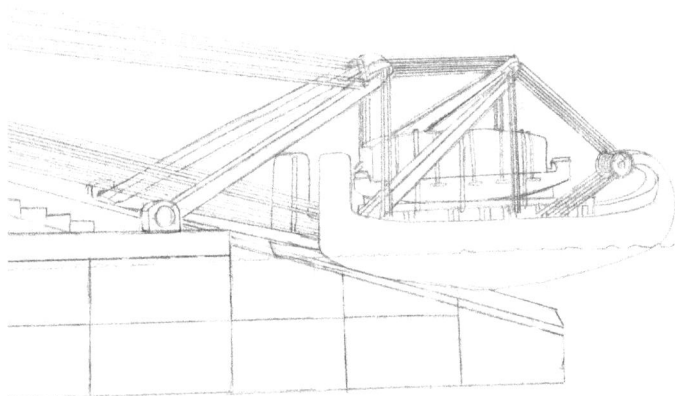

BARGE AND A-FRAME DEBARKING LOAD

Two tall A-frames installed on the ship and riverside moved the sled with the granite block ashore to begin the long trek from the base of the ramp to the northern platform.

In one master stroke, the middle group of pullers managing the land-based A-frame tugged on their lines to make the scaffold stand up straight then tilt slightly backwards toward the Great Pyramid. When the combined energy of two A-frame devices achieved maximum force, assisted by the power of hundreds of workers marching down the incline, it jumpstarted the forward momentum. And in short order, the collective effort behind the great heave dragged the sledge off the barge. Now the crew assigned to the back of the ship began to earn their keep, because they had to provide the countervailing force. Grasping the lines coming over the roller mounted on the hook at the stern, the crew held on tightly to maintain tension on the ropes. Only a taut line would hold the boat's A-frame steady and prevent it from falling over onto the deck, due to the enormous amount of pressure coming from the other end.

One of the greatest challenges the Egyptians faced in charting the sled's progression was how to overcome inertia. Luckily, the forward motion triggered by the two frames working in concert actually caused a momentary shift in the sled's massive weight, which became a tiny bit lighter as the force increased. Recognizing this reality, the builders' goal was to keep the load steadily advancing uphill, no matter what. With that singular objective in mind, once the sledge had traveled down the ship's bow-ramp, off the barge, and reached the edge of the A-frame onshore, workers removed the ropes that connected both frames to the sled. In a remarkable turn of events, this unhooking was accomplished while the vehicle was still in motion — but before it had surpassed the distance the tie-lines were able to stretch. Because the sled was traveling at a snail's pace, disengaging the ropes while it was moving did not present a major problem.

Above all else, the team wanted to prevent the sled from having to stop along its uphill journey. Consequently, they had choreographed the pull-teams to follow the rhythms of a well-rehearsed, highly synchronized dance as they progressed down the steps alongside the ramp. At a certain point, the first group of workers handling the ropes from the pulleys on the step-pyramid would have walked forward toward the river as far as they could go, having reached the bottom of the stairs. With the load still only partway up the incline, the lead team simply ran out of room to pull. The most logical solution to the problem was to have the groups of pullers continuously shift their positions on the staircases. Engineers had designed the system so that when the first group of eight on the ropes east and west reached the very last step, they would unhook their harnesses, walk back up the hill, and join the rear of the column to continue pulling.

Row by row, the people in front disengaged themselves, then made their way to the back of the line to keep lugging the sled forward. Another 592 workers followed behind the lead pullers on the ropes on either side. Deploying the sledge and successfully moving the massive piece of granite to its final destination meant every individual and detail had to be in its allotted place at the correct moment. Only then would the throng of pullers be able to step forward effectively and keep the operation on track. As the job progressed, most, if not all, of the 1,200+ workers involved would reposition themselves at least once during the course of the pull.

One additional facet of the process also demanded attention. As the pullers proceeded down the ramp, their end of the ropes kept getting longer while the ropes on the opposite side of the pulley fastened to the double-decker sled grew increasingly shorter as the vehicle crawled up the slope. As a consequence, a separate team assigned to the work zone near the river gathered up the lines the workers had abandoned when they relocated. After the pullers unhooked their harnesses to clamber up the stairs, leaving the unattended ropes behind, a ground crew looped up the ends to move them out of the way.

Keep in mind that the ropes the two pull-teams controlled were much longer than the ramp itself because the lines had to extend from the river's edge all the way to the top of the plateau before climbing up to the pulleys mounted on the utility pyramid. Coiling the enormous lines in an orderly fashion not only cleared a path for the people descending the staircases, but also staged the equipment so it was readily accessible for future pulls.

Into the Pyramid

The counterweight was a vital component of the process at this stage, but the notion of dispatching it did not even enter the realm of possibility until the loaded sled was about 100 yards away from the northern platform. Because the Descending Passage is 357 feet long from end to end, the team was only able to call on the services of the counterweight for the final 300 feet or so of the ramp. Connecting it any further out than that simply would not have worked.

A specialized team outdoors on the north side of the pyramid had always managed the ropes connected to the stone in the underground channel. They were the ones tasked with resetting the piece of granite by pulling it back up the passageway to a spot just below the opening to the First Ascending Passage. But now circumstances had changed, since work crews had redone the rigging to allow the counterweight to rise to the top of the Descending Passage. The added force this extra weight would provide was vital to the success of the endeavor, especially during the last several hundred feet of the pull.

As the mid-point of the more than 30-foot-long sledge started sailing past the top of the ramp where it met the edge of the platform and wanted to tip forward due to the gravitational pull, the assist afforded the pull-team from the counterweight was key. It made a critical difference not only in maintaining control of the sled but also in moving it forward from that steep angle — until the final 15 feet of the wooden carrier was resting solidly on the platform's deck.

In this instance, the ancient pyramid builders employed a clever plan. Since the sled was crawling up the incline at a sluggish rate, they chose not to halt its progress, but sidestepped the issue entirely by having workers connect the counterweight to the vehicle as it crept forward. They took the ropes tied to the counterweight, which came through the hole at the top of the platform, and slid those lines beneath the carrier — in between the two runners — as it moved uphill. Then they hooked the ropes onto the back end. Why? If the ropes were attached to the sides, the sledge would run into its own lines when it reached the top of the ramp and started tilting forward onto the deck. Placing them under the bottom allowed the counterweight to keep dropping down the Descending Passage until the sled had tipped forward at the upper edge of the ramp, directly onto the flat surface in front of the construction entrance.

With the counterweight now part of the process, the power behind the pull intensified greatly. But countless factors were involved and all of them had to work together without a glitch for the builders' audacious plan to succeed. As the pullers on the steps slowly moved downhill, dragging the sled up the incline, the heavy counterweight beneath the pyramid was also dropping down the Descending Passage, carrying the load with it, drawn forward by the workers turning the king-sized wheel in the Subterranean Chamber. Due to the heft of the counterweight and collective power of the crowds of people along both sides of the northern ramp pulling in sync, the sledge ultimately reached its destination at the top of the incline at Course 25. The Egyptians had captured the biggest prize yet: a sled carrying a titanic piece of granite sitting at the mouth of the Great Pyramid.

The Griffith theory asserts that the Egyptians transported enough granite for a complete floor/ceiling for one Relieving Chamber during a single season. And in the interim, before transferring the slabs inside, they stored the entire fleet of eight or nine "boat-sleds" (separated from their toboggans) at the east end of the platform built against the north wall. There the line of carriers would remain until the time came to begin hauling the multi-ton granite blocks into the Great Pyramid one by one. In the meantime, as the flood waters receded and the river returned to a level too shallow for the barges to navigate properly, pyramid-building more or less reverted to business as usual. Work gangs returned the rigging for the pulleys and counterweight to their regular positions so the lift had the benefit of the big block of granite in the Descending Passage to fuel its journey up the Grand Gallery, and the pulleys atop the utility pyramids, which normally elevated the stones, were fully functional again.

Post-Rollers

The Egyptians must have installed several wooden post-rollers inside the space by the main entrance as well as outside the building at the east end of the platform. Crafted from rollers inserted vertically into holes in the floor, the post-rollers created pivot points against which the workers could pull to direct a load at the other end of the rope. Crews probably inserted a couple of them near the lift at the bottom of the Grand Gallery and at least two more on either side of the route the sled with the granite would take through the open area inside the main doorway.

As soon as the first bi-level sled was in position at the top of the platform after its trip from the river's edge, a team uncoupled the two units by moving the one holding the granite off the toboggan it sat on. To lower the boat-sled on top, crews must have placed a small temporary ramp of wood or stone directly in front of the sledge to bridge the height discrepancy and transfer the vehicle on top down to the floor. The workers took a separate set of ropes, tied them to the front of the upper sled, then guided the lines around the two post-rollers set up inside the wide alcove that was the staging area.

When the ropes tied to the sled were in position and the pull-teams on the northern ramp were hooked up to the lines, they began to walk down-hill, tugging on the other end. Soon the combination of the pullers' exertion plus the assistance of gravity caused the sled containing the granite to shift forward and slide down the short incline at the front end. The boat-sled kept advancing until it cleared the toboggan and squat ramp, and was standing on its own on the 25th course — ready for another work gang to shuffle it over to the east end of the platform.

Two more post-rollers, similar to the ones installed much earlier by the bulge at the platform's northwest corner, were mounted toward the east end of the deck. The crew will employ this set to maneuver the now-separated boat-sled over toward the storage area on that side. Every time one of the sleds carrying a piece of granite made its way to the top of the hill and shed its toboggan, workers manipulated a set of ropes circling the post-rollers mounted on the platform to ease the vehicle eastward. Setting it alongside one of the companion sleds also carting a granite slab, the collection grew, until all eight or nine carriers from the current season were lined up in a row.

Modifying the sledge by splitting up the top and bottom sections afforded the Egyptians several advantages. The gently rounded underside on the upper sled made it easier to swing the nose around and/or rock the vehicle back and forth if necessary.

While the upper sled must have been more than 28 feet long, it was only about five feet wide and four feet tall — compact enough for a group of strong workers to be able to scoot it around a little or spin it in a circle. Secondly, the weight of the unoccupied toboggan, which was considerable, meant the builders could use the lower portion of the two-part sledge to help them reset the pull-ropes during that season's operations. After tying several smaller lines to the back end, the team will drag the toboggan down the ramp into the vicinity of the barge. And since the wooden contraption was heavy enough, the ropes already attached to it would follow suit.

A similar benefit accrued for the counterweight, whose lines remained fastened to the toboggan's back end. The toboggan's bulk as it worked its way down the slope created enough force to help reset the fat stone in the Descending Passage. Once the toboggan had raised the counterweight as high as it could go inside the channel, a work gang undid the ropes from the toboggan and the crew stationed near the hole at the top of the ramp locked them off. When the apparatus finally reached the bottom of the hill and the gang had disengaged the ropes, they loaded the toboggan onto the empty barge, preparing to sail upriver for another load.

First One In

Once the last sledge of the season had arrived at the platform and was uncoupled from its toboggan, attention turned to transferring the inaugural boat-sled and its burdensome cargo over to the lift parked at the top of the First Ascending Passage. This phase of the operation involved rearranging once again the positions and angles of many of the ropes and pulleys crisscrossing the pyramid to take advantage of every available ounce of pulling power.

Early on, workers had reattached the lines removed from the counter-weight when they were revamping the rigging for the big pull. During the period when the Egyptians were in the process of erecting the Relieving Chambers, in the interregnum between the few short months of river flood-ing every year, the counterweight went back to its original position — in the shaft immediately below the opening to the First Ascending Passage. With the counterweight fastened to one end of the ropes, crews took the other end of the lines, which wended underneath the lift, and directed them across the open space inside the construction entrance on Course 25. (In the past, this set of ropes had continued up the Grand Gallery and circled around the pulley stand inserted midway up the ramp before turning back and hooking onto the lift's front end.)

Subsequently, the lines curved around the outside edges of a couple of post-rollers mounted on either side of the route that the loaded sled was going to take, somewhere between the lift and the main entrance. The next step involved fastening those same ropes, which had come through the First Ascending Passage, to the front of the sled hauling the granite. Having direct access to the substantial counterweight in the underground tunnel made it possible for the builders to achieve the goal of moving their monster load closer to the lift, onto its deck, and eventually to the block's final destination.

Assisted by various pieces of equipment, the workers slowly rotated the wooden sled toward the target area. The post-rollers created pivot points that allowed the team to gradually maneuver it into position, lined up with the great lift. Then a separate work gang, after attaching additional ropes for a longer reach, took the sled sitting at the entrance and, just as they had done thousands of times before, connected it to the machine in the niche inside the Queen's Chamber. Still operating after all those years, the hard-working mechanism with the interlocking gears was regularly employed to help pull an unending succession of heavy blocks and sleds into the building toward the lift.

With the expertise of master builders schooled in handling enormous loads, crews pulled the boat-sled onto the lift and then tied it down, hemming in the sides with wooden wedges to hold it steady and upright. Once the carrier with its granite block was safely ensconced on the lift platform, the team restored the ropes from the First Ascending Passage to their original positions. Detaching the lines from the sled, they wound them around the pulley stand mounted on the Great Step. When the ropes were reconnected to the front of the lift, the massive transporter was ready to climb up the gallery corridor again.

Five Openings

As soon as the Egyptians had installed the ceiling in the King's Chamber, the foundation for the Relieving Chambers was fixed. The next step was to haul in a collection of relatively lengthy but fairly short granite blocks and set them along the edges on the north and south sides of the roof, similar to the rails for a train track. Polished on at least three sides (top, bottom, and the side facing the center), the series of blocks had an important function to perform. Their purpose was to leave a void in between the giant slabs of granite used for the floors and ceilings, creating the cavities that became the Relieving Chambers.

The best guess is that the builders had installed the short blocks lined up along the edges for the lowest opening, the same way they had installed the granite for the walls in the King's Chamber. First, crews took limestone filler blocks that were not quite as tall as the existing ceiling slabs and deposited them on the course adjacent to the roofline. Then, after transporting the edging blocks up the Grand Gallery on individual sleds, crews maneuvered them into position next to the roof. Because the bottom of the wooden sled made up for the difference in height between the filler stones and the chamber's ceiling blocks, it formed a level plane even with the edge of the roof. Piece by piece, work gangs slid the edging blocks directly onto the rooftop, setting them in long rows down the two sides. This initial set of "tracks" created the north and south walls for the lowest Relieving Chamber. But its ceiling would have to wait until the Egyptians had completed more courses.

One puzzling feature of the five voids or gaps in between the horizontal layers of granite is the cavities' floors, which are bumpy and uneven. Matching the style of the blocks used in the ceiling of the King's Chamber, the builders appear to have dressed and polished the bottom and east and west faces of the stones quarried for the ceilings in the Reliving Chambers. But they did not level off the tops of those same slabs, which became the floor blocks for the succeeding chamber. Rather than being smooth and even, the floors look almost as if the rock were simply chiseled out of a cliff and dragged into the pyramid — with a few minor exceptions. Crews had trimmed back a flat strip on the north and south sides on top of each ceiling/floor block. Designed to hold the edging stones for the next opening, these narrow bands along the rim had been leveled off and polished.

Taking into account the way the blocks were excavated and dressed, it is not surprising that the chunks of granite in the floors of the five chambers differ markedly in terms of the depth of the slabs and their distinct undulations. In fact, the height of the floor stones not only fluctuates from chamber to chamber but even within a single chamber, which explains why the openings between the different levels of the Relieving Chambers vary in size from top to bottom. At the same time, because the undersides of the granite slabs were polished, the ceilings inside the five cavities are remarkably uniform in look. One obvious conclusion is that the Egyptians felt no need to dress an entire piece of granite that huge when most of it would never be seen. But they went ahead and smoothed off the underside to help slide the outsized blocks into position down the short rails formed by the edging stones. Buffing the granite so it would glide more easily is probably why the edging blocks were also finished off at the top and bottom.

Some pyramid enthusiasts have theorized that the cavities in the Relieving Chambers were actually constructed for their acoustical properties and that the Egyptians employed the structure to create sounds or vibrations for specific rituals and attunement exercises. They claim the overall design was meant more for the tonal qualities and harmonic resonance it produced than anything else. If that is true, such a distinct purpose might account for the stones in the floor having furrows in the peculiar shapes and sizes we see today.

With the first set of "rails" in place, the scene was set for an astonishing process that has the Egyptians depositing a group of gigantic granite slabs to enclose the very first Relieving Chamber. Lying side by side north to south on top of the parallel rows of edging blocks, the initial layer of granite rests just a few feet above the roof of the King's Chamber. As the work progressed, the builders would call on the same technique of setting down two lines of edging stones, then sliding the giant blocks of granite into place to develop future cavities. Contrary to what one might assume about the Relieving Chambers, their east and west walls are not composed of granite but are made out of limestone.

In addition, the primary difference among the five openings is the type of edging stones the Egyptians employed. The short blocks placed along the north and south sides for chambers four and five are also composed of limestone instead of granite. No one really knows why.

Moving the Unmovable

The building process unquestionably became much more arduous and problematic during this period when construction began on the ceiling of the first Relieving Chamber — with multi-ton stones involved. Now another intricate sequence of ropes and pulleys enters the picture. Two sets of ropes came from the pulleys mounted at the top of the utility pyramid associated with the north side of the Queen's Chamber. Those lines circled the pulley that sat near the east end of its upper step, traveled over to the double-pulley stand mounted behind the hole in the Antechamber's back wall, then moved roller to roller from one end of the room to the other before dropping down the Grand Gallery and attaching to the lift. The team would use the ropes around the second pulley positioned on the same step, but mounted further west, to assist them in hauling the sled off the lift and rotating it to ensure that the front end was pointing in the right direction for the climb up the hill.

Two more pulleys high overhead at Course 98 on the top step of the King's Chamber utility pyramid on the north side controlled another collection of ropes. They, too, were part of the system involved in heaving the heavy sled off the lift. Moreover, the lines passing over the pulleys positioned on this utility pyramid would be responsible for the grueling job of transporting the vehicle with the granite up the wide center channel, then lowering it down to the active course. At the other end of those ropes were more than a thousand workers standing outdoors on the northern ramp, ready to hook themselves up to the lines and pull.

A different set of ropes altogether was the group coming from the south end connected to the extra counterweight riding up and down the shaft in the southern utility pyramid. Stretching across the site, they crossed over one of the pulleys atop the King's Chamber pyramid at the north end and continued down the center channel to meet up with the lift. Once the lift landed at Course 49 but before its freight could be unloaded, work gangs would attach the boat-sled carrying the huge granite block to the ropes from the southern counterweight and the various lines designated to rotate the vehicle and raise it up the incline.

• Moving the Granite •

Looking down from above the building site on the north side, three sets of ropes would have been evident. Their layout was designed to help position and elevate the sleds carrying the massive granite blocks for the Relieving Chambers. The lines at the far left and in the middle extended up to a pair of pulleys mounted on top of the original utility pyramid on the north side of the Queen's Chamber. The ropes connected to the easternmost pulley traveled through Antechamber before descending into the Grand Gallery, where they were attached to the lift.

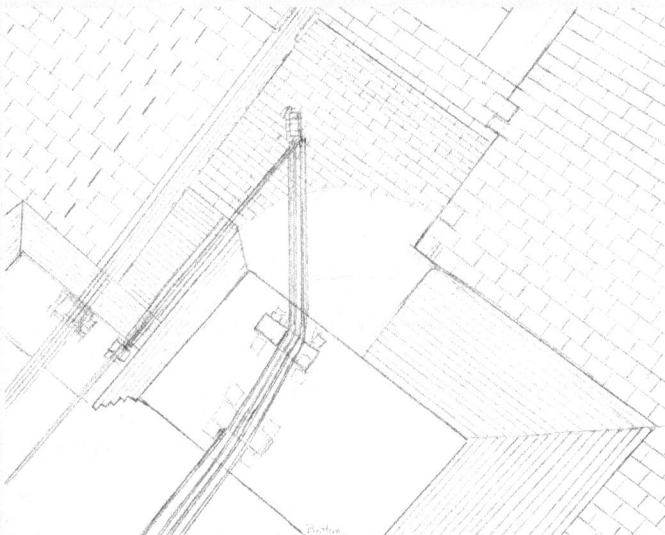

GRANITE BLOCKS IN MOTION

The center set of ropes was not involved in the actual pull except to assist in moving the loaded sledge off the lift and rotating the front end to ensure that it was facing in the right direction and at the proper angle — northwest — for the ride uphill. The set of ropes to the right, which were mounted on the upper utility pyramid linked to the King's Chamber, were responsible for three crucial tasks. First, assist in pulling the sled off the lift. Second, raise the extraordinarily heavy vehicle up to the top of the center channel. And third, lower the sled down the narrow ramp behind the channel's west wall to the course under construction.

Hauling the boat-sled with its colossal load inch by inch across the short distance between the spot where the lift stopped and the start of the smooth rise that was the center channel, the individual teams worked in sync. The operation would gradually raise the granite-laden carrier as high as possible up the wide shaft, then let it descend to the level that crews were in the process of assembling. As mentioned previously, the sled's gently rounded underside meant only a fraction of the vehicle actually touched the floor, which helped eliminate some of the drag. One crucial aspect of the Egyptians' strategy was the setup near the top of the center channel.

While the channel had a wall built along the west side, it stopped partway up the incline, reaching only as high as the last course crews had completed. To avoid having to pick up the front end of the heavy vehicle and move it over that obstacle, the workers outdoors on the ropes continued pulling the load up the shaft until the back end slipped past the point where the wall ended. After maneuvering the sled to angle it more toward the west (the opposite side of the wall), the pullers slowly lowered it down to the targeted course.

Once the carrier had arrived at the correct level, a separate team took charge of moving the huge load in stages toward the vicinity of the King's Chamber. The sled had to cross at least 30–40 feet to reach the chamber's west end, but there was plenty of room for any number of workers tugging on ropes to heave the load further south and maneuver it into position for unloading. Work gangs may have also inserted post-rollers into holes dug out of the floor to assist them in the pull as well as to help adjust the sled's positioning if and when that became necessary. Pulling on the lines attached to the vehicle's front end, the team slowly drew it forward across the level surface of the latest course and lined up the longest side parallel with the room's west wall.

The giant granite slab quarried for the roof of the first cavity sat lengthwise down the center of the sled — polished side down — atop a wooden cradle built into the base. The wood underneath the block was sized to sit flush with the tops of the edging stones on the north and south sides of the chamber's roof. Expending an extraordinary amount of effort and energy, and assisted by some sort of lubricant spread between the stones, workers pulled the massive granite piece forward, sliding it all the way down the edging blocks to the east end of the structure. It no doubt took a long time, and every element of the procedure had to be executed with precision, but the process would repeat itself slab by slab until the entire length of the lowest cavity had its ceiling.

Curiously, the total number of blocks found in the ceilings and floors of the five Relieving Chambers varies between eight and nine. Scholars do not yet have a credible explanation for this anomaly. No one knows why the Egyptians designed the openings that way or why some of the blocks are narrower than others. It could be that the builders chose slabs of different widths for purely practical reasons, and it was merely a matter of the quality of the rock found in certain sections of the quarry, which determined the size of the piece stonecutters felt they could extract.

One other notable difference among the various chambers is the type of stone the builders will use later on. In addition to the edging blocks laid down for cavities four and five, the slabs above the fifth Relieving Chamber — its gabled roof — are composed of limestone.

Peak

Luckily, once all of the granite for the five chambers was in position, the amount of energy the Egyptians would have to expend to transport any single piece of stone into the Great Pyramid would never reach that level of intensity again. How were they able to create the unexpected peak located above the fifth Relieving Chamber? One after another, workers had built up the courses until they reached the level where a series of limestone edging blocks now sat along the rim of the fifth and final layer of granite.

In preparation for constructing the peak, workers had established a small well or pocket along the north and south sides of the structure by leaving out some of the filler stones next to the walls. (This was essentially the same method the team had employed previously to erect a roof for the Queen's Chamber.) The Egyptians may have also used bracing in the form of a wooden platform constructed inside the empty space between the north and south walls. Workers would have been able to keep moving their work deck further west as each ceiling block was installed, to assist them in controlling the next one.

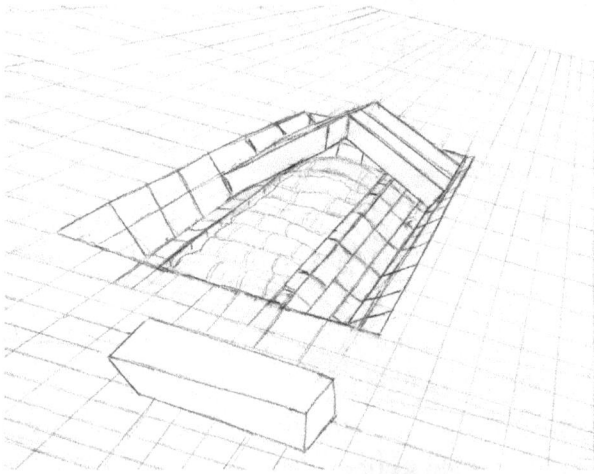

RELIEVING CHAMBERS · GABLED ROOF

The layout during construction of the gabled roof above the Relieving Chambers.

A total of 11 blocks on each side comprise the gabled roof above the uppermost Relieving Chamber, but the individual pieces are not all the same size. Measured roughly, the blocks are about three feet across east to west, yet a few of the matched-up pairs are a little wider than the others. The method the construction team used to haul in the blocks for the peak followed the same general pattern they used to transfer the granite blocks for the levels installed below the roof.

Riding up the Grand Gallery on a sled and carried up the northern center channel, one of the large limestone slabs for the roof — estimated to be at least 15 feet long end to end — was offloaded on the west side of the Relieving Chambers. Balancing the bulky piece on the blocks along the north or south side of the unfinished chamber, workers slid it east along the top of the row of short, polished edging stones. When the ceiling block reached its destination, the team tipped it up and held it in place temporarily by setting the slab in the pocket behind the wall.

It is also conceivable that they lodged wooden beams underneath the heavy gable stone to brace it up. After the block on the first side was ready, crews fetched the corresponding slab, slid it east along the edge of the opposite wall, then inserted the limestone into the pocket and paired it with its mate.

Pyramid researchers have documented several strange, circular holes that appear to be manmade, scooped out of the floor of the fifth Relieving Chamber. They have also observed sets of parallel grooves carved into the undulations in the granite floor blocks. It is possible that the grooves were there so workers could wrap ropes around the floor stones and strap them to the sled. A related hypothesis suggests that the circular holes in the floor may have held the short timbers used to support the ceiling blocks before the roof slabs on the two sides were pushed together.

Once the blocks were situated inside the small well next to the walls and balanced tip to tip for the peak, crews placed standard filler around the bottom of the blocks to weigh down the lower end and hold them in place. Finally, in a nod to the aesthetics of the gabled room, they took wedges composed of limestone and tucked them into the empty space between the top of the edging stones and the ceiling blocks, leaning in overhead to cover that small gap and create a finished wall.

• Corners •

The great care with which the ancient Egyptians constructed the Great Pyramid leads us to believe that they also took extra effort in dealing with the corners of the building. Pyramid researchers seem to agree that the polished Tura limestone in the cladding did not display ugly seams along the edges where the outside walls meet. Rather, the builders quarried and installed the blocks at the corners on each level according to a specific pattern that would both retain the unmarred beauty of the façade and contribute to the stability of the monument as a whole.

The Griffith theory maintains that the corner blocks in every row of Tura limestone covering the exterior alternated from course to course. Examining the east wall and using a single course as an example, the outward-facing surface on every casing stone was slanted at an angle of 52 degrees to match the slope of the outer wall. The other five sides of the blocks were flat, which allowed them to sit level and butt up perfectly against each other in a straight line. The exception to this general rule applied to the pieces used at the corners on either end. Since the cladding spread all the way to the edges of the pyramid, the blocks bookending every row were always slanted on a second side too. For example, in this instance the block found at the building's southeast corner — part of the east wall — was angled on the long side that faced east. But workers had also shaved the narrow end of the block, forming the corner at a 52-degree angle because it faced south and had become part of the south wall.

Turning the southeast corner and heading west, the slanted casing stones on that same course continued along the building's south side. But when the cladding reached the southwest corner, the short front end of the last block in line, which faced west, was angled because that side of the stone now belonged to the west wall. Circling the remainder of the pyramid, the pattern repeated itself at the northwest and northeast corners.

Conversely, the setup of the casing stones on the next level up reversed the pattern. Still viewing the issue from the perspective of the east wall, this time the arrangement moved counterclockwise. On the course found immediately above the one in the previous example, the block visible at the southeast corner was actually the last block in the row of casing stones from the south wall. As a result, the end that faced east was trimmed at a 52-degee angle because it was now part of the cladding for the east wall. The same thing happened at the northeast corner where the final casing stone in the row on the east side of the building ended up becoming part of the north wall — and so on and so on, around the other two corners of the pyramid. The course that followed next returned to the original configuration. Then the setup reversed again on the subsequent level. The alternating pattern in the cladding continued for more than 200 courses.

Engineers had good reasons for not stacking up the corner blocks on the façade as if they were erecting a tower. It seems that they wanted to ensure that the joints where two sides of the Great Pyramid met were reinforced and stable. Setting one stone atop another in a perpendicular fashion helped them achieve that goal. By interchanging the blocks so the stone inserted at the corner overlapped the one beneath it, which lay in the opposite direction, not only forestalled the problem of having four weak seams running up the outside edges of the building but also helped tie the layers together.

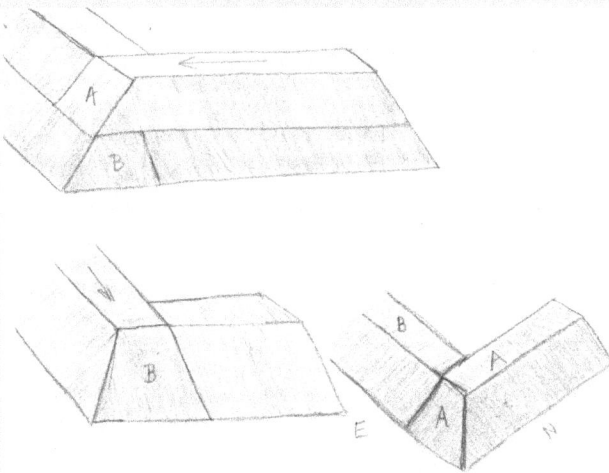

CORNERS OF THE PYRAMID

The ancient Egyptians designed a unique configuration for reinforcing the casing stones at the corners of the Great Pyramid.

CHAPTER 14

TOWERING CORRIDOR

To INITIATE THE NEXT phase of pyramid construction, the Egyptians had formulated a process that would unfold in stages. Judging from what we see now — more than 12,000 years after the fact per the Edgar Cayce timeline — every single aspect of the Great Pyramid reflects a staggering amount of exactitude and planning. Engineers must have charted the systems involved in the buildout down to the minutest detail, bringing all of the moving parts together in a meticulously timed operation that ensured essential crews, tools, machinery, and supplies arrived on site the moment they were needed. For example, overseers would have known well in advance the size of the blocks designated for the various layers and no doubt were quarrying materials for upcoming courses many years before their actual construction.

While decades of work still lay ahead, an end was in sight, and the team may have even been able to imagine the day when they would place a capstone atop their monumental structure. For now, the King's Chamber was finished and the very largest blocks found inside the Great Pyramid were stacked up in tiers above that room, forming the sequence of mystifying cavities commonly known as the Relieving Chambers. No more stones that size would ever enter the building again, which meant the Egyptians could finally finish walling off the Grand Gallery.

It is important to recognize that a level surface formed by layers and layers of courses amassed over many decades now covered a majority of the building site — primarily to the east, south and west. The flat expanse rose as high as the peak of the Relieving Chambers around the 85th course and enveloped the sharp edge of its pointed roofline until the gabled roof had wholly disappeared from view. A wide, horizontal plane on a level somewhere between courses 85 and 90 overlay more than three-quarters of the developing pyramid. It had encased the entire King's Chamber, terminating at the north end in a fairly narrow band of course blocks piled high beside the chamber's north wall. The compact section on the north side would have been wide enough for the workers standing on it to manipulate a sled. But it was still narrow enough not to impinge substantially on the amount of unobstructed space available on Course 49 for unloading and transferring the materials that entered the building.

While a majority of the emergent structure was now covered over by multiple courses, one area the layers of stone had not encompassed was the space that the Grand Gallery occupied. In truth, the gallery had always stood apart from other sections of the building, surrounded by its own unique configuration. To provide some general bearings: The pie-shaped cutout on Course 25, which accommodated the construction entrance and converged at the north end of the gallery near the entrance to the First Ascending Passage, was still wide open and full of activity. A heap of courses bordered both sides of the triangular notch, forming a set of vertical walls that towered over the giant gap and busy work area many stories below.

A Gallery Grows

For generations, the walls flanking the Grand Gallery had reached no higher than the third corbel, making them approximately 16 feet tall. (The third corbel is the one with the shallow, 6-inch-deep groove, which served as the track for the revolving disks on the arms at the back of the lift, to help steady its movement.) The colossal stones used in places such as the Relieving Chambers had prevented the builders from extending the sides of the long corridor all the way up to the Great Step any earlier, or from adding panels to create four additional corbels atop the partially built walls. The upper panels would ultimately raise the sides to their present height of 28 feet. Enclosing the southern portion of the gallery prematurely or building the walls any higher would have impeded the construction process.

The three-corbels-high gallery walls had slowly crept southward — up the slope — as the number of courses kept increasing. While crews continued to construct new levels, including filling out the step-pyramid on the north side of the Queen's Chamber, the northernmost portions of the gallery walls took shape. As the buildout proceeded, it became possible — with the development of one or two additional courses — to insert the L-shaped base blocks on both sides of the corridor, the squared-off pieces on top of them, and perhaps the lowest corbels east and west. By the time the next few courses were installed, workers were able to slide corbel blocks for rows number two and three into place. Slowly the side walls moved up the corridor without ever overtaking the workspace set aside for handling the raw materials too soon.

One relevant but little-known fact about this period of time before the sides of the gallery were fully built is that the upper edge of the walls bordering the corridor met the back end of the lift when it was parked at the top of the ramp. As a result, it would have been possible in theory for someone to walk directly from the main workspace on Course 49 onto the upper edge of the third corbel. Understanding the layout from the perspective of that era, the longest portion of the gallery actually sat below the 49th course, which was why Course 49 was still accessible and had enough space to accommodate workers, blocks, and sleds. Not only would finishing the sides at the beginning have cut off access to the available space on that course, but higher walls would have constricted the ramp, making it too narrow to handle some of the mega-blocks. The flat, open area at the upper (south) end of the gallery's ramp had long been reserved for offloading and conveying the raw materials once the lift had stopped.

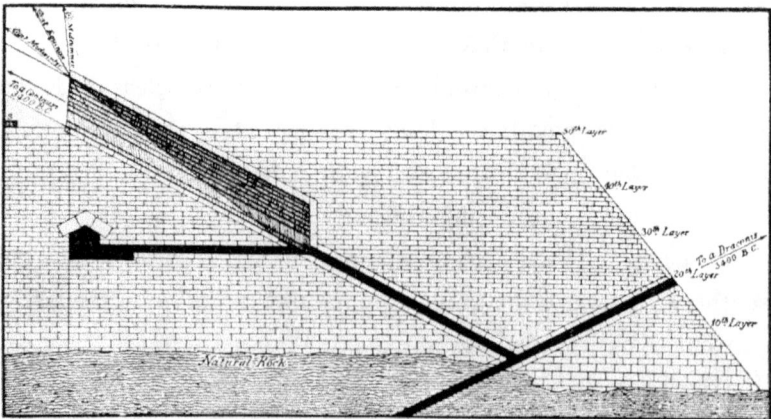

GRAND GALLERY BELOW COURSE 49

Slightly more than 50% of the Grand Gallery lies below the 49th course.

Augmenting the vertical walls by erecting another four corbels will add tremendous height to the Grand Gallery and eventually make it almost three stories tall. Yet even after workers insert the first few sections of the upper panels and the roof, beginning at the gallery's north end, most of this passageway would still sit lower than what was then the principal workspace. Now the question was: How could the Egyptians elevate the remaining limestone blocks to construct corbels number four through seven along the entire passageway — while the walls they planned to build on kept growing taller?

The Build-Up

It is always risky to speculate about specific moves the Egyptians may have made in assembling the Great Pyramid, especially considering the operation from the perspective of the 21st century, many millennia after the fact. Trying to map out the procedures the builders followed to construct the multistory walls of the Grand Gallery is particularly fraught because the stones ride at a 26-degree angle. The wall blocks framing the gallery are some of the few ever discovered inside the Great Pyramid that are set on a slant. No doubt the task was extremely challenging. Yet this ancient people not only found a way to enclose the steep corridor; they succeeded brilliantly.

By now, crews had removed the extensive collection of ropes and pulleys from the Antechamber because that equipment was no longer necessary. The extra lines were gone and only the pulley-stand mounted on top of the Great Step remained. Strange as it may seem, enclosing the Grand Gallery was the first concrete step the Egyptians took toward sealing off large portions of the pyramid even as they were laying the groundwork to complete the final half of their monument.

Because the back ends of the wall blocks lining the Grand Gallery are hidden from view, scholars have yet to determine the exact dimensions of every piece of the smooth, high-grade limestone lining the passageway. A reasonable guess is that the blocks comprising the corbels are about three feet high, at least four feet wide east to west, and approximately eight feet long measured end to end (south to north). As mentioned earlier, many pyramid researchers believe that the sizes of the blocks vary by three inches front to back, which is one way to account for the series of slight overhangs evident inside the corridor. But the Griffith theory maintains that the blocks are exactly the same size and each row was pushed forward by three inches over the one beneath it to produce the projections in the walls. This assumption is based in part on the concept of industrial efficiency: It is far easier to quarry and cut multiple blocks of the same size than to adjust the dimensions of the individual pieces intended for different rows.

The fact that the stones in the walls are set at a 26-degree angle presented a discrete set of issues for the builders. By design, the bottom row in each section of the wall incorporated blocks in the shape of a capital L whose upper edge was cut square to the block. Then a second, rectangular piece of limestone about three feet tall was positioned on top of the base block, followed by the initial three corbels positioned above the two lower stones. Since the entire stack was sitting on a ramp with a 26-degree incline, what prevented the blocks from sliding downhill and tumbling off the slope onto the floor when gravity compelled them to keep moving? The setup included a barricade at the lower (north) end of the corridor to obstruct the wall blocks and hold them in place: the filler stones stacked alongside the east and west walls of the First Ascending Passage.

In working their way up toward the future roofline, the builders also had to contend with two huge piles of course blocks several feet behind the Grand Gallery, forming sheer walls on both sides. The bottom of the gallery was on Course 25 or the same level as the Queen's Chamber. And the courses that sat a short distance away from the gallery walls were the byproduct of workers partially filling in the stepped levels on the original utility pyramid in the northeast quadrant.

The space that the Grand Gallery occupied was similar to the area the builders had set aside for the construction entrance because, for all intents and purposes, it had cut that utility pyramid in two. Years earlier, crews filling in the tiers on the internal pyramid left a few feet of empty space between the stepped levels and the gallery's walls. At this point, the stacks of course blocks, which defined the two aisles beside the outer walls of the corridor, reached as high as the 49th course.

The lower portion of the Grand Gallery had bisected the original utility pyramid on the north side between the 25th and 49th courses at an angle. The mass of blocks built up on either side could have touched the gallery walls. But out of necessity, engineers had decided not to allow the gallery and the layers of courses filling in the step-pyramid to meet. Rather, they purposely maintained a pathway for their work crews. Similar to a catwalk just a few feet wide but broad enough for a worker to stand on and turn, the narrow bit of open space behind the gallery walls acted as a work platform. From there, the team would be able to install the remaining corbels and someday even enclose the long passageway with a roof.

While sufficient space existed east of the Grand Gallery between the already completed courses on that side and its outer wall to position several laborers to handle the new stones, the catwalk area was so tight that it left little room to store anything else. Therefore, as work proceeds, the blocks used to finish the gallery's east wall will pass over a series of temporary bridges. Fabricated by laying down long blocks of stone or constructed from wooden planks sturdy enough to hold the substantial weights, the connectors were placed intermittently across the top of the roofless corridor from the west side. Work gangs assigned to that side of the gallery would transfer the blocks designated for the east wall via these portable bridges.

Wall Slide

Assembling the walls of the Grand Gallery below Course 49 adhered to a regular routine. First, after the dressed limestone blocks for the corbels came up on the lift, workers would retrieve the correct piece and place it in the work/storage area at the south end of the gallery on Course 49. Then one after another, alternating east and west, the crews delegated to manage the blocks made use of the 26-degree angle to slide the piece down the upper edge of the existing wall and into the appropriate position. As soon as a block was situated properly, a different team packed the narrow space behind the latest corbel — between it and the wall of course blocks several feet away — with filler.

Imagine a series of small peaks formed by the original rows of wall blocks that had been in place for decades: corbels number one, two and three. The method the Egyptians followed was merely a matter of taking the initial block for the latest row and pushing or pulling it onto the first tip formed by the edges of the blocks sticking up at the south end of the unfinished corridor.

Then, using the next two peaks to help stabilize the piece of limestone and keep it from wobbling back and forth like a seesaw, workers balanced the new corbel for a moment on all three peaks. Once it inched forward again and started to move past the tipping point on the final peak, the weight shifted and the block headed downhill.

GALLERY WALL BLOCKS ON PEAKS

When parked at the top of the gallery ramp, the back end of the lift met the upper edges of the wall blocks sitting below Course 49. Theoretically, someone would have been able to step onto the walls from the lift's deck. By employing the peaks from the corbels already in place, the crew was able to balance the latest block on the tips jutting up from below in preparation for sliding it down the sloped gallery wall.

With the angle of the wall blocks a mere 26 degrees, it was unlikely that the heavy piece of limestone for the new corbel would take off and run away on its own. Nevertheless, the crew looped a strong rope around the front (north) end to help manage the placement process by hand from above. They may have also wrapped the lines around the pulley-stand atop the Great Step as a precautionary measure, using that device to help break the momentum of the deadweight. The rope let them control the block as it unhurriedly made its way along the upper edge of the third corbel toward the bottom of the ramp.

Erecting the fourth corbel was arguably the easiest part of the upper gallery walls for workers to complete. Corbel number four was also very likely to be an exception to the rule that all of the slabs for the east wall arrived from the west side on temporary bridges. Since the top of the corbel block in row three was readily accessible from Course 49, this section of the walls was probably constructed from materials previously stored on that level. The open space on the 49th course would have provided unencumbered access to enough blocks to insert the fourth corbel on both sides of the gallery. Workers just took the blocks for that row from the short-term storage area and moved them closer to the walls.

Once the bulky corbel block slid down the edge of the wall and reached the barricade at the far end, crews maneuvered it into position consistent with previous corbels: offset three inches from the front edge of the block below it and leaning in approximately five degrees toward the center of the gallery. Workers had also slipped a narrow wooden wedge between the north end of the latest corbel and the stopper blocks to retain some space for removing the work-rope. Because the two stones were held apart before they made contact, crew members were able to pull back the line, which permitted the full weight of the latest corbel block to push downward. Then, by pounding on the wedge with mallets, they worked the wood out from between the stones. Significantly, the very first or northernmost block in every row had a slightly different shape from the slabs lined up behind it. The front edge of the lead block in the series — the edge closest to the bottom of the ramp — was not squared off but shaved at an angle to make it sit flat against the stopper blocks at the lower end.

Work gangs did not pack the narrow lane between the gallery's outer wall and the lofty stack of course blocks a short distance behind it by converting the space into a flat, horizontal surface. Instead, they constructed a sequence of steps running up to the tip or south end of the corbel that the crew had just set into place. Sets of stairs had existed for some time on both sides of the gallery up to the height of the third corbel. By elevating the workers, these staircases made it possible for them to install corbel number four.

All of the stair-steps were temporary, functioning only as long as it took the crew to finish work on a specific row. By erecting steps behind each new block added to the wall, the builders were able to slowly but surely gain the necessary height to keep adding to the sides of the corridor. And later on, after the newest portion of the stairs had served its purpose by providing access to the section under construction, a separate team converted it into the base for more steps. The old staircase faded away as the succeeding one, which would raise the crew even higher, took form.

As soon as workers had deposited the initial (northernmost) corbel block in each row and filled in the space behind it, they would slide the next one down the incline. When the second block in the current row was in position, a small group trailing behind the team handling the first piece of stone packed the space next to the gallery wall with filler blocks. Their charge was to construct fresh steps that reached as high as the upper (south) edge of the latest corbel inserted into the wall. Block by block and corbel by corbel, crews on both sides of the giant passageway steadily built up its sides — and in the process of overlaying the stepped walkway they had used to finish the previous portion of the wall, they simultaneously developed a higher work platform from which to erect another row.

The process was exactly the same for the crews assigned to the east wall whose blocks were transferred over from the west side on portable bridges composed of wood or stone. They, too, ended up elevating their own work platforms in conjunction with the evolving walls. As the sides of the gallery grew taller, so did the catwalk. By essentially repeating the same actions over and over again, the Egyptians would erect the balance of the Grand Gallery's corbels below the 49th course and in the process, raise the side walls almost three stories high.

A Ceiling and a Roof

The overwhelming size and majesty of the Grand Gallery mask many of its core elements, which may be deceptive to the naked eye. It is easy to overlook the fact that the size from east to west at the widest point along the passageway is less than seven feet (6' 10") — not a tremendous expanse, considering the magnitude of the Great Pyramid of Giza. Moreover, the upper portion of the walls comprise a series of seven corbels stacked on top of one another, with each corbel set three inches closer to the center of the corridor than the one below it. A simple calculation multiplying three inches of reduction by seven corbels means that the walls narrow down by a whopping 21 inches on each side as they climb toward the roof. Due to the reduction in width associated with the side walls, a total of 42 inches, the Egyptians only had to cover a relatively narrow gap (3' 5") to construct its ceiling.

It is also worth noting that at this stage of the game, crews were still working on just that portion of the Grand Gallery below Course 49, which covers a little more than 50% of the total length of the passageway. The part of the walls found above that level were not under construction yet. By the time wall-building below the 49th course reached the height of the seventh corbel, circumstances would compel engineers to make minor adjustments to their operations to account for the fact that the corbel blocks in the uppermost row also had to support a roof.

If someone were to stand inside the Grand Gallery today and gaze upward, they would notice that the ceiling is not entirely smooth. The surface resembles a shallow set of stairs whose treads form tiny peaks roughly five inches tall, pointing northward. Each of these peaks signifies a niche cradling one of the roof slabs. Despite the fact that the top row would bear a ceiling, construction of the seventh corbel followed the same basic pattern as before. One after the other, alternating west and east, the wall blocks traveled down the incline along the upper edge of the sixth corbelled row to the spots where they belonged.

The major difference in this situation was that the blocks designated for the uppermost row of corbels were not flat on top but had a jagged edge. While stonecutters had quarried previous corbels as perfect rectangles, with the level surface on top serving as the base for the block positioned above it, the upper edges on the pieces intended for the highest row in the wall were precut in a sawtooth pattern and resembled the stringer for a staircase. Spread uniformly across the surface of the stones when linked together, the cuts had enough space between them to form the necessary slots for supporting the roof slabs. Otherwise, the length north to south echoed the size of prior corbels at approximately eight feet long, end to end. The underside of each piece was left flat and smooth, which allowed the builders to slide the blocks for row seven along the top of the existing walls and set them into place.

Pyramid scholars can only estimate the exact dimensions of the thick pieces of high-quality limestone lying across the gap at the top of the Grand Gallery since it is impossible to gauge how long the ceiling blocks are east to west. Accounting for a decent amount of overhang, a fair assumption is that the roof slabs are at least eight feet across. In short order, workers set these heavy blocks across the open channel and began putting a lid on the corridor — a cavity now more than 28 feet deep.

According to what is observable from inside the 157-foot-long gallery by counting up the obvious peaks in the ceiling, its roof includes at least 40 individual roof slabs. Based on the length of the corridor and assuming each block comprising the seventh corbel to be approximately eight feet long, 20 corbel/stringer blocks must line the sides of the passageway. This calculation further implies that every wall block supports two slots, resulting in enough saw teeth for a total of 40 pieces of polished limestone covering the ceiling. Since no one knows the precise measurements north to south of the blocks seated above the seventh corbel, the projected numbers and the conclusions drawn are only hypothetical. But what we do know is that the ancient Egyptians ended up incorporating at least that many slabs, if not more, into the Grand Gallery's roof.

Installing a roof over the lower end of the passageway involved taking the initial blocks in the row for corbel number seven and sliding them into position down either side. As soon as that job was done, a crew collected one of the roof slabs. After hoisting the piece up from the floor, they deposited the ceiling block atop the sixth corbel by laying it across the chasm from west to east, resting the limestone on the upper edges of the two walls. Using the rim as a slide, workers employed ropes to lower the slab down the incline until it reached the first sawtooth block in the seventh row, where a separate crew awaited the stone.

Once the initial roof slab approached the back of the jagged-edged block at the far end of the gallery and stopped, workers pulled it onto the small peaks by employing wooden rails or smaller blocks cut on the diagonal as a temporary ramp. Balancing the slab for a moment on the pointy saw teeth on both sides of the corridor, the crew cautiously kept sliding it forward before easing the ceiling block into the lowest (northernmost) slot. Work gangs repeated the process until the two slots linked to the initial corbel in the seventh row held a roof slab. Then a second team took over to pack the open areas behind those sections of the walls, east and west, with filler stones. But this time, instead of erecting more steps on the catwalk, crews stacked the blocks in vertical piles, fashioning a horizontal plane as high as the new roofline.

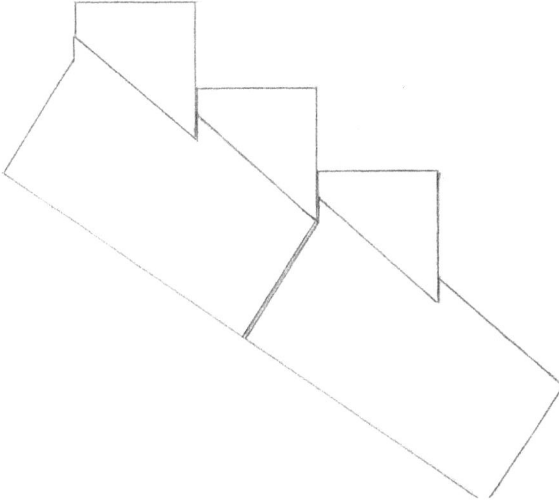

GALLERY CEILING SLABS

The top of each corbel block in the seventh row contains a sawtooth edge to support the limestone slabs for the ceiling inside the Grand Gallery. One of the two slots associated with each corbel block was formed by the angle cut into the block sitting next to it on the north side.

Work advanced as crew members took the next pair of sawtooth blocks off the lift and moved them into the prime workspace. After transferring the stone for the east wall across the movable bridge, they slid the two in turn down the sides of the gallery. When the second corbel block for the upper row was in position on each wall, the workers laid another roof slab across the gap from one side of the sixth corbel to the other.

The sets of roof slabs intended for the succeeding sections were all delivered in this same manner by sliding them along the upper edges of corbel number six. One by one, a work gang would deliver the next block for the ceiling down the incline to a spot just short of where the slab might bump into the one with the peaks in row seven lying in its path. As the latest slab approached the piece in front of it, the team heaved it up on top of the sawtooth limestone using a short ramp, then slipped it into the appropriate slot. When both slots contained a slab, they proceeded to add another pair of jagged-edged corbel blocks to the side walls.

Construction of a roof over the lower portion of the Grand Gallery between Courses 25 and 49 steadily progressed with the introduction of every wall block and ceiling slab related to the seventh corbel. Equally important was what was happening outside the unfinished corridor as the different sections of the ceiling came together. With a good portion of the gallery going under the roof and formally sealed off from above, and the need for the catwalk diminishing with every section that workers completed, the builders started the process of filling in any outstanding nooks and crannies below the 49th course in the area immediately surrounding the gallery. The idea was to eliminate all of the empty spaces that engineers might have introduced to augment construction and put the final touches on the courses closest to the gallery walls.

An Even Plane

As the inaugural sets of roof slabs made their way down the sloped walls and were supported in their slots, workers on both sides of the corridor kept packing the area behind the walls with filler stones. That activity would eventually result in a level surface even with the roofline and stretching as far as the tunnel above the lift at the north end of the Grand Gallery. Section by section, the process of adding a ceiling atop row seven progressed, while the flat plane at the top expanded north and south. For example, when the time came to fill in behind the second corbel block in the upper row, crews did not stop at its northern edge but kept moving in the same direction with more filler. Why? The Grand Gallery ascends through the Great Pyramid at an angle. As a result, the workers who had just packed filler behind block number two created a drop-off because it sat higher than the filler stones arranged in back of the first and lowest corbel block in the row.

Likewise, when the next section was ready to go, the level of the limestone filler piled up behind the third wall block would be taller than the height of the elongated area associated with blocks one and two. Stacking filler stones on top of the two previous piles of filler not only lengthened the flat surface behind the walls, which now ran from the southernmost edge of block number three to the north end of the passageway, but also bridged the gap between the gallery's outer walls and the sheer wall of courses standing a few feet away.

To maintain a flat surface across the narrow lane, which up to now had served as a walkway and work platform, crews will keep adding filler stones behind the seventh row as they move along, dropping chunks of standard limestone on top of the pieces already in place. The cycle was ongoing: Set a corbel block in the wall, insert the ceiling slabs, then pack the space behind the row as high as the roofline and as far north as possible. By the time the Egyptians were done, filler blocks on both sides of the long passageway encompassed the entire length of the lower portion of the Grand Gallery, including its roof, creating an uninterrupted plane that now met the level of Course 49.

CHAPTER 15

STEPS INTO COURSES

WHILE THE EGYPTIANS WERE hard at work constructing the seventh corbelled row and filling in behind the side walls, a strategy was already in motion to bring the next chapter in the saga of the Grand Gallery to a conclusion. The builders had installed walls and a roof for the gallery up to the 49th course but stopped there — approximately 40 feet short of the Antechamber — without fully enclosing the corridor end to end. Furthermore, walling in the final portion of the long passageway presented a special set of challenges.

The operation undoubtedly had to change direction once the walls of the Grand Gallery had breached Course 49 and emerged from below. The blocks for future sections of the walls clearly would continue to ride at an angle, but since they were no longer able to travel downhill; i.e., slide down from a spot overhead on the 49th course, determining an effective way to overcome gravity played a much larger role in the construction process. Equally daunting was that in time, as the builders planted the base blocks for the walls along both sides to support the upper corbels, those additions would close off access to the primary work area, which had been available since the great lift first came on the scene.

Soon workers would no longer have the luxury of moving directly from the gallery ramp onto the wide-open space on Course 49 to unload sleds or rearrange the building materials because the newest portion of the gallery's west wall would be standing in the way, barring passage. That being the case, how could the Egyptians possibly retrieve a sufficient number of stones to not only complete the Grand Gallery but also build the remainder of their Great Pyramid?

The workspace on Course 49 where the supplies were delivered was a flat area, extending approximately 40 feet west (a little longer than the King's

Chamber) and roughly 40 feet north. The boundary line at the north end was where a band of deep stair-steps began, formed by the original layers of limestone deposited for the Queen's Chamber pyramid on the north side. The set of stairs essentially covered the space between the Grand Gallery and the center channel connected to the upper utility pyramid on that same side. Since crews had not yet packed the space in between those two "bookends" with filler stones, the stepped levels still ascended to the apex of the original northern utility pyramid at approximately Course 70.

It is worth noting again that the Egyptians had not built the northern utility pyramid associated with the King's Chamber directly on top of the one linked to the Queen's Chamber. Instead, they placed the upper one further west. The very first internal pyramid ever built, located in the southeast quadrant, had to be operational as early as possible to erect critical spaces such as the Antechamber. But even as that utility pyramid fulfilled its original purpose, its steps were slowly subsumed under layers of course blocks. Over time, workers turned the internal pyramid at the south end into the base for the upper utility pyramid at the same side.

Conversely, to successfully implement the larger building strategy, engineers had to maintain functional pulleys at the other end of the site around the 70th course — the eventual height of the Queen's Chamber pyramid on the north side. For many reasons, the team could not afford to completely bury the structure in the northeast quadrant until almost two-thirds of their massive project was done. Plans required the pulleys mounted on the top step of the original northern utility pyramid to assist in executing thousands of pulls. The machines had also added a crucial element to the Egyptians' ability to handle the mammoth granite blocks used in the Relieving Chambers. Viewing the layout of the construction site from the north, the two internal pyramids — upper and lower — on that side would have resembled a couple of peaks in a small mountain range.

By this stage, the vast plane of filler that had entombed the Relieving Chambers and its gabled roof somewhere between Courses 85 and 90 spanned approximately three-quarters of the building site, including almost the entire area west of the wide center channel from the upper utility pyramid on the north side. In addition, most of the stair-steps west of the center shaft were completely gone since work crews had already covered them up with filler blocks. One exception was a number of steps immediately west of the channel near its base, which remained open. Much later, as construction progressed, workers would connect this narrow strip of leftover steps to the tiers from the Queen's Chamber pyramid on the other side of the center channel by integrating them into the same courses, but that process would not happen for a while. One reason for the delay was the vital role the set of stairs north of the main work area still had to play.

It was readily apparent to the builders that as soon as the Grand Gallery rose above Course 49, fencing in the final piece of the corridor would cut off access to critical avenues for resupplying their operations. The solution to this dilemma was to find a way to stockpile the construction materials beforehand in those sections of the larger pyramid that remained accessible. As a result, the relatively few stepped levels that endured west of the upper utility pyramid's center channel and the wide set of stairs adjacent to the narrow pile of courses behind the Grand Gallery's west wall would serve as both interim storage areas and work platforms for the teams charged with finishing the corridor's walls and roof.

During this interval, the lift was available to transport the raw materials. With the center shaft on the northern utility pyramid still open, pullers positioned on the exterior ramp would be able to raise the high-grade limestone for the remaining corbels along with enough roof slabs, filler stones, and assorted bits and pieces to complete the job. By arranging the necessary supplies on the still-open stairs east and west of the center channel, before access to the lift was closed off, the team had the capacity to store a considerable cache of blocks and gear for use down the road. With the right provisions and planning, they would be able to bring the work on the Grand Gallery to a successful conclusion.

Shrinking Channel

One more reason for stockpiling was to prepare for impending changes to the dimensions of the upper pyramid's center channel, which in the future, would make it virtually impossible to haul in bulkier blocks. As construction advanced over many years, the once-capacious shaft would eventually become an enclosed chute, roomy enough to handle only the smallest blocks found inside the Great Pyramid.

For generations, the substantial center channel on the north side had served as the principal conduit for elevating materials and equipment to the proper courses. But sooner or later, it was scheduled to undergo alterations and start shrinking down. Because the oversized blocks of granite used above the King's Chamber had regulated how wide this passageway had to be, ever since the upper utility pyramid was first developed, the only part of the shaft confined by a straight wall was its west side. The foot of the channel swept out at an angle as it met the 49th course so the eastern edge almost seemed to disappear.

Having the shaft fan out in the area close to the lift had preserved the necessary room inside the prime unloading zone, which had to maintain a sufficient amount of passable space to be able to manipulate the very largest sleds and blocks. Moreover, throughout its long history, the center channel had remained open to the sky. But once work on the fifth and final Relieving Chamber had concluded and the design no longer required a shaft that wide to accommodate such gigantic pieces of stone, the builders planned to not only narrow down the passage but also enclose it during an upcoming construction phase.

As an end to the work on the Grand Gallery drew closer, the distance across the center channel would steadily decrease. Crews were slated to reduce the width of the passageway in the future by joining together the courses on the right- and left-hand sides of the exposed shaft. Furthermore, this process of building up the courses on either side of the channel would also eventually add a roof over the top of the hole, creating a tunnel approximately four feet tall and four feet wide (close to the size of most of the passageways found inside the Great Pyramid).

Obviously, a roof would further constrict the opening by severely limiting clearance in the shaft. Consequently, collecting and storing as many of the gallery's wall slabs and filler blocks as possible on the sets of deep stairs — long before the channel's size was drastically reduced — offered the most efficient and effective method to keep construction marching forward at maximum speed and capacity.

Stockpiles

The ancient Egyptians were both shrewd and farsighted. These builders no doubt had systematically thought through the potential ramifications of every decision they made. For example, the design of the original northern utility pyramid erected decades earlier included steps at the base where it met Course 49, which were deep enough to hold a large collection of sizable blocks for the final sections of the Grand Gallery's walls. Now all the team had to do was haul in those stones and move them over to the stepped levels set aside for storage to ensure that the raw materials indispensable to wrapping up the project were readily at hand.

Up to this point, accumulating building materials on the 49th course had not presented much of a problem. Granted, it would have been difficult, if not impossible, to fit many blocks into the compact space east of the Great Step. Little room remained on that side because, for the most part, it had already been filled in. Unlike the flat expanse on Course 49 west of the lift, which served as the chief venue for unloading sleds and blocks, the space east of the Great Step was more of a narrow alcove squeezed in between the step and a big wall of course blocks.

On the other hand, since none of walls at the southern end of the Grand Gallery existed yet, there was nothing to stop the builders from transporting whatever they needed up on the lift and onto the floor of the primary work area. After setting aside a small collection of blocks in the general vicinity of the lift for more immediate use, workers would slowly transfer the rest of the pieces over to the zones reserved for storage.

The Griffith theory adds an intriguing side note to its description of how the Egyptians laid out their storage system. While the depths of all the steps on the face of the northern utility pyramid may have been equal front to back, the heights of the different tiers varied. One reason these dissimilarities occurred was because each stepped level was built to match the size of a future course. The general idea was to use the steps as work platforms that the crew could stand on while constructing the final 40+ feet of the gallery walls. As the sides of the long corridor grew taller at the south end, teams would be able to drag a stockpiled block over toward the gallery along one of the steps and set it directly on top of the existing wall — without ever having to lift the heavy stone.

The method the Egyptians employed to transport most of the blocks targeted for storage mirrored a process they had perfected years earlier inside the Queen's Chamber. For the smaller filler stones piled up on the lift, four sleds containing individual blocks of limestone were connected back to front like railroad cars and heaved up the center channel together. Picking up each block with a shadoof after it arrived at the designated level, the crew set it on a second sled. Then work gangs quickly pulled the wooden carriers left or right before depositing the limestone on one of the open stair-steps. They would place heavier pieces such as the panels for the side walls on sleds, carried on the lift two at a time, then pulled up the channel as single loads. Besides the blocks used to erect the corbels, the slabs crafted for the unfinished portion of the Grand Gallery's ceiling also rode up the center channel in the same manner to be stored on the appropriate steps.

GRAND GALLERY STORAGE

The raw materials required to complete the Grand Gallery above the 49th course were hauled in and stored on the open stair-steps originally erected as part of the utility pyramids on the north side.

Because resupplying the work gangs with blocks was a continuing concern, engineers wanted to keep the quarried limestone easily within reach course by course as work on the gallery proceeded. The objective was to convey as many loads as possible while Course 49 was still fully accessible, and after moving them up the center shaft, temporarily stash the vital supplies on the makeshift platforms.

Another feature of the multifaceted operation was the presence of any number of shadoofs the team had carted in and set up on the different levels during this period. Employed to lift the blocks from their sleds, the devices would have been fairly easy to move around and/or dismantle and reassemble wherever they were needed throughout a prolonged and demanding construction process.

A Platform Rises

One of the earliest groups of blocks transferred onto the floor of Course 49 consisted of the stones the builders would use in the future to erect a low "shelf" or ledge. Approximately eight feet deep, the ledge would sit directly in front of the stack of courses built against the north wall of the King's Chamber and extend the length of that chamber. After that initial set of blocks, the pieces manufactured to fit around the entrance to the Antechamber and assemble the corbels above it arrived in anticipation of those upcoming projects. So did enough blocks to one day construct a separate corbelled wall directly above the new ledge.

Once the low shelf was built, crews would stow a majority of the stones needed at the south end of the gallery and primary workspace on top of it, as well as on the short strip of stepped levels, which still existed west of the center channel.

During this same timeframe, a steady flow of other types of blocks were also streaming in: rectangular pieces of the smooth, high-grade limestone for the gallery's corbels, including the sawtooth stringers for the seventh row; base blocks for the side walls; a succession of roof slabs; an assortment of smaller cubes to plug into the gaps where the sides of the gallery meet the Antechamber wall; angled chunks of limestone to serve as temporary ramps; and an untold number of filler blocks.

Transporting the raw materials for the Grand Gallery up the ramp on the lift, workers sorted and positioned the blocks on predetermined storage levels. To be sure, the staging and layout of the stockpiled blocks were central to the efficiency and success of the job. Since the collection of stones was both numerous and wide-ranging, the tiers designated for storage must have extended almost to the top of the lingering band of stairs that belonged to the Queen's Chamber utility pyramid on the north side.

Making use of the lowest levels on the workspace's northern boundary first, crews laid out the hefty limestone pieces in neat rows along the steps according to the order in which they would be needed. Engineers had also allocated a fair amount of the building materials for the higher tiers because construction would eventually necessitate having supplies positioned as high as the gallery's roofline to permit the team to fully enclose the corridor. In general, the location of the individual blocks corresponded to the sequence, timing, and height at which crews required access to the stones to bring their enormous endeavor to a close.

Under the rubric of stashing as many blocks as possible west of the gallery before it was too late and access to the lift became severely limited, the builders hauled in stones and equipment as if they were on a factory line, because when the side walls at the south end of the gallery went up, only smaller blocks would be able to enter the work area and then just one at a time. Along with everything else unloaded and stored, teams had carried in a hodge-podge of rudimentary filler stones, which they immediately deposited on some of the utility pyramid's mid- and upper-level layers — again for use later on.

Similar to the wall blocks and roof slabs, the chunks of filler limestone were considered temporary "residents" of the huge staircase, since most of them would be moving downhill to fill in the space left behind by the missing blocks once an individual storage step was emptied. When that moment arrived, workers would transfer filler blocks to the lower stations by sliding them down from one step to the other along the backs of a couple of overturned stringers made out of wood or stone.

In a stroke of pure genius, the process of packing the now-unoccupied stairs with filler meant that the crews would also be raising and expanding their own work platform as they proceeded.

Work Platforms

The southern end of the Grand Gallery presented the Egyptians with two essential problems: 1) elevating their teams as the walls grew higher, and 2) preventing workers from having to physically pick up the weighty wall panels to set them in place. The solution was to create work platforms that would keep evolving as the gallery continued to develop. Every time the blocks stowed on one of the lower steps were carried away, a group of laborers followed behind to pack the unoccupied space with filler stones. Consequently, the flat surface where the crew had previously been standing, which began as a single step at the bottom of the staircase, was now chock-full of limestone filler and as a result, much taller.

Simultaneously, the work platform also kept getting longer north to south as each tier overlaid with filler reached the front edge of the step immediately above it, joining the levels together to create an even plane now two steps deep. Step number one disappearing into step number two meant a sheer wall was rising at the north end of the open space on the 49th course, and the height of this wall along the border of the main work area would continue to increase as the blocks on each storage step were cleared out and replaced with other stones. This was the method engineers had formulated to both store essential building materials at the correct levels for expediency and ensure that once the blocks on any given step were gone and the vacated area packed full, workers had a platform tall enough to access subsequent sections of the walls.

After most of the raw materials were stored in the correct zones, the new platform would also slowly start creeping southward as a separate team laid down rows of limestone blocks in front of the growing wall along the work area's northern edge. The series of blocks stacked up on Course 49 would lengthen what had been the lowest step from the original utility pyramid and elongate every level thereafter. As crews drew down their stockpiles and packed the empty tiers with filler, they would attend to the south end by depositing blocks of standard limestone on top of the ones already in place on the floor, eventually covering a good portion of the primary workspace.

If the team had not started building up the flat surface on Course 49 with blocks to deliberately extend the original set of stairs further south, the emerging platform would have stayed well north of where they ultimately needed it to be to conclude work at that end of the Grand Gallery. Bit by bit, as labor on the unfinished gallery advances, the sheer wall at the bottom of the storage steps slowly closed up the distance between the stairs and the King's Chamber. By the time the job was done many years later, the open square footage on the 49th course would have contracted to a meager 12 feet across north to south.

The Griffith theory notes one more striking feature under this scenario. The stair-steps the builders had developed when they were erecting the Queen's Chamber utility pyramid on the north side must have been sufficiently deep to store the blocks for the gallery's walls longways, front to back. Having the capacity to stow them with the longest side running north-south permitted many more pieces to fit on each tier than if the stones deposited on the row were sitting horizontally down the length of the step. Arranging the limestone in this manner also presented one more substantial advantage: Workers would not have to pivot the bulky blocks to line them up with the gallery walls.

Steps in Between

Warehousing the blocks for the final portion of the Grand Gallery was complete and the formerly empty steps west of it were loaded with a mixture of limestone pieces large and small that had traveled up the center channel. Despite the headway the Egyptians had made, it is important to point out that the process of packing the stairs with building materials had not yet converted that channel into a tunnel. One day, this passageway was bound to get a roof or the builders would not have a foundation on which to construct the courses above it. But enclosing the shaft was slated to occur much later — as work on the gallery was officially concluding.

Equally significant was that work gangs methodically covering the area between the center channel and the gallery — level by level — would inevitably result in all evidence of the lower half of the northern utility pyramid disappearing from sight as its broad steps were progressively swallowed up by and assimilated into the different courses. The apex of the interior pyramid where the pulleys were mounted would remain accessible for a lot longer than that, however. The pinnacle would only begin to fade from view after the Egyptians' buildout finally reached Course 98. For the moment, the mutating staircase merely reflected the promise of things to come. It held what the Egyptians needed to achieve the next milestone in pyramid construction: assembling the remainder of the Grand Gallery's dramatic side walls.

[CHAPTER 16]

A GALLERY REALIZED

BESIDES THE COUNTLESS OTHER elements involved in the massive building operation, erecting the balance of the Grand Gallery demanded equipment specifically designed to meet a new and exacting set of circumstances. Before the southernmost segments of its walls went up, the Egyptians had crafted a special shadoof, which they planned to use far into the future, and positioned it in the available space on Course 49, west of the lift. Not only would the device aid them in the short term by lifting up some of the blocks designated for the gallery's walls and roof, it ultimately would provide the means by which the rest of the stones entering the site would make their way upward toward the summit of the Great Pyramid. To be sure, every aspect of the operation from this point forward was laying the groundwork for that final step.

Pulling Power

The next item on the agenda was to start building the Antechamber's front wall, because the sides of the gallery depended on the existence of a solid structure at the south end of the corridor. But enclosing the Antechamber had repercussions in terms of the team's ability to raise additional blocks. By now, the ropes coming though the chamber's back wall were long gone and its rollers and portcullis stones out of commission. On a more positive note, since the heavy panels destined for the gallery's walls and roof along with hundreds of other stones were already stockpiled, the builders could adjust their equipment to reflect the revised set of circumstances, which no longer included elevating 70-ton granite blocks.

For the most part, the blocks the builders would use in assembling the upper half of the Great Pyramid would be substantially smaller than the stones incorporated into many of the lower courses. But bear in mind that the overall pulling capacity on site was smaller, too. During the previous era, the power required to convey the lift hauling blocks up the Grand Gallery had depended primarily upon hundreds of pullers stationed outdoors and the heft of the counterweight in the Descending Passage.

Now, without having access to pulleys on top of the northern utility pyramids, which were not in alignment with the gallery, and without the assistance of any pulleys in the Antechamber or a counterweight moving up and down the center channel on the south side, the force available to the team had lessened considerably. Such changes meant that a successful effort to move the project forward by continuing to carry supplies up to the 49th course was contingent on either decreasing the amount of weight to be lifted, adding more muscle power — or both.

The diminished capacity to efficiently raise heavy piles of stone blocks must have prompted engineers to reduce the overall size of the lift in the gallery corridor. Because it no longer had to sustain the burden of gigantic pieces of limestone and granite, such as the giant blocks used in the Relieving Chambers, they could decrease the weight of the transport vehicle itself by dismantling the old lift and manufacturing a new, lighter version as wide from east to west as the original one. A lighter lift traveling up and down the ramp would lessen both the mass and overall weight of the loads work crews had to elevate.

Until the Grand Gallery was finished and the next phase of construction began, it would be the substantial granite counterweight sitting underground that would allow the builders to raise equipment and raw materials to the top of the gallery ramp. Since the moment when the pyramid builders first deployed their giant lift, ropes tied to the counterweight had traveled up the Descending Passage and around a pulley at the mouth of the First Ascending Passage to scale that channel before snaking their way through the scaffolding underneath the lift platform. Continuing up the gallery ramp and around the pulley mounted on top of the Great Step, the lines circled back and turned downward, proceeding toward the lift, where a work gang hooked them onto the front end.

Now, with various alterations to the system, and to keep the ropes out of the way, the lines wending through the lower passageways were split into two groups beneath the redesigned lift. Short posts had been installed inside the wooden frame to guide them toward the right or left. The rollers attached to the substructure were there primarily to direct the ropes toward a couple of oval-shaped openings cut into the floorboards on both sides near the outer edges of the wooden deck.

At the front end, crews had erected two more posts with pulleys mounted on top to slot in the lines emerging from below the lift through the oval-shaped holes in the floor. After passing over those two pulleys, the ropes climbed upward toward a tall pulley-stand, planted in the square holes on top of the Great Step. Circling around the grooves cut into the right- and left-hand sides of the roller turned the lines back while funneling them away from the middle of the Great Step as they continued their journey downhill.

This time, workers did not tie the ropes to the front of the lift but attached them to the pair of uprights affixed to the deck. Once the carrier was rigged correctly, the people standing inside the revolving wheel in the Subterranean Chamber were able to pull the counterweight down the Descending Passage to move the vehicle up the corridor. A band of pullers posted on the northern ramp would return the lift to its start position at Course 25 as they pulled the heavy block back up the underground shaft to reset it.

Around the Antechamber

Five limestone blocks frame the entrance to the Antechamber. The grouping includes two blocks, each approximately four feet square, stacked on either side of the doorway, and a much larger block resting horizontally atop the two short towers. The longer piece acted as a header, lying east to west over the entrance. We can only estimate the exact size of the block resting above the threshold because its back end is hidden beneath other stones. A realistic guess is that it is at least eight feet long from end to end and between three and four feet wide from north to south.

It is also reasonable to assume that the blocks surrounding the entrance were originally carried up on the lift and stowed somewhere out of the way on the flat surface of Course 49 since, for the moment, there was no need to raise them any higher. Accordingly, to begin arranging the limestone pieces on either side of the doorway, a small team must have shoved or dragged the base block for the east side around the Great Step by crossing the empty space between it and the front end of the lift. Workers would have kept the block moving until they had brought it all the way behind the step and deposited the square stone next to the entry. Transferring the one for the base position on the west side was equally straightforward. A work gang would have been able to simply slide the block across the floor of Course 49 and set it into place by the Antechamber's door.

The next part of the project required a little more effort. Once the initial block on the west side was in place, crews took a series of limestone pieces the same size and laid them out in a long row. Starting about three feet away from the base block and continuing west down the length of the King's Chamber, the line of stones became the first layer for a shelf that the Egyptians would initially use for storage and later as the foundation for another corbelled wall. The three-foot-wide gap left between the block by the doorway and the ledge's east end was a small but critical factor in the building process. Many years into the future, this insignificant hole would serve as the sole escape hatch for the people sealing up the interior of the Great Pyramid.

Fashioning a ledge did not solve a related problem. If the builders hoped to stack a second pair of blocks on top of the first two adjoining the opening for the door and create the walls inside the Antechamber's entrance, they had to find a way to raise those stones up from the floor. Not surprisingly, based on historic patterns, their strategy involved deploying a series of temporary ramps. When workers were stockpiling the rest of blocks for the Grand Gallery, they had carried in separate chunks of limestone already cut on an angle and/or built short ramps or rails out of wood in preparation for moving the higher pieces into position.

At least one of these ramps would have spanned the space between the floor in the main work area and the recently constructed ledge, which at this point was only a single block tall.

After wrapping a rope or choker around the mid-section of the upper block quarried for the east side of the doorway, a small group of workers standing somewhere overhead dragged it up the small ramp onto the ledge and across the top of the Great Step. (The crew would have temporarily set something inside the ledge's three-foot-wide gap to create a smooth path for the new block.) From there, it would not be too difficult to push or pull the stone further south and set it atop the base block already situated on the east side.

Once the short stack of limestone east of the doorway was assembled, the crew again made use of the small ramp at the foot of the ledge to lift the upper block for the west side from the floor and deposit it on its base block. A few crew members positioned higher than the stone they were trying to raise merely heaved it up the short incline and onto the block at the bottom. At this juncture, the ledge in front of the King's Chamber also began to grow taller as workers using the same ramp proceeded to pull up a series of blocks, including the longer stone that would straddle the break for the escape hatch, as well as enough pieces to arrange a second full row on top of the initial line of blocks leading west.

ANTECHAMBER ENTRANCE
The entrance to the Antechamber.

Due to the variations in height and assorted angles, the operation no doubt required the builders to increase the size of the original temporary ramp and install a few more small inclines here and there. They needed at least one ramp tall enough to transfer the large block of limestone quarried to fit above the Antechamber's entrance to the ledge — now two rows high. That position would allow workers to push its nose onto the upper block on the west side of the doorway. When the front end of the header stone landed there, a team was able to slide it across the gap left open for the entryway to the other side. Furthermore, this latest ramp, which reached as high as the second row on the ledge, was how workers were able to add a third row of blocks on top of the long shelf.

Looking at the situation from the perspective of the 21st century, for the the ancient builders to take the time to fashion a ledge three rows high at the south end of their central work area may seem an odd choice, but its purpose was twofold. First, the platform would serve as provisional storage space for most of the blocks designated for the forthcoming corbelled wall at the front of the Antechamber. And much later, this shelf would form the foundation for a separate wall that continues the pattern of those same corbels by extending them further west. These extensions will eventually form the south wall of a vital yet comparatively short-lived interior room — a room that in due time, would enable the Egyptians to construct the uppermost portions of their Great Pyramid.

Breaching the 49th Course

Before raising the gallery walls any higher, the team needed a foundation upon which to build. And they would approach that job in different ways on the east and west sides of the corridor. Crews started building the base for the remainder of the Grand Gallery's east wall first because the blocks on that side would not be in the way to hinder any of the activities related to the lift.

For expediency, while they were stockpiling other stones, workers had transported the base blocks for the missing sections of the walls and set them off to the side on Course 49 until they were ready to install them. With the stones close at hand, the workers would be able to push or drag the pieces one by one toward the vicinity of the lift. For the most part, the base blocks at the upper end of the gallery east and west replicate the dimensions of the ones framing almost the entire length of the corridor.

The primary difference among them is that the lower edges of the two southernmost blocks flanking the Great Step are not L-shaped but were cut straight up and down. The reason for this slight variation will become apparent later — when the Egyptians temporarily reconfigure some of the blocks at the south end to provide access to the lift from the west side.

One feature inside the pyramid, which a visitor might overlook, is the fact that the ramp running up the center of the Grand Gallery ends in a landing that starts a little more than five feet north of the Antechamber's front wall. This is why the space the Great Step occupies is flat. Yet the walls on either side of the step are not perpendicular to the horizontal plane of the pyramid. Similar to every other section of the gallery, the wall blocks in that area are slanted at a 26-degree angle. While the short stretch of floor with the Great Step in the middle of it is level, the ramp actually continues toward the back of the landing on either side. Dealing with a slanted floor unquestionably affected how crews would be able to fill in the walls along the corridor all the way up to the Antechamber.

Since the exit from the lift and the busy workspace were both on the west side, it made sense for the Egyptians to install the base blocks and the row of squared-off stones on top of them in the east wall sooner than later. The builders had good reason to begin there, since it would have been easy to drag the L-shaped pieces from where they were housed on Course 49 and set them one by one at the upper end of the ramp on the east side before sliding them downhill. In addition, by stopping the lift near the spot slated to receive a wall block and raising the vehicle up the ramp a little at a time, the team would be able to park it next to the area where the latest piece of limestone belonged. The lift's wooden deck became a short-term work platform for the gangs assisting in the installation.

Using a rope looped around the bottom end of the first eight-foot-long base block for the east wall, and circling the line around either the pulley on the Great Step or a new one mounted on top of the lintel over the Antechamber's door, the crew started lowering the piece down the incline. They controlled it with the rope, letting the block fall until it was a few inches away from the one already in place and hit a slim wooden wedge placed against the lower stone. Removing the rope, workers pounded on the edge of the wood with mallets to force the wedge out from between the two blocks, ensuring that the latest addition to the bottom row was permanently fixed.

The length of the unfinished portion of the side walls north to south at the base was about 40 feet, which would have required crews to lower a total of five blocks in sequence down the ramp, including the only block that was not L-shaped at the south end. Although at first glance the critical importance of this base row is eclipsed by the sheer drama of the awesome structure towering overhead, it formed the footing for the final series of corbels that would enclose the long hallway.

The second row of blocks in the east wall, which rest atop the base blocks seated directly on the ramp, matches the size of all of the other stones in that same row along the length of the gallery corridor. With the bottom row in place, it is certainly possible that the big shadoof positioned in the main work area on the west side may have merely picked up the blocks for the second row from the floor and set them one by one on top of the highest (southern-most) base block, allowing the team to drop them down the slope. When row number two was whole, work on the east wall halted. It would start up again only when it was time to begin the painstaking process of inserting the seven corbelled rows above it to finish off that side.

Tackling the next incomplete section and preparing to build a cliff-like wall of corbelled rows on the west side was a more complex operation. First, the job involved a partial remodel of the floor alongside the lift. Many years earlier, the builders had replaced the top layer of ramp stones next to the lift's platform with blocks that were angled on the bottom but flat on top. The idea was to connect the vehicle to Course 49 whenever it was parked at that end of the gallery by fashioning a contiguous level surface for transferring the sleds, blocks, and supplies. Now it was time to swap out the replacement blocks for the original ramp stones.

After removing the flat-topped pieces, workers took two four-foot-long blocks angled at 26 degrees on top and set them inside the trench that the replacement blocks had previously occupied to restore the missing sections of the ramp. Then they lugged the next base block for the wall toward the lift and set it on top of the rebuilt incline west of the Great Step. The crew followed the same general routine they had employed in addressing the east wall by using ropes from a pulley mounted at the south end and sticking wooden wedges in between the stones to create an opening for removing the lines afterward. One after the other, the work gang let the L-shaped blocks slide downhill. They would add the single straight-edged piece when they reached the southernmost position in the row. Soon the formerly empty space where the base for the gallery's west wall was supposed to be had its blocks.

For the first time since the builders had established a critical work area at the center of the Great Pyramid, there was a barrier between the 49th course and the lift. The recently installed set of base blocks on the west side had created a wall approximately three feet high that not only cut off direct access to the transfer/storage area but also extinguished the team's ability to convey more stones. The Egyptians planned to develop a workaround for the situation, but would not be able to do that until the buildout reached the level where they could insert the first corbelled row.

The most immediate issue the team faced was adding the series of squared-off pieces on top of the base blocks on the west side. In this case, the crew probably made use of the shadoof in the primary workspace to drop the second row of blocks one by one on top of the base block at the upper end of the ramp, which permitted a separate work gang to lower them downhill. Or they may have dragged the blocks for the next row over from storage to the bottom of a temporary ramp pushed up against the short west wall, pulling each piece on top of the highest base block to start its slide down the edge of the angled wall. Ultimately, similar to what had occurred on the east side, the height of the unfinished portion of the west wall grew until it was two rows tall.

Over and Up

Arguably the most formidable obstacle hampering the team's ability to complete the Grand Gallery was the fact that once construction had breached Course 49, the underlying circumstances changed dramatically. Constructing the remainder of the walls was going to require crews to move the blocks uphill, which meant gravity would compete against them. Closing up the two sides demanded a carefully orchestrated procedure with an initial focus on erecting the corbelled wall above the Antechamber's door. The speed at which that single wall rises would set the pace for the balance of the corridor because placement of the side panels depended to a large degree on the progress made at the passageway's upper end.

A definite strategy drove the builders forward. The cornerstone of their plan was erecting the south wall. From the beginning, engineers would have wanted to position a set of blocks at that end of the gallery because the prospective side walls had to fit tightly against a solid mass to retain their rigid structure. Similar to the filler blocks piled up next to the ascending passageway tunnel at the bottom of the ramp, which provided a supportive framework for the corbels along the sides, the south wall would play a critical role in guaranteeing that the 157-foot-long corridor was stable at the other end, too. Consequently, in every instance, the crucial variable will be work crews adding one more corbel above the entrance into the Antechamber before tackling the next corbelled row in the gallery itself. Only when the anchor piece was in place could the sides of the passageway grow.

The approach the ancient builders took in sealing off the gallery with walls higher than the two rows of blocks for the base east and west stuck to a fairly rigorous routine. At the onset of the process, they installed the bottommost corbel in the wall above the door into the Antechamber, setting the block on top of the header stone lying across the entrance. The team must have stored the blocks for this first corbel and the ones they would subsequently add to the south wall much earlier by placing them along the short ledge that overlooked the main workspace. They had also used some of the lower stairs still open and available west of the center channel to stow additional blocks. In terms of corbel number one for the south wall, a group of workers standing on the storage ledge west of the block may have shoved the slab eastward and onto the lintel stone from behind; a second team could have wrapped a rope around the far end of the new piece and pulled it across the header from a location on the east side — or both.

The Antechamber wall — a single block wide east to west — is referred to as corbelled because the limestone slab comprising each row overhangs the one beneath it by at least three inches. In this instance, the builders had fashioned the overhangs by increasing the size of the individual blocks, i.e., quarrying a slab that would be three inches longer front to back than the one sitting below it. As a result, the blocks were offset by the correct amount to create the projections on the north side of the wall while the opposite (back) side was flat.

The Griffith theory posits that unlike the corbels projecting inward along the length of the Grand Gallery, which workers had manipulated manually by pushing them forward, the dimensions on the interior of the Antechamber had dictated the multi-sized blocks used in the room's north wall. If every block had been cut the same size and crews merely thrust them forward, the three-inch difference in their placement would have produced a step-like configuration inside the tiny room. But the interior wall at the north end is flat. Granted, the builders could have packed a stepped wall with pieces of filler, but since the setback on the lowest tier would be three inches deep with the succeeding levels expanding to a mere 21 inches, the steps would have been far too narrow to permanently hold filler blocks.

Once the initial corbel in the Antechamber's front wall was in place, workers extended it westward above the ledge along the south side of Course 49, creating the first row for a future corbelled wall in that area. The next step was to identify the blocks missing from both sides of the Grand Gallery and install them.

To understand the full picture of how events may have transpired, it is instructive to set the larger scene. At this point, if the more than 30-foot-long lift had come to a standstill at the top of the ramp, the back end would have been sitting next to sections of the unfinished gallery walls on both sides. What was visible from its deck were the upper edges of a stack of wall blocks riding at an angle and jutting up from below the floor of the 49th course. The cluster of uneven ends marked the spot where work on the corbels in the gallery had stopped — and the place where it would begin again.

Matching the Angle

One way to initiate the process of building up the walls was to identify the stored blocks meant for the bottommost corbels in the side walls. Starting with the lowest storage step on the north side of the central workspace, a gang removed the piece of limestone closest to the gallery, which lay parallel to the wall, and dragged it east. While it is possible that the step where the block had been stowed rose as high as the lowest block in the stack sticking out from below the floor, it seems more likely that there were minor differences in the heights. Workers may have used levers similar to crowbars to elevate one end of the slab they had just hauled over to raise it up to a suitable position. Employing a series of controlled motions, they jimmied the piece of limestone to create a gap between it and the step it sat on. Then they shoved a smaller chunk of filler under the block to hold the south end off the ground.

The smaller stone resting inside the gap between the bottom of the wall block and the storage step became the new leverage point for forcing the corbel block higher if it had not yet reached an acceptable elevation. Using their crowbars, the team pried up the edge again and jimmied the slab before putting a second chunk of limestone on top of the first piece of filler in the stack beneath the new wall block. The process continued until the block on top attained the requisite height.

To create an angle, the upper edge of the very last stone in the short column holding up the slab was slanted to make the new block match the angle of the one already in the wall. This tactic allowed the crew to basically slide the piece eastward and lay it on the wall.

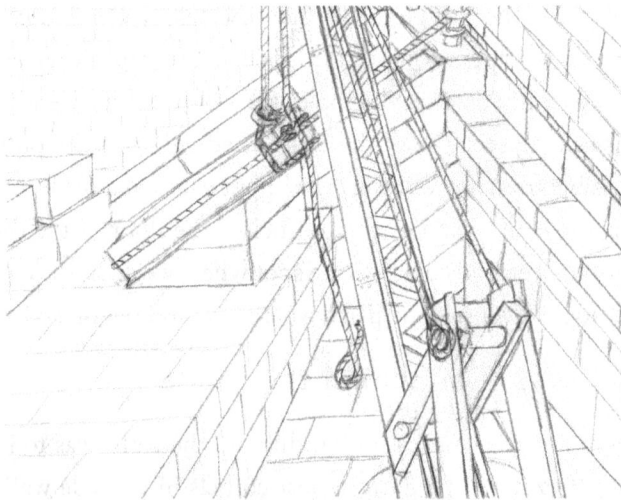

FROM STORAGE TO WALL

An industrial-sized shadoof erected in the main workspace west of the lift assisted the builders in elevating the pieces of limestone for the southernmost sections of the gallery walls above Course 49. After work gangs moved a corbel block across the storage step eastward toward the Grand Gallery, the shadoof elevated one end. Lowering the block atop a stone wedge slanted at 26 degrees put it at the same angle as the sides of the corridor, which allowed the crew to slide the slab onto the existing wall. By the time the buildout had reached the uppermost row of corbels, the height of the evolving work platform had increased to the point where the team was able to move the blocks directly onto the walls from that flat surface.

While the first method may have helped at various points along the way, it was the shadoof standing in the central workspace that was regularly called into service to construct the final segments of the side walls. For the majority of the eight-foot-long blocks hauled over from storage and placed next to the gallery, the hook on the shadoof would catch the choker wrapped around the south end of the piece of limestone and lift up that side. The machine held onto the block and slowly raised it up from the step until the angle was a little higher than the existing corbel in the wall. Then it laid the slab on top of a stone wedge cut at a 26-degree angle.

The result was the latest slab resting on an incline equal to the angle of the sloped wall. Because the wedge underneath it was shorter than the block, there was enough space at both ends of the new corbel to rig it with ropes. Alternating the pieces in sequence, workers would rig one block at a time from each pair designated for the same row on either side of the gallery, first preparing the piece that belonged in the east wall for its journey across the corridor.

East Side, West Side

Installing the corbel blocks designated for the west wall would prove to be a straightforward proposition, but the procedure for moving the materials for the east wall out of storage and over to the other side of the gallery was not quite as simple. Workers had to grapple with transferring the blocks for the rows of corbels in an alternating sequence, introducing the block for the east wall first before inserting the one on the west side. The general idea was to take advantage of the peaks formed by the uneven ends of the existing walls projecting up from below by manufacturing a portable wooden overpass. A temporary bridge designed to sit among the peaks is how crews would convey the blocks targeted for the east wall across the almost seven-foot-wide corridor.

The team had already assembled the materials and equipment for their wall-building exercise, and the next part of the project was scheduled to begin with the northernmost corbels on each side. Workers laid a thick, heavy beam against the right angle formed by the lowest corbel block in the west wall and the base block underneath it. The beam was about half the size north to south as a regular eight-foot-long slab used to create a corbel, yet long enough east to west to span the gap between the walls. Pushing the timber forward (east), brought it to rest in the right angle formed by the blocks at the same height and position on the other side of the corridor. Notably, the wood was as thick as the right-angled corner was tall (three feet), which made it level with the top of the block it rested against. The altitude was important because the limestone slab had to ride across the gallery high enough to avoid hitting the side as it drew closer to the east wall.

Transferring all the pieces for that side across the "valley" that was the Grand Gallery also required the services of a couple of post-rollers. As soon as workers had installed the initial corbel in the wall over the Antechamber door at the south end of the gallery, they had dug holes on top of the block near its east and west ends. The cavities may also have been precut into the limestone at the quarry. Then the crew proceeded to thrust post-rollers into the two depressions. Offset by a slight amount north to south to accommodate separate ropes, each of the thick wooden poles mounted vertically in the floor sported grooves at the top and bottom.

The addition of the two devices established a routine that would repeat itself block by block until the evolving gallery walls reached the roofline. The slab holding the post-rollers also provided a short-term work platform for several members of the crew who were assigned to keep an eye on the ropes passing over the grooves. As construction proceeded, both the work platform by the Antechamber and its post-rollers would gain elevation when the number of corbels increased with every block introduced into the south wall.

The workers handling the pull-ropes stood toward the west, on top of the first corbel erected above the ledge along the south side of the workspace on Course 49. Developed in concert with the installation of the Antechamber's front wall, the series of blocks running parallel to the King's Chamber was designed to extend every corbelled row further west. The crews stationed on top of these extensions managed the lines rounding the post-rollers, and were tasked with moving the blocks for the gallery's east wall from one side of the corridor to the other. When the time came, they would also provide the muscle power to maneuver the individual slabs of limestone into position on the unfinished walls east and west.

Once the shadoof had raised the south end of the newest wall block and laid it on the stone wedge, the builders initiated one of the methods described earlier to set it on the bridge. A work gang with levers piled small cubes of workaday limestone underneath the block headed for the east side, using each chunk as a leverage point to jimmy up the block a little at a time. The piece of filler on top of the short stack was cut at the same angle — 26 degrees — as the angle of the slanted west wall. The objective was to elevate the block higher than the upper edge of the lowest corbel on the west side. Following that process, and with incredible persistence and effort, the crew proceeded to raise the piece of polished limestone even higher — the height of another whole corbel block — and pushed it onto the temporary bridge. Situated lengthwise north to south on the incline, the slab was balanced on its mid-section atop the wooden crossbeam.

The pull-teams assigned to the corbel extensions west of the Antechamber would be responsible for methodically tightening and loosening the lines that crew members planned to wrap around the wall panel to move it eastward. Before the project began, a gang had plaited a loop into one end of the ropes that workers would employ to drift the corbel blocks across the gallery corridor. The idea was to capture and manipulate the piece of limestone through the use of a choker. Pulling one end of the rope through the eyelet to create a wide circle, the gang would lasso the blocks around their eight-foot-long sides.

The first rope had curved around the post-roller mounted toward the west by passing over the grooves then dropping down to the wall block balanced below. Looping the lasso around the stone longways, it circled the block on the east and west sides. After making any adjustments to ensure that the choker was centered at the top (the face closest to the Antechamber), the crew yanked hard to constrict the loop, pulling it taut around the slab. The pivot point was the post-roller, which caused the rope's free end to make a right turn toward the west and the pullers standing on the corbel extensions. The lasso associated with the second post-roller followed basically the same track in circling the block before employing the eastern post-roller to send the line west toward the pull-team. In the end, the position of the two chokers side by side at the top of the block made it possible to control and transfer the heavy stone.

Separate sets of pullers worked the two ropes but operated in tandem in a continuous process of tightening and releasing the lines as they walked back and forth on top of the corbel extensions. The closely coordinated procedure shifted from one post-roller to the other as the block suspended on the wooden bridge inched across the chasm. For example, as the rope on the east side tightened, the pullers handling the one on the west side let some slack into their line and vice versa. Their strategy was to maintain an equal amount of pressure on both sides while using the post-rollers to stabilize the block and prevent it from rocking back and forth. As the new corbel block approached the east wall, the angle of the rope connected to the eastern post-roller gradually straightened out.

GALLERY WALL BLOCKS · TRANSFER

Building the east wall of the Grand Gallery above the 49th course required workers to use the post-rollers mounted over the entrance to the Antechamber to move a corbel block from the west wall across the breach to the other side of the corridor.

When the slab arrived at the east wall, it was met by a small crew waiting on the catwalk in back. Soon the pullers working the line around the western post-roller loosened their lariat, allowing the gang on the east side to remove the rope, which was no longer necessary. Then the process shifted and it became a matter of using the eastern post-roller to pull the block forward (south) along the wall by an amount sufficient to clear the bridge. The problem lay in the fact that the corbel block was sitting on the wooden beam a good three feet above the wall's upper edge. If the workers handling the rope drew the piece southward immediately, it would tumble off and crash into the blocks below.

To forestall such a situation, workers had placed a wooden wedge on top of the wall directly in front of the beam to act as a temporary ramp. The brief incline was designed to provide a soft landing for the slab's back end. The laborers working the eastern post-roller would continue to lug the block forward until it was far enough beyond the removable bridge and the wedge for the people on the other side of the gallery — behind the west wall — to pull the thick crossbeam back across the corridor while a separate crew on the east side removed the wedge. Then the team of pullers posted on the extensions eased the block back down the edge of the wall and into position. With the latest corbel for the east wall set, the work gang on the opposite side of the gallery dragged a matching block from the storage step, raised one end, and slid it onto the west wall.

The current operation only accounted for first two blocks in the lowest row of corbels from the missing sections of the walls. It would take many more blocks of limestone for the Grand Gallery to become whole. Tackling the remainder of the walls involved a recurring course of action with the next corbel block waiting in the wings and consigned to the east side. This time, the team would start by placing the wooden beam in the right-angled corners atop the pair of blocks they had just installed. And when the new slab reached the east side, they would use the top of the previous block to slide the latest one forward. The methods the Egyptians employed to transfer materials from one side of the gallery to the other would remain the same for a total of seven corbelled rows.

Walls and Wedges

The critical variable in terms of the ability to finish erecting the Grand Gallery was what happened to the blocks after they arrived on the edge of one of the walls. Ever efficient, the builders would apply the same techniques in constructing both sides of their magnificent passageway. Beginning with the bottommost set of corbels and completing a single row before moving upward, crews would close up the break between the gallery and the Antechamber one corbelled layer at a time.

As a rule, once the crew slid a stone onto the flat back of the lowest wall block in the pile on either side, they made arrangements for the next stage of its journey. From their elevated positions overhead and standing on one of the corbels at the south end, workers made sure that the ropes on the appropriate side were adjusted properly for a straight-on pull. A straight pull was possible because the two post-rollers mounted above the entrance to the Antechamber were aligned with the gallery walls. The free end of the lasso, which wound around the bottom (north) end of the new corbel block on the edge of the wall, stayed on its post-roller before turning west toward the pullers.

At the same time, to compensate for the variation in height from row to row and be able to slide the unwieldy corbel blocks forward along a smooth track, workers always inserted a wooden wedge into the drop-off between the top of the southernmost block already in place in the angled wall and the block in the row below it. The triangular object, carved from a solid piece of wood, went directly in front of the highest block in the latest row and functioned as a temporary ramp.

With the wooden wedge in place, the eight-foot-long stone had an easy ride downhill when the pullers on one of the post-rollers tugged the corbel block toward them, instead of it tilting and falling off the short cliff. Obviously, as workers kept heaving the piece forward, the back end faced a similar issue of potentially falling off the block it was riding on. The wedge also kept the back end of the stone-in-motion from dropping off the small precipice and banging down hard on the standing wall.

Drawing the slab ahead, the pull-team balanced the weight for a moment on the tip formed by the upper edge of the last block in line. While dragging the stone further south, they kept pulling until the new corbel had cleared the small ramp. Then another gang carried away the wedge. That done, the people on the corbel extensions slowly stepped forward — walking east — to allow the block to drop back down the incline. A crew had also placed the noses of a couple of much narrower wooden wedges in the shape of a long, slender "V" against the front end of the corbel sitting farther down the slope to hold the blocks apart as the latest one moved closer.

Taking the rope into account, the workers had to leave enough space in between the blocks to be able to pull out the line before the two slabs met and gravity bound them together. When the rope was finally gone, the gang assigned to deal with the separators sandwiched between the blocks picked up mallets and pounded on the outer edges of the hunks of wood, causing them to work their way out of the slits.

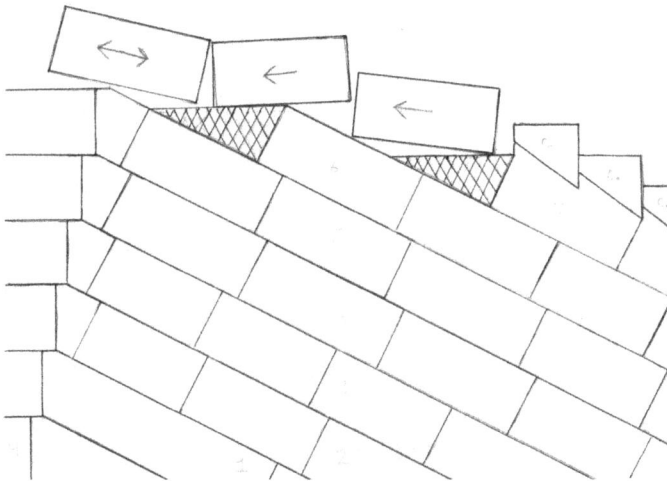

GALLERY WALL BLOCKS · SLIDING

A wooden wedge set on the edge of the wall in front of an existing block provided a smooth pathway for the next corbel as workers pulled the heavy piece forward to clear the wedge before lowering it into position.

While the walls of the Grand Gallery are both awe-inspiring and breath-takingly beautiful, in the final analysis, the approach the Egyptians took to set the corbels in place was not overly complicated. In terms of the general operation, it was mostly the tops of the blocks previously inserted into the walls that served as the tracks for installing the corbels to come. To sum up, the way they constructed the final, southernmost sections of the gallery walls involved dragging a limestone block over from the storage area to either lever it up or raise one end with the shadoof and move the piece from the stair-step onto what was currently the bottommost row of corbels. If the block belonged to the east wall, pullers transferred it to the other side of the corridor via a portable bridge.

Then, employing a rope looped around the lower end of the slab, workers pulled it south by moving the piece of limestone up the sloped wall until it cleared the wooden wedge placed in front of the block it was sliding over. Once the wedge-ramp — and later the wooden separators between the stones — were gone, the latest corbel block settled to the bottom of the incline with its front (north) end flush against the back (south) end of the last piece that the crew had installed in the row.

Lintel Stone

All that said, it is important to add that the way the Egyptians handled the very first block in the lowest corbelled row in the west wall was distinct from the way they would assemble the succeeding rows, east and west. The process had to be different because, in time, the southernmost block in the first corbelled row on the west side would act as the header or lintel stone above an unusual doorway to the lift. Preparations for injecting this key block butting up against the Antechamber wall had required engineers to make a few modifications in terms of their methods and equipment.

The southernmost corbel block was an outlier as far as the overall system the ancient builders had developed was concerned. One crucial detail stands out with respect to completing the unfinished portions of the Grand Gallery: the contours of the blocks. The stones that will eventually become the corbels in rows number two through six were shaped like large rectangles with perfectly flat surfaces on all six sides. The seventh row was the exception since those blocks had a sawtooth cut along the upper edge to support the ceiling slabs. The blocks quarried for row number one, the lowest corbelled row in the wall, were rectangular too — except for the very first block on the west side adjoining the Antechamber wall.

The front edge of this single block — the edge leaning against the wall — was slanted. Why? All of the blocks in the gallery's side walls rest at an angle of 26 degrees. Consequently, if the initial block in the row had been cut straight up and down and it, too, was tilted 26 degrees, the vertical plane at the front end would not sit flush against the flat surface of the wall above the

Antechamber's door. There would have been a gap between the two. Yet, it was only the initial corbel block on one side of the corridor that the builders had treated in this manner, by angling its southern face. The Egyptians had already developed a separate but equally creative solution to the problem of eliminating the breaks between the sides of the gallery and the south wall, not only for the first corbelled row on the east side but also for rows two through seven east and west. They would apply that tactic row by row as the walls inside the Grand Gallery continued to develop.

In this case, the central focus of the builders' grand plan for the gallery's west wall was to, one day, make use of the first block in the lowest corbelled row as a lintel beam. From the beginning, this particular piece was targeted to carry the weight of a future opening on that side of the corridor. As construction advances, the team would temporarily remove the base blocks beneath the new header stone to open up a doorway for transferring materials to and from the lift. But for their strategy to succeed, the initial block in line had to be composed of a single, solid piece of limestone fixed firmly against the Antechamber wall to immobilize the header and make it permanent.

The more immediate problem was how to insert the series of blocks comprising the first corbelled row for the west wall into the tight space allotted to them without the benefit of any real "give" to maneuver the stones into position. Of necessity, the missing sections of the walls on both sides of the gallery had to fit precisely into their slots — securely against each other and the south wall — never to move again.

With the rope wrapped around the lower (north) end of what would become the third block in the bottom row of corbels on the west side, the team stationed on the corbel extensions followed the same procedure of using the western post-roller to pull the stone forward before slowly lowering it down toward block number four, which was already part of the wall. Once crews carried away the wooden wedge that had provided a navigable slope and removed the rope, the third block sank back until it was frozen in place.

Next, taking the block cut to be the lintel occupying the lead position in the first corbelled row, crews repeated the process of depositing the wooden wedge on top of the wall then pulling block number one toward them as far as it would go — firmly against the lowest corbel above the Antechamber door. But this time, they either attached the rope to a stationary object nearby or anchored the stone in its current position using brute force. The objective was to leave a gap wide enough for the second block in line to be able to slip in between the third piece of limestone and this latest one.

A separate group of workers quickly picked up several short timbers and set them inside the hole, sandwiched between the two stones, to maintain the separation and correct amount of space for block number two. This dunnage served a number of purposes. Pressure from the chunks of wood not only held the higher block with the angled front end touching the Antechamber hard against that wall, it also allowed a work gang to remove the rope around block number one. With the wooden braces preserving the split, the builders would be able to drop the middle stone into position while keeping everything else taut. Hauling the second block in the row over from storage, the crew set it on top of the timbers in the gap. They may have also used the shadoof in the main work area to lower the stone into the cavity from above.

The process was no doubt painstaking and slow because the dimensions of the opening were precise and inflexible. Its size left only a fraction of an inch to play with as workers attempted to maneuver the second stone in line into position. Starting with the top layer of wood, they removed the initial group of timbers while steadily pushing down on the piece of limestone. Once that layer had fallen further into the cavity, the next layer was eliminated, and so on and so on until the block sat securely in its hole and the first and lowest corbelled row in the west wall was complete.

Gaps in Between

Work on the gallery's walls proceeded apace. With the lowest corbelled rows on both sides set, the team could begin assembling the uppermost sections of the missing panels. Starting with the wall above the Antechamber, they installed its second corbel, then extended the ridge by adding another series of blocks to erect row number two above the ledge on the south side of the primary workspace. Concurrently, workers were preparing the blocks to construct the next corbelled row inside the Grand Gallery.

As described earlier, the stones quarried for the first block in the lowest corbelled row in the east wall, as well as every succeeding row on both sides of the passageway, except for the saw-toothed blocks in row seven, were the same size and shape: rectangular. The fact that they were not slanted at the front end predictably presented a problem. It is impossible to push the side of a squared-off block leaning at an angle flat against an upright surface. The planes do not meet, resulting in a cleft or gap between the two objects. The challenge for the ancient Egyptians was figuring out how to fill in the breaks between the southernmost blocks from every corbelled row in the gallery and the vertical plane of the Antechamber wall.

Not surprisingly, they had long foreseen the predicament and made allowances for it. During the interval when the builders were stockpiling stones, crews must have carried in a collection of smaller "cubes" already sized for a close fit, based on the estimated dimensions of the series of future gaps. At the very least, the compact chunks of limestone, which workers would slip into the openings from the side, were beveled on their southern faces but left flat on the other five sides. The gap-filler's north face was designed to butt up against the first corbel block in the row sitting behind it. Cut to fit tightly against the front of the Antechamber, these customized inserts would eradicate the breaks between the sides of the gallery and the wall at the south end.

The angled face of each small piece the team planned to install might have been cut at the quarry, but it was more likely that crews waited until a row of corbels was in place to trim the chunks of limestone. By accurately measuring the size of the gap at the corner where the two walls met, they would be able to tailor the block intended for a specific cleft to an exact fit. Stonecutters could have made use of the remaining open space on the 49th course or the developing work platform on the gallery's west side to shape the blocks, which would have permitted them to stand at the level of the fissure to finish dressing the stone. (Note: The builders had addressed the gap between the Antechamber wall and the lowest corbelled row in the west wall much earlier — when the block serving as the header was originally quarried and angled on one end.)

Bringing the gap-filling process to a successful conclusion required an extra but not trivial step. Because each new corbel in the wall above the Antechamber overlapped the one beneath it by at least three inches, the pieces of limestone tucked into the gaps on either side of the gallery could not protrude higher than the blocks they abutted. If the inserts plugging up the breaks projected past the top of the existing block in the Antechamber wall, they would hit the overhang when workers introduced the next corbel at the south end. Since the southern face on the limestone plug was slanted, the angled side created a slight rim along the upper edge, and because this rim extended a tiny amount above the top of the block, the tip would have bumped into the slab it adjoined. Arguably the easiest way to solve the problem was for workers to wait until a keystone had been slotted into the gap, then trim back the small peak by shaving it off. Eliminating the tip created a smooth, level surface ready to receive another block for the wall at that end of the corridor.

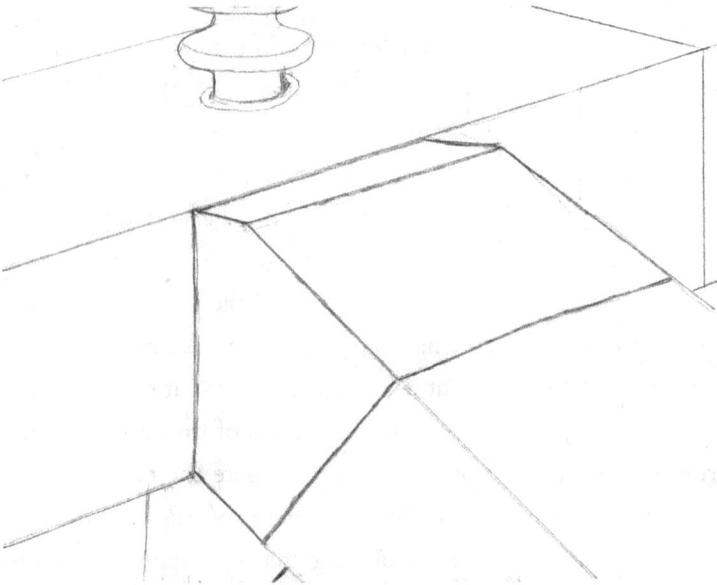

GAP-FILLER

Gap-fillers were inserted between the Antechamber and the sides of the Grand Gallery to eliminate the breaks between the two structures.

The rising walls linked to the Antechamber and Grand Gallery sparked another welcome phenomenon: an increase in the elevation of the team's work platform. Their deck kept growing longer north to south, as well as higher, with every additional row of corbels and every vacant storage step subsequently packed with filler stones. At the same time, concentrated activity was also occurring above the short ledge (previously used for storage) in front of the narrow stack of courses adjacent to the King's Chamber on the north side.

With each corbelled row incorporated into the Antechamber wall, workers had also added a row of corbels above the ledge, carrying the pattern more than 30 feet west. And for the moment, the pull-teams were using those corbelled levels to maneuver the blocks for the gallery walls. The principal reason for this unexpected corbelled wall at the south end of what remained of the open space on Course 49 would become apparent as work on the Grand Gallery drew to a close and the builders prepared to open up a remarkable new door to the lift.

GRAND GALLERY - EAST WALL

Illustration of the Grand Gallery's east wall as seen from the west, showing the gap-fillers and the roof slabs.

Non-stop construction presented a critical need to continue building up the perimeter of the primary workspace in any event. Only by adding new layers of stone around the edges by stacking up more course blocks as the gallery's walls progressed would the work platform on the west side eventually become tall enough to access the roofline. The procedure the Egyptians followed in this situation was rooted in the same principles they had adhered to for previous courses: 1) Develop a layer and use the flat, horizontal surface on that level to move the blocks for the next course into place. 2) Erect each level by never actually lifting the weighty stones, which otherwise could be pushed or pulled into position.

It was no different for the blocks added to the corbelled wall rising above the short ledge. Row after row, as soon as workers deposited the limestone for a corbel in the front wall of the Antechamber, they placed a line of corbel blocks above the shelf. Each row that the gang assembled afforded them a long, flat work deck, stretching all the way from the Antechamber to the western edge of the King's Chamber, which allowed them to drag in an assortment of stones for the succeeding levels.

Most of the blocks used to construct the south wall of the Grand Gallery, and especially the one above the ledge along the south side of the workspace, had been stowed on the lower stairs west of the center channel. Based on the arrangement described here, the builders probably used long boards to span the gap at the corner where the remnants of that stairway, which ran north and south, met the far end of the east-west ledge. These short-term bridges, composed of strong wooden planks, would have allowed workers to simply slide the hefty pieces of stone straight across from a storage step onto the top of the unfinished wall above the shelf.

As was the case elsewhere, after the team had emptied one of the steps on the west side of the center channel, they would transport filler stones into the unoccupied space, thereby elevating and broadening the work platform inside that zone.

Course by course, crews hauled over the pieces of dressed and polished limestone from the various stockpiles around the site to complete not only the sides of the Grand Gallery but also its southern wall. By the time the seventh — and last — row of corbels lining the corridor was in place, the process of assembling the last few sections of the gallery's ceiling was already well underway.

Walled In

Putting the finishing touches on the gallery's roof presented its own unique set of circumstances. The platforms surrounding the primary work space reached high enough to access the roofline, but workers had never blanketed the compact area on Course 49 adjacent to the gallery's west wall with stacks of blocks. As a result, there was no work deck built up to permit contact with the southernmost sections of the seventh corbel.

Since the builders needed to retain a modicum of open space in the main work area for handling the materials to finish the Great Pyramid, they had not amassed blocks over every speck of the floor. Instead, crews had purposely refrained from expanding the ever-growing work platform on the north side as far south as the Great Step, because stacking a giant pile of limestone blocks opposite the step would have obstructed the future opening planned for that spot. Layers of course blocks piled against that part of the west wall would have permanently barred access to the only doorway left for transferring supplies to and from the great lift.

The question now becomes: How did the Egyptians actually finish the ceiling in the Grand Gallery? Luckily, long ago, the team had stored roof slabs on some of the higher stairs north of the central workspace and kept shifting blocks upward with the rising platform any time the need arose. It is important to remember, too, that although most of the empty space surrounding the gallery had already been filled in, a narrow catwalk still existed at the south end alongside the west wall. That walkway provided an entrée for workers who wanted to climb up on top of the work platform or the gallery wall.

A feasible strategy has the team transferring the last few ceiling slabs from their lofty work deck on the west side, which stopped a little north of the opening in the roof, over to a group of workers stationed by the east wall. Then a small crew standing on top of the completed sections of the roof immediately north of the hole, together with a second gang posted on the highest corbel in the Antechamber wall, maneuvered the blocks into their slots on the sawtooth blocks. Upon inserting the final slabs for the roof, the walls on three sides of the Grand Gallery and its lid were finally a reality.

• Hidden Staircase? •

One of the strangest features of the Grand Gallery is its ceiling, which — as observed from inside the corridor — was not constructed as either a flat or gabled roof. Instead, it appears to be composed of a series of short steps running north-south. Few researchers have examined the roof's structural components in great detail (or at least, to date, no one has published detailed data about its specific characteristics and dimensions). According to the Griffith theory, however, a reasonable assumption is that engineers chose to construct the roof in this manner for a specific purpose we have yet to fully understand. The intriguing design also opens a window to additional speculation about what other options this particular type of ceiling may have afforded the ancient Egyptians.

At the very least, the builders would have made certain that the top side of the ceiling slabs, which are hidden from view, sat straight up in their slots — level with the horizontal plane of the Great Pyramid. A series of blocks resting on a slant might needlessly complicate the construction process and slow it down. Tilted blocks would have forced workers to compensate for the peaks and angles before setting any more stones on top of the ones already in place as they erected the portion of the pyramid above the gallery's roof.

The roof slabs must be at least eight feet long, given the distance across the top of the Grand Gallery (3' 5") and the width east to west of the saw-toothed blocks in the seventh row that support each end. Based on the concept that the Egyptians were smart and efficient builders, stonecutters must have shaped the sawteeth for these "stringers" to hold the roof slabs upright and keep everything plumb. Because the gallery walls decline at a 26-degree angle, workers did not cut the slots for the ceiling slabs into the finished limestone at a 90-degree angle to the block. A wedge cut perpendicular to the top of the stone would have caused the roof slab slipped inside it to lean forward toward the north end of the passageway.

On the other hand, cutting each slit at an angle to the upper edge of the corbel block — consistent with the slope of the gallery walls — allowed the slabs to sit straight up in their slots. Without accurate measurements, it is impossible to substantiate, but these cuts are probably about six inches deep.

The success of the unusual setup was predicated on at least part of the ceiling slab matching the angle of its slot. Ordinarily, a rectangular block placed in a slanted hole will tip over. That said, to go from a 26-degree incline back to level, workers must have trimmed away part of the roof slab along its base. Significantly, the shaved-off section on the underside, which cuts across the stone east to west, did not extend all the way to the top of the block. The incline started at the bottom of the slab but was not steep enough to reach the upper edge and divide the block in half. It stopped below that point, which left all four sides at the top still squared off. This clever design meant that when workers placed a ceiling slab into the slot atop one of the corbel blocks in the seventh row, the angle along the bottom fit firmly against the side of the opening, but the slab's upper edge remained level with the horizontal plane.

Equally important was how the stringer blocks with the sawteeth linked up within the seventh row. The Griffith theory estimates that every corbel block incorporated two slots on top to support the roof slabs, and the higher (south) face of each stringer block had been trimmed back at the quarry along the upper edge on that side. About six inches deep (the same depth as the sawtooth slots) and running east to west across the block, the cutback left a lip or rim at the south end. As a result, the southern face was not completely flat. The flat part started about six inches below the top of the block. Not surprisingly, the angle of this rim perfectly matched the angle of the slots intended for the ceiling slabs (26 degrees). When the builders lined up two of the corbel blocks end-to-end in the wall, together they formed a complete slot.

The slight setback created by the angled lip on each sawtooth piece fulfilled an important purpose: As work crews lowered the corbel blocks for the seventh row down the top of the gallery walls one by one, lining them up north to south, the flat, even surface on the north face of one block fit neatly into the indentation underneath the lip at the south end of the previous block. The single exception to this basic design was the very first stringer block on both sides at the lower (north) end of the gallery. To account for the gap that occurs when a quadrilateral object resting on an inline meets a vertical plane, stonecutters had angled the north face of the lead pieces to make them sit flush against the stopper blocks at the bottom of the corridor.

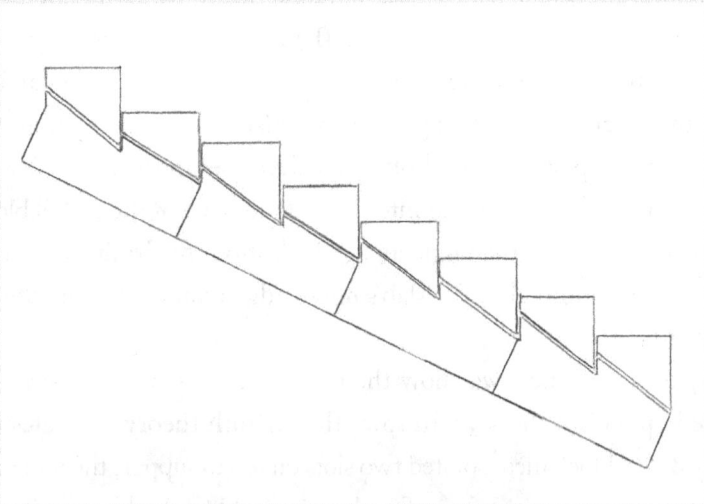

GALLERY CEILING SLABS · STRINGER

Ancient Egyptian stonecutters developed a unique design for the blocks comprising the seventh corbelled row in the Grand Gallery's walls. The jagged upper edges are configured as a sawtooth, which created a series of slots for the roof slabs — two to a block. The southern face on each piece was also shaved back near the top to create the rim that links the individual corbel blocks together.

The suppositions put forward by the Griffith theory beg a separate, even more fascinating question. If the top sides of the ceiling blocks are a sequence of level surfaces climbing from north to south, could they possibly serve as the treads for a hidden staircase above the Grand Gallery? If so, do these steps lead to some sort of concealed chamber or secret route into and out of the building? We can only wonder, but the mere possibility of a hidden set of stairs opens up yet another area of study for anyone seeking to understand the many confounding mysteries of the Great Pyramid.

CHAPTER 17

LEVER ROOM

BY THE TIME THE walls in the Grand Gallery had reached as high as the seventh corbel and it was under roof, the builders' work platform was a tall stack of courses surrounding the compact staging area on Course 49 on three sides. As a result, the square footage inside the prime workspace had contracted to a mere 12 feet across north to south and 30 feet long east to west, leaving little room for either transferring or rearranging blocks and sleds. The big shadoof was still in place, but with the gallery's west wall now standing in the way, work crews had no direct access to the lift to receive the incoming stones for the moment.

It was also during this period of time, in concert with the intense activity to complete the wall at the gallery's south end and build up additional courses, that the team had reduced the size of the northern utility pyramid's center channel. Working their way up level by level, they had narrowed down the shaft and deposited blocks on top of it to enclose the trough, because capping the opening was the only way to build additional courses overhead.

What formerly was a wide, open passageway had become a constricted four-foot by four-foot chute — not much larger than the Horizontal Passage. Although workers would not convert the uppermost portion of the passageway near the top of the utility pyramid into a tunnel for a while, shrinking down the last fully operational center channel marked a major turning point in the construction effort. From then on, conveying humongous blocks of granite and limestone directly into the heart of the Great Pyramid was no longer a possibility.

Defining the Lever Room

The once-spacious work area on Course 49 might be compared to a giant hollow that had been scooped out of the center of the Great Pyramid — but now that space was in the midst of a major transformation. Crews were in the process of turning it into an efficient internal chamber called the Lever Room that was designed to raise the next sequence of limestone blocks up the northern shaft. Although the new chamber was transitory, it would reside at the heart of the Egyptians' construction activities for many decades to come — until work on the monument reached the summit and was nearing completion. Erecting the Lever Room not only launched another memorable chapter in the story of the Great Pyramid; it also offers insight into some of the remarkable techniques the ancient builders employed to overcome seemingly intractable problems.

When the day came to seal up the Great Pyramid, this room would disappear, but in the meantime, it was the reason they were able to keep adding more courses.

Engineers had designed the new chamber for maximum efficiency with a minimal footprint. When fully built out, the space would contain a stepped platform at the center capable of supporting the principal shadoof, as well as a broad ledge or shelf at the north end where the quarried blocks raised by the shadoof would drop onto sleds. The west end of the ledge was where the last vestige of the broad center channel — reduced in size and enclosed like a tunnel — would still exist as a hole above the shelf in the room's north wall. And it was through this aperture that the workers posted outdoors on the northern ramp and harnessed to the ropes would elevate an unending succession of stones.

Work on the Lever Room probably began with the team finishing out the wall delineating the east end of the new chamber. The portion of Course 49 the crew planned to renovate was actually the back side of the Grand Gallery's west wall. And because that wall was corbelled, the surface they needed to rework was not flat. Seven rows of finished Tura limestone blocks stepped back from the spot where the work gang stood, since the wall blocks lining the gallery were pushed inward toward the center of the corridor. Consequently, the reverse side of the wall was a series of narrow steps that the team had to stuff with filler stones to produce a smooth sided Lever Room. Standing on the last vestiges of the catwalk next to the gallery, crews would work their way up, filling in the narrow walkway as they packed the tiered levels to erect an interior wall.

It is important to highlight again that the builders had not deposited any blocks at the east end of the new chamber in the space reserved for the small doorway they wanted to open next to the Great Step. This meant the room's evolving east wall would not be very long north to south, since it could only extend from the blocks on the north side of the reconstituted workspace to the edge of the future opening in the gallery wall. The wall on the opposite (west) side of the Lever Room already existed as the stack of courses that had previously marked the western edge of the center channel. Similarly, the corbelled wall constructed above the ledge on the south side of Course 49 was in place, too.

Over the years, as the courses on the north side of the primary workspace continued to grow taller, those layers had also been stealing further south, until eventually, the pile of blocks reached a stripe on the floor similar to a modern-day chalk line demarcating the northern border of the forthcoming Lever Room. This was also the place where the blocks in the work platform on the north side had made a slight transition. By the time the room was fully constructed, the stacks of filler set along the boundary line drawn on the floor, which were several rows deep at the base, had formed the flat vertical plane of a normal wall.

But approximately 20 feet up from the floor, the mound of filler stepped back to establish a wide ledge in front of what would become the room's actual north wall. In others words, the Lever Room would have a built-in shelf at the north end.

Advance Work

A crucial aspect of the shelf's development was preparing for the featured role it was destined to play many years down the road in joining together the different segments of the air shaft originating from the King's Chamber. Meandering through the course blocks behind the corbelled wall on the south side of Course 49 was a prefabricated portion of that tight passageway. After the air shaft first exited the chamber through the hole in the wall, it traveled north in a straight line for about eight feet, then came to an abrupt end.

Later, the builders lengthened the channel during the process of assembling the narrow band of courses built alongside the King's Chamber. Crews had used those growing layers as their work platform when constructing the granite-lined room and the Relieving Chambers above it.

Exchanging some of the regular filler blocks for pieces precut with a rectangular notch front to back on the underside of the stone, workers set the notched-out pieces end to end, thereby extending the squared-off opening through the line of blocks. After leaving the King's Chamber and crossing the first eight feet, the shaft wended its way piece by piece through the stack of course blocks piled up beside the wall on a slow, upward trajectory and in a general northwesterly direction. The rectangular shaft (5" x 7") eventually ended in a small hole in the corbelled wall above the ledge on Course 49, approximately six feet up from the floor in what would later become the Lever Room's south wall.

Ultimately, the segments of the air shaft previously constructed had to connect with the center channel, which originally ran up the front of the upper utility pyramid on the north side but by now had turned into a much narrower, enclosed chute. Recently reduced to a regular-sized passageway, the reconstituted center channel still climbed upward at a 32-degree angle. But due to the void on Course 49 retained for the Lever Room, it now began at a hole in the room's north wall. The lower edge of the four-foot-tall shaft was even with the top of the built-in shelf on that side, which put it about 20 feet above the floor. As a result, the entrance into what used to be the northern center channel was several feet west and almost 14 feet higher than the opening for the air shaft that came through the corbelled wall on the south side of the new room.

In the future, the ancient builders would connect those two ends. But not yet. Work to join them together and put the finishing touches on the northern air shaft was still many years away. The Egyptians' more immediate concern was making the Lever Room functional because its operations were central to their ability to complete the Great Pyramid.

Yet before they went any further, workers had to assemble the components that would make it possible to join disparate sections of the northern air shaft together down the road. Necessity had required them to put many of the pieces in place beforehand — before ever completing the ledge on the north side of the Lever Room. It appears that the builders had decided to do what they had done at the south end and prefabricate a portion of the anticipated air shaft as they were constructing the shelf. The distance this next segment of the shaft had to cover would extend from the front of the new ledge to the back wall where the four-foot-wide opening representing the former center channel was.

Moving west to east, workers set the first row of blocks for the ledge on the Lever Room floor by overlaying the space from the chalk line to the base of the north wall. Following the placement of course blocks in that relatively small area, a gang laid a second layer over the initial group of filler stones before continuing on up. When the crew reached the row almost directly across from but slightly higher than the hole in the south wall, they took a block cut at an angle on top and added it to the mix, with the slope rising toward the north.

The next steps involved setting a thin slab of a harder material over the ramp stone to act as a liner and installing an insert block on top of the liner. Sporting a squared-off groove seven inches wide and five inches tall and notched out along the bottom, the upside-down U-shaped insert positioned above the angled block was designed to continue the air shaft on the north side of the room. In fact, this block, installed in the ledge's base, would form one of the air shaft's mysterious bends years later, after it hooked up with the segment coming from the opening in the south wall.

Since the bottom of the insert was flat but rested on an incline, the piece tilted downward. As a result, the block the crew added to the row above the insert block was slanted on the bottom to bring everything back to level with the horizontal plane. An even surface was an essential factor in the Egyptians' ability to build the rest of the shelf.

The team packed the next layer for the northside shelf using basically the same procedure. In this instance, they filled in the row up to the point where they wanted a second insert to line up with the first one and reach the opening in the north wall. Given the ledge's dimensions (approximately six feet deep north to south), a logical assumption is that it only took the initial prefabricated section and the current piece to bridge the space. The latest insert would constitute the fourth and final surprising turn in the King's Chamber air shaft, with a small jog toward the northeast.

After depositing an angled block on a slight diagonal in the correct position within the developing row, workers covered it with a hard stone liner. Then they set the notched-out piece of limestone with the rectangular channel directly over the incline. By that time, construction had reached the top of the ledge. The concluding step in fashioning the future air shaft was to lay a limestone block — slanted on the bottom — directly over the latest insert and bring everything back to level.

The extensions to the air shaft that the crew had integrated into the recently completed ledge ended in a small squared-off hole in the floor right below the opening to the channel inside the north wall. True, it sat in an area where team members would have to stand to feed the loaded sleds into that chute, but the size of the cavity in the floor was minimal and would not have interfered with their work. Eventually, the builders would connect the two openings — the one coming through the top of the ledge and the squared-off opening in the north wall — when they begin to close down the Lever Room. Moreover, the relative position of the most-recent sections of the new "pipeline" incorporated into the shelf anticipated future segments traveling across the room from the hole in the south wall and trekking further west at a slight angle — the final links in the chain tying the northern and southern halves of the King's Chamber air shaft together.

The finished ledge was designed to be a little less than 30 feet long east to west, stopping just shy of the far end of the evolving room. Measured north to south, it was wide enough to hold two short stacks of sleds parked side by side near the east end. In addition, in preparation for the time when the loaded sleds would have to make a right turn toward the opening in the north wall, the builders had tweaked the general area around the hole while construction was still underway. Adjustments may have included softening the corner on the east side of the aperture by shaving off the sharp edges on individual wall blocks or adjusting that particular section of the wall by creating a slight curve to produce a gentler angle for rotating the sleds toward the shaft.

Engineers had also devised the ledge to be tall enough for a worker to stand on once the room had its ceiling, by introducing a series of corbels overhead. The extra headroom they created above the shelf, which would reach a height equal to the upper row of corbels in the room's south wall, left a sufficient amount of vertical space to accommodate a worker. This detail is particularly pertinent, especially in terms of the available workspace on either side of the chute that contained the ropes connected to the pullers outdoors. In the end, the workers positioned next to the hole inside the Lever Room who were continuously feeding loaded sleds into the passageway would permit the ancient Egyptians to finish erecting their pyramid.

LEVER ROOM INTERIOR
The interior of the Lever Room.

Final Touches

As soon as the Lever Room's fourth and last (north) wall was set, the moment arrived to enclose what little remained of the unoccupied portion of Course 49 by roofing over the revamped space. Erecting a ceiling would once and for all put a cap on the gaping void at the center of the Great Pyramid that had made construction possible. At this juncture, the Grand Gallery, the corbelled wall above the entrance to the Antechamber, and the wall at the south end of the Lever Room were all seven corbels high. Likewise, the recently completed wall with the stepped-back ledge at the north end of the incipient room climbed that high. Now it was just a matter of work crews placing roof slabs across the approximately seven-foot-wide fissure they were converting into the Lever Room. The Egyptians had bridged much deeper, larger, and far more daunting gaps before.

In terms of practical floor space, the distance across the Lever Room north to south was about six feet, but the dimensions of the room as a whole are deceptive, due to the extra footage added to the total from the presence of the ledge. It had both shrunk the actual floor space and pushed back the rear wall by another six feet or so. These measurements also fail to take into account an additional, unique factor affecting the ceiling's design: the south wall. While the bottom of this wall was a smooth vertical plane, the upper portion consisted of a series of seven corbels, projecting three additional inches toward the center of the room with every row. As a result, the top of the south wall was almost 21 inches closer to the north side of the room than its base.

As far as the north wall was concerned, it culminated in three rows of corbels, which also protruded toward the center of the space and the corbelled wall located on the south side. When crews were erecting the portion of the north wall behind the ledge, they had pushed each block in the last three rows forward so the piece of stone jutted out from the one underneath it by at least a foot. A 12-inch overhang was possible because workers were able to cover the back (north) end of the blocks with enough filler to make them stable as the work platform was being developed on that side. In other words, the weight of the stacks of blocks surrounding the corbels prevented them from falling forward. Not surprisingly, the proximity of the uppermost corbels at both ends of the room had a bearing on the size of the roof slabs since the hole the team needed to cover — a gap approximately seven feet wide — was not huge.

The limestone slabs for the Lever Room's ceiling were long enough to span the length of the space north to south, with some hangover at either end to help hold them securely in place. Given the size of the slabs, the team would have hauled in the pieces beforehand and stowed them on the storage steps with all of the other bulky blocks before enclosing the south end of the Grand Gallery. The prospect of roofing over the Lever Room also seems more plausible when viewed from the perspective of the bigger picture. On the whole, the method the team employed to add a roof was primarily a matter of using the horizontal surface of the work platform behind the north wall — currently as tall as the roof of the Grand Gallery — to transfer the stored blocks one by one over to the appropriate spots in the ceiling. Another feature to consider is that work gangs also had access to additional shadoofs and sleds situated on the uppermost steps of what remained of the original northern utility pyramid. Such equipment would have assisted them in relocating the roof slabs crews had transported on-site years earlier as the need arose.

Before the Lever Room's ceiling going on, the Egyptians had gathered filler stones and fabricated a platform for the big shadoof in the middle of the chamber. The deck they assembled probably had steps on three sides to help crew members climb on top more easily. The value of such a sizable shadoof to the success of the enterprise cannot be overstated, and positioning it correctly was key.

First, raising the equipment off the floor shortened the distance between the device and the ledge where the blocks delivered into the room ultimately were headed. Second, the room measured 30 feet east to west, and although the bulky shadoof was only able to pivot a few degrees back and forth, it had a long arm. The back end, which held the counterweight, required enough unobstructed space to clear the west wall and at the same time, permit the apparatus to turn freely. No doubt the builders also wanted to leave some room near the back end to be able to store the extra stones they would add to or subtract from the counterweight as the size of the loads shifted. All told, the setup imposed any number of constraints, but the condensed space the Egyptians had developed as their Lever Room seemed to resolve them all.

Gateway

A ceiling was in progress, but the Lever Room was not done yet. Since from now on, access from above would be impossible because the space was covered, the builders had to provide a way for both workers and materials to gain entry into the room. In an incredible act of foresight and creativity, they solved the problem by fashioning a doorway from a standing wall: the west wall of the Grand Gallery. Removing the two blocks adjacent to the Great Step on the west side directly below the "lintel" block (the southernmost block in the first row of corbels), the ancient pyramid builders would expose an opening whose primary purpose was to transmit the stones brought up on the lift.

Workers removed the upper wall block from the stack of two under the header first. To begin the process, they placed a pair of rectangular filler stones side by side on the Lever Room floor, next to the gallery wall, to create a foundation for the procedure. Then they arranged a couple of wooden wedges cut at a 26-degree angle — the same angle as the sides of the gallery — on top of the foundation stones to receive the eight-foot-long wall block. Imagine a single wedge resembling a right triangle approximately six feet long with a hypotenuse of 26 degrees. Then imagine it cut in half. When the pieces were reassembled and set end to end lengthwise to become one long wedge again, they formed a continuous 26-degree angle along the top. The reason for cutting the wedge in two was to permit workers to remove it in stages as the operation unfolded.

Pushing the upper block for the new doorway forward (west) toward the interior of the Lever Room, workers slid it onto the wedges, maintaining the same 26-degree angle as the wall. Because the wedges were not quite as long as the piece of limestone, almost one-quarter of the block at the south end had nothing underneath it. This gap between the filler blocks at the base and the underside of the wall block was where a work gang set chunks of wood to use as leverage points. Taking long-handled levers, the crew jacked up the wall block high enough to remove the original wedges one at a time as they slowly lowered the slab down until it lay in a horizontal position on top of the blocks at the base. Then, by employing wooden rails or a temporary stone ramp, the team slid the block they had just removed from the wall down to the Lever Room floor before shoving it toward the middle of the space to make room for the next one.

For the block that sat lower in the side wall, the crew carried away the filler stones used as the foundation for the previous piece and set the wedges on the floor. After that, they simply pushed the block forward onto the two wedges to free it from its slot, jacked up the stone, and — after pulling the wedges out from underneath — laid the slab on the floor. Once both wall blocks were inside the room, the workers pushed them together flush with the Great Step to form a short platform or runway.

It is also worth noting that the upper and lower wall blocks and the Great Step had something important in common: The blocks from the gallery wall were as thick as the step is tall (36 inches). As a result, when all three blocks were lined up in a row, together they formed a smooth plane stretching from the top of the Great Step to the far end of the brief runway, jutting into the Lever Room. Since the blocks in the west wall show no signs of undue wear and tear today, the Egyptians may have also added a layer of protection on top of the stone platform.

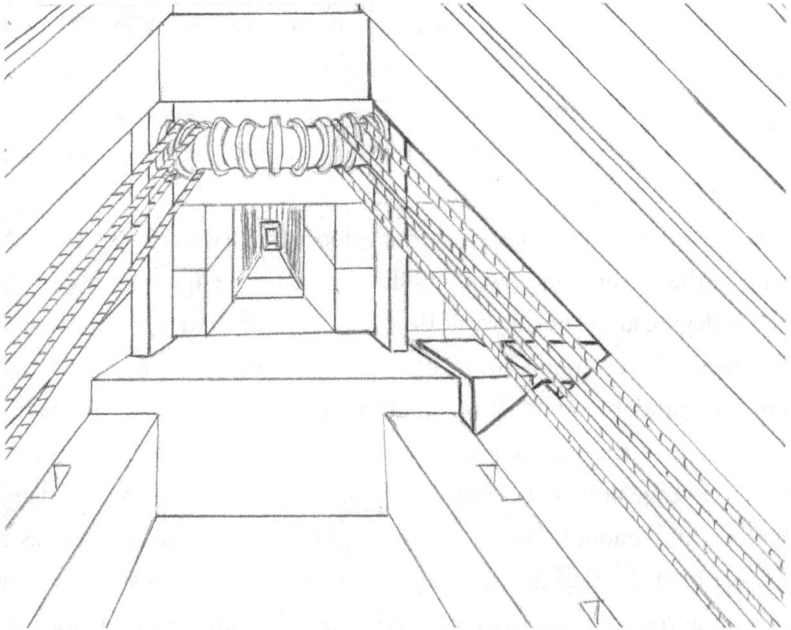

LEVER ROOM DOORWAY

According to the Griffith theory, the ancient Egyptians created an opening in the Grand Gallery's west wall, which led to the Lever Room (see area outlined in black on the right). The blocks for the later courses, along with other supplies and raw materials, would pass through this small doorway on their way to the upper levels of the pyramid.

New Routes

The team was simultaneously in the midst of adjusting the configuration of the ropes and pulleys to take advantage of the altered set of circumstances. For many years, the two rectangular holes at the back end of the Great Step had held a pulley-stand with a set of ropes dedicated to helping raise the lift. The revised operation, now oriented toward the Lever Room, also demanded the use of a pulley atop the Great Step. But this time, the Egyptians could not merely repurpose the old one because that stand was not tall enough. Ropes coming from the prior (shorter) pulley would have draped across the new doorway and/or drooped onto the middle of the step, impeding the crew handling the incoming stones. The upshot was that the builders mounted a different pulley-stand — taller than the header block located above the door in the west wall — so the lines dangling from its roller would stay above the opening during their descent down the ramp to connect to the lift.

Earlier modifications to the rigging, which steered the lines down the sides of the lift, had turned out to be an auspicious move for one more unexpected reason. The spot at the top of the ramp where the lift normally parked was about to change.

The reality was that the vehicle had to move up a little higher for the blocks it carried to be able to take the quickest and most direct route through the doorway into the Lever Room. From now on, the lift would ascend the gallery ramp as high as possible until it was resting against the Great Step. Instead of stopping a few feet back, the vehicle would keep inching forward until its deck sat head-to-head with the step's front edge, forming a contiguous, even plane. Obviously, if the ropes were allowed to drop down into the middle of that space, they would become entangled with the workers attempting to transfer the blocks.

The lift's new termination point allowed the team to move a pile of blocks transported up the gallery ramp more efficiently, since they would be able to push the stones across a flat, unbroken surface before dispatching them through the hole in the gallery wall. Arguably, this latest phase of the construction process was less challenging in terms of the overall size of the limestone pieces work crews had to manipulate. Nevertheless, the process was time-consuming because the undersized entrance into the Lever Room meant the blocks had to be inserted one by one.

In and Up

Systems were now duly organized to begin erecting the next 100+ courses of the Great Pyramid. Once the piece of limestone started down the short runway leading into the new room on the opposite side of the gallery's west wall, a work gang stationed near the doorway prepared to put a choker around it. It may be that workers had positioned the two wall slabs on the floor to leave a few inches of space between them. The gap would have provided enough room to wrap a length of rope with an eyelet at each end around the middle of the block and prepare to elevate it. Then the crew would hook the loop at the top of the choker onto the shadoof.

At the same time, the crew assigned to the ledge by the north wall was pulling another sled into position. The shadoof's job was simple: Take the blocks coming through the hole in the gallery wall and deposit them one by one onto the sleds stowed on the ledge. After the shadoof picked up the piece by its choker and made a slight rotation northward, it set the limestone into the wooden cradle built into the bottom of the carrier. When the sled had its block and the crew on the shelf had removed the choker, they made use of the pull-ropes coming down the chute to drag it west toward the opening in the north wall. Then, a second work gang attached the latest sled to the back end of the last one in line.

After setting four loaded sleds in a row and linking them together in a chain, the team positioned the vehicles directly below the entrance to the chute. A worker standing on the ledge stationed by the hole in the wall made certain everything was aligned before the signal was given and the short train began moving uphill through the passageway. As had happened countless times in the past, the innovative techniques the Egyptians had perfected prevailed as they raised four heavily laden sleds up hundreds of feet — to the debarkation point on Course 98.

The setup for raising blocks to the higher courses was in the midst of a makeover but similar to the techniques applied over the course of many years. The builders would rely on the strength of an army of workers based outdoors to provide the critical pulling power. The pulley-stand on the 98th course, which held the long set of ropes extending down the north side of the pyramid, was still functional. At one end, the lines dropped through the chute into the Lever Room and were fastened to the sled-train. At the other end, they proceeded along the exterior wall to the teams of pullers lined up on the steps of the northern ramp.

By now, the blocks were following a well-worn path through the Lever Room and the shaft ascending behind its north wall. After the stones exited that tunnel on Course 98, a shadoof assembled on the same level as the pulley-stand picked up the blocks in sequence and placed them on other sleds positioned nearby. Then the work gangs took hold of the newly loaded vehicles and pulled them over to their assigned quadrants, positioning the Tura limestone for the corners and façade around the pyramid's circumference before packing the space behind it with filler stones.

Bear in mind that the sleds coming up the chute eventually had to return to the Lever Room to receive more blocks, which added a fresh dynamic into the situation. Because the enormous ropes used for construction were so thick and heavy, and an empty sled so light, workers may have tied a weight behind the last sled in line or attached a smaller work-rope to the back end to help them drag the short train back down the shaft after it was unloaded.

The process of handing off the blocks to a shadoof at the top of the chute and loading up individual sleds worked for about five or six courses — as high as the device's arm was able to reach. The pole on the shadoof up top did not extend very far, which rendered it impossible for the apparatus to make contact with a small sled situated many levels above the course where the machine stood. The Egyptians faced a dilemma: How to get access to more courses?

One possible solution would be to deposit angled blocks along the edge of subsequent courses and create ramps to continue moving additional stones to the upper levels. But by its very nature, any useful ramp would have to keep growing at a formidable angle as the layers of new courses grew. Consequently, when the shadoof at the top of the shaft on Course 98 had attained its limit in terms of how high it could realistically reach, the builders reconfigured their operation again.

CHAPTER 18

SCALING THE WALL

Up to now, the Egyptians had been able to construct about 50 percent of the Great Pyramid's courses by sheer pulling power as sleds and supplies wended their way through the rooms and passageways that existed within the interior of the structure. For the final portion of their monument, the builders would use one of the exterior walls to convey the course blocks skyward and, layer by layer, bring them closer to the peak. Granted, the surface area the team intended to cover with stones would steadily shrink on the way up to the top, but the length and breadth of the mammoth pyramid meant that it would still take many decades and an extraordinary amount of material and persistence to complete.

Course 98 was a flexion point. It held the critical pulley-stand at the top of the Lever Room shaft that supplied the blocks, and a shadoof to transfer them from one sled to another. This was why the builders had never encroached on the flat area near the chute where the two devices stood. Even as Courses 99 through about 106 were taking shape, crews had maintained an even surface around the machines — an area large enough to contain the equipment and accommodate the succession of loaded sleds surfacing at the top of the channel from the Lever Room. Workers had isolated a sufficient amount of space by packing each layer only up to the edge of the floor in that limited area.

The buildup of filler stones eventually resulted in a high wall spanning three sides of an approximately 20-foot-wide expanse, with the courses rimming the east and west ends following the contours and angle of the exterior wall. The outcome was that two of the walls bordering the open space were slanted. In short, the Egyptians had purposely engineered a chink in the north wall by leaving out blocks to create a setback halfway up the side of the

Great Pyramid. Workers would deposit the casing stones for the façade and the lower-grade limestone filler to close up the hollow at a later date — when construction no longer required the use of a pulley and shadoof on Course 98 or the flat surface where the equipment was mounted.

The general idea was to send the rest of the blocks arriving at the setback from the Lever Room to the exterior wall on a specially designed sled. The niche in the side of the pyramid was the spot where the transfer from inside to outside would occur. The decision to use the angle of the outer wall as a ramp and launch a sled transporting blocks up the pyramid's northern face was eminently practical. The team had organized the process knowing that they were running out of options since the single remaining incline from the tallest internal utility pyramid had risen as far as it could possibly go. The same question that has confounded scholars for centuries confronted the ancient Egyptians then: What kind of ramp would permit them to construct their Great Pyramid? In this case, the answer was staring them in the face. The ramp they needed was already there.

Equally relevant was that the amount of force required to raise a stationary load from the bottom of the pyramid up a 52-degree incline — the slope on the exterior wall — was enormous. On the other hand, having the ability to deploy that same burden from a starting point halfway up the side of the building gave the Egyptians' plans a significant boost. It was also true that to initiate this revised approach, the team first had to haul a sizable empty sled up the wall from the northern platform. And if the strategy to employ the side of the Great Pyramid as a ramp were to be successful, it also demanded further accommodations.

Longboat

The style of the 15-foot-long sled the builders would deploy to scale the north wall was different from previous versions they had engaged. Picture a sleek vehicle with a wide, flat section down the middle. The bottom was composed of a thick piece of wood, beveled on both sides, with a pair of low runners underneath. The sled's "stern" was fenced in by taller boards fastened to the back end, as well as halfway down each side, leaving free space near the front to transfer the blocks it conveyed onto the various courses. The three-sided box ringing the back half of the vehicle was there to prevent the stones from falling off and tumbling down the wall as it crawled uphill. In addition, holes drilled along the backboard's upper edge provided openings for attaching a set of pull-ropes. Workers had also wrapped the sledge's underside in a rug or other type of soft material to cushion the bottom and protect the polished limestone in the cladding from scratches.

Perhaps the most significant addendum to the description of the wall-sled was its connection to the pyramidal structure itself. It is no great surprise that much of the research on the Great Pyramid has traditionally focused on the interior spaces, including its most prominent passageways and rooms, such as the Grand Gallery or the King's and Queen's Chambers. But the key to accurately analyzing this monument is understanding that every one of the spaces currently identified as representing the core of the pyramid — from the Subterranean Chamber to the apex of the Relieving Chambers — sits off-center. They reside in the eastern half of the edifice almost 24 feet away from the building's actual north-south centerline. The significance of that offset was far-reaching.

In the case of the Lever Room, the opening for the chute was near the room's west end, which placed the shaft with the pull-ropes much closer to the authentic midpoint of the Great Pyramid. As a consequence, the Griffith theory maintains that the two exterior sleds the Egyptians deployed (they would put a second, smaller version into service later) traveled upward along the true center of the north wall. This position placed the vehicles in a direct line with the peak of the capstone yet to come. Assuming the hypothesis is correct, it explains one more noteworthy detail about the exterior sleds. Because the Great Pyramid is in reality an eight-sided building, all four faces contain indentations where separate sections of the walls meet — precisely at the center on each side. That shallow wedge is where the wall sleds were going to ride. For this reason, each vehicle was slightly beveled on its port and starboard sides, which allowed the flat bottom to sit inside the narrow groove and use the concave line down the middle of the wall as its guide.

The only sensible way to safely transport a fully loaded sled up the steep angle of the outer wall, especially one as cumbersome as what we are calling the longboat, was to build in a few stopgap measures. The builders needed a guarantee that in the event their equipment ever failed, the sledge would not fall too far or, even worse, slide downhill like a runaway semi on a mountain road and crash to the bottom. To that end, they constructed a stone barricade at Course 98 to function as an interim docking station.

The overall plan of attack was to position the exterior sled west of the setback on the 98th course and proceed up the north wall. With that approach in mind, crews took several blocks of the Tura limestone cladding west of the setback on the same level as the floor and exchanged them for different pieces. Workers replaced the white casing stones from the exterior wall with blocks of the less-valuable, standard limestone, which they turned in the opposite direction to make them slant outward — square to the 52-degree angle of the pyramid. The new line of blocks installed a few feet over from the edge of the recess in the wall formed the barrier or stopping point where the wall-sled would rest.

Pulleys at Each End

The reformulated systems and procedures spawned by the Lever Room coming online, and the decision to have a large sled ascend the outer surface of the pyramid, obliged the Egyptians to reconfigure equipment and rigging across the site. The set of ropes suspended from the pulley on Course 98, which was connected to the chain of sleds moving through the chute from the Lever Room at one end and a team of pullers on the northern ramp at the other, did not change. But now two more pulleys entered the picture when workers placed a stand on the north side and a second one on the south side of the latest and highest available course. Supported inside substantial four-legged wooden frames, each pulley-roller was outfitted with its own set of lines. The team would use the north- and south-side pulleys to raise the large sled loaded with quarried blocks up the outside wall to erect the uppermost layers the Great Pyramid.

Workers had also surrounded the devices, made to be strong but trans-portable, with heavy blocks piled around the base to brace the apparatus and stabilize its movement as they proceeded to assemble each course. Laying down blocks from the outer edge of the pyramid toward the center, the groups filling in the new level always stopped a little bit short of the pulleys, which left a deepening hole around the legs of the two frames. After assembling a few courses, then taking some of the tension off the ropes, crews dismantled the pulleys by lifting the parts out of the shallow cavities and inserting filler blocks into the depressions in the floor. Once the work gangs had built up the bottom of the cavity so the pulley-stand was able to sit higher, they set the machines back inside their holes and began constructing more layers. Besides using assorted filler blocks brought up on the sled, the team probably left the stabilizing blocks at the bottom of the holes thereby incorporating those stones into the surrounding course before moving on to assemble the next one.

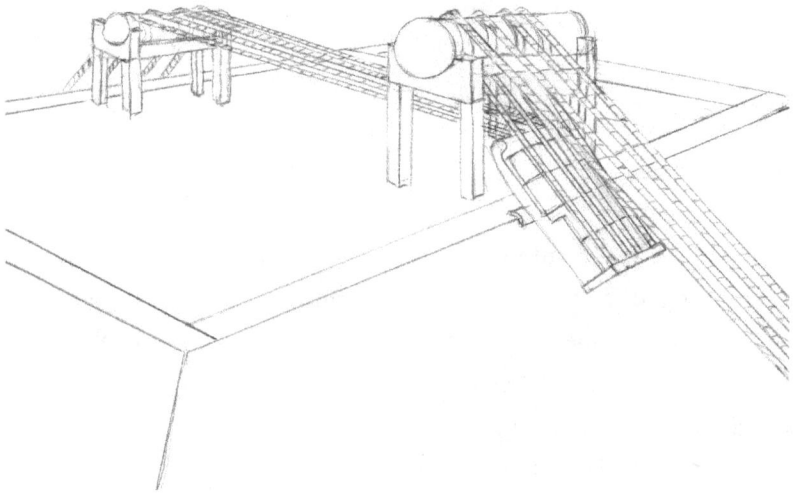

PULLEYS FOR WALL SLED

Pulleys mounted on the north and south sides of the latest course were used to raise the wall-sled from its docking station at Course 98.

The amount of strength required to pick up and relocate a pair of pulleys carrying the weight of extremely heavy ropes was formidable. Yet while the exercise required a significant amount of preplanning and occasional modifications, it, too, eventually became routine. Pulleys across the building site included braking mechanisms to slow down and/or lock the ropes into place, which gave workers some degree of control over the massive lines.

Furthermore, the Egyptians, who were experts in rope-making and its applications, were not only proficient in the art of improvised rigging but conversant in all sorts of hitches, loops, and knots.

For example, the team no doubt employed a knot similar to a stopper hitch to draw up enough slack to be able to repeatedly dismantle, rebuild, and reconnect the pulley-stands on the north and south sides. Laborers around the site would occasionally use ropes to rig up swings or other types of lines to hang from equipment such as a pulley-stand whenever the situation called for it. In other words, similar to the ironworkers and rock-climbers of today, these ancient builders understood the most efficient, effective — and safest — methods for managing their gear to achieve the ultimate goal.

Maintaining a pulley at the south end of each level dramatically increased the available pulling power due to the presence of hundreds of people stationed outdoors on that side of the building. A set of ropes connected to this pulley extended down the pyramid's southern face. After passing over the rollers mounted on the exterior wall as they descended, and weaving through the pulley-stands on the ground, the lines continued toward the south and the throng of pullers assigned to haul up the load. The set of pulleys at the base of the pyramid on the south side, which were secured between large stone blocks planted in the ground, had been there since the very first utility pyramid was erected behind the Queen's Chamber.

The other end of those same ropes stretched all the way across the course-in-progress to a roller installed at floor level on the upper edge of the opposite (north) wall. Made from stone or possibly acacia wood, the roller was similar to the one located at the top of the northern ramp where the incline intersected with the horizontal platform in front of the construction entrance. To lock the new roller in place, crews left out a piece of the façade and the chunk of filler directly behind it. Then they used the empty space for the specially designed block cradling the fat dowel. After the southern ropes passed over the roller on the edge of the floor, they continued down to the big sledge resting against the side of the building, where a work gang attached the lines coming from the south to the vehicle's front end.

A separate set of ropes managed by a crew assigned to the opposite side of the pyramid climbed up the north face. Two sets of pullers occupied the northern ramp. The first one lifted the chain of sleds through the shaft in the Lever Room while a second group was tasked with the job of raising the loaded sled up the outer wall. Once the ropes associated with the team handling the wall-sled reached the pulley-stand mounted on the north side of the current course, they circled around it, turned back, and proceeded down the face of the building toward the longboat.

Aiming this bunch of ropes toward the sled's back end, workers tied off the lines by threading them through the holes drilled into the wooden backboard. Securing the ropes to the highest part of the carrier achieved a couple of objectives. First, the way the sled was outfitted held the lines above the blocks moving on and off its deck, which meant the pull-ropes would not hinder the process of transferring stones directly onto the level under construction. Second, higher lines would provide greater maneuverability when it was time to pull the sled onto the even surface of a course.

Loading Up

The same shadoof, which had been hard at work removing blocks from the sleds that arrived at Course 98, also loaded the giant sled hanging on the exterior wall. Instead of turning to drop the pieces onto smaller sleds standing by on a neighboring course, the shadoof grabbed each of the four stones landing in the setback by their chokers and lined them up inside the wall sledge from front to back. As part of the operation, workers probably removed the chokers from the blocks and sent the lengths of rope back down to the Lever Room in the empty sled-train so the people working below could reuse them.

At a signal, the army of workers posted outdoors on the north and south sides began to pull, raising the load up the north wall to the current course. When the sled arrived at its destination and its nose was peeking over the edge of the wall, the front end reached a natural tipping point where the vehicle balanced for a moment on the rim before tilting onto the floor as the pullers dragged it forward.

Besides keeping the lines away from the sides of the vehicle to remove the blocks it transported more efficiently, tying the ropes coming from the north side to the sled's back end also permitted the workers to inch the carrier onto the course without having it run into its own lines. And strange as it may seem, the dimensions and design of the longboat actually allowed it to move between the legs of the northern pulley-stand. When the crew on the northern ramp stopped pulling and let the rope slack off slightly, the southern team was able to draw the sled onto the surface of the course without the other set of pull-ropes interfering with its progress.

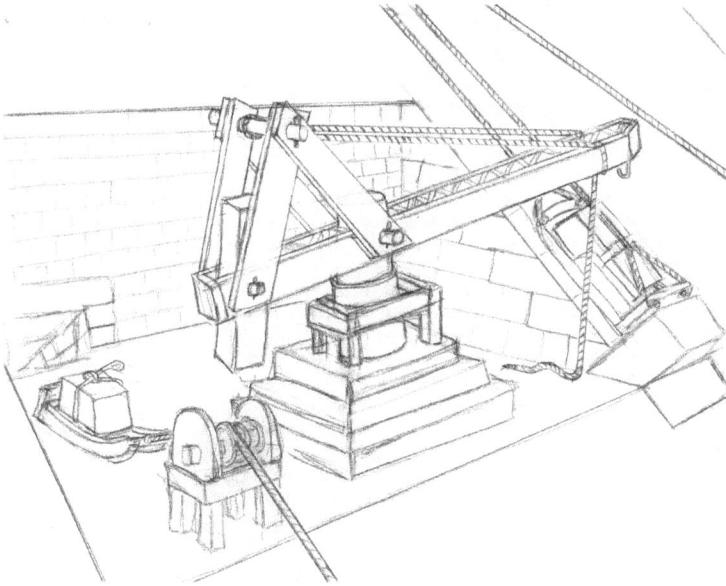

WALL SLED - LOADING

The niche on the north side of the pyramid at Course 98 was the transfer station for the raw materials moving up the outer wall.

Once the vehicle had tipped forward and moved far enough into the open space so its stern was stationary, sitting solidly on the level surface of the floor, the pull halted. In truth, workers never moved the sled very far from the edge of the north wall because another shadoof mounted nearby was available to unload the blocks it carried. Similar to most of the shadoofs at the site, this one could be taken apart and reassembled course by course.

The process of unloading and distributing the building blocks for the upper levels of the pyramid was not very complicated. Whenever the sledge conveying a load of limestone reached the course-in-progress and was firmly grounded, crews prepared the stones for the next leg of their journeys by wrapping chokers around them. Then the local shadoof picked up the blocks individually and deposited them on smaller sleds, which the work gangs took in hand and transported to the appropriate zones.

Sending the longboat back to its docking station probably involved adding more bulk for the return trip to help stabilize the vehicle by overcoming the weight of the heavy ropes as it traveled down the side of the pyramid. Several members of the crew would have initiated the process by pushing the sled over the edge of the wall. Sometimes a few people may have climbed into the carrier to add more heft, using their bodies as ballast for the trip down the wall. The more likely scenario, however, has the builders attaching a length of everyday rope to the back end, which a team standing at the setback at Course 98 would tug on to assist in lowering the empty sled toward the dock.

Meanwhile, up on the developing course, a familiar pattern had kicked in. Work gangs transported the sleds carrying single blocks over to their assigned quadrants to either insert a piece of Tura limestone for the cladding or add filler to the rows of blocks they had already amassed. Once the new pieces were in place, workers moved their empty sleds carrying only the chokers back toward the shadoof near the edge of the wall to await more stones.

Course after course, construction continued as the Great Pyramid rose ever skyward. The builders' methods would essentially remain the same for as many as 100 courses — until approximately Course 207, when the team faced a unique set of circumstances. The reality was that every time crews removed the pulley-stands from a completed course only to reassemble them in anticipation of erecting more layers, the square footage on the next course under construction would be a bit smaller than the one they had just finished. As a result, the two devices were slowly creeping closer to each other with every completed level. Given the situation, as the buildout neared the pyramid's summit, the square footage on top would gradually shrink down to a size where the pulley-stands literally stood back-to-back. When the machines almost touched and thus were in too close a proximity to be able to operate properly, the Egyptians switched out their building methods again.

CHAPTER 19

THE SUMMIT

THE ANCIENT EGYPTIANS HAD finally built up to Course 207, only three courses below what scholars believe was the apex of the Great Pyramid. During this period of construction, the surface area on top had contracted to a 10.5-foot by 10.5-foot square, which was compact enough to launch the next phase of the buildout. If someone could stand on that small platform after the pyramid was finished, they would have been able to reach up and touch the bottom edge of the capstone. The builders had also replaced the 15-foot-long sled sometime earlier with a smaller, more agile version about six feet long to carry the supplies up the exterior wall.

Rather than dismantle the pulleys on the north and south sides, the builders would continue to employ the one at the north end to raise a majority of the remaining blocks and equipment. The pulley on the south side, while for the most part no longer tasked with lifting, would nevertheless play an important role in what happened next. Before their work was done, the Egyptians would make use of the solid frames and industrial-sized rollers on both pulley-stands in a variety of inventive ways.

The most significant change made to the pulleys before the scaled-down sled was deployed was to reduce the number of pull-ropes, leaving a single rope on each machine. Not only did a total of eight thick ropes eat up valuable space in an extremely tight area, the weight of the upcoming loads did not warrant such massive lines. Three ropes on the south side were the first to go. But before the crew let them drop, the workers at the base of the pyramid moved back, stretching the lines as far south as they could be extended. And when the lines that remained on the summit finally slid down the side of the building, resulting in three enormous heaps at the bottom, crews prepared to gather them up for storage.

Similar to snatching one end of a ball of twine to unwind it, the workers had maintained access to a free end on each line because the pull team had drawn the ropes straight back from the south wall. As a consequence, the cleanup crew was able to efficiently address what otherwise might have been an intractable mess. The pull-rope decommissioning process took some time because the gangs stationed on the ground had to manipulate the heavy ropes by coiling them into a series of loops, which they placed in an orderly fashion in the direction of the pyramid. The layout resembled long rows of coiled-up garden hoses, with each mound small enough for a worker to carry it on a shoulder. On the north side, the pull-ropes would remain as is for a while. The team would not eliminate the initial three lines by sending them down to the platform at the bottom until they had elevated the necessary materials to erect the apex of the Great Pyramid.

ROPE CIRCLES

A wall painting in the tomb of Pharoah Seti I depicts workers carrying sections of a long, coiled rope.

Walk-Boards

The first item on the agenda was to determine workspace for the crews so they could keep building. An approximately 10-foot-square area holding two oversized pulley-stands did not offer a lot of room to maneuver, much less install additional courses or mount a capstone. The builders' strategy was to haul up exceptionally strong boards — at least 14 feet long, two feet wide, and four inches thick — and create a walkway around the top of the unfinished pyramid. A span of 10 feet across provided an extra two feet at either end, since the planks extended beyond the corners of the floor.

In anticipation of assembling a set of wooden pick boards, the wall-sled had transported the necessary hand tools, climbing ropes, and related equipment to the top.

While the general supplies had ridden up on the sled, the boards for the new catwalk were bound together and came up the north wall on their own. Included in the bundle were the planks for the north and south sides, which had straps or metal U-brackets attached to the undersides at both ends. Two more boards without any hardware on the bottom, designated for the east and west walls, accompanied them. Workers had cushioned the bundle by wrapping it in some sort of soft material before winding the pull-ropes around the package. Employing the northern pulley, the crew assigned to move the load raised the set of walk-boards up to the top, where a second team dragged it toward the center of the space. Removing the pull-ropes and the outer covering, they separated the pieces of wood and tied shorter lines around the set of planks with the brackets.

To give the new platform greater stability and strength, the Egyptians had made another tactical decision: to brace the catwalk. Four units of pre-fabricated lattice-style scaffolding designed to fit beneath the two-foot-wide walk-boards and sit 90 degrees to the platform were banded together in a bundle, swathed in thick fabric, and raised up the north wall. Once all of the necessary equipment and materials reached the summit, workers locked down one of the ropes on the northern pulley and freed the other three before signaling the group on the ramp below to pull and let them fall to the bottom.

The plan was to create a narrow platform for the work crew in preparation for bringing up a quartet of heavy beams longer than a telephone pole and erecting a pyramid-shaped structure overhead. The tall pyramidal frame was where the builders planned to install a reconstituted set of pulleys for the next part of the job. Soon, after attaching themselves to ropes fastened to the legs on the two pulley-stands, a couple of work gangs swung a short distance down the sides of the building and got into position to catch the first two planks dropped from above. Using brute strength, the crew standing on top of the finished course lowered the initial pair of boards for the work platform down the north and south sides, halting when the wood was about two feet below the upper edge of the wall. Then they tied off the planks.

After the pieces dangling over the edges were in place, the people at the top let down the board for the walkway's east side. And while that one was still suspended in the air, the workers hanging from the ropes by the northeast and southeast corners took hold of the new plank and pushed the ends into the brackets fastened to the bottom of the initial two boards. Knotting lengths of rope around the corners where the planks overlapped hitched them together and secured the joint. The process repeated itself on the west side until all four sections of the platform were connected. With each board pressed firmly against the side of the pyramid, which flared out, the tops of the planks sat level to the horizontal plane.

When the package holding the X-bracing reached the top, crew members separated the individual units in preparation for the next step. Now they lowered the braces one by one over the outside edge of the catwalk toward the workers hanging from the ropes anchored to the pulley-stands. The job of the teams suspended below was to maneuver the scaffolding into position underneath the walk-boards on all four sides. One method for attaching the walkway on top to the struts underneath involved carpenters pre-drilling a series of holes down the length of the platform's 14-foot-long planks when they originally trimmed the boards. The precut slots allowed the work gangs to insert the short wooden slats jutting up from the support frames into those holes and pin the two pieces — the plank on top and the scaffolding underneath — together.

When the walk-boards had their supports, it was time to tighten up the bracing to maintain the rigidity of the platform and hold the wooden substructure firmly against the walls. In this case the Egyptians' extensive knowledge of knots and hitches proved to be the solution. Operating in tandem, the people on the swings wrapped a couple of ropes all the way around the scaffolding until both loops encircled the entire pyramid. The distance involved was not significant — the workers on the ropes were hanging a few feet below a course that was only a 10-foot square.

Then the crew introduced a dowel between the lines near the midpoint on all four sides, employing the same principle as what in modern parlance is called a come-along. Rotating the heavy sticks in sync on alternate sides of the pyramid (north-south/east-west) twisted the ropes and made them tighter, which, in turn, pulled the wooden latticework closer together and stiffened up the frame. When the lines finally became taut and the walkway was as solid as if it were bolted down, workers locked the four turn-sticks into place so nothing would slacken off or sag.

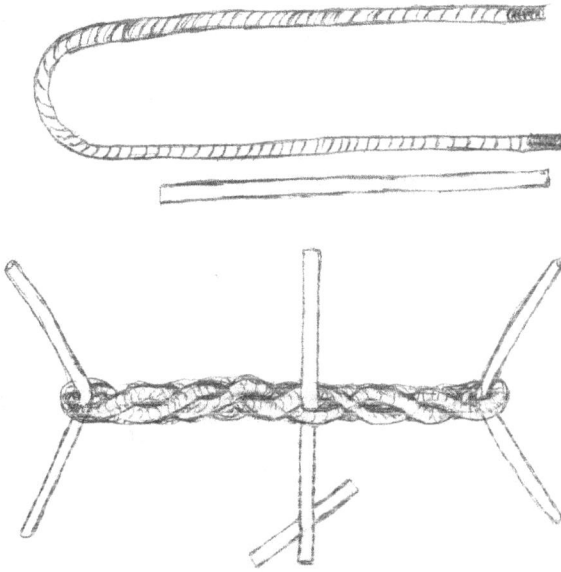

COME-ALONG

Modern construction workers employ a device now called the come-along, defined as a hand-operated winch with a ratchet that is used to pull objects. Often employed to help pull two joints together, the come-along tightens up the space in between them. The ancient Egyptians applied the same principle by using a wooden stick inserted between a double-looped rope wrapped around a couple of objects. Twisting the stick to shorten the rope drew the items closer together by slowly eliminating the space that separated them.

Pyramid Over Pyramid

Another prominent feature distinguished the boards set on the north and south sides of the walkway. They must have come from giant, old-growth trees because in addition to being at least four inches thick, they featured a pair of knobs with holes drilled through the middle jutting up from the boards at either end. The knobs carved out of the plank were designed to hold a set of extremely tall wooden beams. When inserted at the corners and leaned toward the center of the uppermost course, these beams would form a peak higher than the apex of the Great Pyramid was going to be someday. But first the builders had to transport the massive timbers up to the flat area at the top of their unfinished pyramid.

Now that the catwalk — their work platform — was a reality, the team had to make a series of adjustments before the next stage of construction could proceed. Because the new walk-boards projected out from the sides of the building, the two-foot-wide outcropping produced an obstacle for anything riding up the outside wall.

Engineers had to find a way to move a loaded sled and the related equipment over that hump. The answer was to build a short wooden ramp and connect it to the walkway at the center of the north wall.

Such a wedge lying against the outer surface of the pyramid, bridging the gap between the wall's 52-degree slope and the overhang resulting from the catwalk, would create a smoother route for transporting blocks and supplies. The cargo would still have to make an approximately two-foot-high "jump" from the top of the walk-boards to the floor of the highest course, but given the size of the sled and the length of the wooden beams, their front ends would probably start protruding over the edge of the wall as soon as they arrived at the level of the platform. Hauling an object up from that point onto the floor would not present a major problem, considering the amount of pulling power the builders had at their disposal.

About 25–30 feet long and as durable as a telephone pole, the lumber for the pyramidal frame above the summit came up next. The top of each industrial-sized beam was cut at an angle to sit flat with the matching beam pushed against it, and also had a hole drilled through the base. Slipping the bottom end of the poles inside the knobs at the corners of the catwalk and lining up the hole pierced through the base with the one in the knob on the walk-board provided a way to fasten the pieces together. Hollowed out of the inside edge near the top of each wooden beam was a semi-circular indentation in the shape of a quarter moon. These depressions were intended to support the "handle" at one end of a pulley roller.

The most feasible setup has workers wrapping a patch of carpet or other supple material around both ends of the tall beams to protect the casing stones on the pyramid's exterior. The cushioning at either end would also hold the center section — the portion of the shaft in between the pillowed ends — slightly above the side of the building. In this case, because the very first beam was targeted for the south side of the pyramid, the crew planned to pull it up bottom-end first. Rotating the pole on the northern platform at the 25th course to have its base facing the wall, workers took the rope from the northern pulley and fashioned a choker at the far end of the wooden pole. Then they added a half-hitch somewhere past the midway point on the shaft. The rope had to sit above the center of the beam for a straight, uncomplicated pull. If the line were placed too low, the unwieldy timber might have a tendency to flip-flop or twist around as it ascended.

A long piece of everyday rope was also affixed to the back end to trail behind the wooden girder during the trip up the side of the building. Approximately 200 feet long, this line is what crews would use to return the pull-ropes to their original positions once the beam was delivered to the summit.

Finally, when all of the preliminary work was done, the team raised the first piece up the north wall as high as Course 98, where it paused. With the pull halted, the crew staffing the setback transferred the southern rope that was attached to the sled parked at the docking station onto the beam. Using a half-hitch, they tied it around the shaft just above the middle. The inclusion of the line from the pulley on south side added a considerable amount of momentum to the pull.

When it reached the top, a sequence of carefully orchestrated movements maneuvered the initial girder into position. Because the beams were so heavy and long, not even the entire team of laborers would have been strong enough to manipulate them by hand. As a result, the builders instigated an unusual use for the pulley-stands. Each pulley-stand was four feet long north to south. Since the two devices were lashed together back-to-back in the approximately10-foot-square space, they were only about a foot from the edge of the pyramid.

As the wooden beam nosed its way forward over the edge of the wall, aimed toward the pulley-stand on the north side, it slowly started traveling up the frame. Because the ropes were attached at least 10 feet down from the top of the more than 25-foot-long piece of timber, crews could only bring it partway up before they were forced to stop, which left at least 15 feet still hanging over the wall.

Winding security lines around the beam to hold it in place in the interim, the work gang repositioned the two pull-ropes, then had the people on the ground start tugging on them again. Soon, the cumbersome pole managed to move high enough up the side of the pulley-frame to reach the tipping point where it began to list and lie down horizontally on top of the stand on the north side.

The teams continued to pull, advancing the piece toward the south, until it was reclining across the tops of both stands. Because the lines wrapped around the two pulleys would soon lose their ability to pull any further, the crew had tied smaller ropes around the beam to control its descent toward the catwalk. A few members of the crew managing the lines for the drop had positioned themselves on top of the stands. Moving forward again, the wooden beam eventually tilted down the edge of the frame on the south side and slowly proceeded toward the gang stationed on the platform below. The group overhead had to meet the challenge of safely lowering the unwieldy girder without letting it crash into the workers preparing to catch it. Using a type of knot called a round turn allowed them to release the rope in incremental stages and thus manage the beam's progress as it inched downward.

Tying the beam loosely to the pulley-frame on the south side after it had descended as far as the crew wanted it to slide, left the lower end free to swing a short distance back and forth. (The pull-ropes remained on the piece of timber as an extra safety measure.) The small group standing on the walkway grabbed the wooden girder by the security lines still tied around the shaft and fitted the bottom end into the slots protruding from the southeast corner of the walk-board. Lining up the holes in the brackets with the hole in the beam, they pushed a short dowel through the openings and attached the base to the knob on the plank. Then they removed the pull-ropes and any other unnecessary lines. After the initial piece was lodged in its slot, workers propped up the pole and secured it against the southern pulley-stand, where it would stay until all four corners had their beams.

Laying the groundwork for pulling another beam up the side of the building had begun when the first one reached the summit and the crew had set aside the "tail" fastened to the back end. When the initial girder was reclining on the pulley-stands, a work gang detached it and tied the line around one of the stand's legs, letting the tail hang down the north wall. The pull-ropes north and south had carried the wooden girder to the top, and when it was safely in its slot, those same ropes had to return to their start positions to transport the next load. The tail's length was significant because it was approximately half as long as the pyramid was tall.

The beauty of the Egyptians' strategy lay in its simplicity. These clever builders knew that if they fastened the ends of both pull-ropes to the tail-line that had accompanied the beam to the top, it would reach all the way down to the niche on the 98th course, where a small team would be able to pull it toward them — which is exactly what they did. Once the pull-ropes arrived, workers staffing the setback undid the one from the southern pulley and fastened that line to the front of the docked sled to immobilize it. But the rope from the pulley on the north side had to descend at least another 200 feet to reach the platform at Course 25.

Luckily, the northern pull-rope was already at the halfway mark down the wall, which meant the tail-line was long enough to accomplish this second task, too. The smaller rope dropped down to the northern platform where a work crew grabbed it and, walking forward, lugged the weighty pull-rope to the bottom.

Shortly thereafter and echoing the same basic procedure, the Egyptians raised the beam at the northwest corner of the catwalk. Their choice of corners reflected the larger goal of ensuring that the pick boards remained balanced throughout the construction process. The effort involved in elevating and inserting the wooden girders on the north side of the pyramid was less taxing than mounting the initial beam. Instead of leading with the bottom end, the northern pair came up the wall one after the other head-first. And because workers did not have to transfer the second set of girders to the other side of the building, the installation procedure, while not as complicated, generally mimicked the routine executed so effectively with the original pole installed on the south side.

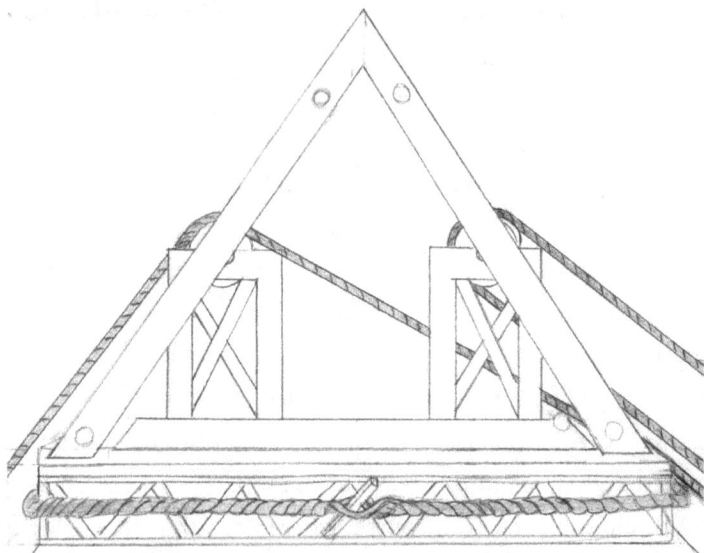

SUMMIT WITH N-S PULLEYS

The four-legged pulley-stands on the north and south sides, which were put into commission when the Egyptians began using the wall-sled, rose higher with every course the builders completed until they reached the summit. Employing a single rope, the machines assisted in hauling up the blocks and equipment that preceded the capstone. In time, workers would transfer their rollers to the pyramid-shaped, wooden structure erected above the peak before dismantling the two stands and sending them down to the bottom.

Crawling up the northern pulley-frame after the piece of timber had arrived at the summit, workers connected the girder to the stand with security lines, repositioned the pull-ropes, then raised it higher. After those maneuvers, the group posted on top of the stand slowly lowered the wooden beam toward the people waiting on the platform below, with the lines rigged so the base swung loose. This allowed the work gang on the catwalk to insert the shaft into the knob and affix it to the corner slot before leaning the latest beam against the northern pulley-stand and tying it down.

Soon, crews had installed beams on all four corners. Now it was time to fashion A-frames from the girders propped up on the north and south sides.

Subsequently, by drawing the pieces together at the top directly over the center point of the uppermost course, the builders would produce wooden scaffolding simulating the shape of the Great Pyramid.

Pulleys in the Air

Using push rods similar to a staff, the crew on the summit — aided by a small group standing atop the pulley-stands — carefully leaned the pairs of beams north and south inward, matching up the beveled edges at the top to fit neatly against each other. When the pair secured to the knobs on one of the walk-boards met and was held steady, workers shimmied up the shafts and fastened them together with ropes. The result was a triangular frame on two sides of the pyramid.

The team followed up by tilting the triangles toward the center of the upper course and, as the points touched in the middle, strapping the two units together where they converged at the top. The outcome was an outline in the shape of the Great Pyramid taller than the peak of the future capstone. Because the four-sided, open structure had to handle a tremendous amount of weight and pressure, workers were also scheduled to place a series of wooden supports beneath the girders — between the wooden beams and the exterior walls — as soon as the sides of the pyramid were a little taller. And they will continue to insert extra supports as the number of courses increases.

This was also when the Egyptians began to deconstruct the pulley-stands they had counted on ever since the first loaded sled climbed up the outer wall. But before dismantling the stands altogether, workers would take the grooved rollers from inside the heavy frames and transfer them to the new structure towering overhead. Using the stands for elevation and assisted by a work gang who had shimmied up and were hanging from the girders installed over the summit, they mounted the rollers between the beams on the north and south sides.

The team deposited the handles at either end of the roller into the semi-circular indentations carved into the inside edges of the thick beams. Engineers had placed the hollows near the top of the scaffolding on purpose to set the rollers as high as they could possibly go beneath the peaks of the A-frames. Besides keeping the rollers out of the way of the pull-ropes, this setup also

anticipated the height and position of the forthcoming capstone. Their placement left a sufficient amount of space overhead — between the rollers and
what will soon be the final block at the apex of the Great Pyramid — to be
able to pick up the capstone and set it down on the peak. To prevent the
repositioned pulleys from jumping out of their slots as the ropes ran across
them, the crew secured both ends with a wooden clasp.

At the same time, work gangs using stopper hitches had secured the
two bulky pull-ropes to keep them from plummeting down the walls before
the lines to the newly mounted rollers on the scaffolding could be rerouted.
Workers probably draped the rope over the roller on the north side first,
because it was the one they planned to use to lower the parts from the dis-
assembled pulley-stands to the bottom. The configuration on the north side
would not change with the introduction of a higher pulley. When the builders
begin hauling up blocks again, the pull-rope would still climb the side of the
building from the northern ramp, circle the pulley at the top, and travel back
down to Course 98, where a team would attach it to the back of the wall-sled.
For a very brief period, however, the Egyptians were going to modify that
arrangement to drop some of the gear to the bottom of the building.

After crew members at the top of the pyramid had dismantled the two
pulley-stands, they attached the parts to the line on the north side and sent
them down the wall in condensed loads, with the largest components descending individually. In this case, instead of the rope at the north end only
going as far as Course 98, it continued on, transporting the assorted parts
down to the northern platform.

When all of the extraneous equipment had been removed from the
10.5-foot-square area on top of the pyramid, the northern pull-rope returned to its stationary position at the docking station at Course 98. Crews
subsequently hooked a separate work-rope to the latest wall-sled by looping
it from the left side to the right side of the backboard. The idea was to tie
the pull-rope to the center of this semicircle and establish the conditions for
a straight-on pull. A mere six feet long, the new wall-sled was much lighter
and narrower than the previous model due to the ever-shrinking amount of
space at the top of the pyramid.

In a similar fashion, the pull-rope climbing up the south wall was strung

over the top of the roller set into the A-frame on that side. When the rope
from the south side reached the summit, the pulley turned the line downward,
angling it toward the north. Since the southern roller sat high enough, the
line coming from that end enjoyed an unobstructed path over the edge of the
north wall where it curved downward — heading toward the sled docked
at Course 98.

Clean Edges

At this point, the floor on the highest course was a little less than 15 feet
from the future peak of the pyramid. Most researchers believe that the Great
Pyramid was approximately 480 feet tall when originally built, but because
the monument's highest levels and capstone have been missing for centuries,
we can only speculate about the type of blocks incorporated into the last few
levels. The Griffith theory maintains that the exacting nature of the summit
caused the Egyptians to use finely cut pieces composed of the higher grade,
polished Tura limestone — not only for the exterior cladding, but also for
the interior of the uppermost courses — instead of the usual filler blocks.

Since the builders wanted the blocks comprising the courses immediately
below the pinnacle to fit absolutely square (edge-to-edge), they did not rely on
imperfectly shaped chunks of limestone. Mismatched blocks at the top might
cause the peak to be unsteady. The objective was to achieve precision in the
placement of every block and pack them together so tightly that the summit
was fixed and virtually solid. It is also logical to assume that for the courses
closest to the apex, the Egyptians had sculpted shallow depressions into the
tops of the blocks. By scooping out a portion of each piece of limestone at the
quarry, collectively they formed an indentation that helped secure the blocks
on the succeeding level when crews slid the stones together.

Stonecutters had shaved back the bottom of the pieces quarried for the
next few layers to create a small protrusion on the underside of the stone.
This outcropping was designed to sit neatly inside the shallow "bowl" cut
into the tops of the blocks from the previous course. To further guarantee
maximum stability, workers may have copied a bricklayer's running bond
when installing the blocks for the final set of courses. No one really knows
how many of the upper levels were treated in this manner, but it may have

been as many as 10 — a sufficient number to ensure the top of the pyramid remained rigid and immobile.

Because the smaller wall-sled had to both navigate over the walk-boards and, once the pyramid grew higher, climb further up the north wall, engineers must have limited each load to one or two blocks. After the shadoof on Course 98 dropped the stones into the wall-sled, the teams stationed on the ground north and south began to pull until the vehicle made its way up to the level under construction. Heaving the sled onto the floor, the work gang began to position the white Tura limestone for the cladding. Since the area they had to fill in was so compact, most of the blocks for the façade came up first, which allowed them to set those pieces around the edge of the latest course while leaving an opening on the north side just wide enough for the sled to slip through.

Workers did not have very far to go in laying down blocks on the constricted courses near the pinnacle of the pyramid. When they had inserted the angled casing stones and reached the front of the vehicle, with just a few slots left to complete that particular level, slack in the pull-ropes let the sled slide back down the wall. It is reasonable to assume that this small crew temporarily stored the last few blocks for the current course on top of the ones they had just installed, since the pieces in the floor were less than two feet tall. Standing atop the brand-new course, they wedged the final chunks of Tura limestone into the gaps from above. After assembling a series of these meticulously executed courses on the way up to the summit, the buildout finally arrived at the second level down from what would soon be the peak of the Great Pyramid.

Based on the available square footage, the second-to-last course encompassed only three blocks on each side, including the blocks at either end, which shared the corner of an adjoining wall. The stones were three and a half feet at the base, 22 inches high, and narrowed down to about three feet at the top, due to the slope of the exterior wall. Workers set a total of nine into place with one at each corner, one sitting in between the corners on all four sides, and a single square piece at the center. The lone block in the middle filled up the modest amount of interior space behind the angled stones that formed the pyramid's façade. Two of the faces on the blocks placed at the corners were slanted at 52 degrees, since the sides creating the corner belonged to different walls.

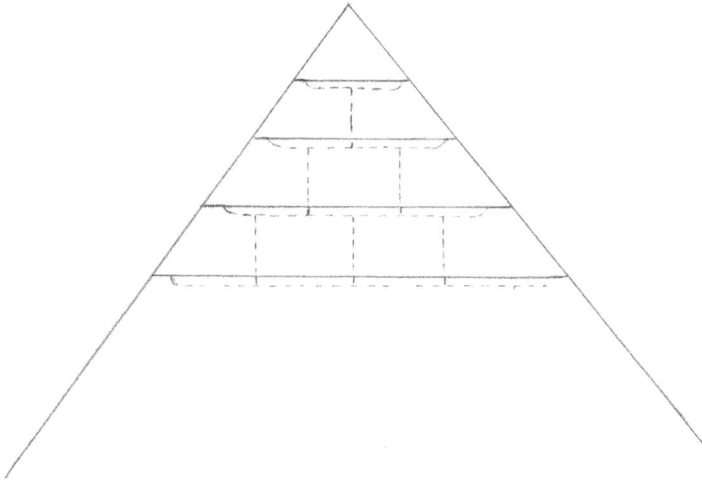

SUMMIT BLOCKS

To ensure the structural integrity of the pyramid's summit long term, stonecutters had carved shallow depressions into the tops of the Tura limestone blocks for the last eight to 10 courses. In addition, the bottom of each block was shaved back to create a protrusion that would fit securely into the bowl underneath it.

By the time construction had reached the 209th course, one layer below the level containing the capstone, the surface area had contracted to a trim square approximately six feet by six feet. Because the space was so tight, its dimensions made it impossible to insert separate blocks for the outer walls and inner core. In this case, the team took four individual blocks of the white limestone from Tura and prepared to shove them against each other. Each three-foot square had one-quarter of a shallow bowl dug out of the top for seating the capstone. Before a piece left the quarry, workers had also cut the block's two outward-facing sides to an angle of 52 degrees because those sides would represent the cladding on the summit's exterior walls. Trimming the outer faces left the interior edges square on all four pieces — able to sit flat against another block. Similar to previous courses, the bottom of each piece was partially cut away to create a small bump on the underside that was designed to sit neatly inside the depression carved into the prior level.

Engineers had provided a hollow on top of the group of four to help contain the pyramidion they wanted to plant on the uppermost point of the building. Such an indentation promised to add stability to the peak. It was the Egyptians' insurance policy against wind or some other type of natural disaster sweeping this solitary beacon off the top of their soaring pyramid. With the final course in place and ready to receive the penultimate block, it was time to raise the capstone.

Pinnacle

Jubilation must have permeated the job site when word spread that the overseers had declared all systems go for placing the capstone on the summit. True, the presence of a capstone did not mean that the monument was finished and the work was done; the Egyptians still had to dismantle the equipment at the top, repair the niche in the north wall at Course 98, shut down the Lever Room, and fill in the pie-shaped cutout, which served as the construction entrance, before sealing up the Great Pyramid for good.

Nevertheless, to have attained the pinnacle at last was a mind-boggling achievement and must have signified an emotional moment for a people who, for generations, had looked forward to this day with great anticipation. Their triumph had taken almost 100 years to achieve. It is not hard to imagine thousands of workers, joined by residents from the surrounding communities, gathering on the north side of the building and tilting their heads upward to watch the small sled carting the capstone climb up the wall — and when the crew at the top finally dropped the topmost block onto the peak of the Great Pyramid, rejoicing at the sound of a bell reverberating throughout the site to mark the auspicious moment and begin the celebration.

The ascending sled was much smaller than all of the others that the builders had employed over the years because it was specially designed it to carry that one iconic block. Like previous wall-sleds, it was high-backed to prevent the pyramidion from plunging down the angled wall. Following the normal routine, a single rope from each pulley would convey the sled with the capstone from the northern platform upward to the summit. To equalize the weight by pulling the load from the center, workers had again strung a half-loop of rope from the backboard and connected it to the northern pull-rope.

The line from the south side was fastened to the middle of a separate
"rope-handle" attached to a low board across the sled's front end. The crew
had also wrapped the runners on the underside in soft carpeting to protect
the casing stones from scratches. Tied down to the sled with everyday ropes,
the capstone and its carrier moved as a single unit. Arguably the strangest
feature associated with the special sled was the size of its wooden base, which
was narrower side to side than the width of the block it transported.

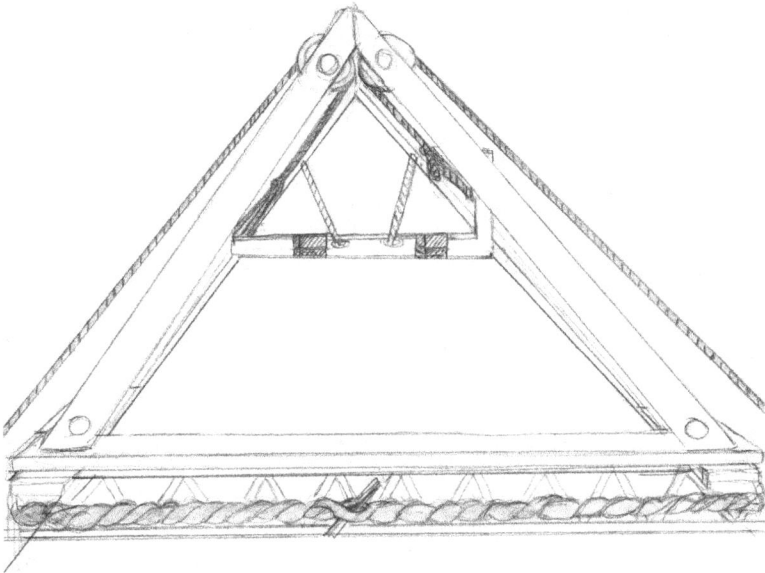

CAPSTONE PLACEMENT

The capstone was pulled up to the peak of the transitory wooden
structure that crowned the top of the pyramid. Then it was
lowered onto two rows of wooden shims, which allowed workers
to remove the special sled that had carried it up the wall.

Since there was no room to stand on the course-in-progress, the workers
at the top waited on swings similar to painters' chairs or window-washer
platforms, which hung over the sides of the building from ropes lashed to
the pyramid-shaped scaffolding overhead. Dropping the capstone into place
would be a more delicate operation than most. When the sled arrived at the
top, workers placed a line of short wooden blocks along the east and west sides
of the shallow recess in the floor. Raising the load as high as it could possibly

go left five or six inches of clearance between the bottom of the vehicle and the floor. And since the width of the capstone east to west extended past the edges of the sled, a small overhang existed on both sides. These ledges meant workers would be able to set the pyramidion directly onto the rows of wooden shims, leaving the sled in the middle.

Control of the pull-ropes was now in the hands of the small team at the top of the pyramid who had the ability to pull down on the lines to fine-tune the sled's orientation. With the capstone and its carrier still suspended, drifting gently above, the signal came to start lowering it down. As the load slowly dropped, the people balanced on the hanging chairs guided the piece into position over the chunks of wood lined up below the overhangs on either side.

As the shims temporarily held the capstone off the floor, other members of the crew cut the ropes wound around the sled and prepared to pull it out from underneath the capstone. To get rid of the vehicle, the work gang first had to undo the pull-ropes on the south side and tie them off. Then, with the front end untethered and the cords that had immobilized the triangular block detached, the team handling the removal process finessed the carrier out from between the chunks of wood. They must have left the empty sled hanging off the side of the building near the walk-boards until they were ready to lower it down to the bottom.

Once the group suspended from the ropes had removed it, workers next to the east and west walls stuck their levers below the pyramidion and jimmied up the piece, prying it high enough for other members of the team to slip out the wooden shims. Next, they replaced the shims with narrow wooden wedges set along the edge of the depression in the floor. After carefully lowering the block that they had just jacked up, they could settle the capstone at the pinnacle of the Great Pyramid into its hole. The final step involved crew members clutching mallets and hammering on the wooden wedges to force the tips out from beneath the edge of the stone.

Down the Sides

Now that the capstone was up, the equipment on the summit could come down. Dismantling the gear would not be easy, especially considering that the only place left to stand at the top of the pyramid was on the walk-boards. Yet, despite the potential pitfalls and obvious challenges, the ancient Egyptians were equal to the task. While we can only speculate about how the work proceeded, it probably started with the people hanging from the ropes lowering themselves down to the catwalk, then shimmying back up the beams on the A-frames to untie their swings. While they were up there, this group also undid the lines at the peak of the scaffolding that were binding the two A-frames together. The swings and other superfluous equipment were piled onto the sled and/or attached to the pull-rope for the trip downhill.

It is important to mention that during this phase of the operation, the team standing at the bottom by the northern platform had to be extremely mindful of what was at the other end of the pull-rope. The loads during this relatively brief window of time were much lighter than the enormous rope warranted, so crews had to adjust conditions accordingly. For example, when the sled that had previously carried the capstone arrived back on the northern platform more than 630 feet below and workers detached it to set it aside, they must have added extra weight to that end of the line. (The distance from the peak to the bottom of the Great Pyramid along the angled wall was more than 700 feet, but because the northern platform where the sled landed was 70 feet high, the sled only dropped about 630 feet.) Without increasing the mass to counterbalance the heft of the heavy rope, they would not be able to control the line as it scaled the wall. Even worse, a loose rope traveling up the side of the pyramid at high speed might slap into and wipe out the workers and equipment at the top.

The builders' deconstruction and removal plans for the tools and supplies that remained on the summit made the rope from the south side unnecessary, so it was probably the next thing to go.

By this time, crew members had untied the A-frames strapped together above the peak and removed the roller traversing the beams on the south side. Now they were able to unpin the two girders by disconnecting them at the base from the slots at the corners of the southern walk-board and laying them down on the planks along the east and west walls. Fortunately, there was no need to transfer the heavy timbers over to the opposite side of the pyramid before letting them drop to the bottom. Shortly thereafter, workers prepared to lower the pieces from the southern A-frame down the north wall using the rope on that side. After swathing each end in a soft material, tying a work rope above the center of the shaft, and stringing the beam to the pull-rope, they could let the lengthy girders descend the side of the building one at a time.

Repeating a pattern from the past, the core work on the Great Pyramid once again shifted to the north end of the site This was also — while the roller installed inside the northern A-frame was still operational — when the builders released the wooden ramp that hung down the wall to help haul the sleds over the edge of the walkway. A small crew secured the giant wedge to the line and sent it down the wall on the pull-rope. As soon as it was gone, the team took the last pulley-roller mounted on the scaffolding above the peak out of service. Tying off the pull-rope to secure it temporarily, workers climbed up the A-frame, disengaged the roller, and lowered it down to the catwalk. Then they tackled the base of both beams — still attached to the walk-board — by unpinning them from their brackets and setting the posts on the platform.

Circlets

Eliminating the single roller left at the top of the pyramid meant engineers had to find other ways to eliminate the remaining equipment from the summit. They improvised a solution that proved to be both resourceful and an effective way to ensure that every bit of evidence associated with the construction process would disappear. A work gang looped two ropes around the top of the pyramid in concentric circles, making the summit the common center. They also stuck some sort of padding or softener underneath the lines at the corners of the building to prevent the sharp-edged limestone from slicing through the ropes.

The two circlets, which dropped as low as the second or third course down from the peak, served distinct purposes. The bottom rope was designed to hold the pulley over which the pull-rope would pass, permitting the team to keep lowering objects to the ground. Before closing the lower loop, workers had threaded the rope through a hole drilled lengthwise down the center of a large grooved roller. The builders also realized that they would need some-thing to distance the roller from the exterior wall to maintain some space between it and the fragile cladding.

To solve the problem, carpenters took a thick board longer than the roller and fastened two short wooden slats a few inches away from the east and west ends. These "arms" projected out from the backboard at a 90-degree angle and had holes cut through them to accommodate the rope holding the roller. Set flat against the side of the pyramid, the contraption not only prevented the pulley from bumping into the building; it provided plenty of room for the bulky rope passing over the grooves to move freely.

As soon as the backboard and roller were ready, the crew cinched work-ropes around the beams from the second A-frame now lying on the walk-way and attached them to the pull-rope one at a time for their journeys down the wall.

At this juncture, the Egyptians were ready to finish the cleanup process. Work crews had positioned the lower rope looped around the summit by placing the roller at the center of the wall on the north side. By contrast, the upper loop served as their lifeline. The higher rope was the cable from which workers would suspend themselves to disassemble the walk-boards. By now, it was pretty much a skeleton crew laboring near the peak — other members of the team had either ridden or walked themselves down to the 98th course by holding onto the stationary pull-rope.

Affixed to individual lines connected to the upper circlet and hanging off the side of the building, the people posted up top began the next part of the operation by undoing specific sections of the lattice-like supports underneath the walk-boards. The first step was to remove the ropes encircling the substructure, which had firmed up the bracing and tightened it against the walls. Moving section by section around the sides of the pyramid, the team approached the job initially by securing each unit with a safety rope to prevent it from breaking loose and setting off in a sudden freefall. Then they removed the pins that had attached the bracing to the top of the catwalk. Once they had attached the initial unit to the pull-rope, it rode down the north wall. Circumnavigating the pyramid, the other three supports were lowered one by one to the bottom.

Dealing with the unstable walk-boards required caution and dexterity as the workers hanging from the upper loop began dismantling the wooden platform. Before the catwalk could be taken apart, however, the crew had to secure the pieces to a fixed point to prevent the boards from plummeting down the sides of the pyramid before they were ready to deal with them. That spot was the lower loop of thick rope tied around the summit, which supported the only pulley-roller left at the top. The gang on the walkway took smaller ropes connected to the rope-circle and wrapped two of them around the planks on the east, west, and north sides, a few feet away from each end. While the suspension ropes did not firm up the platform to any great degree, someone would still be able to gingerly navigate the catwalk. With ropes securing the boards, crew members undid the knots at the corners that held the platform together.

The outlier was the plank on the south side of the building. It was going to be the first one they discarded and due to its location, was rigged differently. A couple of lines were cinched around the board, then strung over the top of the lower rope encircling the summit. One neat trick was to tie the working ropes a bit off-center because that way when the team attached the lines to the pull-rope and let them go, the plank would upright itself to travel down the wall vertically.

The first order of business was to disconnect the 14-foot-long walk-board by slipping the planks along the east and west walls out of the brackets on the underside. Once the hangers no longer joined the pieces together, the crew would be able to convey the southern plank over to the north side where the pulley was. A pair of workers on swings clutching the free ends of the lines hanging down from the circlet slowly pulled the board east by dragging it along the cable overhead. Rounding the southeast corner, they prepared to maneuver the drag lines over the suspension rope holding up that end of the plank against the east wall.

With the help of someone standing on the catwalk, the lead puller let a little slack into a line, which allowed it to slip over the initial rope supporting the eastern plank. Then the partner on the next swing repeated the process. They kept going, progressively moving the heavy board dangling down the side of the building further north. Soon the pair was lifting their ropes over the second suspension line on the eastern plank as they approached the edge of the north wall. There was no need to pull much further because after turning that corner, the crew working from the swings on the north side was in a position to bring the pull-rope over to the southern walk-board and rig it for the descent to the platform below.

It is safe to assume that the walk-board on the north side followed shortly thereafter. Situated directly beneath the pulley-roller, this portion of the platform involved a deconstruction process that was fairly simple. With the suspension ropes still around it, workers attached the big pull-rope somewhere above the plank's center point, eliminated the lines supporting the walk-board, and let it go. The team waiting below on the northern ramp took things from there by lowering the plank down the wall. The walk-boards on the east and west walls were probably just pulled forward (north) one at a time — far enough beyond the corners for the people in the swing chairs at that end to attach the pull-rope. Removing the suspension lines released the board so that once the overseer gave the signal, it would head downward in much the same way.

Two Lone Men

By the time the walkway had disappeared, so had most of the crew at the top. The time had finally come for the builders to leave two lone workers on the summit. Their colleagues had shimmied or walked down the north wall using the stationary pull-rope as a banister, climbing off when they reached the recess to the interior of the building at Course 98. As agile and sure-footed as mountain goats, the pair who remained on the peak climbed up and stood on top of the lower loop tied around the pyramid — the one with the roller. After securing themselves to the lower loop with safety lines, they reached up and prepared to cut the upper circlet. But first, they warned the crowd below what was coming before slicing through the rope and letting it tumble down the wall.

Somewhere along the way, the builders had dealt with a crucial component of their plan to erase every sign that human beings had ever roamed near the peak of the Great Pyramid. Much earlier, when they were assembling the backboard to keep the pulley away from the wall, carpenters had attached two short arms with holes drilled through them to support the rope threaded through the center of the roller. In the same vein, they had also fabricated a third arm just a few inches east of the one already installed at that end, which also had an opening to accommodate the line. This extra, third arm was not there to keep the pulley from slapping against the building — its purpose was to cordon off a narrow section of the rope for a knife-like device to sever the line by cutting it in half when the project was done.

ROPE-RELEASE CUTTER

Artist's rendering of the rope-release cutter shaped like an Egyptian shen.

From the beginning, a specialized tool mounted in between the two arms at the east end of the backboard was part of the design. Knowing that someday they would have to get rid of the loop around the summit supporting the pulley roller, the Egyptians had fashioned an extremely sharp cutting instrument expressly for this purpose. In a nod to a symbol considered sacred to their culture, the device was crafted in the shape of a shen. Represented in hieroglyphs as a stylized loop of rope, a shen is drawn as a circle with a tangent line at the bottom touching the curve.

Fastened to the backboard to project outward, the rope-release cutter looked as if someone had rotated a basketball hoop without a net to hang it vertically. The stationary ring placed between two wooden arms a few inches apart from each other surrounded, but did not touch, the rope. The instrument was made out of copper with a razor-sharp, circular knife blade composed of iron or obsidian set into the interior of the frame. The horizontal bar at the base, which extended past the edge of the circle on both sides, had holes pierced through each end to hold the plaited leather bands that workers would attach to the tool. The straps controlling the cutter were extremely long, extending as far as down the wall as the setback on Course 98. But they would not be fastened to the shen until the last two workers were ready to abandon the summit for good.

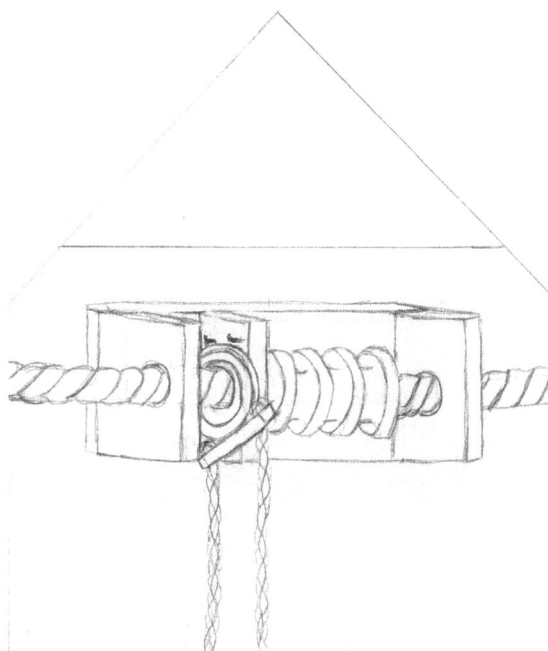

ROPE-RELEASE CUTTER AND BACKBOARD
The rope-release cutter was mounted on the backboard set against the north wall to support the pulley-roller.

Positioning the shearing device around that tiny portion of the rope found between the arms at the east end of the backboard produced the conditions for an accurate cut. The invention had created a way to avoid slippage and ensure that the small, targeted section of the rope would not slide back and forth with the cut only partway through. As workers yanked on the straps from below, the blade was in a position to make continuous contact with a single spot. This ingenious arrangement was meant to be fail-safe — a guarantee that the knife-blade would actually sever the circlet around the peak.

With their tasks completed, the last two people at the top, having tied the leather straps to the cutter and made their way down to Course 98, alerted everyone on-site that the roller carrying the pull-rope to the summit, along with all of the other paraphernalia near the peak, was ready to come down. Then a few members of the team stationed in the niche began tugging on the straps — alternating from one side to the other as if they were ringing a chapel bell. Pulling the knife edge back and forth across the line eventually sawed through the thick cable until it hung by a thread and suddenly collapsed, causing the backboard, pulley, and hundreds of feet of heavy rope to crash to the bottom.

Due to the location of the roller and the ropes, which were aligned with the indentation at the center of the north wall (the former track for the wall sleds), the gear probably fell straight down, almost as if it were in a sluice. Luckily, the huge pile of rope accumulating on the northern platform created a buffer for the other equipment as it landed.

The very last rope that had traveled up the side of the pyramid, more than 200 courses to the summit, was no longer necessary. From this point forward, the lines linked to the pulley on Course 98 would be the only set of major pull-ropes the Egyptians need to fill out and seal up the rest of their Great Pyramid.

• Angles and Bends •

The Griffith theory posits that the small passageways in the Great Pyramid thought to be air shafts are actually the remnants of the center channels that ran up the front of the northern and southern utility pyramids. These channels were the main conduits for hoisting up the heavy sleds loaded with blocks. During the decades it took to erect the Great Pyramid, the Egyptians had built two separate sets of internal pyramids, which essentially served the same purpose but at different levels. Similarly, at various stages of the construction process, and especially as the massive building operation was drawing to a close, workers sealing up the interior of the structure narrowed down these channels, primarily using precut blocks, which left behind the small openings we see today.

It is worth noting that in general the new theory considers the label "air shaft" to be a misnomer. While it is true that at the time the Egyptians were erecting the Queen's Chamber the channels on either side of that room were still open to the sky, which would have allowed circulating air to reach the people working below; refreshing the atmosphere was never their primary purpose.

In any event, the two passageways in that chamber do not reach the outer wall of the pyramid today.

One little-known fact is that while for centuries people were aware of the shafts in the King's Chamber, no one knew that any existed inside the Queen's Chamber because the openings were masked and the shafts hidden behind the interior walls. It was not until 1872, when a British engineer and explorer named Waynman Dixon and his friend Dr. Grant noticed a crack in the south wall and pushed a wire through it, exposing a void, that the presence of the first shaft in the Queen's Chamber finally came to light. Knowing the King's Chamber had two shafts and guessing that the Queen's Chamber had a similar design, the pair of explorers measured the same distances on the north wall of the lower chamber and, after chiseling through the limestone, found the second opening.

We can only hazard a guess about how the ancient Egyptians determined where to place the shafts inside the two rooms. They were remarkable architects and based on their past history, it is easy to imagine them making whatever accommodations were necessary to ensure that the position of the openings corresponded from chamber to chamber. It seems clear that the builders had made certain that the locations of the sets of holes in each room matched.

Scholars have observed that none of the shafts retain their original rectangular shape from bottom to top, nor do they extend upward from the chambers in perfectly straight lines. In fact, each tunnel includes at least one bulge or bend. Why did the meticulous Egyptians, who scrupulously monitored every detail of the Great Pyramid for its beauty and precision, alter what could have been straightforward passageways by having them deviate off-course? They must have had specific and very logical reasons for the designs, but to date, pyramid investigators have not been able to crack that secret code.

As far as researchers can tell, the shaft on the north side of the Queen's Chamber travels straight out from the room for approximately seven feet. Then it turns upward at a 39-degree angle and appears to make a slight jog around the bottom of the Grand Gallery before once again heading in a northerly direction as it continues to climb at a 39-degree angle toward the perimeter of the building. Curiously, a camera mounted on a small rover revealed that the shaft on the opposite (south) side of the chamber includes a small step-down in the floor near the top of the small tunnel — close to the stone door with two copper handles that blocks the passageway. The dip in the floor is a couple of inches deep and experts do not know why it is there. Moreover, both shafts linked to the Queen's Chamber (each at least 200 feet long end to end) stop short of the exterior walls and consequently, never break through the outer surface of the Great Pyramid.

While for the most part, the air shaft in the south wall of the King's Chamber climbs steadily upward in a straight line after the first several feet, this opening contains its own peculiar set of anomalies. Over the years, researchers have discovered at least three different types of bulges inside the channel. The first was a hole at the bottom by the chamber wall in roughly the shape of a pear, which pyramid robbers had chopped out of the granite in the distant past. While visitors cannot see the cutout today due to later repairs, the cavity was once large enough for a man to crawl inside.

A second anomaly found further up the southern shaft is an oval-shaped area that appears to be dug out of some plaster. The reason for the plaster is anybody's guess because once you move past that short section of the passageway the flat limestone walls begin again. Lastly, near the upper end, the tunnel widens out on both sides for a couple of inches then quickly returns to its former shape. In general, the shaft on the south side of the King's Chamber rises at an angle of 45 degrees until it exits the exterior wall of the Great Pyramid at Course 101. Why or how the various irregularities occurred remains a mystery.

Arguably the strangest sir shaft found inside the Great Pyramid is the one located on the north side of the King's Chamber. Although archeologists have known for centuries that the rectangular opening (approximately 5" x 7") extended in a straight horizontal line through granite and limestone for at least eight feet or more behind the inside wall, no one knew exactly where it went after that. Then over the years, explorers hacking their way through different portions of the pyramid made a startling discovery. After the small tunnel leaves the King's Chamber and crosses that short distance in back of the north wall, it begins to meander as it climbs higher.

Pyramid-ologists often refer to the curves and bends in the shaft as an S-curve. But the route the northern shaft follows is more akin to a series of dog-legs or elbow turns, which wander a distance of about 30 feet from the hole inside the room, gradually carrying the opening upward and farther west. Beginning on the horizontal, the small tunnel shifts first to the north-northwest then back to the north, followed by a turn toward the north-northeast, and finally back to true north again. This somewhat semicircular diversion bores through several courses before finally reaching the upper stretch of the passageway. At the point where the two sections meet, it straightens out and ascends on a 32-degree angle toward the exterior wall, ending at Course 102 in a small opening to the outside world.

The critical question is this: Why would the Egyptians create a shaft with so many twists and turns? According to the Griffith theory the chief reason was the original location of the center channel from the upper utility pyramid on the north side. The western edge of that channel sat at the far end of the main work area on Course 49 about 40 feet away from the Grand Gallery. Consequently, when workers began to narrow down the channel during the course of assembling the Lever Room, the opening for raising the blocks sat over on that side. Given its placement, the shaft should have "punctured" the wall of the King's Chamber somewhere near the northwest corner—at the other end of the room from where it sits today. But it doesn't do that. The original hole for the air shaft is toward the east end of the King's Chamber near the doorway.

Evidence suggests that the builders' goal was to keep the position of the openings for all four shafts consistent from chamber to chamber. In this instance the ancient Egyptians had already established a hole for the northern air shaft in the King's Chamber directly above the one in the Queen's Chamber when they originally constructed the room. Work gangs had inserted two precut granite blocks into the north wall to create an outlet for the shaft near the doorway.

But much later when the builders developed the Lever Room, the opening above the ledge in the room's north wall represented the upper portion of the same shaft. Yet it sat toward the west. This hole (a remnant of the former center channel) was the place where workmen fed the loaded sleds into the chute leading to the 98th course. The result was a pre-fabricated opening inside the King's Chamber positioned many courses below and much too far east to easily join the two sections together.

Further complicating the situation was the fact that for decades a large open area existed right in the middle of the space where the lower portion of the northern shaft from the King's Chamber was supposed to go. Initially it was the builders' primary workspace on Course 49 and much later the Lever Room.

In addition, the Egyptians would be using the passageway that started above the ledge on the north side of the Lever Room nonstop or until the highest block reached the summit of the Great Pyramid. The need to keep the chute that delivered the stones continuously in operation must have had some bearing on the contours and position of this particular shaft.

An even greater challenge to erecting the bottom portion of the northern air shaft was the high wall of courses standing in the way. The new theory maintains that when the King's Chamber was constructed, the method the builders used was to fill in the courses immediately surrounding the area set aside for that room one level at a time. This allowed crews to use a completed course as their work platform and simply drag the sleds with the granite blocks over the flat surface to assemble the next level—until all four walls, the ceiling, and the Relieving Chambers were complete.

The layer-by-layer approach to the buildout included erecting a somewhat narrow band of courses along the north wall of the King's Chamber to serve as a work platform on that side. The growing stack of limestone filler blocks elevated the workers higher as the number of levels increased. Gradually this group of courses filled the space alongside the wall as far north as an imaginary line extending west from the front edge of the Antechamber to the other end of the King's Chamber. Similar to the rest of the courses on the east, west and south sides of the building site, the stack next to the chamber's north wall eventually reached high enough to cover the peak of the Relieving Chambers at approximately Course 101.

Could the sequence of turns and bends, which little by little carry the northern air shaft upward at a slight angle, be the result of the Egyptians' best attempts to make the two ends of their passageway meet? The Griffith theory submits that this is the case. The ancient builders must have known from the beginning that one day a big gap would develop between the upper and lower portions of that small tunnel and no doubt had been planning a way around the problem for a very long time.

The series of elbow turns imply that they were adjusting the trajectory of the shaft by degrees to start closing up the distance as their "pipeline" snaked its way through the wall of courses in front of the King's Chamber and across the Lever Room. Needless to say, preparing years in advance to lay disparate segments of a long channel through a solid wall—and end up in the correct position to link all of the pieces together—was not an easy job.

It is important to note that from the start workers had constructed the lowest section of the air shaft adjacent to the King's Chamber in its final form, i.e., as a compact rectangular tunnel seven inches wide and five inches tall. And they had fabricated this segment of the passageway early on—during the process of assembling the courses next to the chamber's north wall. Conversely, the upper portion of the shaft represented by the opening above the Lever Room ledge would remain approximately the same size as most of the other internal passageways found inside the Great Pyramid (3' 5" x 3' 11.5") for some time—until this conduit was no longer required for the pull-ropes and loaded sleds.

Instead of just depositing row after row of rectangular blocks to erect the courses along the north side of the King's Chamber, crews had incorporated specially designed blocks into the different layers to extend the air shaft beyond the spot where it had exited the room. While it is difficult to determine the precise number of regular course-blocks each section of the shaft replaced, the buildout followed a uniform pattern: 1) Similar to other ramps and inclines, the limestone pieces used for the base of the angled passageway were slanted on top. 2) A harder, more durable rectangular stone slab was set atop the base block, lying at the same angle, to act as the shaft's floor and keep the height of the opening consistent from beginning to end. 3) The next block up had a long rectangular indentation notched out of the bottom front to back, forming the shaft's roof and walls. The underside of the upside-down-

U-shaped block was flat and sat directly on the floor of the passageway. 4) Finally, the uppermost block in the group of four was slanted on the bottom to bring the top back to level with the horizontal plane. Because only by reestablishing a flat surface on which to build would the team be able to erect additional layers above the tiny shaft wending its way through the narrow stack of courses.

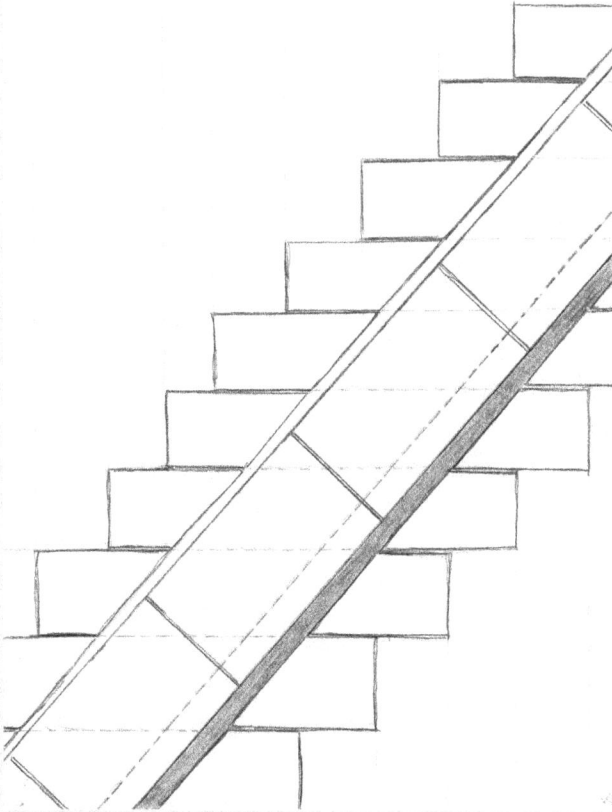

AIR SHAFT IN SITU

Displayed within the general context of the blocks that surround them, the air shafts were created from four separate types of blocks. The most significant were the upside-down U-shaped inserts that narrowed down the passageways and produced the small openings (represented here by a dotted line) that bore through the Great Pyramid from inside King's and Queen's Chambers.

As the number of layers increased, the lower portion of the passageway
on the north side of the King's Chamber (the south end of the work
space on Course 49) got progressively longer as it steadily moved higher
and further west. In assembling the band of course blocks in front of
the chamber's north wall, the crew kept lengthening the lower section
of their "pipeline" by adding additional pieces to bring it closer to the
spot where it ultimately needed to be. The Griffith theory maintains that
after making at least three turns using blocks specifically quarried for
that purpose, the lower portion of what is called the air shaft temporarily
ended at a hole in what would become the future Lever Room's south
wall—a bit east and a little lower than the opening situated above the
ledge across the room.

The Egyptians would have to wait until they were closing down the
Lever Room and putting the finishing touches on the Great Pyramid to
link up the hole at the room's south end with the one above the ledge.
Until that time, the corbelled wall on the south side would have a cavity
in it, an ever-present reminder of exactly where the northern air shaft
associated with the King's Chamber was going to be.

CHAPTER 20

A RECEDING NICHE

ALMOST 100 YEARS AFTER initiating their extraordinary project, the Egyptians were preparing to close up the Great Pyramid for posterity. The precipitating activity was filling in the recess in the north wall at the 98th course. Approximately 20 feet wide and 20 feet deep, the setback presented a host of challenges for the workers attempting to seal up the hole. Not only did the team packing it with blocks have to contend with finishing off a section of the pyramid's sloping outer wall, work crews also had to complete the project while literally covering over the only available space to stand on.

The process began with the removal of the docking station developed years earlier for the wall-sleds, located at floor level several feet west of the cavity in the north wall. The shadoof, which had picked up the blocks coming from the Lever Room and transferred them onto the sled riding up the side of the pyramid, sat at the center of the alcove on top of a mini step-pyramid three levels high. The recess in the outer wall also contained the pulley-stand with the only set of functioning pull-ropes on the building site at that time.

Connecting the hook dangling from the shadoof's arm to the chokers wrapped around the docking-station stones protruding from the wall at a 90-degree angle, the crew picked up the blocks and set them aside to use as filler as the job progressed. In short order, a couple of blocks of the highly polished white Tura limestone arrived at the top of the Lever Room shaft and were placed inside the hole that the docking station had previously occupied to repair that minor slice of the façade. The new blocks inserted into the cladding had not traveled up to Course 98 on sleds because adding unnecessary equipment at the top would have crowded out the team's work area. Space around the opening to the shaft was at a premium and, in general, the limited conditions inside the niche, which soon would become even more constricted, dictated a different approach to the job of raising additional course blocks.

Circumstances called for a pared-down process, which meant ejecting three of the four ropes around the pulley. From this point on, the team would rely on a single line to raise the blocks up the chute — just as they had done at the summit. The loads were not tremendous and the unavoidable fact was that the square footage inside the niche was shrinking with every advance the builders made. In a carefully timed maneuver, the three unnecessary ropes were pulled to the bottom one by one, landing in a heap on the northern platform.

Instead of depositing the latest chunks of limestone onto sleds, workers stationed on the ledge in the Lever Room took the pull-rope and looped it around the base of the block. None of the stones were huge, which made them relatively easy to control and drag through the passageway in sequence. Due to the heft of the pull-rope, the workers also tied a thin line to the loop catching the bottom end to keep the rope from flying off the outside wall as the work gang overhead in the setback undid each small load.

With the docking station gone, the team had also decided to alter the position of the shadoof to permit the arm to swing the other way, since the first stage of the buildout would occur from the back of the niche toward the front. The device was normally set up with the counterweight — the low end — pointed toward the back of the recess, but work gangs turned it around so the weight at the rear faced the breach in the exterior wall. Reversing the direction allowed the arm to rotate from the opening in the floor at the top of the shaft on the east side, all the way over to the southwest corner of the alcove, spanning the south wall.

One additional detail is worth noting. There was a narrow lip along the top of the back wall, formed by the front edges on the line of casing stones from the course directly above the niche. The fresh cladding that crews were going to insert on the next row down would slip underneath the narrow rim formed by the white limestone installed years earlier for the north wall.

To further set the scene, the hole at the top of the shaft where the blocks emerged from the Lever Room sat just a few feet over from the niche's angled east wall. The primary pulley-stand, which held the rope that scaled the side of the pyramid from the northern ramp, was positioned several feet back from the edge of the building in a straight line roughly eight feet north of the hole in the floor. Moreover, the long arm of the shadoof was able to reach the top of the setback — almost 25 feet high — in an arc that encompassed an area from the delivery channel to a spot on the west wall across from the opening in the floor. As the work progressed, however, and filler blocks started crowding out what little space remained inside the recess, the Egyptians would have to shorten the shadoof's arm to keep building.

Up Then Out

Once again, the simple structure of a step-pyramid served as the foundation for the construction process. Beginning by the hole at the upper end of the shaft, the shadoof lifted the first block landing on Course 98 from the Lever Room, swung over, and deposited it in the southwest corner of the setback. Soon it was lowering a few more blocks into the same corner, which workers shoved up against the sides of the initial block. The process repeated itself as the team kept building up, then out, layer by layer, creating a series of staggered steps across the niche's back wall, spreading north toward the center platform. The area the steps covered north to south was fairly compact since the gap in the wall was only 20 feet deep and the deck with the shadoof stood in the middle of the space. The newly constructed stepped levels, which quickly approached the southern edge of the shadoof's platform, also stretched some distance down the side walls.

The inescapable question was how the Egyptians could possibly construct a precisely gauged, sloping exterior wall over this large cavity in the side of the pyramid. To the untrained eye, their installation technique was not self-evident, but in truth, the answer was not complicated. The decisive moment came when the upper step at the south end of the alcove had increased in height to one level below the narrow lip formed by the casing stones peeking over the back wall. When step construction had attained that height, the team could begin to address the missing rows of cladding.

First, the crew in the Lever Room conveyed additional casing stones to the top of the shaft. Then, row by row, using the individual steps they had just developed as a base, workers standing on the north side of the latest piece of cladding would push it into place. To insert the upper row of new casing stones along the back wall, the shadoof swung the block over to the correct spot where a small work gang slipped it partially in between the top step and the front edge of the finished course above it. Once they undid the choker, workers shoved the piece further south until it hit against the filler in the back wall and was matched up perfectly with the cladding overhead. The builders' ever-present concern and paramount goal was to consistently maintain the exact 51° 50' slope of the outer wall.

The blocks quarried for the façade were long and flat on the bottom but slanted on the outer face. Viewed from the side, they resembled right-angled trapezoids. Consequently, because the flat surface on top was not very long north to south and the team only slid the stone partway into its slot at the start, they may have used a wooden wedge to temporarily hold up the front end. The wedge prevented the piece of limestone from tipping forward as the job proceeded. Workers would remove the support once they took off the choker and pushed the casing stone to the back of the cavity. Only when the blocks situated above and below the latest piece of cladding were binding it in place would the team eliminate the triangular prop. Crews normally reused the same set of wedges to install the rest of the blocks in a particular row.

The back wall crept steadily forward as, one by one, the steps received their casing stones — until this stage of the project had gone as far as it could go. With blocks spanning the distance across the niche east to west now lined up next to the southern edge of the center platform that held the shadoof, the builders had successfully sealed up the setback in the north wall as far down as Course 104.

Fading Away

The next phase of the operation involved filling up the negligible amount of empty space by proceeding in the opposite direction: working back from the edge of the exterior wall toward the center of the niche. This change meant the large pulley-stand in service for more than half a century had become an impediment that would hinder progress. Mounted on the 98th course a short distance back from the north wall, it stood in an area that workers were ready to pack with filler. The time had come to eliminate it. After tying off the pull-rope and disassembling the machine's component parts, workers swathed the pieces in bull hides or some other type of cloth to avoid scratching the surface of the pyramid and prepared to send them down the side of the building. But because the basic rigging on-site was not designed to carry equipment descending to the ground, the team had to readjust the pull-rope first.

The team posted on the northern ramp let the line go slack, which allowed the gang in the Lever Room to tug on the other end and gradually cause a couple hundred feet of rope to pool on the floor. As soon as enough rope had collected inside the room, the people up top standing inside the niche took smaller lengths of rope and, using a stopper hitch, tied the bundles holding the legs, roller, and other assorted pieces of the pulley-stand onto the pull-rope. As workers slipped the first few packets over the edge of the wall, their weight carried them downward toward the base of the pyramid, dragging the excess rope in the Lever Room behind.

The crew staffing the room must have attached some kind of bar to their end of the rope and set it across the opening above the ledge to prevent the line from completely disappearing as it traveled up the chute and down the wall. Once the initial packages landed on the northern platform and were untied, the process repeated itself several times: Draw a pile of rope into the Lever Room, affix the leather-covered bundles to the line, and let the equipment drop over the side. When the very last parcel had descended, the heap of rope moving through the shaft inside the Lever Room became taut again, leaving all of the elements in place to raise another block.

Abandoning the critical pulley-stand at the top of the elevation channel on the north side compelled the Egyptians to readjust, causing them to raise the remaining blocks for the next stage of construction using the pull-rope alone. But such a dramatic changeover presented its own set of issues. For example, the builders had to take measures so the single line coming over the north wall on its way to the Lever Room shaft — scraping against two hard, limestone edges — would not fray and prematurely break.

The solution was to cap those sharp corners with thin, removable strips of metal, which would not only soften the bends where the angle of the rope shifted but also keep it from catching on any rough spots in the stones. To address the problem, the builders put metal shields over the edge of the north wall and the threshold to the chute. Later, the crews charged with sealing up the recess in the wall would transfer the metal caps on an ongoing basis by moving them up, course by course, with every level they completed.

After the activity had switched over entirely from the pulley-stand to the bare rope, the next order of business was to start filling in the last remnants of the setback, including the missing rows of cladding for the façade. Signaling for more blocks, a work gang standing on Course 98 started packing the minuscule portion of Course 99 that had lain vacant for decades. True to form, the team approached the job by following the tried-and-true method, which had proven so effective in the past, by setting the white casing stones along the edge of the outside wall first, and then depositing rows of filler stones behind them.

Workers were also going to incorporate the three-step platform erected for the shadoof into the developing levels as they loaded up the alcove with blocks. Because the dimensions of the target area had already shrunk north to south, they had shortened the shadoof's arm. Disconnecting one piece, the crew detached the lengthy pole and replaced it with a shorter version, hanging the hook to grab the chokers further down the neck. The modifications allowed them to continue using the device for the last unfilled sections of the niche before the confined space would require the team to jettison the machine for good

Multiple Moving Parts

Work gangs must have pushed or pulled most of the blocks for the initial level into place by hand to complete Course 99, but that was merely the first in a series of steps to advance construction toward the ultimate goal. Since the floor of the niche was on the 98th course but the so-called air shaft on the north side of the King's Chamber exits the pyramid at Course 102, the builders had to finish off courses 99, 100, and 101 before they could fashion the hole in the outer wall.

Adding the raw materials for the next course (100) required a slightly different approach. The team would have to ramp up using angled blocks to elevate the pieces of limestone higher. In many cases, creating a temporary ramp was merely a matter of turning around one of the blocks cut for the façade to access its slanted side. As the 99th course spread west to east and the filler blocks approached the opening leading into the Lever Room, crews also had to reckon with the hole in the floor. Their ability to fill in blocks for the subsequent course — or any course thereafter — was predicated on extending that shaft.

The lengthening process involved placing a block that was angled on top directly in front of the hole to extend the passageway's floor. Then rectangular blocks from Course 99 were positioned on either side of the new "ramp stone." When work on Course 100 got underway, the team would place a fourth block — this one slanted on the bottom — over the initial add-on by having it straddle the stones sitting on either side of the opening. Workers would replicate this routine as they proceeded to build up courses 100 and 101, extending the angled passageway even further north toward the outer wall.

The ancient builders' unwavering attention to detail resulted in a tunnel whose internal height, width, and slope never deviated from top to bottom. And when the series of extensions finally reached the 101st course, the mouth of the shaft was just a few feet away from the edge of the outside wall or the depth of a single piece of the Tura limestone cladding. In the end, the hole would breach the north face of the Great Pyramid at Course 102.

By employing the shadoof and a sequence of temporary ramps, workers had also managed to increase the height of the wall in front of the set-back by another three courses as they blanketed the space east to west with casing stones and rows of filler blocks behind. When the buildout finally reached the upper step of the center platform, it was primarily a matter of attending to Courses 102 and 103 — the only levels still lacking blocks before the unexpected cavity halfway up the side of the pyramid disappeared forever. A tricky maneuver still awaited the builders, however. In a test of their creativity and mettle, the Egyptians had to solve another riddle: How to seal up and permanently secure their massive monument, yet leave an opening in the form of an air shaft behind?

Courses 102 and 103

With the operation in the niche having progressed to the degree that the team was ready to set blocks directly on top of its center platform, a work gang dismantled the shadoof. Wrapping the gear in cloth or leather, crews sent the pieces down to the ground via the same method they had employed to shed the pulley-stand. Since the counterweight at the rear of the apparatus was composed of heavy blocks, those stones remained up top to be reused as filler on one of the evolving courses.

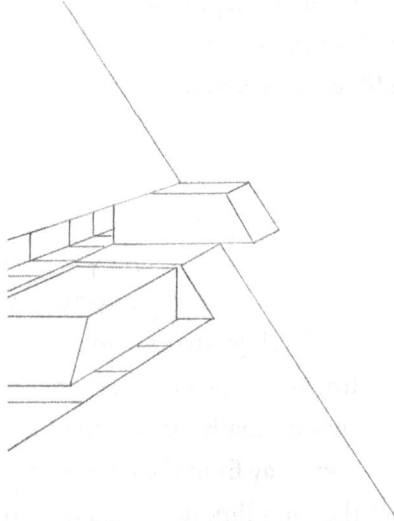

CLADDING · COURSE 98

Work crews inside the setback on the 98th course used the slanted edge on a casing stone turned sideways as a short-term ramp to elevate the piece of cladding for the next row up.

Plugging up the last fissure left over from the niche in the north wall now became a process of inserting a couple of rows of casing stones for the façade. Earlier work on the steps associated with completing Course 104 had produced slots for the next row down to slip into — the cladding on Course 103. Likewise, inserting a single row of the polished white limestone into the outer wall was the only trace of the 102nd course still left undone. For the most part, wrapping up the final two rows proceeded in a zigzag fashion, almost as if workers were crafting the teeth of a zipper as they tackled the exterior wall on that thin sliver of the building. (The Egyptians would not officially seal up the rest of the pyramid's north wall until much later — when they closed down the spacious construction entrance on Course 25.)

Starting with the initial block for the missing section of the façade on Course 102, a few workers pushed the piece over from the top of the Lever

Room shaft until it was flush with the west wall, making sure the edges lined up properly with the existing casing stones. After that, a separate group took the next block intended for the same course (102) and shoved it up against the first one. But this time, they arranged it so the beveled edge was facing east. The second stone in the row would serve as a temporary ramp for the piece that belonged in the 103rd course, now making its way westward. Standing on the pair of blocks they had just set on the lower course and pulling the new chunk of limestone up the short ramp, workers maneuvered it into the open slot at the far end of the row to pack the unfinished portion of Course 103.

As soon as the initial block on the higher row was in place, workers spun around the casing stone from the course below it that had created the temporary incline and returned it to the correct position with the slanted edge facing north. At the same time, the team made certain that the latest blocks on both 102 and 103 were perfectly aligned and the exterior angle stayed true. With everything in order, the developing row of cladding on Course 102 — two stones wide east to west — was ready for its third block. Once again, when the crew lugged in the block, they initially turned it sideways to ramp up and gain access to the row immediately above it. The third block on the 102nd course allowed them to transfer and install a second block for Course 103.

The cycle kept repeating itself. Back and forth, block by block, the workers moved, adding stones for the façade to one level then the next, until Courses 102 and 103 were walled in all the way over to the tiny bit of open space around the entrance to the shaft.

Men on the Rope

It was at this juncture — when the team was preparing to add the second-to-last casing stone in what was formerly the niche — that they took measures to stabilize the future cavity in the pyramid's north wall. Engineers had included the installation of a header block as part of Course 103 to solve a major structural problem: How to retain a void while safeguarding the integrity of the wall? Integrating a lintel stone into the cladding above the hole where the course blocks exited the chute would provide the necessary support to maintain a permanent opening in the outer wall and create a solid base for the casing stones above it.

To visualize the scene, workers had filled in the cladding east and west across Course 102 up to the edge of the entrance to the shaft, leaving that row short by the width of a single casing stone. Resting a header block atop the pieces from Course 102 on either side of the gap would preserve the rectangular aperture at its normal height and width. The builders' decision was advantageous because maintaining the cavity's original dimensions meant that they would be able to narrow down the passageway using regular-sized blocks. To put the final touches on their infamous air shaft, the crew was going to take a series of blocks (3' 5" x 3' 11") sporting seven-inch by five-inch cutouts along the bottoms and inject them into the passageway. A long, tight line of these insert blocks with a squared-off groove thrust inside the channel from below would produce the baffling air shaft tunnel, which ends in the small opening visible on the north side of the Great Pyramid of Giza.

One little-known fact about the upper portion of the northern air shaft associated with the King's Chamber is that it does not ascend at a 32-degree angle in a straight line before piercing the side of the building. Besides the twists and turns evident in the channel's lower echelons before it heads upward on a steady incline, the last approximately four feet of the passageway run horizontally toward the outer wall. In other words, when the angled shaft reaches a certain elevation, it changes to a level plane — similar to when a staircase reaches a landing. According to the Griffith theory, this anomaly was the result of the steps the Egyptians took to extend the original shaft to the outside wall during the period when they were filling in the niche.

The abrupt change in direction within the confines of the close-fitting tunnel would pose a serious challenge to anyone trying to maneuver a block of limestone into position through the last part of the passageway. Without some extra space above the bend where the shaft suddenly goes flat, there would not be enough room overhead for a block inside the channel to turn the corner.

The solution was to leave out part of the ceiling over the transition point to allow the stone to make the turn and reach the outer wall. Consequently, engineers must have left out at least one block in the area directly above the crook in the shaft.

The extra space overhead permitted the builders to pull the latest casing stone — the header block — up to the top of the shaft and balance it so about two-thirds of the piece of limestone lay in the horizontal section of the tunnel. The objective was to leave a modicum of space between the block's front end and the exterior wall. Because the width of the gap in the façade on Course 102 was slightly more than three feet and the lintel straddling the hole needed at least six inches at either end to stay put, the header piece must have been almost five feet long. While perhaps more elongated than usual, the block was identical in outline and composition to the thousands of other casing stones coating the outside walls: angled at 51° 50' on one side and made of highly polished, white Tura limestone.

Once the block sat securely on the flat section at the top of the shaft, the next step in the procedure was to grab hold of the pull-rope looped around the bottom and draw the line back toward the Lever Room. Then crews locked off the rope at both ends — on the interior of the pyramid and on the pulley-stand overlooking the northern ramp. Immobilizing the line would afford the gang putting the finishing touches on the setback an opportunity to hang off the side of the building from the stationary pull-rope and tackle the last part of the job from there — an approach very similar to how they had handled construction at the summit.

The narrow smidgen of space between the leading end of the header block and the exterior wall meant a couple of workers could stand on what remained of the niche within the limited amount of space at the top of the shaft. The job of the two-person team was to lever up the lintel stone by several inches and loop a work-rope around the middle. They were also charged with setting a wooden beam — flat on the bottom and rounded on top — across the gap near the back edge of the pair of casing stones from Course 102 that flanked the opening. If the beam were too close to the front edge, it might fall down the side of the pyramid. After the temporary pulley was in place, they dangled the work-rope coming off the block over its curved side and dropped the line down the tunnel into the Lever Room.

Meanwhile, after connecting themselves to the rigid line to avoid falling, a few of the workers outdoors scrambled up from the northern platform toward the opening, using the lone pull-rope as their ladder. The two people up top had also fastened lanyards around their waists for safety reasons before lowering themselves onto the locked-down rope that scaled the outer wall. Hanging just below the gap where the permanent hole on the north face of the pyramid would be, the small group suspended down the side of the building had a specific job to perform: They were supposed to rotate the header block when it surfaced from the shaft and help maneuver it into position.

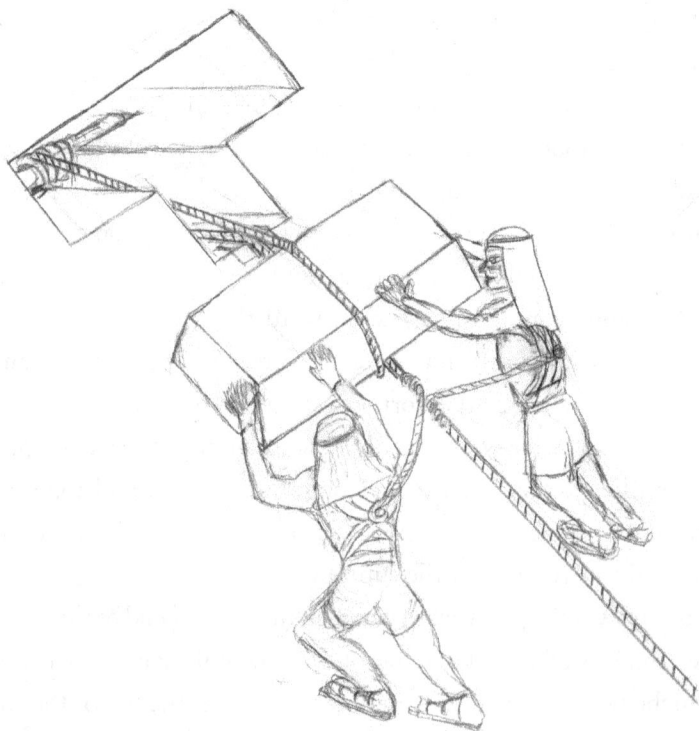

HEADER BLOCK · NORTHERN AIR SHAFT
Workers attached to the pull-rope on the north side of the building assisted in the placement of the header block above the opening for the air shaft on the north side of the King's Chamber.

The lintel stone came out of the chute longways (north-south), partially propelled by a worker (perhaps more than one) who had climbed up the locked down rope inside the tunnel and pushed it from behind. The team in the Lever Room also assisted by pulling on the work-rope tied around the block's mid-section. Tension on that rope, which made it taut across the makeshift pulley, helped drag the stone forward the last few feet until it had exited the passageway and was suspended down the wall. The crew inside handling the work-rope held the header block in place over the side of the pyramid, then started raising it the short distance back up the wall toward the gap in the cladding where it belonged.

The most plausible setup has the gang outside connected to the rope kneeling against the side of the building. This position provided greater stability than if they tried to stand upright while attempting to manage the stone. Clearly, the job this group had undertaken was difficult, but they were never tasked with carrying the full weight of the piece of limestone. The team in the Lever Room clutching the work-rope served as a counterweight to balance the bulk of the burden and permit the block to swing. Handling both ends of the header stone hovering beneath the hole in the wall, the crew on the ropes manipulated the block by rotating it to hang lengthwise east to west with the angled face pointing toward the north. After that exercise, it was primarily a matter of lifting the new lintel high enough to start sliding it into the slot above the opening into the shaft. The work gang would keep pushing on the block until it sat snugly inside its hole, flush with the casing stones that surrounded it.

As the team posted in the Lever Room tugged on the work-rope, the header slowly rose higher, guided toward its cavity by the people tied to the pull-rope. The crew inside the room many courses below was responsible for heaving on the line hard enough to get the header's bottom edge over the top of the blocks bordering the gap in the wall. The objective was to ensure that at least a narrow strip along the lintel stone's back end was actually in the hole. Setting the block on the front edge of the opening stabilized the piece of cladding momentarily, which took most of the weight off the line. Steadying the block, in turn, allowed the workers on the wall attached to the pull-rope to reposition themselves for the final push.

But before the crew was able to slide the header fully into position, the work-rope had to disappear and the temporary pulley be removed. Because the header lay over the open space that was the gap in the wall, a crew member crawling inside the tunnel could have simply sliced through the line and let it fall down the shaft, or the team may have tied the work-rope around the wooden beam to tug it out from wherever they had wedged it and slid the temporary pulley down the chute. Another possibility was to saw the beam in half, affix the chunks of wood to the work-rope, and lower them down to the Lever Room ledge.

KING'S CHAMBER · PEOPLE ON COFFER

The Griffith theory maintains that the original — and central — purpose of the shafts leading from the King's and Queen's Chambers was to elevate the blocks used in pyramid construction. Yet the two channels found inside the King's Chamber may have also played an important role in terms of their value as air circulators. One possible reason why these shafts do not stop short of the exterior wall but break through to the outside may be the tiny amount of radon gas emitted by the granite in the chamber's walls and ceiling. Natural products, including many types of stone, often contain trace amounts of radioactive elements such as radium, which, when broken down, turns into radon gas. Without proper air flow to release this toxic substance, individuals inside the room breathing in the gas over a prolonged period of time might damage the cells in their lungs or develop other health problems.

The header block was now partway in and partway out of its slot, forming a minor projection on the pyramid's otherwise glass-like exterior wall. But the stone was no match for the strong workers whose job was to fit it into place with optimal precision. Moving in concert and employing brute strength, the team secured to the pull-rope slipped the header block into the only empty spot left around the cavity where the future air shaft would be. The result of their labor was a rectangular opening, three feet, five inches wide and three feet, 11 inches tall, and more than 100 courses up the north wall.

The hole in the side of the massive structure did not remain that size for long. The reality was that the Egyptians were approaching the end of the construction process and would not have to elevate either filler materials or casing stones to such extreme heights ever again. Conditions were primed to reduce the scope of the northern shaft once and for all. But the builders would not seal up this passageway completely because, just as researchers have speculated for centuries, retaining a permanent opening was the end goal — to let fresh air into the pyramid and toxic gases out. One example of such toxicity was linked to the granite lining the King's Chamber, which naturally emits minute amounts of radon gas.

Insert Blocks

As described previously, the Egyptians' approach to reducing the parameters of the former northern and southern center channels, which had served as conduits for delivering the building blocks for the Great Pyramid, was as clever as it was unique. The northern shaft linked to the King's Chamber was the last one that the builders had to narrow down. After quarrying pieces of limestone sized to fit the tunnel's internal dimensions, stonecutters had notched them out to create a squared-off groove along the center-bottom of each block. The crew on-site planned to drag a succession of these precut blocks up the close-fitting passageway to reduce the interior of the original channel to a tight hole.

The northern pull-rope would draw the inserts up one by one, with a worker trailing behind to secure them in place. Rigging the blocks properly was the key to the project's success. The team in the Lever Room took a board longer than the width of the groove on the block's underside and attached it horizontally to the line. Then they laid the indentation along the bottom of the first insert over the rope and positioned the board, which stopped short of the stone's outer edges, to sit flat against the southern face (the side toward the low end of the tunnel).

Tugging on the line would force the board hard against the block, catch it, and move the load forward. The wooden plank also had holes bored through each end with a length of work-rope fastened to either side. Those lines held a seat or swing where a crew member would be able to kneel and follow the insert up the passageway.

The initial insert block, quarried from the white, polished limestone and cut at a 52-degree angle on one side, represented the final piece of cladding for the space that the setback in the north wall formerly occupied. The first and uppermost insert was also the only one that had to turn the narrow internal corner inside the passageway. Since this block would come to a stop on the horizontal portion of the shaft, the team did not have to worry about it falling backwards. But they did have to make certain that the new casing stone with the notched-out base fit precisely inside its slot. For that reason, before the workers on the north wall hooked to the pull-rope depart, they would climb up to assist in the installation process and confirm that the outer edges of the new piece lay flat and even with rest of the façade.

Shortly after the first piece with a notched-out base was in place, crews lowered the worker who had been following it back down the tunnel and began outfitting the next insert block for its journey upward. Composed of standard limestone, the second one would sit right at the bend in the passageway. Since this position placed it at the intersection where the incline encountered a vertical plane (the back end of the insert at the top), the north face of block number two was beveled. The slanted surface would allow the second stone in the queue to sit flush against the initial insert. Similar to what had occurred when filling in the gaps between the sides of the Grand Gallery, which rest at an angle, and the vertical Antechamber wall, the crew may have also shaved off the upper edge of the second insert to eliminate the small tip above the seam where the two blocks met.

Before the builders could shrink down the rest of a shaft rising at a 32-degree angle, they had to find a way to lock the insert blocks into place. Otherwise, gravity would cause them to slide downhill. The strategy engineers had devised relied on wooden pegs about six to eight inches long wedged into the sides of the tunnel to prevent the blocks from dropping back down the hole. To that end, the crew's toolkits must have included pegs of varying lengths to achieve the correct fittings.

The procedure involved preparing the block by chiseling shallow cavities on its east and west faces before the insert started up the slope. Workers chipping out the rock considered where the depressions would fall relative to the insert's front (north) end, centering the hollows between the two edges. Then, taking into account how far the carved-out sections were from the back end of the previous insert, plus adding in the length of the stick of wood, the crew measured the same distance down the sides of the shaft. After marking the exact point where the bottom end of the dowel would fall, they hacked concave gashes into those spots on the tunnel walls.

When a new insert block traveled up the shaft and was flat against the back end of the stone in front of it, the worker on the swing would slip the pegs into the upper pockets (the depressions on the sides of the block). As soon as the pegs were in place and the pullers released some of the tension on the rope, allowing it to go a little slack, the heft of the stone slid the hunks of wood slightly downward until they were firmly lodged inside the nicks in the walls.

No one knows exactly how much space there might have been between the insert blocks and the tunnel walls, but the Griffith theory suggests that the process required only a couple of inches to work — enough room to fit someone's hand or a pair of long-handled pliers or tongs squeezed together. The worker on the mobile seat may have also had a partner who climbed up behind him, and after steadying himself, waited for the order to begin the installation. When the crucial moment came, those two workers, each attending to a single peg, inserted it on their side of the block at the same time, which cemented the insert in place.

The dowels wedged into the walls were not intended to carry the weight of the entire column of heavy stones forever; they only had to last as long as it took to install the series of insert blocks between the Lever Room's ledge and the 102nd course, which is one reason why they may have been made out of wood instead of stone. Wood will deteriorate after a certain amount of time, and when it fell apart, gravity would force the blocks inside the shaft more tightly together, thereby eliminating any gaps between the stones. Over the centuries, the sheer volume of blocks incorporated into almost every inch of the Great Pyramid's interior locked all of the elements of the northern air shaft into a permanent position.

[CHAPTER 21]

A CHAMBER VANISHES

Construction moved in a new direction, with the lowest insert block plugged into the tunnel above the shelf on the north side of the Lever Room. The longest segment of the air shaft was finished and now the issue was connecting the opening at that end of the room, which was built into the base of the ledge, to the hole in the corbelled wall on the south side. At this stage, progress was no longer predicated on workers raising additional blocks up the northern shaft because for all intents and purposes that elevation channel was gone. The passageway was only wide enough for the pull-rope to get through. Operations were switching over to packing the open space inside the Lever Room from floor to ceiling with filler — and in the process, joining the two ends of the air shaft together. After that, the Egyptians would seal up the room for good.

A second significant change was also on the horizon. The builders were getting ready to abandon the pull-rope on the north side of the building, which had been central to their operations virtually since pyramid construction began. Removing the last rope located high up the north face of the pyramid meant that from now on, the builders would have to rely almost entirely on the counterweight in the Descending Passage to move the necessary building materials upward. But before the team withdrew the rigging that dropped down the side of the building, the group hanging onto that line would perform one final task from their perches below the minute opening in the outside wall.

Still attached to their tag lines while slowly climbing down the rope, these workers were going to detach the roller stands and stanchions affixed to the outer wall, which had corralled the pull-ropes for decades and prevented them from slapping against the fragile exterior. They planned to send the equipment to the bottom and patch up the holes in the façade as they descended. As the people clinging to the heavy line slowly lowered themselves down the side of the building for the last time, they polished the casing stones that had held the various rope-guides. The goal was to erase as many of the marks on the brilliant white cladding as possible until every speck of evidence related to the construction process had faded from view. In truth, because the height and breadth of the Great Pyramid of Giza is so immense, minor imperfections in the outer walls would mostly have been invisible to the naked eye.

As a rule, the pull-ropes were tied off at both ends whenever workers were using them as ladders to climb up and down the side of the building. In this case, once the people connected to the single line had landed firmly on the northern platform again, the crew inside the Lever Room disconnected their end. They made additional modifications by removing the swing-chair that had followed the insert blocks up the passageway, along with anything else that might impede the line traveling back up the air shaft. When someone gave the signal, the pullers stationed on the ramp started tugging, which caused the freed rope to shoot quickly through the tunnel and fall to the bottom in a massive heap.

The method the builders had adopted to raise additional blocks was also undergoing a significant change. The single pulley-stand mounted on the Great Step remained in place, connected to a much lighter, smaller version of the lift, which still functioned as the primary carrier for the building materials. The pulley at the top of the gallery ramp would continue to help elevate the loads for a while, but the real power for the next phase of the construction operation was slated to come from the workers rotating the big wheel inside the Subterranean Chamber, which was hooked up to the heavy counterweight in the Descending Passage.

The team stationed outdoors controlling the ropes attached to the high end of the underground weight, which exited the pyramid at Course 19 before meandering beneath the northern platform, was a critical component in the reimagined system. Once the lift had climbed up the Grand Gallery and unloaded its cargo, this group was responsible for dragging the counterweight back up the descending passageway to reset it — just as they had done thousands of times before.

In general, the pieces of limestone quarried to fill in the Lever Room were smaller than most of the other building blocks and thus a little easier to handle. Smaller also meant they were lighter, which had a direct impact on the amount of weight the lift in the Grand Gallery had to carry. The chunks of filler would enter the room as they always had: through the small doorway in the corridor's west wall. Even taking into account the stones' somewhat diminished size, it is reasonable to assume the crew continued to employ the shadoof mounted on the stepped platform at the center of the room to assist them for as long as possible.

Chock-Full

The machine's arm was able to pick up individual blocks coming through the gap in the wall one at a time and deposit them on top of the ledge to begin packing that area up to the ceiling. To prepare the space, workers had already dismantled the sleds on top of the shelf and sent the parts down on the lift, along with other extraneous tools and equipment. Since the shadoof had a very short rotation arc due to the confines of the room, it merely lifted the filler blocks and dropped them on top of the shelf. Then the gang assigned to that work zone took the individual pieces and pulled or shoved them toward the far wall.

Working their way west to east, they slowly filled in the first row with standard limestone, overlaying the ledge. Using the same technique, the crew would keep adding more and more layers to the flat surface until the stack of filler reached the ceiling and they ran out of space to work.

The bottommost row of blocks included one crucial accommodation. The Egyptians had originally built a short segment of the air shaft into the ledge's base, and it culminated in a trim hole (5" x 7") on top of the shelf, directly below the lower edge of the rectangular opening in the north wall leading into the chute. The result was a small cavity in the floor in the area where the workers stood to direct the loaded sleds into the shaft. Consequently, before packing the entire ledge with course after course of filler, the team had to install a uniquely shaped piece of limestone specially designed to join the two holes together on top of the ledge. Otherwise, per the new theory, the northern air shaft would have had a nearly foot-long break in the middle of it. After workers had added this important linkage to the first layer of filler, they resumed the job of loading up the remaining space above the shelf with rows of squared-off limestone blocks.

It was also incumbent upon the Egyptians to start extending the air shaft from the opening built into the front of the ledge's base southward — to begin its trek toward the prefabricated hole in the corbelled wall on the other side of the room. But they could not initiate that project until the work gangs had increased the height of the Lever Room floor. The cavity in the room's south wall sat several feet east and a little lower than the one on the north side built inside the ledge. The repercussion was that the last few sections of the air shaft would span the room on the diagonal.

As soon as the team joined the holes on the north and south sides together, lengthening the small opening by another six feet or so, the northern air shaft would finally be complete. This mysterious passageway, which started in the King's Chamber before wending its way behind the south wall of the future Lever Room, would finally become a single, unbroken channel extending hundreds of feet up — to the outer face of the Great Pyramid.

Work proceeded as more filler blocks arriving from the lift were delivered through the small door and workers started covering almost three-quarters of the floor with chunks of limestone. The space that the team wanted to pack was only about six feet wide north to south and 20 feet long east to west. The room did not extend as far as the west wall of the King's Chamber but stopped short of that boundary. Moreover, engineers had always planned on retaining a modest amount of open space near the entrance to the Lever Room to leave enough room to replace the blocks from the Grand Gallery's west wall and preserve a pathway to the escape hatch. As a result, a limited area around the runway formed by the tipped-back wall blocks remained free of filler.

The plan was to build up the floor as close to the ceiling as possible and incorporate the steps from the center platform into the new courses as they developed. The technique the builders employed was reminiscent of the approach they had taken in closing up the niche in the north wall at Course 98. But in this case, the team would not have to contend with the 52-degree slope of an exterior wall or worry about handling pieces of the precious Tura limestone cladding.

The most efficient method for filling up the room was to create a series of stepped levels and use angled blocks as temporary ramps to raise the raw materials up to the higher rows. Since it was impossible to turn the shadoof around due to the size of the room, a safe assumption is that by this time, workers had pulled the machine apart and transferred the pieces onto the lift for the trip down the Grand Gallery to the construction entrance. In the interim, the system of transmitting blocks to fill up the Lever Room carried on like a conveyor belt. Beginning at the west wall and using ramp stones, jacks, ropes, levers, and wooden wedges, the team constructed a series of tiered levels, which grew taller as the steps slowly crept eastward toward the middle of the space.

The construction team may have also employed a couple of portable, single-rope pulleys mounted on an upper row to hoist the blocks from step to step. With a simple pulley available to assist them in moving the stones up the short ramps, workers would not have to handle them using physical strength alone. The buildout continued until the steps inching forward from the west wall reached the vacant center platform, and the scene was set for the two ends of the northern air shaft to meet.

Hooked Together

The uppermost level of the deck at the center of the room was slightly lower than the opening built into the base of what previously constituted the ledge, which by now was fully assimilated into the flat north wall. This made it an ideal height for installing the final approximately six-foot-long segment of the air shaft. Because the distance in between the north and south walls was so minimal, it would require only two blocks of limestone positioned end to end to cover the expanse. In addition, since the southern opening sat lower and further east than the northern one, the differences in position and height meant the last section of the shaft would traverse the space at a slight angle. The work gang assigned to the south side of the room had started the process while they were adding a row of filler by inserting a block that was slanted on top directly in front of the hole on that side. To match existing segments of the air shaft, they had also placed a thin slab of a more durable material over the ramp stone to serve as the passageway's floor.

While constructing the next level, the team slid a second block that was also angled on top into the space between the initial one sitting next to the hole at the south end and the cavity in the north wall. This latest block, which crews lined up with the opening originally built into the ledge, received a hard stone liner on top, too. As the work progressed, crews would set the same type of upside-down U-shaped insert blocks they had installed in other sections of the shaft over the two ramp stones. Since the southern opening sat a little lower than the northern one, putting this portion of the passageway on an incline, the notched-out blocks were resting on a slope. To compensate for the angle, workers would set a couple of blocks slanted on the bottom in subsequent rows, above the pair of inserts, to bring everything back to level. With the final two pieces of their "pipeline" in place, the Egyptians had cause to celebrate. After countless decades and a remarkable amount of effort, the air shaft on the north side of the King's Chamber was whole.

Still, the workers laboring to fill in the remaining space in the Lever Room did not let up. It is impossible to say for certain whether the tiny portion of the Great Pyramid the Griffith theory has labeled the Lever Room contains any voids now. Crews must have stuffed as much of it as possible with blocks while leaving an unobstructed area around the slabs on the floor, which were part of the Grand Gallery. They needed enough space to be able to restore those blocks to their original positions and close up the gap in the side wall. Before shutting down the room forever, the builders may have also stashed smaller chunks of limestone cut to an exact fit into any lingering crevices and corners.

Shutting the Door

A pivotal moment occurred when the team was ready to eliminate the doorway from the Grand Gallery, which opened into the miniscule portion of the main work area that still existed on Course 49. They would seal up the entrance even before their project to eradicate the Lever Room concluded by restoring the blocks removed from the gallery's west wall. Before permanently shutting down the entrance, however, workers must have brought in as many filler stones as possible to keep packing the space full. They recognized that before long, the only option left for delivering additional blocks would depend on them taking the pieces in hand and literally pushing them one by one, through the "manhole" located at floor level, toward their colleagues standing inside the room.

Originally created via a carefully calibrated procedure, the solitary doorway into the Lever Room had evolved from two wall blocks set beneath a special lintel or header block installed on the west side of the Grand Gallery corridor. The upper piece the team had removed to create the entrance had come out of the wall first and was lowered down to Course 49. The lower block, which was also shoved forward (west) and laid on the floor, was the second one out. The two pushed together against the Great Step had formed a short runway for sliding chunks of quarried limestone into the room. The order of the wall blocks' removal would be reversed during their restoration.

To be clear, workers had never rotated the hefty wall blocks or turned them on different sides. Both lay in the same direction north-south as when they had emerged from the gallery wall. The issue that confronted the builders was not only how to slip the finished limestone back into place but to do it in a way that maintained the 26-degree angle of the side walls. Once again, the solution to the problem involved a series of wooden wedges cut flat on the bottom and at a 13-degree angle along the upper edge. Since the first block the crew wanted to elevate was the lower one situated next to the gallery wall, they did not have to reposition it. They could simply raise the slab in small increments until it was high enough and at the correct angle to slide back into its berth.

Taking long levers in hand, a work gang stationed at the south end of the block jacked it up and slipped in the first wedge, which was shorter north to south than the piece of limestone, ramming it underneath the back end to hold the block off the floor. After placing wooden shims directly below the portion of the stone overhanging the wedge to use as the new leverage point, the group jacked up the block higher and forced a second wedge — also angled at 13 degrees — on top of the first one. By this time, the lower wall block was even with the edge of its slot, resting on an incline of 26 degrees. This position allowed the crew to slide it sideways into the wall.

Because the upper wall block sat further west on the floor, the crew members had to move it closer to the gallery before they could begin the replacement process. And since this piece was originally positioned higher in the wall, it necessitated lining up a few filler stones to create an approximately three-foot-high base from which to elevate the piece to the same height and angle as its hole. The team also took a separate block of filler limestone with a slanted face and used it as a temporary ramp to move the wall slab onto the base blocks.

GALLERY WALL BLOCKS · RESTORATION

Restoring the blocks taken from the Grand Gallery's west wall permanently closed off access to the Lever Room from the lift.

Then, taking their levers in hand, workers lifted the south end of the stone and shoved one of the 13-degree angled wedges beneath it. After that maneuver, they placed chunks of wood below the overhang on the underside. Employing their levers again against the wooden shims, the work gang lifted the south end higher and shoved the second wedge into the space below the slab. By then, the block lay on a 26-degree incline parallel to its slot, which allowed the crew to simply push it into the pocket. And with that final thrust, the entrance to the Lever Room vanished forever.

Escape Hatch

Long before the Lever Room had come into existence, the Egyptians had arranged a way for their workers to be able to close up the chamber and leave.

Decades earlier, while designing and building the low shelf and corbelled wall at the south end of the work area on Course 49, engineers had left an opening three feet wide and three feet tall at floor level on that side — between the east end of the ledge and the Antechamber. It was enough space for someone to crawl through. The hole survived because the builders had also placed a couple of header blocks back-to-back above the opening, incorporating them into the south wall. During the era when the Lever Room was operational, the escape hatch would have been visible near the southeast corner of the floor.

The opening went back (south) almost six feet. The initial four feet had a very short ceiling because that part of the tunnel lay below the pair of header blocks. A person would have been forced to slide on their belly to traverse the initial portion of the passageway. The roof above the next section — less than two-foot-long — of the hatch was higher, with a sufficient amount of vertical space for a worker to kneel or squat before standing up because one of the three-foot-high blocks overhead was missing. At a mere 21 inches plus or minus north to south, turning around or maneuvering was definitely a tight squeeze.

Viewing the exit corridor from a more spatial perspective, it existed between the edge of the corbelled wall at the south end of the Lever Room on the west side and the north end of the Antechamber to the east. A little less than six feet back from the point where workers exited the Lever Room, they would make a left turn toward the Antechamber and eventually end up inside that area, standing on the north side of the Granite Leaf.

During this timeframe, the escape corridor was by no means a straight, even plane all the way out. Someone surfacing from underneath the header blocks who turned east would have had a three-foot-high limestone block, the northwest corner of the Antechamber's floor, staring them in the face. They would have to scramble on top of that block to make their way back to the lift. The slot the Griffith theory says that the workers came through was the width of one of the two matching pieces of limestone situated at the north end of the otherwise granite-lined Antechamber. This opening on the west side, which no longer exists, foreshadowed one more place in the Great Pyramid where the ancient Egyptians would mask what was once a necessary hole.

Before the great exodus from the Lever Room happened, crews had to finish up the job of packing the last quarter of the chamber with filler. Now that the entrance from the Grand Gallery was closed off, construction activity had become a handheld operation. Removing blocks from the lift, workers carried each stone through the small maze around the Antechamber entrance before handing it off to someone in the escape corridor who pushed the limestone underneath the header blocks and through the opening toward the work gang stationed inside. The group inside then added the latest piece to the stacks already piled up around the ever-shrinking space. By the time the rows of filler had reached the opening in the southeast corner, the chamber known as the Lever Room did not exist anymore and the very last worker had crawled out.

The next item on the agenda was a project bent on eliminating every trace of what had existed within this small portion of the Great Pyramid. First up were two blocks three feet tall, three feet wide, and approximately 21 inches thick — narrow enough to fit through the slot at the north end of the Antechamber. Another block three feet by three feet but only six inches thick would be the third one in line as the job proceeded. Together, this trio would close off the four-foot-long space beneath the pair of lintels above the escape route. After pushing the first slab through the slot by the Antechamber, the team lowered it down into the passageway leading to the Lever Room. Then they pushed the block forward (north) until all four edges were flush with the front of the opening, sealing that exit point. The second block followed the same general track and routine. And once the third and narrower three-foot-high block was set into place, the longest part of the escape corridor had been permanently locked off.

Securing that fragment of the escape hatch south of the header stones also involved a set of precisely cut blocks, which ultimately would do away with the access route altogether. Crews began by sliding a slab (3' x 3' x 21") through the slot at the north end of the Antechamber and dropping it off the edge into the hole before pushing the block up against the escape route's west wall. Slipping a second slab the same size through the gap and into the small chasm below made the top of the three-foot-tall piece of limestone even with the floor block from the Antechamber, thereby eliminating the drop-off. The position of those two blocks situated side by side, plugging up the narrow corridor on the 49th course, had laid the groundwork for the escape route's complete eradication.

As they maneuvered a third three-foot-high stone through the tight slot near the front of the Antechamber, the crew pushed it west onto the lower block next to the far wall. Block number four comprised the concluding piece of the jigsaw puzzle. True to form, the builders were extremely fastidious in the way they inserted this final block, hoping to camouflage the opening that heretofore had led to the Lever Room. Similar to the methods used to insert the wall blocks inside the Queen's Chamber that contained the rectangular openings for the air shafts, stonecutters at the quarry had slightly beveled all four edges to ensure an exact fit once the precisely cut stone was inserted into its slot.

The idea was to make it appear as if the limestone had been there from the beginning and thus preclude any possibility of seeing past the edges and deducing that a gap had once existed there. It is impossible to know for certain how the original block was cut or inserted into the wall because this is one of the places inside the Great Pyramid where Captain Giovanni Battista Caviglia, an explorer in the 1800s, dug and dynamited his way through the rock in search of new chambers and treasure.

With the final block in place, leaving behind a flat, even wall, the escape hatch from the Lever Room was nothing more than a memory.

Down the Passageway

Attention now turned to sealing up one of the primary working shafts inside the Great Pyramid of Giza: the First Ascending Passage. For the moment, the pulley mounted on top of the Great Step was still standing and the lift remained operational.

The real work commenced as crews prepared to transport three heavy granite blocks — approximately three and one-half feet wide and 47 inches thick — into the Grand Gallery, together with a fourth block of about the same dimensions but composed of limestone. The limestone and two of the granite slabs were five feet long while the third block of granite was shorter than the other three pieces. Notably, the granite slabs were tapered slightly on the two sides that would end up facing east and west. The builders planned to arrange the blocks in a long row down the gallery corridor until workers were ready to drop them, one by one, into the ascending passageway.

Starting with the initial, shorter granite block traveling through the construction entrance on its own sled, a work gang transferred it onto the lift by placing the slab on the deck longways with the tapered sides facing east and west. Once it was in the correct position, the lift rose as high as it needed to go based on the amount of space required to accommodate a total of four slabs lined up end to end along the gallery ramp. When the lift reached its mark, workers lassoed the piece of stone around the lower end from above and, using a temporary pulley mounted in the floor holes on either side of the corridor, pulled the granite off the lift and partway up the incline. A squat wooden barrier fitted into a couple of ramp holes at the back end prevented it from sliding downhill. The second block in line, designated to sit behind the first one further down the incline, was delivered in the same manner, followed by the third piece of granite and finally the outsized limestone slab.

The Egyptians' preparations for closing the down the First Ascending Passage sparked some dramatic changes to their operations. Soon the lift, which had raised countless loads up the Grand Gallery, would be out of commission. Anticipating that day, crews had begun detaching the ropes affixed to its sides and substructure, and torn apart the pulley-stand that had crowned the Great Step for decades. Separating its beams from the roller, they carried the parts away. Hot on the heels of those developments, the lift itself was dismantled board by board, and the pulleys mounted underground at the intersection of the First Ascending Passage with the Descending Passage were removed.

The one significant object that did *not* disappear was the wooden bridge built over the entrance to the Horizontal Passage, which spanned the gap between the notched block above the doorway into that tunnel and the entrance to the ascending passageway on the 25th course. The north end of the bridge was pushed against the small lip in the floor, a couple of feet in front of the opening to the First Ascending Passage. The wooden structure would remain in place for a while because it was essential to the process of closing down the ascending passageway.

With the area where the lift had been parked now empty, there was nothing in the upper portion of the tunnel to connect with the bottom edge of the Grand Gallery and extend its floor. In reality, the cleared-out space at the top was nothing more than a six-foot-wide void that made an abrupt break from Course 25 into a deep shaft. The channel descended at a 26-degree angle for 128 feet (a distance almost as long as a 13-story building is tall) until it ended underground at the junction with the Descending Passage. Luckily, the interior slope offered the perfect setup for the next part of the builders' strategy. Sliding three giant slabs of granite and a giant piece of limestone down the incline and into the breach would make the channel virtually impassable by jamming it up with bulky blocks. Which is exactly what they intended to do.

The idea was to push all four blocks waiting in the wings farther up the ramp into the ascending passageway to permanently secure one of the potential entry points into the Great Pyramid. The contours of the First Ascending Passage were promising because the tunnel contained a collection of large stone girdles, and each of them had a large square hole with a beveled interior cut through the middle of it. The series of girdles stood upright to the horizontal plane.

The three girdles located toward the passageway's upper end were quarried from single slabs of high-grade, finished limestone and sat about 17 feet (17' 2") apart from each other. Conversely, stonecutters had fashioned the string of girdles near the bottom of the tunnel, set close together in a dense row, in two pieces. Engineers had designed the lower group as half-girdles to provide some give, by allowing the top of the square "doughnut" to separate from the bottom. The two-part configuration was critical to the success of the Egyptians' plans since the blocks hauled in earlier and stored inside the gallery corridor would shoot through the holes at the center of the girdles as they descended. The need to pass through these openings on the way down was also why the hard granite blocks used to plug up the channel were tapered on two sides.

The piece of limestone positioned at the lower end of the line of four inside the Grand Gallery sat near the high (south) end of the wooden bridge atop the entrance to the Horizontal Passage. Slated to be the first piece to take the plunge, it was in the start position. Limestone is much softer than other types of rock, so it seems that the builders were not as concerned about this block making its way down the chute, and had decided to leave it as is without tapering the sides. It was also the case that the first piece out of the gate was intended to fulfill a specific purpose. The Egyptians had chosen limestone because it was the best choice for disguising the opening between the lower portion of the First Ascending Passage and the Descending Passage.

Their strategy was bold and ingenious. The team knew that when the limestone dropped more than 100 feet and hit the far end of the tunnel, the force would be sufficient to start pushing the block's front edge through the hole directly above the Descending Passage. Then, one after the other, as the three heavy chunks of granite were pushed down the shaft and banged into the back end of the previous block, the sequence would act like hammer blows to shove the limestone even farther through the opening. Moreover, during the course of getting hit from behind, the limestone's soft edges would begin to conform to the shape of the surrounding rocks in the walls and ceiling, making it appear as if it had been there forever.

The method for releasing a block up top was straightforward. First, the crew removed the short wooden barrier sitting behind the piece of stone. Using muscle power, workers pushed from the back end to propel the slab forward and start it sliding downhill. The weight of the block plus the height and angle of the gallery ramp and wooden bridge provided the necessary momentum for the piece to begin plummeting down the shaft. With the floor underneath the slab a mere 41.5 inches wide, the side walls were narrow enough east to west to keep the descending projectile in its lane and on a relatively straight path downward. The three blocks of granite followed the limestone into the tunnel, with the shortest piece the last one in.

By the end of the operation, after the granite blocks had struck their heavy blows by knocking into each other from behind, a transformation had occurred: The hole in the ceiling where the Descending Passage met the First Ascending Passage no longer existed. The old opening was completely plugged up with almost a foot of limestone that protruded into the intersection from above.

In addition, the series of girdles at the bottom end of the ascending passageway had a long string of granite blocks wedged inside, which reinforced the value of fabricating them in two pieces. The half-girdles could withstand the pressure from the onslaught of the falling stones because they were able to split apart.

The final step in securing the First Ascending Passage was carried out by a work gang assigned to the Descending Passage whose job was to shave back the limestone outcropping — a scheme meant to fool the eye. The problem was that it would be impossible for them to reach that area if the counterweight were in its normal position. However, since the pulleys and ropes converging at the bottom of the First Ascending Passage were gone, the reset team outdoors handling the lines for the counterweight was able to raise it higher inside the channel.

The temporary relocation allowed a small crew entering through the Well Shaft to gain access to the Descending Passage and climb up that passageway to complete the lock-down project. (The workers would use the same route to exit from the underground tunnel when the job was done.) Sanding down the limestone's jagged front end to create a smoother surface was a clever ploy to thwart potential intruders by concealing the fact that an opening had ever been there in the first place.

PASSAGEWAY INTERSECTION
It is almost impossible to tell that the Descending Passage ever opened into the First Ascending Passage.

CHAPTER 22

FINAL COURSES

THE ANCIENT EGYPTIANS MUST have looked forward with great anticipation to the day when their enormous construction project would draw to a close. They were poised to bequeath an engineering marvel to the world. With the end in sight, the focus now shifted to filling in the pie-shaped slash on the pyramid's north side that had served as the construction entrance.

Plans were also underway to construct a formal entry into the building, as well as install safeguards to prohibit access to potential interlopers who tried to get inside. Culminating efforts to seal up the Great Pyramid were in full swing, beginning with a series of renovations to the upper end of the First Ascending Passage.

According to the Griffith theory, during this era, the top of the passage-way had a different configuration from what the channel looks like today. And while the shaft was entirely closed off by limestone and granite plugs at the bottom (north) end, workers had not yet built out the upper section near the entrance where the ascending passageway joins the Grand Gallery to make it conform more closely to the gallery's appearance as a whole. After finishing work on the tunnel's interior, the team would bookend the larger corridor by adding corbels over the entrance to the First Ascending Passage that corresponded with the wall above the Antechamber's door.

The process of revamping the portion of the First Ascending Passage just below the Grand Gallery was primarily a matter of narrowing down the space east to west by adding panels to the side walls and installing a ceiling inside. The builders had originally lined the initial 34+ feet of the passageway with dressed limestone blocks because that area was where the great lift parked, capping a deep hole. A short, triangular wooden wedge inserted between the vehicle's blunt-nosed front end and the top of the 25th course had extended its deck, which made the wooden lift part of the flat, unobstructed surface that materials and equipment rode in on as they entered the building.

Similar to the rest of the gallery ramp, which had functioned as a track for the lift transporting loads toward the Great Step, the upper end of the First Ascending Passage included a pair of matching ledges on the east and west sides. In the beginning, crews had set a series of blocks (20.6" x 6') on the floor inside the tunnel to extend the lift track below Course 25 by continuing the 26-degree angle further down the shaft. These platforms were as wide and tall as the ones hugging both walls along the steep, 157-foot-long gallery ramp. The limestone blocks used for the lowest portion of the track also sported a series of recesses on top to hold the stone rollers that supported the lift's "wings."

Prep Work

Imminent renovations to the ascending passageway were also the catalyst for more changes. Crews had dismantled the lift months earlier, before they had sent a sizable hunk of limestone and three large granite blocks down the tunnel to close it off at the bottom. The lift's departure had resulted in a more than 30-foot-long, sloped chasm in the floor of the 25th course — at least 15 feet deep at the north end and almost seven feet wide east to west. The problem the ancient Egyptians faced was how to compensate for the fact that there was a big hole where the lift's wooden deck and substructure used to be, and still deliver the necessary blocks from the quarry to jumpstart the next phase of construction. The solution was to either jury-rig the top of the old lift to turn it into a temporary bridge straddling the gap in the floor or cobble together a brand-new deck and lay it across the cavity.

Since the refurbishing work was occurring in the same general area where stones and equipment had always entered the building, the delivery process was predictable. The limestone panels to cover the walls and narrow down the upper section of the passageway were smaller than the blocks lining the sides of the Grand Gallery, and were probably transported to the site on individual sleds. Then the team transferred the blocks intended for the interior walls and ceiling, along with the pieces that would surround the entrance, and stored them inside the gallery. With the raw materials available near the top of the shaft, workers would be able to rely on gravity to help them move the wall panels and ceiling slabs down the slope and into the tunnel. After the collection of blocks and equipment was stockpiled in the Grand Gallery corridor, a separate work gang broke down the temporary wooden deck and carried it away.

Refurbishing

Composed of smooth, high-grade limestone, the panels arriving to overlay the First Ascending Passage's interior walls were the same width as the lift track (20.6"). Each piece was about three feet long and almost four feet high — the current height of the passageway from floor to ceiling. To judge from the seams still visible on the walls, it appears as if the builders had removed the pair of ledges that were part of the lift track before renovating the space. Taking a page from an earlier playbook, the group tasked with covering the walls with another sheet of stone took the first block targeted for the west side from the supply stored in the gallery and lassoed it around the bottom end. Then they lowered the slab into the shaft until it bumped into a wooden wedge set against the highest girdle in the passageway where another crew was waiting.

The wedge holding the two objects apart provided enough room for workers to remove the rope from around the piece of limestone. Once they knocked out the hunk of wood, the wall block settled back into its permanent position. The teams at the top and bottom repeated the process on the other side of the tunnel before continuing to thicken the walls panel by panel, alternating west and east. As usual, because the wall slabs sat on a sloped floor, the front ends of the northernmost (lowest) blocks on both sides were beveled. The slanted edges allowed the pair to rest flat against the vertical stone girdle. Covering the original limestone walls piece by piece gradually shrank the passageway from just under seven feet across to about half as wide (3' 5") — the size of the tunnel as it exists today.

To an observer standing in the Grand Gallery studying the entrance to the First Ascending Passage, an obvious but critical feature stands out: While the tunnel descends sharply downward from the 25th course, heading "underground" at a 26-degree angle, the threshold is even with Course 25.

If the ascending passageway were still open at the bottom and a first-time visitor able to climb up the shaft from below, they might reasonably expect the opening at the south end to be nothing more than a hole in the floor overhead, similar to the opening for the Well Shaft. Instead, the ceiling above the doorway is almost four feet higher than the top of Course 25 — tall enough for someone to bend over and scoot through.

This design was partially the result of the newly installed interior walls, which, at that time, approached but never actually reached the upper end of the passageway where the Grand Gallery begins. Construction of the line of wall blocks had stopped just short of the 25th course, several feet back from the edge of the floor, because before the team could install the last two panels in the side walls, they had to tackle the next part of the operation. This phase entailed finishing off the recently condensed space by erecting a roof overhead. Since the distance inside the channel east to west was now so minimal, it would have been fairly easy for crew members to use the standing walls as rails to slide the ceiling slabs down the incline as far as the uppermost girdle. Again, the initial ceiling block lowered into the hole was not entirely rectangular but shaped to fit tight against the upright girdle, and cut on an angle at the front end.

Placement of the first few roof slabs, in turn, was the impetus for a second procedure to get underway. The lengthy slot originally set aside for the lift was shaped like a right triangle whose hypotenuse ran from the top of the 25th course at the south end to approximately 15 feet below the surface at the north end. After the team had inserted the initial ceiling block, a crew up top stationed on the north side of the hole began lowering down blocks of standard limestone to a work gang standing on the new roof slab.

Since the chunks of stone were not huge, it would have been relatively easy for the group at the northern edge of the pit receiving the raw materials from the exterior platform to lower each block on a rope to the people below. The hand-off set in motion the process of installing a roof slab, then packing the empty space above it with filler as ceiling construction advanced southward. The idea was to keep adding filler blocks on top of the roof until the packed area eventually reached high enough to be even with the floor of Course 25 and the cavity disappeared.

While the length of the ceiling gradually increased with every new slab that the crew installed, the gang packing the roof kept building up, then out, toward the south. This method created stepped levels, which enabled them to raise both the blocks — and themselves — higher as the stacks of filler grew. The gap between the top of the passageway's roof and the 25th course, which was gradually diminishing, was fairly deep at the north end but narrow east to west. Covering its width may have involved inserting only two or three small blocks side by side. It is worth noting that because the ceiling itself was on a slope, the blocks forming the first or lowest layer of filler were always slanted on the bottom. The angled pieces brought the base back to level, producing a flat, horizontal surface for the succeeding rows.

The people piling filler above the roof worked back from the north end of the hole, adding more blocks each time the group at the south end introduced another ceiling slab. As the operation proceeded, the dimensions of the unfilled space would fluctuate. Due to the angle of the roof, which brought the ceiling closer to the top of the hole as it advanced southward, the distance between the highest layer of filler stones and the edge of the floor decreased with every section the team packed. The smaller angle reduced the amount of filler required on top of the ceiling. The unique building methods the Egyptians employed permitted workers to not only regularly move up step by step along with the newly installed course blocks but also add filler as high as it had to go, until it was even with the top of Course 25.

Entrance

Slab by slab, the ceiling inside the initial 34 feet of the tunnel came together until the roof was a single block-length away from the bottom of the Grand Gallery and the job came to a halt. The final ceiling slab was still missing, but before crews could set that piece into place, they had to fabricate the framework for a more impressive entrance. Sometime earlier, when workers were demolishing the ledges inside the ascending passageway, they had removed the southernmost blocks from the lift track on the east and west sides and the ramp stones underneath those two pieces.

The idea was to create a flat surface in the area where the interior walls would meet the future entrance. The slope in the tunnel meant that stonecutters had to compensate for the inevitable gap that occurs when a slanted object joins a vertical plane. As a result, they had angled the south end of the second-to-last block in the ceiling and the front edges of the highest wall panels on both sides. The beveled faces on those three blocks would fix them hard against the doorframe once it was constructed.

GRAND GALLERY NORTH END

The north end of the Grand Gallery includes a pair of header blocks above the entrance to the First Ascending Passage.

To assemble the doorjamb. workers slipped rectangular blocks about 30 inches high, 20.6 inches long, and 20.6 inches wide into the flat-bottomed slots on the right- and left-hand sides of the gap left open for the entryway. The crew dropped the first two blocks into the slim breaches between the spot where the interior walls had stopped and the edge of the 25th course began. Similar to several other places inside the Great Pyramid, this arrangement put the bottom edge of the initial pair of stones bordering the doorway below the Grand Gallery's floor. Then workers set a second pair of blocks approximately the same size but cut at a 26-degree angle on top, above the first two, to create a doorjamb three feet, 11 inches tall.

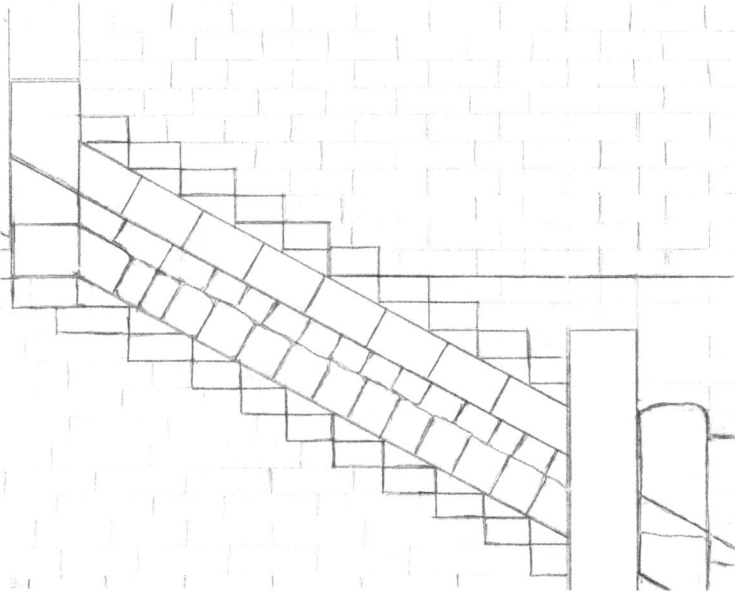

FIRST ASCENDING PASSAGE · BLOCKS

A diagram of the east wall of the First Ascending Passage shows the blocks at the upper left that comprise one side of the doorframe, and the ceiling slabs inside the tunnel descending from behind the header block over the entrance. The illustration also depicts the filler stones stacked on top of the roof when the passageway was being refurbished. Blocks that were angled on the bottom made up the first layer of filler to bring the courses back to level. By packing the space between the passageway's roof and Course 25, the ancient Egyptians gradually eliminated the deep cavity they had fabricated for the lift.

The final component surrounding the doorway was also the final ceiling slab. If someone were to stand inside the Grand Gallery and look north, the next piece the builders installed was the substantial header block that sits directly above the opening into the First Ascending Passage. Later, the ancient Egyptians would install a second lintel stone above this first one seated over the entrance, which ultimately would reduce the number of corbels in the gallery's north wall from seven to six. Contrary to how the other blocks quarried for the renovations were hauled in and stored inside the gallery before the ascending passageway's transformation, workers handling the initial header block had to revise that strategy to maneuver the bulky chunk of limestone into position.

By now, the work gang setting filler above the tunnel's roof had packed it to the upper edge of the hole. Because more than 90% of the cavity originally developed for the lift was located below the level of the 25th course, only the small fraction constituting the entrance to the ascending passageway rose higher than that — three feet, 11 inches high to be exact. As a consequence, the sloping walls jutting up at the south end of the shaft by the gallery were akin to a small ramp. This incline is what the team would employ to help pull the first lintel stone onto the doorjambs.

The size of the header and confined space within the narrowest portion of the construction entrance afforded the workers no room to rotate the stone. The reality of the situation warranted an unusual installation procedure. Measured to fit precisely between the Grand Gallery's east and west walls perpendicular to the block beneath the lowest corbel on either side of the corridor, the lintel stone entered the building from the north, traveling along a straight path southward and facing the same direction as it does in the wall. With the assistance of a pulley mounted inside the gallery to draw the stone forward, the crew would move the final piece of the doorframe into position.

The initial block slated to lay across the entrance rode in on a shallow sled designed to provide a sufficient amount of space underneath the stone for workers to tie a long rope around the middle of it. Traveling over the short incline formed by the walls that jutted up from inside the tunnel, the rope extended southward into the Grand Gallery toward a temporary pulley mounted partway up the ramp in couple of floor holes. After the line had circled around that pulley, a group of workers grabbed it in hand and started walking downhill, propelling the weighty block forward. As soon as it was partway into its slot, the team at the north end standing behind the stone slipped the rope out from underneath and took the sled away. Meanwhile, a different work gang using levers and other tools inched the piece forward until one good push slid the initial header block firmly into its berth.

The underside of the first header stone had been shaved off at a 26-degree angle, which matched the tops of the two short columns comprising the doorjambs. The slanted faces above and below permitted the block to rest flat across the entrance, transforming the final segment of the passageway's ceiling from sloped to level in anticipation of the buildout to come. The giant header stone resting horizontally above the entrance would play a major role in the Grand Gallery's future by becoming the foundation for the series of corbels erected at the north end of the corridor. Balancing out the architectural features found at the top and bottom of the gallery ramp, the corbels that one day would grace its fourth wall were destined to add even more luster to an already magnificent space.

By the time the refurbishing project for the First Ascending Passage was done, the look and interior dimensions of the shaft had undergone a dramatic change. Yet true to form and in keeping with the pyramid's architectural precision, the extensive alterations the Egyptians had labored over made it appear as if the tunnel had been that way since the monument was first constructed.

To the North

With the makeover of the ascending passageway wrapped up, the plan to close down the construction entrance was ready to make some headway. A visitor in the 21st century might find it hard to imagine being able to stand inside a deep cutout on the north side of the pyramid, look straight up, and see nothing overhead but clouds and sky. In truth, that was the layout during this period of the Great Pyramid's history. The triangular-shaped notch extending back almost 60 feet from the outer wall was the byproduct of a sizable section of the original step pyramid associated with the Queen's Chamber that had never been built. Since the beginning of the Egyptians' massive project, the open area on Course 25 adjoining the platform at the top of the northern ramp had been the primary inlet for equipment and supplies. But now work had progressed to the point where that situation was about to change.

On a parallel track, workers posted outdoors had initiated a separate project targeted at the exterior ramp on the north side. The job of closing up the giant gash in the Great Pyramid where workers and provisions arrived would require a steady stream of filler to complete. Instead of spending time and effort chiseling out and transporting thousands of freshly cut blocks, engineers had chosen to make use of the limestone already incorporated into the massive access ramp that led to the northern platform. Eventually, they would have to break down the incline to remove it from the landscape anyway, so why not start demolishing it now?

The first stage involved dismantling the outermost sections of the staircases on both sides while leaving a pair of narrower steps and the ramp's smooth center section intact for the moment. Starting from the bottom of the western staircase first, crews would work their way up, using the elongated structure as the source for a regular supply of stones.

This period when the Egyptians were putting the final touches on the Great Pyramid was also the time when workers began to clear out the building by shedding unnecessary paraphernalia from the interior. The more immediate activity included pulling apart the wooden bridge over the entrance to the Horizontal Passage, as well as disassembling and removing the geared mechanism from the niched wall in the Queen's Chamber. They also carried away inessential ropes, tools, pulleys, scaffolding, and rollers.

Because the area under construction represented the aftermath of an early decision to leave out a huge segment of the original step pyramid, the surface workers would fill had a unique configuration. Since the pyramid's inception, the project had required setting aside space for delivering materials into the building. The team's solution was to bifurcate the step-pyramid on the north side of the Queen's Chamber. The open area retained access to the 25th course from the ramps abutting the structure on three sides and the quarries on the plateau.

In the past, as new courses rose to the left and right of the open supply lane cutting through the internal utility pyramid, a set of sheer walls more than 100 feet tall had taken shape. The west wall extended in a straight line north from the lower end of the Grand Gallery toward the northern platform. But before it reached the front of the building, 40 feet away from the edge, it stepped back, moving approximately 20 feet farther west before continuing on. The small bumpout was part of the space architects had set aside for an official entrance into the Great Pyramid.

On a parallel track, the wall developing along the other side of the inlet stretched north in a straight line 128 feet from the bottom of the Grand Gallery before fanning out toward the east. The layout the builders had conceived left a broad expanse on Course 25 to accommodate the blocks, sleds, and associated equipment entering the site. The length of the gap at its widest point along the pyramid's north side was at least 100 feet east to west.

A few facts are relevant to discussing the supply area's evolution. The walls bordering the construction entrance had developed in concert with the pyramid as a whole, and the Grand Gallery was not built all the way to the ceiling until many decades after its construction began — only when the humongous granite blocks for the Relieving Chambers were in place. In the beginning, engineers had left a couple of feet of empty space, or the width of a narrow walkway, behind the gallery's walls for their workers — space that crews would gradually fill in once they were able to make the sides of the corridor taller.

After the walls had reached the height of the seventh corbel, a 28-foot-high ceiling covered the lengthy gallery as well as the area above the lift, carrying the roof further north. It continued for another 128 feet atop the two vertical walls flanking the part of the inlet allocated for the people and cargo entering the building. The extension was a critical element in the pyramid's development because it created the base for building the monument higher. While a roof stretching that full length had turned a good portion of the construction entrance into an enclosed passageway, the Egyptians had no other option. Fabricating courses as far north as possible as early as possible was central to the success of the project writ large.

The team needed a solid foundation upon which to build more layers or construction would never have reached Course 98, where a critical pulley-stand was mounted. The only way to start building higher and one day finish the upper portion of the Great Pyramid on the north side was to assemble courses above the gallery and around the construction entrance, which meant stacking blocks on top of the gallery's roof extension. No doubt the resulting tunnel, which was only 28 feet high and little less than seven feet wide (the width of the Grand Gallery east to west), constricted the access route for the raw materials at the point of entry. Blocks and equipment arriving on-site were forced to pass through the tunnel before they could be loaded onto the lift.

Building out the original portion of the pyramid left exposed to accept the supplies would proceed in a manner consistent with the methods that the Egyptians had employed when they closed up the gash in the north wall at Course 98. In that situation, engineers had left out blocks to produce a setback in the wall because they needed a place to hold an essential shadoof and pulley-stand on the north side. When the time finally came to seal over the recess hundreds of feet up the wall, workers had packed it with filler and installed the cladding as they proceeded to cover the area around the machines and the hole in the floor (now an air shaft) where the blocks emerged from the Lever Room. Mimicking this successful method, work gangs shutting down the construction entrance would start with a line of white casing stones set along the front edge of each course, then load up the empty space behind it with standard limestone filler. In general, construction would move from north to south, building upward as it followed the slope of the pyramid.

Delivery Channel

The creative decision undergirding the Egyptians' current strategy was to extract the filler for the project from the staircases built into the northern ramp by narrowing down the steps and transporting the blocks up the slope on individual sleds. A logical assumption is that the builders made use of the two existing pulleys mounted at the front edge of the northern platform to haul up the stones. Workers handling the rope tied to a wooden sled and circling one of the pulleys, would be able to generate enough power to drag the weight of a single block up to the top of the hill.

A more difficult situation arose when the sleds were still a short distance below the northern platform. The pulleys' height and position made it impossible to move the load onto the deck due to the angle of the ropes. As a consequence, crews had to rely on muscle power alone to move the vehicle up the last several feet, over the threshold, and onto the level surface. When the sled landed, the shadoof picked up the block of limestone and set it down on a storage pile until it was needed.

The Tura limestone cut to sheath the outer wall came on site as it always had: offloaded from ships docked near the Sphinx, deposited on sleds, and pulled up the ramp on the west side of the building. Turning the northwest corner, the sleds transporting the casing stones traveled down the northern platform to the construction entrance. The preliminary stage of the builders' close-down work would begin with a crew overlaying what was left of Course 25 by the entrance with blocks that filled in the last scraps of empty space from Course 26. They packed the initial level by simply taking the blocks delivered to the northern platform and pushing or pulling them into position.

Covering this particular section of the 25th course was significant not only because the original floor inside the decades-old construction entrance would cease to exist, but also because the layout portended what was in store later. Workers had painted a line on the floor indicating where the center of the Grand Gallery would have been if it had continued all the way to the north end of the pyramid. Then they marked off a rectangular area abutting the gallery's centerline to expand it eastward. The other half of the new "box" was the bumpout that crews had incorporated into the construction entrance's west wall as they kept building toward the north. Taken together, the squared-off space that the architects had set aside was about 50 feet wide east to west and at least 60 feet long as measured back from the edge of the outside wall.

When work gangs set the rows of filler stones across the floor of the construction entrance, they would leave the cordoned-off space empty. What began as a shallow cavity in the floor of Course 26 would soon become a deepening hole that slowly turned into a spacious niche. Each new course was going to raise the three sides of the hollow higher until the setback reached its predetermined height — tall enough to accommodate the giant double-layered chevron blocks that would become an archway over the future entrance to the Great Pyramid.

As workers laid down Course 26, they also incorporated several blocks that were cut at an angle on top into the layout, placing them on the east side of the depression in the floor. The set of ramp stones represented the first segment of an approximately 10-foot-wide channel that, in time, would extend southward at a 52-degree angle and climb more than five stories high. Fabricated to carry the sleds and raw materials to complete the unfinished courses, the passage would grow as the number of layers multiplied. In the end, the shaft would be long enough and tall enough to transmit quarried stones to the uppermost reaches of the buildout.

As the next course came together, crews would make use of the lowest portion of the short incline to pull the blocks onto the top of the previous level — Course 26 — since the angle was not yet too steep to bring them up by hand. Slotting a second set of ramp stones into the course-in-progress lengthened the slope by a few more feet. But as soon as the two levels above Course 25 were in place, the angle of the working ramp would have become too vertical to proceed without help. The job required a shadoof.

Staircase for a Shadoof

Setting up the mechanism on top of the course that they had just completed (27), members of the team installed the machine on the east side of the growing delivery channel so that the counterweight at the back end faced eastward and the arm pointed in the opposite direction, toward the west. As efforts to construct the ensuing courses got underway, workers would leave about 10 feet of empty space around the piece of equipment, which they would fill in much later as the project wound down.

In conjunction with the recently assembled shadoof, crews had also mounted a pulley-stand on the same level, with its legs straddling the sides of the budding incline. They had marked off the ramp's dimensions to position the stand correctly but had omitted the angled ramp stones on that particular course. Temporarily retaining a horizontal space in front of the pulley created a small docking station where a sled would be able to rest. Steadying the vehicle by anchoring it on a flat surface also made it much easier to put a choker around the new stone and hook it onto the shadoof. After hitching the piece of limestone to the machine, the shadoof would pick up the block and transfer it to a second sled positioned nearby on the same course.

The builders' core strategy was to create a series of these tiered levels — simulating a step-pyramid — as they worked their way up to the top. At most, the long arm of any single shadoof would only reach as high as four or five courses. Once the height of the stack exceeded the arm's capacity (10–15 feet), the team would move the equipment to access it from a higher level. To that end, work crews would maintain an approximately 20-foot-square open area — 10 feet around the shadoof and 10 feet for the pulley-stand — on every tier.

The portion of each stepped level left open for clearance was located at the front end where the course intersected with the east side of the delivery channel. Since the height of the blocks used for the different layers varied, which, in turn, affected the number of courses the shadoof's arm was able to service, leaving a void on every level allowed the team to assemble a machine wherever they needed it. Retaining a series of relatively small work platforms was a necessary element of a successful buildout. Workers would reclaim the voids where the shadoofs and pulley-stands were mounted by packing them with filler and installing the missing casing stones only when the project was coming to an end.

Switching the equipment from one course to another began with a work gang transporting the pulley-stand straddling the delivery channel several levels up and setting it on top of the last course completed, placing the stand's legs over the area where the ramp stones should have been. With the pulley now gone from the lower course, a small group went back and inserted the angled blocks they had previously left out of the ramp to reconfigure the section where the incline abruptly went flat. Restoration was vital because the next sled making its way uphill would undoubtedly get stuck trying to pass over a break in the channel. The journey upward required a smooth, unbroken pathway for the ride to the top.

The same process of transferring the pulley and shadoof would repeat itself many times during this era. After conveying the parts for the shadoof to the highest new level, workers reassembled the device. The project overall may have required five or more steps equipped with shadoofs and pulleys before the bulk of the construction work was done. That being said, the Griffith theory says that the ancient Egyptians dismantled and reused the same two or three shadoofs on the way up and down. It is highly unlikely that they would have taken the time or gone to the trouble of manufacturing enough components to erect a separate machine on every tier.

Rising Courses

The procedure for elevating the course blocks was simple. Waiting on the northern platform at the bottom of the delivery channel was a small high-backed sled a mere three or four inches off the floor and holding a single piece of limestone. In keeping with the Egyptians' general construction philosophy, the white casing stones would be the first blocks transported for each course. Two long pull-ropes were attached to the sled's front end and strung over the pulley on the highest available tier, with the other end of the ropes dropping back down the channel. The lines were long enough to extend beyond the platform against the outside wall and continue on to the army of pullers waiting on the northern ramp. As they walked forward, the sled slid up the incline toward the level where the shadoof was located. When it reached that step and the team kept pulling, the vehicle's front end tipped forward over the edge of the flat surface where the ramp had temporarily ended.

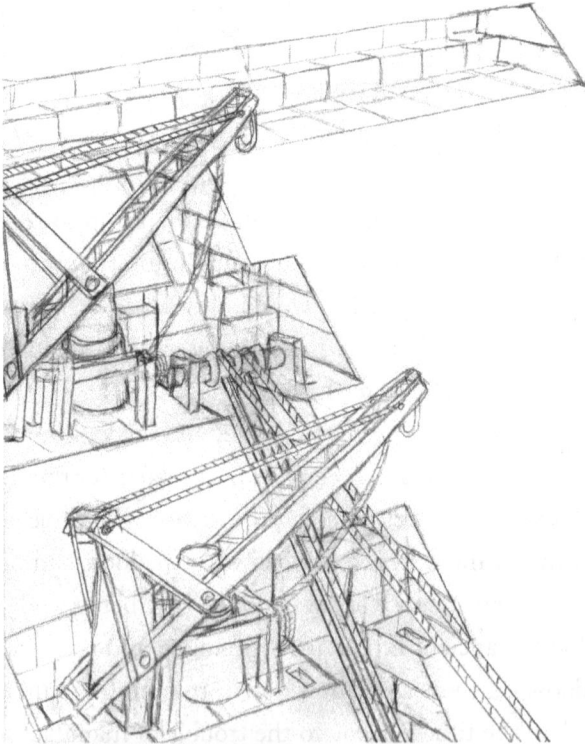

CONSTRUCTION ENTRANCE · SEALING UP

Sealing up the construction entrance involved creating a series of stepped levels, which accommodated the pulleys and shadoofs used to raise the necessary course blocks and casing stones.

Then, with the assistance of the crew posted up top handling the incoming stones, the sled was maneuvered onto the ledge beneath the pulley-stand and unloaded. After wrapping a choker around the block and hooking it to the shadoof, the crew received the signal for the machine to lift it off the small carrier. Once the block was hanging from the arm, the shadoof swung around (south) and set the piece of limestone on a second shallow sled near the front of the course. The work gang responsible for assembling that particular level took over from there.

On each step, when the cladding had been set into place east to west along the course's front edge, workers pushed or pulled the filler blocks toward the walls behind it, working their way back from the south, east, and west sides toward the delivery channel. Maintaining the perfect alignment of the casing stones was paramount while the unpolished, somewhat-misshapen filler did not demand such an exact fit. As the job progressed, crews took great care to pack blocks only up to the boundary lines marking off the area west of the delivery channel where the official entrance to the building would be. Skirting the outline on the floor, crews kept adding blocks around the three sides of the rectangle, increasing the depth of the setback layer by layer.

One reason that engineers had chosen to use sleds instead of hauling the blocks up the delivery channel one by one on their own was to provide some ballast for the pull-ropes. If workers had merely lassoed a lone block and pulled it up the slope, they might have lost control of the heavy lines when that weight was removed. Without a substantial mass at the other end, the load could break free and plummet down the incline, possibly hurting a crew member or destroying something as it fell. On the other hand, a wooden sled attached to one end of the pull-ropes would help balance out the weight and assist the team in lowering both the sled and the ropes down to the northern platform in anticipation of another load. The crew may have also attached a length of a much lighter rope to the sled's back end. Clutching this tail, they would be able to move the vehicle plus the pull-ropes down to the bottom and get them ready to start up the channel again.

The series of courses would continue to grow and spread across the width of the entrance until construction reached the tip of the huge cutout on the pyramid's north side. By the time the Egyptians finish installing filler and cladding all the way up and as far as the outer edge of the edifice, the former inlet for the building supplies (excluding the unfinished area set aside for the forthcoming entrance) would be transformed into a smooth-sided exterior wall. But that outcome was still many years away.

Fourth Wall

Concurrent with the major face-lift occurring inside the construction entrance, work to develop the corbelled wall at the north end of the Grand Gallery now began in earnest. In some ways, the corbelled blocks in its fourth wall were merely another element in the overall transformation, representing the symbiotic relationship between that corridor and the evolving courses north of it. A two-story opening in the gallery's north wall, which stretched from the original header block above the entrance to the First Ascending Passage to the roof, had to be sealed up. As work at the north end of the larger pyramid proceeded, the builders would steadily eliminate this gap by adding a second lintel over the doorway and fashioning six elegant corbels above it.

The stack of courses rising higher inside the shrinking construction entrance was what made work on the gallery's fourth wall possible. The team would apply the same principles and techniques to this operation as governed their approach to constructing the bulk of the Great Pyramid. Its central premise was to avoid, at all costs, lifting a heavy stone by using brute force alone. Instead, crews would rely on the time-honored methods that had served them so well to elevate the blocks for the final series of corbels in the Grand Gallery. That is, after installing layer after layer of course blocks, workers would employ the even surface of the highest available level to transfer the individual corbel blocks into their slots.

The second header intended to sit atop the doorway into the First Ascending Passage, just like the initial one, came downriver from the quarry and eventually landed on the northern platform. The blocks comprising the six corbels above this header, similar to all of the pieces arriving for the gallery's last unfinished wall, were composed of a high-grade, polished limestone delivered to the docks near the Sphinx. After they were placed on sleds, the blocks traveled up the ramp on the pyramid's west side, around the northwest corner of the building, and onto the platform. Once there, the sled would be connected to the pull-ropes circling the pulley mounted on the highest available level of the 10-foot-wide delivery channel.

By now, adjunct crews had cleared out all of the unnecessary ropes and equipment from the central portion of the pyramid, but a single temporary pulley had stayed behind inside the Grand Gallery. As the job proceeded, a work gang lowered into the space on rope ladders through the hole in the north wall would use this device to pull the second header and the remaining corbels into position. Pushing the stand's legs into a couple of the floor holes running down the sides of the gallery ramp, the group set the pulley far enough up the incline so the angle of the rope permitted them to pull the block forward (south) as they walked downhill. Given that the wall they were erecting at the north end grew taller with each new block they inserted, the team inside the corridor would fine-tune the position of the pulley-stand as necessary. After each pull and before climbing out of the gallery, crew members relocated the machine farther up the ramp — closer to the Great Step — to adjust the angle of the lines in preparation for dragging the next corbel block forward.

While the procedure as a whole would prove to be both strategic and effective, the timetable governing various parts of the process was fluid. Progress in closing up the gap on the gallery wall was dependent upon the progress made in constructing the courses on the other side of that wall, within the construction entrance — and a considerable amount of lag time was inherent in the operation as a whole.

For example, it may have taken many months to build the required number of layers for the stack of courses to get high enough to be even with the top of the last corbel installed. As a result, immediately after the crew tugging on the lines from the pulley inside the gallery had finished installing the latest block, rope ladders were lowered into the corridor to let them exit the chamber by climbing up and out through the opening at the north end. The work gang would scramble down again to return to their posts only when the pile of courses had reached the height that made it possible to add another corbel block.

As expected, when the courses under construction had achieved a level equal to the top of the original header block over the doorway into the First Ascending Passage, the groundwork was laid to install the second lintel. In accordance with the core tenet of never physically lifting a block, the builders would again use the latest course as an even plane to convey the heavy piece of limestone to its spot. By now, workers had connected the sled carrying the new header block to the pulley mounted at the upper end of the delivery channel. Then the people controlling the pull-ropes that dropped down to the northern ramp raised the sled up the incline to the recently completed course.

When the sled reached the top, a crew disconnected the original ropes and attached the vehicle to a separate set of lines circling a couple of strategically placed post-rollers inserted into precut holes in the floor. The vertically mounted, grooved posts helped the crew rotate the sled slightly while dragging it in a westerly direction. As they continued pulling, the load gradually crept closer to the target area until it was lined up with the Grand Gallery. The idea was to move the awkward vehicle as close as possible to the gap in the gallery's north wall. Once it stopped about three feet back from the opening, the team used levers to take the header block off the sled and set it on the floor. Then they tweaked its orientation until the lintel stone was positioned perfectly east to west, corresponding to the way the header block was supposed to sit in the wall.

While one work gang stood by in the gallery corridor, its partner gang up top on the opposite side of the breach in the wall rigged the stone. At this point, the spot where the overhead crew was located was not very high since the bottom edge of the gap in the wall was only the height of the first lintel block above the entrance to the First Ascending Passage. Taking one end of the strong rope coming from the gallery, the small team lassoed the piece around the back end. The pull-rope may also have had a length of work-rope fastened to it to assist them in hauling up the line. As soon as every aspect of the procedure was coordinated and set, the gallery crew took their places and started down the ramp, carefully drawing the upper header stone forward toward its slot.

When the second header block crossed the threshold of the cavity and was partway inside the opening, the people below stopped pulling. Before the block settled into a permanent position, the gang up top had two tasks to perform: 1) Remove the rope; and 2) use lever bars, poles, and manpower to shove the piece the short distance into its hole from behind. Unlike upcoming corbels that would jut out beyond the blocks underneath them by three inches, the upper lintel stone was aligned with the lower one, resulting in a flat surface on that portion of the north wall.

The Griffith theory suggests that the blocks at the north end may not be as wide east to west as the slots surrounding them. The scantest amount of space between the piece of limestone and the cavity's side walls would have provided enough room for the Egyptians to accommodate a rope and slip it out later. While it is impossible to peer behind the walls of the Grand Gallery and observe whether this hypothesis is true, such a setup supports the process described here and makes the approach that the ancient builders took in fabricating the fourth wall a viable one.

The next step occurred when the block was approximately halfway inside its slot and the crew stationed in the gallery let some slack into the rope. By removing the tension on the line and locking it down, the team overhead managing the piece of limestone from behind was able to lift the rope wrapped around the back end up to the top of the stone and gently pull the lariat loop north. Their objective was to retain the same configuration for future blocks and avoid having to re-rig the entire setup every time a new piece arrived.

Six Not Seven

When the stack of courses under construction during the overhaul had attained a height equal to the top of the initial header stone, workers had slid the upper lintel into place. But the six corbels scheduled to fill in the rest of the north wall would come later — synchronized with the progress made in developing additional courses. While the process of inserting the rest of the blocks to plug the gap in the gallery wall would follow the same general pattern, the builders had to delay their installation until the floor got taller. As new courses continue to pile up level by level, the horizontal surface on top would provide the route for depositing specific corbel blocks at the proper elevations.

Although at first glance, the blocks protruding from the gallery's north wall may appear to match the corbels in its east and west walls, closer inspection reveals that the first corbel at the north end actually sits higher than the lowest corbels on either side. In fact, it is almost the same height as the second corbel in the side walls. The root cause for this anomaly does not seem to be a design flaw but rather, the outcome of the deliberate decision to put not one but two header blocks over the entrance to the First Ascending Passage. The question is why. No one really knows the answer to that mystery or the ostensible purpose of the double lintel except to speculate that the Egyptians may have desired a more solid foundation for the corbels they planned to erect on top of it. By contrast, the gallery's east and west walls, and the wall above the Antechamber, all contain seven corbels.

The six corbels at the north end rise 28 feet high, but their widths decrease in size east to west with the blocks becoming shorter as they ascend the wall. The lowest corbel measures more than six feet across (6' 10") while the one near the roofline is considerably shorter (3' 5") east to west. On the other hand, the Griffith theory maintains that, although the back ends of these stones are tucked behind the walls and not visible, their dimensions north to south are the same. Consistent with the corbels along both sides of the Grand Gallery, the ones installed in the north wall were pushed forward (south) to overhang the blocks underneath them by three inches. The cumulative effect of these projections puts the top of the north wall 18 inches closer to the south end of the corridor than the bottom.

As the number of layers increased and the courses kept rising higher, workers continued to install the final series of corbels one by one. The process kept advancing, with the opening in the gallery's north wall slowly shrinking, until the crew was ready to insert the sixth and final corbel block in the up-permost slot. Granted, closing up the fourth wall was a precursor to closing down the construction entrance for good, but it was only a preliminary step among a wide array of concluding activities. Workers still had to complete the courses at the center of the construction entrance up to the top, raise and distribute batches of filler to cover the tiers holding the shadoofs, eliminate the delivery channel, and install the casing stones absent from the façade. Most important, however, before the builders plugged up the only void left in the Grand Gallery's north wall, sealing up that lone exit point forever, they had to extract the people and equipment from inside the corridor.

Handling the final corbel compelled the crew to modify its approach because the current backdrop for their work presented a unique set of chal-lenges. Luckily, the uppermost block for the gap in the wall was small enough that it did not require the power of a pulley to lug it into place. In this case, a group of strong workers would be able to push the corbel into its hole from behind. But given the circumstances, they first had to make preparations for hauling the pulley-stand and roller out of the gallery corridor. The procedure was relatively straightforward since the work gang posted below could easily attach the roller and beams to the rope at hand.

Then, one after the other, the crew at the top would heave up the parts, pulling them over the lip of the opening. When the corridor was cleared, with the last bit of debris from the construction operation gone, the team overhead lowered the rope ladders. Grabbing hold of the rungs, workers climbed out of the passageway through the only hole left and departed the Grand Gallery for the last time.

The multiplying layers had put the top of the most recent course extremely close to the roof of the 128-foot-long tunnel at the gallery's north end. The claustrophobic dimensions inside the enclosure meant that the group working behind the single remaining breach in the corbelled wall was forced to squeeze into the minimal amount of space available. With the roof so low due to the height of the stack of new courses, their heads almost brushed the ceiling when they sat down. The side walls must have made it feel as if they were sitting at the far end of a long tube.

The space was much too confined to transport the sixth corbel block on a sled, and the crew would not have been able to stand up anyway. With a great deal of effort, the small team crawling around on their hands and knees moved the block through the tunnel to the edge of its slot before pushing it southward from behind. Once they had succeeded in propelling the corbel forward and projecting it the mandatory three inches beyond the block below it, the hole in the north wall no longer existed. All that remained for the work gang to do was to stuff the rest of the tunnel with filler. Starting at the south end and moving north, they inserted standard limestone all the way to the other end of the empty "tube."

By the time workers had finished packing the long, narrow passageway, every trace of the old interior tunnel above the lift had been wiped out. Installing the uppermost and last corbel in the fourth wall and eradicating the tunnel marked the conclusion of a significant chapter in the story of the

Great Pyramid. After decades of grueling work and countless hours spent overcoming formidable odds, the Grand Gallery was finally complete.

Filler and Cladding

To understand how the next stage of construction unfolded, it is important to understand the placement of the elements involved in the buildout relative to one another. The peak of the construction entrance where its angled east wall met the entrance to the former tunnel at the north end of the Grand Gallery was more than 50 feet high. But the tunnel's roof was the same height as the Grand Gallery's ceiling: 28 feet. Taking into account that the side of the pyramid ascends at a 52-degree angle, after packing the tunnel with filler stones, the builders still had a good distance to go and many more levels to complete before a full-fledged exterior wall would reach the apex of the construction entrance.

The upper portion of the huge gash on the north side of the pyramid would not fade away until crew members had added piles of blocks at least 50 feet high — filling out the empty portions of the otherwise-completed courses. Since the buildout had already surpassed the height of the setback where the Egyptians were slated to develop the pyramid's official entrance, that area was not a factor in the equation.

Level by level, work gangs had loaded the space between the east and west walls with filler positioned behind the row of white limestone set along the front edge of each course. But workers had intentionally left two stretches empty as construction moved higher. The plan was to go back and fill in the set of deep stairs where the shadoofs were mounted, along with the delivery channel when the project was close to shutting down.

The system and pattern the team tracked in erecting the topmost section of the five-story opening on the north side was a familiar one. One group of workers transferred the pulley-stand higher while a separate crew assembled a shadoof on the next usable level to raise the blocks up to the course under construction. Then, when the height of the mound of courses exceeded the length of the shadoof's arm, the transfer/setup process for the equipment repeated itself. Higher and higher the layers climbed until the team had attained the summit of the pie-shaped gap and was ready to turn around.

Now the strategy became a matter of covering all of the spots left empty on the way up that had supported the building process. The list included the tiers performing as mini work platforms and the angled channel where the blocks rode up the incline. Reversing the original order, work gangs would slowly work their way down to the bottom, trimming out the last unfinished strips of filler and cladding on the pyramid's north wall (minus the recess for the formal entry) as they descended.

The turnaround began when the pile of courses approaching the peak of the construction entrance met the bottommost layer of the courses originally assembled above the lift tunnel, which workers had recently packed full. Due to the angle of the construction entrance's east wall, the unfilled area at the summit requiring attention was just 25 feet wide east to west. In addition, the size of the opening top to bottom was insignificant or the average height of a single casing stone. The cavity represented the break between two levels — the most recent course assembled and a much older one. Workers did not have to construct an entire course at the tip-top because the only pieces missing were the blocks of white Tura limestone for the cladding that fit in that slender fragment of the façade.

Conditions were strikingly similar to what workers had encountered years earlier when they were closing down the niche in the north wall at Course 98. The row of polished limestone in the course directly above the one they were in the process of completing overhung the break between the two layers by several inches, forming a small lip along the upper edge of the hole.

Inserting a row of casing stones beneath the lip on the upper row would eliminate the gap at the peak of the construction entrance. It would also be the final chore the crew had to perform before tackling the shadoof-staircase and delivery channel on their way down to the northern platform.

After raising the initial piece of cladding for the construction entrance's summit up the shaft, a work gang standing on the latest course shoved the block west to the far end of the open row. Sliding the piece under the slight overhang, the crew made certain it was positioned correctly and precisely aligned with the slope of the exterior wall. Block by block, the white casing stones traveled up the channel and were pushed against the side of the last one seated further down the line. The team continued to add blocks for the façade until the space inside the hole was full and it was impossible to imagine that a break had ever existed there.

Next up were the tiers crafted to hold the equipment along with the delivery ramp. It's a safe bet to assume that by now, the shadoof near the top was positioned too high for the about-face the builders were ready to initiate, so the crew dismantled it and carried the parts several courses down to a lower step, where they reassembled the machine. The stand for the pulley soon followed to make it available for elevating the necessary blocks. The shadoof would take over the job of not only loading the stepped wall directly behind it with chunks of filler, but also covering that portion of the ramp located immediately south of the pulley. Over time, workers would integrate all of the unfinished sections into the smooth, Tura limestone-lined exterior wall.

The fraction of each course that the team was scheduled to overhaul was approximately 20 feet wide east to west and 10 feet long north to south. On the east side of the delivery channel, the builders had left about 10 feet of empty space on each tier for clearance around the shadoof. That open area merged with another 10-foot-wide expanse, which extended from the east side of the delivery channel to its western edge — the zone set aside for the pulley-stand. Due to the compact nature of their workspace, crews had abandoned the use of sleds during this period and brought the blocks up the shaft individually by lassoing them with a single rope around the back end. When a block drew near the platform and was within reach of the two machines, lying on the flat surface in front of the pulley, workers detached it from the pull-rope, wrapped a choker around the piece of limestone, and affixed it to the shadoof's arm.

With all systems go, the shadoof swung around to place the block at the feet of the work crew near the top, and they started filling in the highest tiered level over to the back wall. After that section had been transformed into steps high enough vertically to hold the casing stones, the gang moved on tier by tier and continued to add blocks in a step-like fashion as far down as the current work platform where the shadoof was.

In concert with handling the squared-off filler blocks arriving on-site on a regular basis, workers were also turning over the angled half-blocks in the floor of the delivery channel. Transposing the ramp stones, they developed a flat surface to build on. Slowly, what had once been a steep incline at a 52-degree angle on the south side of the pulley-stand, became a series of stairs, which the team would soon pack with more filler. The plan was to keep building out toward the north, mirroring the slope of the exterior wall, as the individual levels undergoing alterations were ready to receive their missing rows of casing stones step by step.

Similar to what had occurred on Course 98, when a layer was complete except for the cladding, the shadoof lifted a casing stone up to the correct spot on the highest available level where a group of workers, standing on either the step below or on a ladder, helped guide the piece partway into its slot. With the block of white limestone stationary, sandwiched between the blocks above and below it, the right-angled trapezoid was unable to tip forward, which allowed the crew to remove the choker. After the team had freed the stone, they pushed it southward, slipping the sides into the hole in the façade until the edges were even with the cladding that surrounded it.

The activity was ongoing and continued to move lower as workers attacked the job by sections, putting the final touches on four or five levels at a time. Once the layers had their filler and the blocks for the façade were in place, the crew transferred the shadoof and pulley-stand to begin work on the next sequence of courses farther down. While systematic, the procedure took some time. It only halted when the builders finally reached the platform at the bottom of the north wall — a wall that now glistened as brilliantly as those gracing the other three sides of the Great Pyramid.

One more item colored the Egyptians' immediate plans for the future: the desire to create a formal entrance befitting the scope and grandeur of their magnificent edifice. But such an entrance would not be obvious. The ancient pyramid builders intended to hide it away from the prying eyes of thieves and other potential intruders. Concealing the door from the uninvited would keep out anyone attempting to breach a sacred monument meant to guard its secrets for posterity.

[CHAPTER 23]

GRAND ARCHWAY

ON THE NORTH SIDE of the pyramid, about 10 courses above the cavity that Caliph Al-Ma'mun dug in the 9th century (the opening where tourists enter today), is a somewhat small but intriguing indentation in the wall. Knowing that the building was originally constructed as a smooth-sided structure covered entirely in highly polished white limestone, what becomes immediately apparent to the casual observer is that this niche must have been behind the exterior wall at one time. But since almost 100% of the pyramid's casing stones carried downstream from the quarries at Tura disappeared centuries ago, the original outer walls do not exist anymore.

The notched-out area on the north wall includes a small "patio" in front of a double-decker chevron formed by two pairs of substantial limestone blocks stacked on top of one another. Their mitered tips lean in and touch to create the apex of a triangular arch. According to many archeologists, this odd formation is all that remains of the original entrance to the Great Pyramid.

The multi-faceted operation the Egyptians embarked upon to close down the construction entrance had resulted in a completely flat north wall clad in dazzling white limestone — with one exception: the 50-foot by 60-foot setback. Crews had assiduously avoided filling in this area as they were tackling the large pie-shaped gash in the side of the pyramid. The builders' intention was to assemble a grand, ritual-worthy entrance before sealing up the last remaining cutout in the north wall. Consequently, erecting a double-layered archway inside the unfinished space became the next item on the agenda, but first the team had to gather the proper equipment and prepare the site to make their strategy work.

During the years when workers were in the midst of eradicating the construction entrance by completing courses and adding cladding to the façade, they had largely left the setback alone even as they stacked up blocks around it. The result was an inset with three distinct walls. Engineers had configured the one at the back (south) end, which was about 30 feet high, as a series of steps. The stepped levels would provide not only small platforms for the crew to work from but also a variety of elevations for mounting critical gear. As the project unfolded, this staircase would prove to be a valuable asset, since plans also included building upward to imitate the 52-degree angle of the exterior wall.

CHEVRONS ON NORTH SIDE

Chevrons from the original entrance to the Great Pyramid are located in the north wall, above the hole that Caliph Al-Ma'mun created when he forced his way into the pyramid — the opening where visitors enter the building now.

Besides the stair-steps at the back end, the builders had fashioned two tall ledges on either side along the length of the setback, north to south. Designed to hold essential equipment, the tops of the shelves sported a series of holes carved into the limestone placed a few feet apart from each other. Finally, crews had removed two lines of stones from the floor — the single surviving section of Course 25 that was still vacant — to create a pair of trenches 30 feet long, two feet deep, and two feet wide. The parallel grooves resembled inverted triangles because their sloped sides met in a point at the center-bottom down the length of the channel. These depressions in the floor, situated at least 10 feet apart, began at the south end of the setback and stopped approximately 15 feet shy of the pyramid's outer edge.

Long-Term Storage

The Egyptians were master builders who unquestionably began their massive project with the end in mind. One clue to this ancient people's foresight and ingenuity was how they handled the outsized limestone blocks for the archways that would frame the formal entrance. The Griffith theory posits that about midway through the construction process and shortly after crews had installed the giant slabs of granite for the Relieving Chambers, they had transported the blocks for the arches from the quarry — decades before construction managers actually needed the materials on-site.

When the sleds conveying the granite blocks intended for the Relieving Chambers had first arrived at the top of the northern ramp, the loaded vehicles were parked side by side at the east end of the platform along the pyramid's north wall. Most of the sleds waited there for a long time because work gangs had to build up additional courses before they could transfer the blocks onto the lift to transport them to the 49th course and beyond. It took awhile, but over the years, the platform's parking area finally cleared out. Sometime after the granite was gone, the team made use of the unoccupied space to store a second set of sleds, which held the blocks for the chevrons in the entryway. Yet it was not until the Great Pyramid was nearing completion that this collection of stones would be taken out of storage and used.

Composed of standard limestone, the dressed blocks probably originated from one of the quarries on the Giza Plateau and were hauled up the ramp on the west side of the building. All of the slabs were identical in size and shape, with a beveled face at one end. The angled tip would let the block rest against its twin on the opposite side to form a peak.

Assuming the height of the blocks to be 15 feet, they must have ridden in on low-slung sleds at least 20 feet long end to end. The flat-bottomed vehicles curved up at the bow and stern and had wooden slats built into the interior. The inserts held the limestone a few inches off the floor, leaving just enough room underneath to be able to wrap a rope around the middle of the column and pull it.

A single, intact set of the double-layered chevrons is still visible on the north side of the Great Pyramid. No one is certain how many triangular arches were erected in the beginning, but judging from the depth of the recess and taking into account the 52-degree angle of the outside wall, it appears that the structure included a total of 16 blocks. The lower row would have contained five blocks apiece on each side, totaling 10 altogether, while the row on top had fewer than that. Due to the slope of the exterior wall, the upper set of arches must have included three blocks on each side. Any more than three would have made the configuration too high at the front end, and in theory, caused it to poke through the north wall. That means the upper row had a total of six blocks sitting above the three southernmost chevrons in the lower row.

The sequence in which the crew needed the blocks determined how they organized the sleds for storage. The key was to avoid having to turn them around at a later date or manipulate specific pieces when the time came to erect the series of gables. To that end, stonecutters had alternated the direction of the columns as they were loading them. A pull-rope was tied to the front of each sled, but the way the block lay inside its carrier fluctuated between whether the tip or the base faced forward. Using the post-rollers by the northwest corner of the pyramid where the platform fanned out, a gang of workers raised the sleds up the western ramp one by one. Then, with the help of a couple more post-rollers installed at the opposite end of the platform, the pullers lugged them toward its eastern edge.

From the moment the sled was loaded, climbed up the ramp, and turned the northwest corner, the direction the block pointed — either angled tip or flat base forward — dictated where it was stowed. Workers parked the carriers north to south in two parallel rows on the 50-foot-deep platform by placing them lengthwise (east to west), consistent with a fixed blueprint. The idea was to arrange the blocks in the correct order, according to their positions in the upper and lower rows of chevrons.

Pyramid construction had reached its concluding stages when the tall, pointed blocks for the arches were finally put to use. Installation would proceed from the south wall of the setback northward, establishing the lower row of chevrons first. Construction would also follow a regular pattern, with crews inserting a single block on the west side, then its counterpart on the east side, before leaning the two stones together. When both blocks in a pair were in place, the work crew moved on to the next set by once again fitting out the west side, then introducing a match on the east side. Back and forth the process continued until all 10 pieces were joined together to complete the bottom row. Pairing up the six blocks on top involved a similar routine: progressing from south to north and adding the blocks west to east.

The system the builders had outlined meant that the most efficient way to store the sled carrying the very first block was to have its base facing toward the west and its tip pointing eastward. As a result, when workers dragged the sled further west and lined it up in front of the setback, they could leave the stone pillar as it was to pull it off the vehicle toward the back wall. With the bottom end facing toward the west, workers would be able to easily slip the base into the trench on that side when the column arrived at its intended location.

Conversely, the next block, which formed the other half of the initial pair, started out with its tip facing west. Why? Because the second block was targeted for the trench on the east side, the easiest way to handle the piece of limestone and slide it into the hole was to have the block arrive with the base on the same side as the trench. When crews finally settle the second block into its perch, they would push the tips of the two pieces together until they met in the middle. Back and forth, leading with the base then the tip, the lengthy blocks would flow into the setback until the double-layered archway became a reality.

Uncommon Archway

Before the operation got underway, the builders had arranged equipment around the sides of the setback to help haul in the oversized blocks and set them up. Mounted on one of the lower steps at the center of the back wall was a pulley short enough for the rope to clear the underside of the lower archway as it expanded. A couple of wooden rails similar to train tracks ran down the center of the floor; 12 inches tall and placed four or five feet apart, the rails extended from the back wall to the edge of the northern platform.

The team had also stuck movable post-rollers into the southernmost holes on top of the ledges above the east and west walls. Ropes curving around the vertically mounted rollers would help workers lift the blocks and slide them into the trenches. Two more pulleys positioned at the opposite (north) end on both of the side-shelves would redirect the ropes downward toward the northern ramp and the teams standing by to pull.

Using post-rollers planted in the floor of the northern platform, the team hauled the first sled from the storage area west and lined it up parallel to the setback's front edge. Then a separate crew took one end of the rope from the pulley-stand on the south wall and fastened a hook to it. After looping the line around the middle of the block, they hooked the rope back onto itself. The wooden inserts inside the sled afforded the crew a couple of advantages. First, the column rested several inches above the floor of the sled — high enough to be able to slip a rope around it. Second, its elevation was equal to the height of the rails, which permitted the piece of limestone to slide straight onto the tracks. To transport the block southward, the other end of the rope went underneath and over the pulley-roller before continuing north toward a group of pullers stationed inside the setback, who would grab onto the line and tug.

Taking the rope in hand, the team in the setback walked forward from the pulley along the flat area between the two trenches. As they stepped forward, the block began to creep toward them on the tracks. The bulky stone kept progressing southward while the pullers proceeded north until the first person in line was only a few feet away from the block and the pull halted. The work gang had to reposition themselves by crawling over the piece of limestone to the other side. Since the obstacle was less than five feet tall, including the thickness of the block plus the rails, and they were not dealing with an incline, the switch was easy to perform. After rearranging their positions, the crew continued pulling until the first block had arrived at the back wall with its base next to the inner edge of the trench on the west side.

Disconnecting the heavy block from the rope around the pulley, workers rigged a different line to stand it up. They looped the new rope around the top of the pillar approximately one-quarter of the way down the shaft, and tied it off with a knot or choker that would tighten the line when the team on the northern ramp pulled. The work gang may have also put some sort of cushioning underneath the line at the corners to prevent the block's sharp edges from fraying the cord. The latest rope subsequently climbed up and around the post-roller at the south end of the western ledge before heading north to the pulley mounted at that end, which redirected it downward, and continuing across the width of the northern platform toward the cohort of pullers on the ramp. Walking down the slope in lockstep, this group would provide enough force to make the column stand upright.

Raising the first block for the first chevron was a delicate task. Its base rested a little east of the trench on the setback's west side and ideally was in a position to just slide down the angled inner wall to the bottom of the depression. But since the block was four feet wide, only half of it would actually fit inside the ditch. Consequently, the extra two feet sticking out above the cavity would create an outcropping on that side. The immediate challenge workers faced was not to let the piece scoot further west before it dropped into the slot. The trouble was that when the team outdoors began to pull, the bottom end of the tall, heavy chunk of limestone would have a tendency to keep sliding. To short-circuit the problem, the builders placed a wooden buttress on the trench's west side to prevent the stone from skidding away and potentially bypassing the hole altogether.

With the crew on the ramp tugging, the slab began to budge and ever-so-slowly stand up. They kept pulling on the line until the block stood taller (albeit still at a slight angle) than it eventually had to be. Putting their weight against the rope to keep it taut, the pullers held their positions for some time to maintain tension on the line and freeze the cumbersome piece in place. This brief respite, in turn, allowed the work gang inside the setback to prop up the stone and prevent it from falling over by setting wooden supports against the underbelly. The braces absorbed most of the pressure in stabilizing the block, while the rope tethered near the top was locked off as an extra precaution. Once the first half of the initial chevron was secure in that temporary position, the game plan the Egyptians had set into motion could carry on. They were ready for the next column.

The formula the builders had developed required hauling in the second block with the tip facing forward (west) and proceeding in a manner that, for the most part, was a mirror image of the preceding process. Workers would lug the piece of limestone from the storage area, park it in front of the setback, then pull the block off the sled to ride the wooden rails toward the south wall. The biggest difference and most challenging aspect of this phase of the project was that the newly positioned block for the western half of the arch was now partially in the way. It was imperative that the team modify their approach if they had any hope of clearing that impediment, adding the matching piece of limestone, and standing it up.

Due to the narrow quarters in between the trenches and proximity of the block previously installed on the west side, when workers drew the stone targeted for the eastern trench into the setback, they stopped pulling when it was at least four feet away from the back wall. In fact, when it came to a standstill, block number two only made it as far as three or four inches north of the original limestone pillar on the west side. The reason was obvious: It would have been impossible to raise the second block to its full height if it were deposited directly across from the one opposite it.

The job of shuffling block number two into position commenced with workers pushing a second wooden post-roller into one of the holes on top of the eastern ledge, right behind where the block had stopped. This time, the operation involved winding two separate ropes around the upper end of the block to raise the column and adjust its placement later. Reversing direction from the process employed to elevate the initial block, the lines attached to the stone climbed up to the ledge on the east side.

The upper rope tied around the piece of limestone mimicked the arrangement on the west side by curving around the post-roller at the very back of the ledge before shifting to the north and moving toward the exterior ramp. The lower cinch-line of the two stretched up to the grooved post-roller mounted behind the block. After a half-turn around that device, the crew brought the rope north and draped it over the pulley at the far end of the shelf. From there, it traversed the platform and traveled toward a second team stationed on the ramp who were assigned to pull.

The most efficient and effective method for standing up the column designated for the southeast corner was through a sequence of highly choreographed maneuvers. The team had initiated the procedure by using the lower rope to move the base of the block partway into the trench on the east side while raising it to almost full height. In this instance, with the pullers hanging on to steady the stone, the band of workers inside the setback used long poles pushed against the underside to immobilize the block in its current position. From there, the idea was to gently "walk" the piece further south little by little in a coordinated fashion.

CHEVRON CONSTRUCTION

An array of equipment was installed inside the setback at various points during the course of constructing the chevrons in the triangular double archway on the north side of the Great Pyramid.

Taking one end of the rope connected to the pulley-stand on the back wall, another work gang stretched a third line around the middle of the upright block, then hooked it onto a thick pole stuck into the floor close to the pulley. Fastening the rope to a stationary object meant that when workers picked up the other end of the line and walked forward down the center of the space, the loop would tighten, dragging the piece of limestone toward the south wall. The process was akin to pulling in a big net on a fishing boat.

Later on, the team would continue to enlarge their "dragnet" as the number of blocks on the east side increased. After standing each new block upright, workers would increase the size of the rope-ring catching the row of stones to encompass the latest addition. By enclosing the next column for the east side within the constricting loop, they were able to lug the piece southward and heave it up against the blocks already in line.

By then, crews posted across the site were working in tandem. When it was time to make the first move to walk block number two southward, the pullers on the ramp controlling the lower rope that was stabilizing the block, released some of the tension to let slack into the line. Simultaneously, the pull-team on the upper rope took over and held on. While the lower rope was loosening, the upper one tightened to keep the line rigid and the stone erect. At the same time, the crew inside the setback managing the rope-ring that encircled the block was inching the stone southward by tugging on the line and steadily dragging it toward the back wall.

At the same time, a small crew on the north side of the new pillar was busily focused on the base. Outfitted with pinch bars and other types of levers, they shoved their tools underneath the bottom edge of the stone and pried it up, thereby redistributing the weight by the tiniest amount to help move the block forward. Workers may have also spread a thin layer of slippery tafla clay along the short route to grease the way and assist them in the painstaking process of shifting the eastside block further south. The operation was a grueling exercise and required an enormous amount of patience to execute properly, but in the end, it worked. Walking the stone southward in baby steps resulted in the pair of blocks to create the first set of chevrons fronting each other.

The final variable in the equation was uniting the two columns by having them meet in the center of the setback. More likely than not, when the teams on the east and west sides handling the ropes began to release them, they did so in synch and at a very deliberate pace. As work crews lowered the stones toward the midpoint, they also prepared to insert a wooden wedge in between the blocks before the two sides converged. The wedge served as a safety device that afforded the builders some wiggle room before the angle and weight of the heavy pillars united them in a permanent bond. Their aim was to ensure that the east and west sides were properly aligned and the center seam spot on. When the positioning was correct, a work gang pounding on the edge of the wood would force the wedge out from the middle — binding the blocks together in a picture-perfect triangular arch.

Scheduled to install a total of five pieces on each side, the Egyptians would repeat the same procedures piece by piece by inserting a block on the west side, then its counterpart to the east, until the bottom row of arches was complete. And as construction steadily moves northward, workers would adapt the process by relocating the post-rollers, braces, and related equipment as necessary.

The team was also reckoning with another issue that cropped up consistently: During this period, the very first chevron at the south end of the setback was freestanding, but the rest of the arches were supposed to sit against each other in a dense row. Implementing such a design demanded a few minor adjustments to the original plans.

The reality was that every time a work gang inserted another block into the row, the south face of the new block was not able to touch the north face of the block already in place because the rope wrapped around the latest pillar was in the way. Because the pull-ropes leading to the post-rollers atop the ledges were almost three inches thick, they produced a lump between the columns. The inevitable result was that the new pair of blocks could only come within three or four inches of the previous set that crews had installed.

The pieces would not sit side by side in a flat row until work on the latest pair of blocks added to the north end was almost done. First, the team had to install the column for the west side and crab-walk the one on the east side farther south. Second, they needed to lower the two columns toward the center and stick the wooden wedge between them. Once the wedge was gone, the tips of the slabs touched, and the structure was stable, the effort halted to allow the crew to remove the ropes separating the latest two blocks from the pair immediately south of them. Obviously, eliminating the pull-ropes would leave a narrow channel inside the row. It was up to the workers at the base using the pinch bars to close up this space by prying up the bottom edges and jostling the new columns into place by those last few inches — until stone was flush against stone.

We can only guess about how long it may have taken the Egyptians to complete the five chevrons in the bottom row, but whatever the timeframe, they were not ready to close out the project yet. From the start, the ancient pyramid builders had planned to create at least one elegant entrance onto their massive monument, and a defining feature of that entry point was a second layer of triangular arches positioned above the first.

Upper Row

Preparations were already underway to erect the three chevrons in the upper row. The biggest change to the construction operation involved redirecting most of the activity from the middle of the setback to its flanks. Since the base of the blocks in the lower row stuck out almost 24 inches above the top of the trenches, the team began by hauling up filler stones and constructing a two-foot-high floor behind the pillars to smooth out the uneven areas on both sides. The setback was approximately 50 feet deep and 60 feet wide, which meant there was at least 20 feet of empty space between the outer edge of the trenches and the east and west walls. The portion workers covered with smaller chunks of limestone made the flanks two feet taller than the northern platform and elevated both sides higher than the floor beneath the lower archway.

The next step was to develop a way to transfer the sleds carrying the blocks for the upper arches. The answer was constructing a temporary ramp parallel to the setback's front edge. Since the loaded vehicles would come from the storage area at the east end of the platform, the base of the incline was at that end, with the height of the slope increasing as it extended west. The ramp rose at a gentle grade before leveling off in a horizontal landing in front of the recess in the wall that was two feet higher than the northern platform. The deck's flat surface equaled the height of the recently constructed floors on both sides. The even plane would support the process of unloading the heavily laden sleds.

Equipment needs for the project also shifted during this period of time, causing workers to add to or redistribute the collection of tools at their disposal inside the setback. Crews mounted two additional pulleys on the steps at the back, centered between the trenches and the side walls and set high enough for the pulling angle to work. Work gangs had also put wooden rails down the middle of the level floors on the two sides. Approximately 12 inches square and divided into three sections, the tracks would convey the blocks for the archway's upper row southward. The moveable post-rollers on top of the ledges and the teams of pullers stationed on the northern ramp remained vital parts of the operation.

The first block installed for the initial chevron for the upper row was the one in the southwest corner. Grasping the rope attached to the sled's front end, the team moved it out of storage by looping the line around a couple of post-rollers planted on the northern platform, a short distance beyond the temporary ramp. The vertically mounted rollers served an essential purpose by providing pivot points for pulling the loaded vehicles westward and hauling them up the short incline. Because the first piece of limestone was targeted for the setback's west side, it lay inside the sled with its base facing forward.

Echoing the successful strategy that they had employed to erect the lower row of chevrons, the builders moved the sled up the small hill to the landing and stopped in front of the tracks on the west side. Wooden inserts on the sled's interior held the long pillar off the bottom, which left room to wrap a rope around the middle. Taking one end of the line from the pulley affixed to the step on back wall, the crew circled the block and hooked the rope back onto itself. Then a second group fed the other end of the line underneath and around the pulley-roller before gripping it in both hands and marching north. The block lay prone as they shuttled it southward, sliding the piece of limestone along the rails at a snail's pace with every step forward. Similar to the situation that had occurred while transferring the pieces for the lower row, workers would scramble over the top and reposition themselves on the other side of the block when the pullers heading north and the stone crawling south met somewhere in the middle.

When the first block for the upper row had gone about as far as it could go, the pull halted and a switchover occurred. While a small crew undid the line around the pulley on the back wall, a few more workers took up positions on the western ledge. The tip of the block, which was beveled, lay very close to the southernmost chevron in the bottom row — in a position to slide up its angled side. But before the team was able to proceed with their strategy, they had to set the stage for a smooth transition from the horizontal surface of the reconstituted floor to that sloped plane.

Part of the answer was to use a bunch of wooden rollers approximately five feet long (longer than the width of the stone) to fill in the void that would develop between the block resting on the floor and the slanted side of the lower chevron as it started uphill. The work gang standing on the western ledge had already tied a rope around the piece of limestone about a third of the way down the column and curled it around the southernmost post-roller by the back wall. The rope then followed the well-worn path — making its way north above the ledge, over the pulley at the opposite end, down to the northern ramp, and into the hands of the pull-team who attached it to their harnesses.

Since the wooden tracks that had carried the block were 12 inches tall, it already lay a foot off the floor. Now, a separate crew armed with levers and pinch bars prepared to jack up the front end by at least another foot, starting by cramming the wooden posts underneath the tip as if they were stacking a pile of logs. While the work gang with the levers on the north side of the block jacked up the pillar, the pullers on the exterior ramp raised it by tugging on the rope until the column was balanced on a single edge. This action helped support the weight of the piece while lifting the load high enough to clear the rails. As the group handling the small posts piled them underneath the front end, their colleagues pulled out the first sections of the tracks at the south end and carried them away. Subsequently, a few people climbed onto the roof of the lower archway while several more clambered on top of the eastern ledge.

During this time, the pullers had incrementally slacked off the rope, carefully laying down the block with its tip on top of the stack of wood and the back end leaning at a slight angle. Then the crew working from the shelf on the west side removed their line. The most immediate task for the gang assigned to the other ledge was to loop a different rope around the bottom of the block, almost as if the heavy column were seated on a swing. One end of the rope trailed up the north face of the pillar, passed over to the eastern ledge, and circled a post-roller deposited in the hole closest to that side of the stone. Crew members strung the other end of the rope so it tracked the block's long southern face and curved around the post-roller at the back of the shelf on the east side. After that procedure, the two ends made their way north toward separate teams of pullers waiting on the ramp. Their strategy was to have the ropes from the pair of post-rollers perform in unison during a single pull.

The block's current trajectory was to travel up the angled side of the lower archway — a relatively steep slope — until its tip reached the center point. Acting in tandem by tugging on both ends of the rope at the same time, the pull-teams heaved the block up as high as it could go without overshooting the roof ridge. Then crews locked down the lines to temporarily retain the stone in its current position on the west side, six to eight feet off the floor.

An effective solution to the question of how to restrain the block and secure it permanently atop the lower row of chevrons was to stack filler underneath the base. With that approach in mind, crews would use standard limestone to overlay the area between the bottom of the suspended pillar and the wall on the setback's west side. It is important to note that the chunk of limestone the work gangs inserted directly beneath the hanging block was either notched along the top edge or only half as tall as the piece situated behind it. The builders were not able to cover the bottom of the latest column for the archway completely, edge to edge, because the rope looped around its base was still there. Continuing the layer of filler stones as far as the west wall immobilized the block, which allowed them to remove the line and plug up the small cutout crafted to accommodate the rope.

The Egyptians adhered to the same general course of action on the other side while installing the companion block to the first half of the chevron for the upper row. In this case, the sled transporting the slab (tip forward) stopped in front of the rails on the setback's eastern flank and traveled south using the pulley on that side. Reversing the previous pattern once the block reached the back wall, workers posted on the ledge on the east side fastened a line around the column. Meanwhile, the group with the pinch bars gathered near the tip to lever it up and the team supplying the short wooden posts got ready to insert them beneath the tip.

After the various work gangs had elevated the block and inserted the wood, another crew removed the southernmost sections of the tracks before the eastside pullers lowered it down and left the new pillar waiting at the bottom of the archway. Then a few workers standing on top of the lower row of chevrons to help rig the rope along with the crew assigned to the western ledge took over. Catching the block's lower end in a rope sling, the gang on the west side prepared to slide it upward by wrapping the ends around a couple of strategically placed post-rollers lodged in the shelf and stretching the lines toward the pulley at the ledge's north end.

Tugging on both ends of the rope simultaneously, the groups walking down the northern ramp drew block number two up the side of the lower chevron until the stone's beveled edge was flush against its mate — the solitary piece in the top row. Once crews had locked off the lines, they added filler all the way from the bottom of the suspended block to the east wall, covering the entire area except for the narrow channel underneath the base of the stone that contained the rope. By now, the portion of the floor on both sides behind the new columns in the upper archway had grown taller by six feet or more due to the mass of filler supporting the latest chevron. With the first duo in the top row assembled, the builders were ready to install the next pair of blocks in line.

The pyramid's 52-degree exterior wall imposed a significant constraint on the number of upper chevrons the team was able to construct. The space the architects had allotted only allowed for a total of three sets of blocks in the top row lined up tightly north to south without any breaks between them. The problem this configuration presented was the same one engineers had confronted in the past: how to accommodate a rope but eliminate the gap it produced between the stones.

The first two blocks in the upper row were uniquely situated, with only the stepped back wall on the south side and nothing on the north side to impede the removal of the pull-ropes. But when it came to the blocks for chevrons number two and three, workers would again raise them up the roof of the lower archway as close as possible to the columns already in place — with the same result. A narrow channel the width of a rope that was two or three inches in diameter would separate the most recent slabs from the columns they were supposed to adjoin.

Block by block, west then east, crews would install the next four pillars — two on each side — and repeat the process of adding filler from base to wall. It was only when an individual block was propped up and stationary that they could eliminate the rope used to elevate it. Removing the rope left a break in the row, so now it was up to the people with the levers to attack the problem by adjusting the latest pair of stones to close up the gap before the job proceeded.

Standing on the roof of the lower archway on the north side of the latest block and using a thin, handheld copper wedge, workers hammered the small triangle underneath the edge of the limestone to open up a minute amount of space. By penetrating the tiny gap that the wedge had made, they were able to slip the front end of their tools beneath the edge to pry up the block and move it slightly forward (south). Slow and steady, the work gang persisted in applying levers along the edge to keep the slab advancing. The repetitive actions shifted the column southward until it had traveled the two or three extra inches representing the width of the rope and was flat against the last block in line.

Soon the only piece missing was a single block on the east side — the other half of the third chevron in the upper row. When the builders had succeeded in installing the sixth and final block on top, they turned their attention to the next pressing issue: eliminating the one big gash left in the pyramid's north wall. It was time to cover up the setback.

North Wall

The Egyptians had faced these types of situations before. The challenge always involved the question of how to lift workers and materials high enough to be able to actually do the work. In this instance, they also had to construct a stepped base rising at a 52-degree angle to support the white cladding for the outside wall. Current circumstances demanded that the team fill in an area stretching from the front edge of the northernmost chevron in the lower row to the south end of the setback, as well as all of the space above the dual archway they had just constructed. A portion of the operation involved reconstituting the steps integrated into the back wall of the recess by building them up to the correct height and angle to receive their casing stones in the future.

Given the need, crews erected shadoofs on both sides of the setback in the open area between the double archway and the edge of the northern platform. The machines would be able to not only transfer the blocks southward, but also drop them onto hard-to-reach areas such as the eastern and western ledges. The majority of the filler stones would have been fairly small and easy to handle, since there was no reason to inject larger pieces into the mix when the task was simply packing a hole. The chunks of filler limestone required for the project originated from the northern ramp, which crews were in the process of slowly dismantling. Workers would also transfer the pulleys mounted on the back wall to higher steps and use angled stones as temporary ramps to help them elevate the materials to seal up the cavity in the wall.

Some of the spaces that had to be filled were the uneven levels on the east and west sides, stemming from the differences in the heights of the floors. The filler blocks that supported the three upper chevrons had built up the floors between the archway and the side walls, but because there were only three upper chevrons, the floors behind them were several feet taller than the floors in back of the first two chevrons at the north end of the lower row. They were still in their original state: just two feet high.

As crews tackled the shorter sections east and west, they interjected the first temporary ramps in various spots. Installing small inclines here and there was a good way to raise individual pieces from one level to another without too much trouble.

Over time, the team succeeded in enveloping the entire area around the double-layered, triangular archway in filler up to and including its gabled roof. Then, in short order, workers also started packing the empty space above the double archway they had just concealed by constructing a series of stepped levels across the top. Once the new steps were integrated with the existing ones from the back wall of the recess, the flight of stairs (without any Tura limestone sheathing) extended from the front end of the lower row of chevrons — 15 feet back from the edge of the pyramid — to an imaginary line marking what used to be the setback's south wall.

Once the understory was sufficiently built up so most of the recess had turned into a staircase following the slope of the exterior wall, work gangs were able to start the process of inserting the casing stones to finish off that portion of the façade. In general, the operation proceeded from south to north, beginning with the uppermost level. Because crew members were able to stand on the step right below the one that needed the cladding, the procedure was fairly straightforward and efficient. Moreover, the approach the builders took was akin to the one they had employed to fill in the niche on the 98th course since the circumstances were so similar.

The blocks of white limestone already in place in the row directly above the step where the new casing stone belonged created a narrow rim along the upper edge. Workers were going to slip the next piece for the façade underneath that lip. Setting the block partway onto its step so the slanted front end was unable to tip forward, a small team pushed it southward until the angled face lined up with the block overhead and the edges east and west sat flush with the cladding on either side. Only when every seam was perfectly aligned and a straight edge revealed that the angle was correct would the crew move on to the next block.

By now, for all intents and purposes, the setback had disappeared except for a narrow strip at the front end, representing the last 15 feet of empty space between the northernmost chevron in the lower row and the northern platform. The series of chevrons the team had engineered was impressive, but only a down payment on the entrance the ancient Egyptians had in mind. The grandeur of the triangular double archway would soon be eclipsed by construction of a mysterious inner hallway and a tiny, nondescript door into their massive monument — a covert entrance, which for generations would protect the route into the Great Pyramid by keeping it well hidden from the prying eyes of the world.

[CHAPTER 24]

TRANSFORMATION

THE EGYPTIANS' CENTURY-LONG CONSTRUCTION project was drawing to a close and soon would take on some of the characteristics of a mining operation. The builders were ready to dig down to remove the floor beneath the chevrons, revamp the upper portion of the shaft encompassing the Descending Passage, and fashion a clever door secreted in the façade. Their scheme also marked the beginning of the end for the exterior platform at Course 25. From the time that platform was originally constructed, it had covered the courses at the bottom of the pyramid on the north side, which were already dressed in their casing stones, but due to the presence of the platform, that portion of the finished exterior wall was out of sight.

When workers were filling in the area above and around the chevrons in the dual archway and preparing to install the casing stones for the north wall, the stepped levels they developed had extended all the way from the south end of what was formerly the setback to the edge of the northern plat-form. Yet the result was not a finished structure with a perfectly polished, flawless veneer because the builders had not sealed up every bit of the open space. Crews had left a gap in the wall approximately six feet wide east to west directly in front of the northernmost chevron — a fissure that reached as high as the peak of the triangular archway.

In addition, a narrow band of stair-steps left and right of the hole in the wall also lacked its cladding. The small gap in the side of the building imme-diately north of the chevrons would soon serve as both an entryway for the work crews and an exit point for the materials they planned to remove from inside the pyramid. Later, this opening would become the site of a series of header blocks composed of the same Tura limestone as the façade and form the ceiling over an internal corridor.

After the team assigned to the interior entered the pyramid from the northern platform through the breach in the wall, they prepared to start digging. Beginning underneath the initial pair of chevrons at the south end, workers pried up floor blocks from the 25th course. The purpose of the excavation was to burrow down as far as Course 22 by eliminating blocks directly below the double-archway and beyond — all the way out to the platform's edge. Knowing how shrewd the ancient builders were, they probably did not remove every single stone straight down on all four sides as if they were digging a grave. But as the crew descended, they left a few pieces at the north end of the hole by turning them into a slim staircase. The steps may not have extended down to the bottom at the 22nd course due to the steep angles involved, but even having a few steps near the top of the cavity while they were excavating the upper layers would have allowed the workers to carry tools and smaller materials in and out by hand.

As the job progressed and the depth of the hole increased, a small team stationed up top dropped one end of a rope into the pit. The line came from a new pulley mounted on the northern platform to assist in removing the larger stones. After the gang "underground" attached the rope to a choker fastened around the current block, the group overhead holding onto the other end of the line walked forward toward the ramp and pulled the piece of limestone onto the platform's level surface. Notably, the area in front of the deck had returned to normal because the temporary ramp and the landing erected to haul up the sleds with the chevron blocks from storage was gone. Crews had demolished them before packing the setback in the north wall with filler.

When a block of the standard limestone originating from under the archway landed on the northern platform and was stationary, workers undid the choker and discarded the piece by sending it down the westside ramp. Meanwhile, the excavation work was proceeding along two distinct tracks. The group dealing with the floor below the series of five chevrons was removing blocks from an area approximately 10 feet wide east to west, spanning the distance between the legs of the arches on either side. This team kept going and it was not long before the topmost layer in the floor had disappeared. When the bottom of the hollowed-out space had dropped down as far as engineers wanted it to go (Course 22), the gang in that work zone stopped digging.

At the same time, workers excavating the section of the floor between the northernmost chevron and the edge of the platform would dig down farther until the small area at the north end of the hole dropped lower than the 22nd course to Course 19. It is important to note the placement of some of the features inside the pyramid. The line of chevrons began 15 feet back from the outside wall. While the triangular archway was positioned directly over the Descending Passage situated several courses below it, that passageway did not stop 15 feet back from the pyramid's edge but extended all the way to outer wall at the 19th course. In addition, the deepest part of the new pit at the front (north) end was not as large east to west as the section beneath the chevrons. The portion of the hole by the edge of the platform was only as wide as the gap in the north wall: six feet.

Due to the arrangement below the floor, the team handling the six-foot-wide section would have to break through and dismantle about 18 feet of the upper end of the Descending Passage to be able to drop it low enough to reach Course 19. But rather than demolish everything to the bottom of the hole, the segment that the crew was going to remove would result in at least four feet of the passageway freestanding at the south side of the pit.

As the excavation team at the north end slowly descended, they took apart the passageway's roof and side walls, carefully working around the ropes coming from the counterweight and leaving the tunnel's slanted floor intact. Then, having finally hit their mark and laid the groundwork for the remodeling project to come, the gang that had been jimmying up the blocks used ladders to climb out of the narrow chasm. The space was ready.

Quickly reorganizing, the Egyptians shifted their focus to the next major area of concern: sealing the hole that the crew had just departed by closing up the last break of any significance in the pyramid's north wall.

Tura Limestone Headers

By now, core construction work had moved inside to transform elements of the Great Pyramid that had existed virtually since the construction project began. These changes would prove to be the key to its future. Before any alterations could occur, however, the builders had to figure out a way to roof over the deep chasm that had developed between the northernmost chevron and the outside platform. No doubt attempting to retain a deep hole in the floor, which plunged down to Course 19 at one end, while maintaining the angle of the exterior wall above the pit, presented a singular challenge to closing up the gap.

To further complicate the situation, the underside of the white Tura casing stones workers would insert into the wall also had to serve as the ceiling for the deep trough. Such a risky design choice made it impossible to install that particular set of casing stones in the usual manner. Similar to other locations inside the building, engineering protocols required putting header blocks across the break in the wall because that was the only way to ensure the structural integrity of the roof capping the hole for the long term.

The precisely cut pieces of glossy white limestone quarried for the header blocks were approximately eight feet long, four feet wide, and four feet high, with one side cut to match the 52-degree angle of the exterior wall. Since the peak of the northernmost chevron rose almost 15 feet above the 25th course (the level of the northern platform), the problem the crew had to contend with was how to elevate the heavy blocks that high. Not surprisingly, the answer was to introduce another pulley.

The team had purposely left a narrow band of stairs without any cladding along both sides of the breach. Using ladders, smaller blocks, and other makeshift tools a work gang made its way to the upper level, pulled up the parts for the machine, and assembled it by planting the legs in a couple of holes gouged out of the top step. The device was designed to be especially long east to west because there would be two ropes — one at each end — coming off the header stones. The lines coming from the polished white blocks went underneath then over the pulley-roller before dropping down both sides of the opening toward the platform below.

The job required a total of five header blocks to cover the gap, and the most efficient way to install them, was to start at the bottom and move up. The team's strategy was to use the angled face of a lower block as an incline to help slide the piece into position for the slot above it. While it is impossible for researchers in the 21st century to know for certain, the bottommost header in the group may not have been inserted at this time. Chances are that a portion of the opening designed to hold this initial block, which abutted the

northern platform, sat below the edge of the deck and therefore was not fully
accessible. If this hypothesis is correct, the builders probably modified the
space where the first lintel stone was supposed to go by topping it with some
sort of wooden lid slanted at the same angle as the pyramid's wall. Down the
road, as construction came to an end, but before they totally dismantled the
northern platform, workers would install the lowest header block in that slot.

The blocks designated for the interior ceiling/façade had arrived from Tura
on ships docked near the Sphinx, where they were loaded onto individual
sleds. The vehicles rode up the ramp on the west side of the building, pulled
along by workers tugging on a rope attached to the front end, which rounded
the post-rollers at the northwest corner of the pyramid. After heaving the
initial sled up the western ramp, then east toward the middle of the platform,
they came to a standstill lengthwise (east to west) in front of the rift in the
north wall. Because the gap was about six feet wide but the header blocks
were at least eight feet long, a foot or more was available at either end to sit
solidly on the steps bordering the opening. By dropping a long block across
the gap to straddle the fissure from ledge to ledge, crews would erect a roof
that could not fall into the hole.

Installation work on the succession of header blocks followed a systematic
pattern. Placed horizontally on wooden inserts built into the shallow sled,
the block lay several inches off the floor of the vehicle, which left plenty of
room to fasten one of the pulley ropes around each end. When the crew
had finished rigging the slab, other team members waiting on the northern
platform picked up the opposite end of the lines and began to pull. Heaving
in concert, they tugged on both ropes simultaneously, pushing themselves
forward (north), which caused the long casing stone to slide upward toward
the next step.

Once the base of the stone had cleared the top of the previous block, a
couple of work gangs posted on either side of the staircase began maneuvering
the piece of limestone into the correct position. During the course of adjusting
the block, they also jacked up one end at a time to remove the ropes. When
the alignment was exact, with no deviation between the angled front edge
of the latest header and the one immediately below it (giving the appearance
of a seamless surface), the gangs moved on to the next piece.

After header blocks two through five were safely in their slots, the only task still pending was to address the strips of stairs without their cladding along both sides of the now-concealed gap in the wall. The casing stones included in this next phase were smaller than the eight-foot-long headers because they were sized to fit into the spaces around them. In general, the process resembled the approach that the builders had taken when they were filling in the setback: The crew got rid of the pulley at the top and set up a shadoof on the northern platform to help them lift the remaining pieces for the façade onto the steps one at a time. Occasionally, team members may have also made use of the angle on a second casing stone as a temporary ramp to help elevate a block from one level to another.

Starting with the highest bare step, a small team gathered on the level below it to guide the block hanging from the shadoof's arm into the opening. A narrow lip, formed by the bottom edge of the cladding on the next course up, ran across the top of the hole. The group would slide the new block underneath the tiny overhang to create a uniform surface that visually joined the two rows together.

Shoving the stone back toward the step's riser, they pushed it partway in, then stopped to undo the choker. After that, the crew continued to prod the piece southward until it hit the back wall, always double-checking its placement to ensure that the angles and seams were flawless.

Working their way down from the southernmost header and moving north toward the platform, work gangs gradually enveloped the naked stairs with polished white limestone. Finally, the only exposed breach left in the wall was the six-foot-wide opening adjacent to the northern platform where the bottommost header block was supposed to go.

Platform Overhaul

Ever since the earliest period, when the Great Pyramid reached the height of Course 25, the northern platform had acted not only as an annex to the main construction entrance but also as a staging area — a pathway for workmen, tools, sleds, and supplies entering the site; and the apex of the massive 1,400+-foot-long ramp erected on the north side of the building. But now the platform was about to undergo a major transformation that would alter its contours in the short term and one day, in the not-too-distant future, see it razed altogether.

The next stage of pyramid development revolved around the solitary access point on the north side, where someone could actually enter the building: the opening where the Descending Passage had crossed the outer wall. From the start, the ancient Egyptians conceived of a system driving their massive operation that included an enormous counterweight riding up and down an underground tunnel. A critical factor in the construction equation, the counterweight had proven to be fundamental to the success of the entire enterprise.

At this point, the approximately 25-foot-long block of granite comprising the counterweight — nearly as tall and wide as the channel itself (3' 5" x 47.5") — was locked down. The piece of stone hung just below the bottom end of the shaft known as the First Ascending Passage, now impossible to enter due to the series of outsized blocks plugging up the tunnel's lower end. Ropes tied to the top of the counterweight emerged from inside the pyramid at the 19th course through an aperture in the north wall of the same size as the Descending Passage.

Yet for decades, this hole had been obscured from view because at Course 19, it sat behind the northern platform. The ropes fastened to the counterweight snaked their way underneath the structure by climbing upward through an internal channel and exiting through a hole in the deck. The opening sat behind a wooden roller mounted at floor level on the platform's northern edge, at the point where the center of the primary ramp met the horizontal plane. A team of pullers stationed nearby had regularly used the ropes surfacing from below the platform to reset the counterweight after the lift had transported a load.

At this juncture, preparations were underway to uncover the aperture in the north wall six courses below, where the lines tied to the counterweight exited the building, then refurbish the space around it both inside and out. Reimagining the outlines of the upper reaches of the Descending Passage would eventually transform what was merely a serviceable outlet into an enigmatic portal, portending a whole new era in the story of the Great Pyramid. But before making such a radical change, the team had to dismantle part of the northern platform.

For the second time during a fairly brief period, the Egyptians had implemented a process that involved digging down to reach a lower course instead of building up. Workers were going to remove blocks from the platform to fashion a trench with a sloped floor. The idea was to open up a passageway at the level of Course 19 that started at the hole in the wall and extended to the platform's northern edge. The bottom of the new shaft would ascend south to north in a straight line on a 26-degree angle. By slicing a passable corridor through the platform, beginning at the opening that led from the Descending Passage, the team would be able to move workers and materials in and out of the building with relative ease. In short, the trench currently under construction offered the most direct route to finishing off the monument's interior spaces.

With that objective in mind, the first step was to begin the excavation process by prying up a strip of blocks from the top of the northern platform that would be at least 10 feet wide east to west. The crew on the south side of the deck marked the point on the floor where an imaginary vertical line would hit the center of the opening at Course 19. Then they delineated a rectangular area five feet wide on either side of the chalk mark that went north to the deck's front edge. Since the northern platform was approximately 50 feet north to south, several teams were probably working in tandem, with different gangs tackling the job by dividing it into thirds. Digging down layer by layer, they would pile the chunks of limestone filler onto sleds and send them down the western ramp.

As the hollowed-out space grew deeper, the group laboring at the platform's south end continued excavating until they were within striking distance of the level where the hole in the wall was located (Course 19). This opening — the former threshold to the Descending Passage — was the ticket to getting inside. Once the southernmost work gang had removed enough material so the floor of the trench met the base of the outlet, they stopped. The dig at that end had gone as far down as they wanted it to go.

At the same time, the excavators working on a separate but parallel track near the middle of the trench had eliminated fewer blocks. The floor inside the hole was slated to rise at an angle matching the slope of the underground channel (26 degrees), beginning at the 19th course and stopping about 15 feet short of the north edge of the platform. Consequently, both teams of diggers were installing ramp stones as they worked their way down. In fact, if it were possible for someone to slide down this incline after it was fully built, they would continue downward on the slanted floor and enter the pyramid before plunging down the Descending Passage, headed toward the counterweight. While the low end of the trench touched the bottom of the opening in the outer wall, the depth of the pit steadily decreased on its way up.

The crew at the far end of the trench performed a different task. The builders had calculated the hole's slanted bottom to peak approximately five yards away from the platform's edge. When the incline reached that point, it would level off and the sides of the ditch widen out. Engineers had to compensate for the fact that the original deck was going to have a huge gash through it, which would destroy the only available landing site between the pyramid's egress and the exterior ramp. Work crews needed some type of level surface at the end of the "runway" down the center of the trench to set down the materials conveyed from inside and employ as a staging area for rigging the necessary ropes.

Fanning out east and west, the third group of workers up top eliminated blocks from an area north of the boundary line where the trench-ramp stopped, and began to fabricate a new, more compact deck. The squared-off section they developed — more than 20 feet wide east to west — sat at least eight feet lower than the top of the original platform.

The excavation team kept pushing further north until their makeover activities had also encroached on the northern ramp itself as they also began removing stones from that structure.

After levering up some of the angled blocks on the ramp's summit, workers replaced them with rectangular pieces to transform a defined section at the top of the slope into a level surface. Crews probably recycled some of the rectangular filler blocks previously taken from the platform for this purpose. The result was a deck that began at the upper end of the trench-ramp and extended north 30 feet or more Although the alterations were extensive, they did not force the team to change the basic procedures for transferring blocks. Workers would still be able to tip an object over the front edge of the modified deck onto the northern ramp for the trip downhill.

Decluttering

The builders intended to tidy up the bottommost sections of the pyramid, including the Subterranean Chamber, before remodeling the interior space around Course 19. The reality was that ever since workers had sealed up the Grand Gallery, it had been impossible to get in or out of the lower chambers and channels. Inserting the final corbel in the gallery's north wall had precluded anyone from entering or escaping — even through the Well Shaft. As a consequence, the equipment left below ground was temporarily abandoned. The only other possible way to reach the Subterranean Chamber was by crawling down the Descending Passage but it, too, was choked off as the counterweight obstructed access from the north end. As soon as crew members were able to pull the big chunk of granite through the hole in the wall and get it out of the way, they would let themselves down this shaft to the lowest room in the pyramid. Then they would clear out the tools and machines left behind, along with anything else that didn't belong there.

Enlarging the hole in the wall at Course 19 marked the onset of the next phase of the interior work. This particular area would be bustling with activity in the near term and was scheduled for a major overhaul in the future. Soon, the ancient Egyptians would cover the hole in the exterior wall formerly linked to the Descending Passage with an elegant Tura limestone door. For the moment, however, they were merely going to remove some of the casing stones around the opening to widen it and clear a pathway for the work crews and supplies going in and out of the building.

The primary object engineers wanted moved off-site was the counterweight, and that piece of granite was more than 25 feet long. Luckily, the team had recently erected an exit ramp for the heavy stone when they dug the sloped trench out of the northern platform and altered the deck at the opposite end. The only thing left to do was to re-rig the ropes to draw the block to the top of the underground shaft, up the trench-ramp, and onto the flat surface that had taken a bite out of the upper end of the northern ramp.

Due to the presence of the trench, nothing sat in front of the hole in the wall to impede the counterweight's departure. With that section of the northern platform gone, the internal channel snaking beneath the deck, which had contained the ropes from the giant stone in the Descending Passage, had also disappeared. Although the people constructing the trench-ramp had taken apart the miniature tunnel surrounding the lines, the ropes had not gone anywhere — while dismantling the narrow channel, crew members had carefully set aside the lines as work on the trench proceeded.

The team would soon connect the lines from the counterweight to the pulleys that, for decades, had been standing like a pair of sentinels at the top of the staircases alongside the northern ramp. Those two machines — the workhorses on the pyramid's north side — would once again prove their worth by helping crews drag the counterweight out of the pyramid and onto the deck. Later, the same pair of pulleys would control its journey downward toward the river's edge.

Picking up the set of ropes attached to the counterweight and draping them over the pulleys east and west, workers prepared to extract the lengthy piece of granite from its channel for the first time in almost a century. The block had to cover a fair distance to scale the passageway and emerge from the bowels of the pyramid, but since the slope was only 26 degrees, the process was not overly taxing. Drawn forward from its normal position below what used to be the opening into the First Ascending Passage, the counterweight initially moved more than 90 feet upward to reach the hole in the north wall. Then it climbed another 35 feet or more to the top of the trench-ramp before sliding onto the scaled-down deck and coming to a stop somewhere between the two pulleys.

The pull itself was routine. Teams at the top of the stairs on both sides of the ramp attached themselves to the lines and began walking in sync down the steps. Workers had already carried away hundreds of stones from the staircases to use as filler when they were closing down the construction entrance, but the steps were still roomy enough for a couple of people to stand or move shoulder to shoulder. When the counterweight reached the level surface at the north end of the trench, the pull halted and a work gang prepared to redo the ropes by untying the lines at the center-front of the block first.

The builders planned to release the counterweight by letting it fall to the bottom of the ramp, albeit with some controls. The angle of the slope was not unusually steep (26 degrees), yet a chance remained that given the weight of the granite, the block could take off unexpectedly and speed downhill. To prevent such a catastrophe, workers would remove the set of pull-ropes from the pulleys, then take two more ropes and wind them around the mechanisms in the opposite direction.

The counterweight still had a line fastened around its middle, tucked inside a deep groove that prevented the cord from dragging against the passageway's walls and floor. A crew took the latest two ropes and attached them to the east and west sides of the belt cinched around the block. But this time, they coiled the lines around the pulleys the other way. Instead of passing over the tops of the pulleys, the ropes coming off the stone went under, then over, the rollers before dropping down to the bottom of the staircases. The rigging had changed because the set of ropes was not there to pull, but to act as a braking system to restrain the counterweight as it fell. When the team tipped the stone forward over the front of the deck and it started its descent, the crews controlling the ropes would maintain tension on the lines to break the momentum while slowly climbing up the stairs as the counterweight crept down the incline.

Withdrawing the counterweight from the Descending Passage had opened up a newfound avenue for the work gang appointed to clear out the Subterranean Chamber. The rope that wound around the big wooden spool inside the chamber's doorway was still connected to the counterweight's back end and would have allowed the team to lower themselves down the passageway by holding onto that line — or they may have just crawled down the tunnel by pushing their arms and legs against the walls, since the space was only a few feet wide.

The rope trailing behind the granite block was important for another reason, too: Tying objects to the tail was how the clean-up crew would raise the old equipment and other accumulated junk to the top of the shaft and move it outside the pyramid.

The first articles to go were the pulleys in the lower section of the Descending Passage where it flattened out before entering the Subterranean Chamber. The rollers in that spot had changed the direction of the lines exiting the room horizontally to guide them uphill. The second and largest job the work gang tackled was dismantling the human-sized wooden "hamster wheel" that workers stood inside and revolved to drag the counter-weight down the passageway and move the lift carting a load up the Grand Gallery. After breaking the wheel into smaller pieces, the team grouped the chunks of wood together in bundles and tied the packages to the counter-weight's tail.

The counterweight's descent toward the riverbank must have happened in fits and starts to accommodate the people emptying out the lower chambers. Once they had secured the pulleys from the crook in the passageway, along with the initial bundles of waste materials to the line, a signal alerted the braking team to let the piece of granite drop a little lower. The short drop moved the attachments trailing behind the block farther up the shaft. Then the crew up top locked off the pulleys until another collection of objects hanging lower down the tail was ready to go.

It was not very long before the rest of the equipment, including the bro-ken-down wooden spool, was tied to the rope like tin cans tied to the bumper of a newlywed couple's car. As the counterweight continued dropping and the lead attachments landed on the deck, the downward crawl halted again to allow the team to unfasten the first set of add-ons and transfer them over to the western ramp. When the deck had been cleared of that batch, the counterweight was released to descend a little lower until the next group arrived up top. Stop and go it went until the Subterranean Chamber was emptied and the counterweight reached the riverbank. A good guess is that the Egyptians would load the bulky counterweight onto a ship, then sail around to the docks near the Sphinx to store it in a yard somewhere on the Giza Plateau in anticipation of future jobs.

Years earlier, the builders had employed a specific set of procedures to offload the huge slabs of granite for the Relieving Chambers from the vessels that had sailed them downriver. Now the pattern was reversed. The barge was already waterside with the unlatched gate on the bow lowered onto the solid surface of the ramp. Tied to the dock with ropes knotted around two large posts, one on each side, the vessel was stable and secure. The loading process kicked off with a work gang jacking up the north end of the counterweight and slipping a roller that was a couple of inches in diameter underneath the block. The idea was to start the stone sliding onto a wooden skid that would

provide an exoskeleton for attaching more ropes. Before the team was finished, they made sure the sled was positioned directly in front of the ship at
the centerline.

In a nod to the past, when they had conveyed the Relieving Chamber
blocks into the pyramid, the Egyptians revived the use of the A-frame — the
same equipment that had helped them debark those 70-ton behemoths from
their barges. The granite for the Relieving Chambers had traveled down the
Nile decades earlier and the wooden devices were in storage ever since. For
this job, a flexible A-frame was affixed to the barge's interior walls — port
and starboard — with pins pushed through holes at the base of the legs. But
now, instead of leaning toward the back of the boat as it had done the last
time, the heavy frame would bend southward toward the Great Pyramid.

Tilting the A-frame toward the ramp, workers took a couple of ropes
attached at the corners on the south side of the crossbeam and tied them to
the front of the skid holding the counterweight. Another set of lines secured
to the opposite (north) face of the crossbeam went around the pulley-roller
mounted on the giant hook built into the stern. Meanwhile, crews had installed
two more pulleys further up the center section of the ramp, a short distance
beyond the skid — high enough for the pulling angle to work.

The ropes extending from the roller at the back of the ship went over
the new land-based pulleys before dropping down the incline to the pullers
waiting along both sides, who picked up the lines and attached them to their
harnesses. This time, the cargo would be heading in the opposite direction
from the route the Relieving Chamber blocks had taken — toward the river
versus toward the pyramid. Tugging on the ropes as they walked down the
slope, the pull-teams gradually stood the A-frame upright. From leaning
over toward the ramp and practically touching the floor, they swung it to full
height, hauling the sled forward and onto the ship as the device rotated. The
workers continued pulling until the skid toting the slab of granite was safely
centered in the barge, with its weight evenly distributed. To get the vessel
underway, the ship's crew disconnected all of the ropes and laid the A-frame
down on the deck before setting sail.

One final decluttering chore still waited in the wings: sealing off the
bottom of the Inspection or Well Shaft. Recessed into the west wall of the

Descending Passage, the opening to the Well Shaft sat approximately 25 feet north of the elbow in the passageway where it straightened out — a little less than 30 feet away from the Subterranean Chamber's door. The nook where the Well Shaft started was only about three feet wide north to south and three feet deep east to west as measured from the front edge. Climbing upward from the hole in the wall, the shaft cut through the bedrock and the pyramid's lower courses until it reached the bottom of the Grand Gallery.

All told, the space to be filled probably required two dressed blocks sitting on top of one another to close up the void. Since the chunks of limestone were relatively small, they may have been tucked into a corner of the Subterranean Chamber and been there for years, or the team could have slid them down the Descending Passage once the equipment and debris were cleared out. After a work gang inserted the filler blocks into the opening, they took plaster and covered up the seams, making it impossible to see around the edges or inside the hole. By the time the patching job was completed, any evidence of a hole leading to a vertical channel was gone.

A Walk Under the Chevrons

All systems were go for putting the final touches on the pyramid's interior. Plans included modifying the opening where the Descending Passage had penetrated the outer wall — to transform the area into the principal entrance for the Great Pyramid. There was one problem, however: Currently, people accessing the building from outside through the enlarged hole at Course 19 might fall because they would be stepping onto the passageway's original slanted floor.

When workers were digging down from the 25th to the 19th course, they had removed the ceiling and walls on both sides of the short section of the tunnel near the top, but they had not altered the floor. For cleanup crews to be able to extract the counterweight and other surplus materials from the bottom of the passageway and the Subterranean Chamber, the floor had to continue at a 26-degree angle all the way to the top.

Since a sloped floor was no longer necessary for equipment purposes, the team was able to alleviate the slippage problem by leveling a small area right inside the threshold of the future entrance to the pyramid. Using standard blocks, a crew evened out several feet of the floor near the top. With the sides of the Descending Passage missing, the renovated space was a little more than six feet wide east to west, including the narrow center section (3' 5") that represented the former floor plus bands on either side about a foot and a half wide where the wall blocks had been. The two horizontal walkways extended from the hole in the north wall to the freestanding opening that led into the truncated Descending Passage.

ENTRANCE AT COURSE 19 · STEPS

Two short sets of stairs, which climbed up to the header block over the entrance to the shortened Descending Passage tunnel, led visitors underneath the chevron archway toward the center of the pyramid.

In terms of the general layout, the entrance into the descending passageway that crews had overhauled sat approximately four feet further north than the front edge of the northernmost chevrons found several courses overhead. This put the revamped entry to the tunnel south of the hole in the outer wall at

Course 19. Because the upper end of the original shaft was gone, the opening to get inside resembled the mouth of a squared-off cave with a large header block above it. The Griffith theory states that this header had been there since the passageway was constructed. By contrast, the segment of the Descending Passage that the team had dismantled earlier was composed of smaller, more manageable blocks. Since the builders knew well in advance that they would have to break down the uppermost section someday, integrating outsized header stones into that portion of the tunnel was never part of the design.

Taking into account the height of the passageway (47.5") and the thickness of the limestone slab over the entry, the top of the header block was approximately eight feet off the floor. During the next phase of construction, crews planned to fabricate steps that would allow a visitor to climb on top of the header stone and launch a journey beneath the chevrons into the heart of the Great Pyramid.

ENTRANCE AT COURSE 19 · LAYOUT

Looking south, a confluence of factors is evident in the layout of the interior space near the entrance at Course 19: the opening into the Descending Passage, the steps up to the chevron archway, and the path underneath the chevrons leading to the pyramid's core.

Workers had only flattened out a few feet of the angled floor inside the threshold on Course 19, which meant that an incline still existed between where the modified part of the floor stopped and the redesigned entrance to the descending passageway began. Since the substantial piece of limestone seated above the entry extended to the outer edges of the narrow walkways on both sides of the angled portion (the flat areas where the walls used to be), workers erected two short staircases on those level surfaces east and west. The sets of stairs probably consisted of five steps about 16 inches high each, which fell a little short of the top of the lintel stone over the entrance. The final tread that would take someone up to the height of 96 inches (eight feet) was stepping onto the header block itself.

When someone arrived on top of the header block and strolled southward several feet, they were confronted by a second limestone slab as wide and thick as the one underfoot. The second slab was actually part of the floor underneath the chevrons. Stair-steps erected on top of the lintel above the opening to the Descending Passage spanned the vertical distance between the two large blocks. In an amazing feat of architectural prowess, the builders had arranged it so the people who climbed those last few steps would find themselves walking beneath the dramatic triangular archway.

According to the Griffith theory, an ancient Egyptian would have been able to enter the building during this era, and by following the route laid out on Course 19, experience the double-arched room. Furthermore, visitors could wander even deeper into the monument and access the very heart of the pyramid by passing through an opening behind the southernmost set of chevrons — the site where 21st-century researchers have discovered an anomaly that appears to be a void.

• Strabo Stone •

The Griffith theory contends that for centuries the area behind the chevron-shaped double archway had served as an entry point into the center of the Great Pyramid. (The last two chevrons from the original archway—the southernmost set—are still visible on the north side of the building.) Only much later in the monument's history was this opening sealed up, perhaps when the ancient Egyptians no longer supported a priesthood or when political or other circumstances made it necessary to keep unwanted visitors out.

STRABO STONE
The Strabo Stone

The large white-colored stone evident beneath the remaining chevrons is deceptive. With the pyramid's Tura limestone cladding still intact throughout most of the pyramid's history, and the only door into the structure a mere six feet wide, it would have been impossible to transport a stone of that size inside. The more likely scenario is that whoever covered up the entrance used smaller blocks then plastered over them to make it appear as if they were one large stone.

The tan-colored carving underneath the gable at the top of the arch that resembles the humps on a camel is called the Strabo Stone. This oddly shaped block mimics the contours of the hieroglyph for "akhet," which depicts the sun rising over a mountain. Egyptologists have also translated this figure to mean the "horizon of heaven." At one time this ancient culture may have placed a metal disk in between the two humps to represent the sun.

Given its meaning and significance, the wavy block in front along with the triangular slabs of limestone positioned behind it must have been part of the original construction. Because the Strabo Stone represents the idea of crossing the boundary to heaven it would have been an apt symbol residing directly over the pathway into the Great Pyramid's core. While the purpose of the divided piece of limestone set further back was likely twofold. It would have maintained the privacy of the inner sanctum against anyone trying to peer inside and obstructed access to the interior recesses of the building.

CHAPTER 25

ETERNAL SEAL

THE EGYPTIANS HAD ACHIEVED the impossible, and only two small openings stood in the way of securing the Great Pyramid for good. From the outset, the architects had planned to install at least one door into the building, but that entry would be concealed from the rest of the world. While the massive structure was not a tomb, it still fulfilled a critical purpose and held great spiritual significance in its own right. The ancient builders could never have imagined it turning into a public venue.

Those initiates who understood the rites and rituals that occurred within the pyramid's chambers would be welcomed into the inner sanctum, but not everyone was supposed to wander inside. Whether the builders realized it or not, people who were drawn to the imposing structure yet only able to view it from outside would also benefit from the experience. The monument's mystery and majesty exerted a kind of magnetic pull that was difficult to escape. Shining like a beacon reflecting the rays of a blazing sun, the Great Pyramid spoke to everyone who encountered its presence — even from afar. Just as it does today.

An Extraordinary Door

The moment had finally arrived to close up the pyramid, as well as the ramps and platforms that had defined the Giza Plateau as a construction zone. The initial step in the process was installing a single door made of polished white limestone and tucked into the siding on the north wall — a barrier meant to protect the Great Pyramid's secrets for posterity.

The second-to-last piece of cladding the Egyptians intended to insert into the façade on the north side would be this beautiful door, mounted on hinges and precisely balanced by an internal counterweight. Provisions for the new door included finishing out the frame around the hole in the wall at Course 19, which had acted as a service entrance during the remodeling process. The very last piece of cladding in the wall would be the lowest Tura limestone header block that was missing from the wall in the space between the double archway and the northern platform. The slot for the fifth and final header stone sat right above the gap for the entrance and would function as the top of the doorframe.

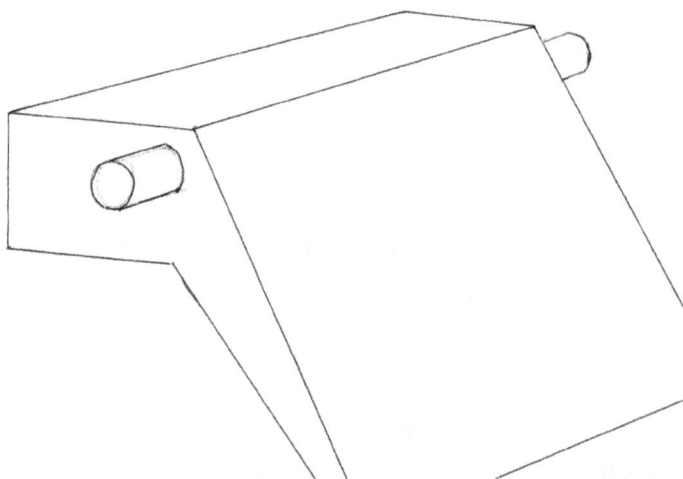

TURA DOOR · CLOSEUP

The six-foot-wide door into the pyramid was composed of the same polished white limestone as the façade and cut to be precisely balanced by an internal counterweight.

The doorframe's base was already in place, formed by the casing stones underfoot on the 18th course. The length of the blocks at the bottom north to south was about four feet — deep enough to stand on. The next two pieces the team deposited around the opening were the doorjambs flanking the hole. Designed to hold a six-foot-wide 10- to 20-ton door, the slabs of white limestone inserted left and right were six feet tall. Stonecutters had scooped out a channel along the inside edge of each block to cradle the hinges jutting out from the sides of the door, which were approximately 12 inches in diameter and at least a foot long. The deep furrows workers had carved into the doorjambs began at the top, six or more inches back from the front of the stone (the face cut at a 52-degree angle), and continued a good 18 inches downward from the block's upper edge. Once the team inserted the hinges into these grooves, the door would be able to swing up and down.

The meticulously engineered door came downriver by barge from the quarries at Tura, but rather than docking near the Sphinx as the ships coming from that region normally did, the barge arrived at the bottom of the northern ramp. Tied to a wooden sled, the finished piece of limestone lay on its face, angled side down, with the base leading uphill and the hinges sticking out east and west. The load was heavy enough for the crew to use the same technique — involving an A-frame — to handle the job of getting it off the boat as the process they had recently employed to move the counterweight onto its vessel. This time, though, the cargo was heading in the other direction.

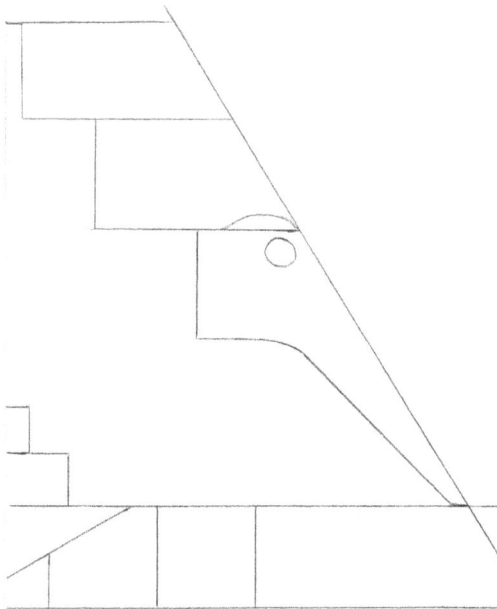

TURA DOOR · SIDE VIEW
The door was mounted to open out. When closed, it appeared to become part of the cladding covering the Great Pyramid.

Once again, the legs of a tall A-frame were attached to the ship's interior at port and starboard, which let the frame rotate and either stand up vertically or lie down over the deck. Four ropes fastened to the corners of the crossbeam on the side, facing the center of the river, were tied to the sled's back end.

Workers had also connected four more lines to the A-frame's legs on the same side: two on the east leg and two on the west one. Those ropes stretched to the pulley mounted horizontally on the giant hook that was built into the stern. When the sled carrying the special door began to move forward, the crew onboard would hang onto the lines curled around the pulley in back to keep them taut as the frame leaned over toward the shoreline to debark the load. They had to maintain tension on the ropes because keeping the lines rigid was the only way to keep the unwieldy A-frame from falling over too far.

The pair of pulleys erected on the riverbank partway up the center of the ramp, which workers had previously used to transfer the counterweight, were still operational. After a work gang had fastened a separate set of ropes to the opposite (land) side of the A-frame's crossbeam, they wrapped those ropes around the pulleys. Clasping the loops woven into the pull-ropes and attaching them to their harnesses, workers walking down the ramp would assist in hauling the sled onshore. The final two lines went around the pulleys at the top of the ramp by the edge of the northern platform at Course 25. Secured to the front of the sled, this set traveled all the way up the incline, over the pulley-rollers at the top, and back down to a couple of teams posted on the staircases along both sides of the ramp.

The signal to start pulling set all three teams into motion. The people at the center of the ramp managing the ropes from the lower set of pulleys walked toward the water, heaving on the A-frame's crossbeam and leaning it toward the pyramid. At the same time, the pullers coming down the steps drew the sled southward as the sailors holding onto the lines curved around the roller at the back of the barge inched their way down the main deck, putting the full force of their weight against the power of the heavy frame tilting in the opposite direction. At some point, the system overcame inertia and the loaded sled slid off the vessel to begin its journey up the slope.

When it touched down on the ramp and momentum took over, crews disconnected the lines tied to the back of the sled as it crawled up the hill, but the crew assigned to the lower set of pulleys partway up the slope stayed on their ropes. Now it was up to them — in concert with the crew controlling the lines at the back of the ship — to carefully set the A-frame on the deck so the barge could sail away.

The job of transporting the sled up to the top of the incline was regulated by the teams of pullers marching down the sets of stairs that ran parallel to the ramp while tugging on the ropes. And when the first group in line had gone as far as they could go in approaching the river, workers peeled off to walk back up to the top and take their place behind the last people in the queue. The process was akin to a relay race, where a member of the squad swaps places after handing off the baton to a teammate. Changing out the positions at the back of the lineup kept the pull going and the sled continuously progressing upward — until it reached the front edge of the revamped deck on the northern platform and was moving toward the trench-ramp.

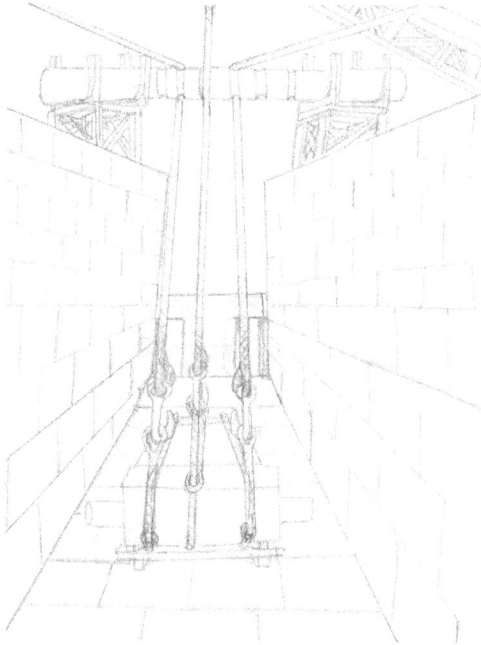

TRENCH-RAMP AND TURA DOOR

A pulley mounted next to the pyramid above the trench-ramp elevated the multi-ton door toward the hole in the north wall.

To make the transition from the primary ramp's 26-degree angled surface to the horizontal plane, the groups handling the ropes just kept pulling, which made the leading edge on the sled rise higher against the platform. Eventually, the weight shifted and, having reached the tipping point, caused the vehicle to lie down flat on the deck. This switchover was feasible due to the angle of the ropes. Since the front end on the modified section of the deck sat several courses lower and farther north than the pulleys on the edge of the original platform at Course 25, the pullers were able to haul the sled southward toward the pyramid.

Once the sled had settled on the level surface, the activity came to a halt to allow the riggers to redo the ropes. A work gang had already positioned another pulley-stand right next to the pyramid, above the opening at Course 19, with its legs straddling the trench's south end. The device sported a single long roller and stood about eight feet tall. To prepare the loaded vehicle for the next stage of its journey, workers detached the original pull-ropes and tied two lines to the sled's front end. Placed near the roller's east and west ends, the new ropes went underneath and over the top of the pulley. Then a couple of pull-teams picked up the lines and walked across the deck and partway down the northern ramp — dragging the sled south toward the bottom of the trench-ramp and the hole in the wall.

Workers had also placed a short, angled stone at the juncture where the trench-ramp met the north wall — with the slanted face aimed up the side of the building. The approximately two-foot-long incline was there to assist them in moving the door from a downward trajectory to drawing it upward above the doorjambs. The team may have also placed some type of soft material on the floor to cushion the area before standing the door upright. The objective was to avoid chipping off fragments of the finely cut, straight-edged limestone, which had to fit perfectly into the Great Pyramid's unblemished façade.

When the cargo reached the wall, a work gang readjusted the lines again in preparation for sliding the door upward and lowering it into its frame. Since the door had been loaded onto the sled with its base facing the building, the team did not have to adjust the piece to set it upright. In addition, the way the wooden sled was designed made it possible to wrap a couple of chokers around the block's mid-section and encircle it from the base to the upper edge. The loops on the chokers were rendered toward the top to ensure that the correct side led as crews lifted the weight. To further assist them in raising the awkward piece of limestone, which may have weighed as much as 20 tons, workers had installed a shadoof on the platform by the north wall in the area immediately west of the trench. Adding that device resulted in a third choker, capable of hooking onto the shadoof secured around the door's midsection between the other two.

Ropes attached to the initial pair of chokers went over the top of the pulley straddling the trench, which was tall enough to elevate the block. At the same time, a second gang had lowered the shadoof's arm and hooked it onto the loop on the middle choker. The first step in the lifting process was to slowly raise the door as workers loosened the skid by cutting the ropes binding it to the underside of the limestone. After separating the block from the sled, the team stood the door on its bottom edge (the one closest to the pyramid), then leaned it slightly southward, letting the hinges rest against the doorjambs. The direction the door had traveled up the ramp from the riverbank meant that when it was standing upright, the face slanted at 52 degrees — part of the cladding — ended up on the north side.

Step number two was to lift the bulky door high enough to suspend the hinges a few inches above the tops of the doorjambs. From that position, and with only minor adjustments, the team would be able to drop both sides straight down into their slots. With the door now in its frame and capable of swinging up and down, workers raised it partway and shoved a wooden wedge beneath the front end to hold it open. Then they removed the chokers.

One Last Void

The doorframe was not whole yet — the section across the top was missing. Every element was duly organized to install the last Tura limestone header above the refurbished space on the 19th course, and in the process, seal up the last big cavity in the Great Pyramid's north wall. Header number five had come off a ship from Tura that had docked at the bottom of the ramp. Oriented north to south on its sled, the block was longer than the wooden carrier, overhanging the vehicle by a few feet at either end. Since the piece was composed of limestone and only about four feet high, four feet wide, and eight feet long, it wasn't exceedingly heavy. A group of workers pulling on the ropes around the pulleys on the northern platform would be able to haul the load off the barge and raise it up the slope.

When the sled eventually made its way up the incline and was sitting on the level surface of the lower deck, the crew up top rotated it east to west

— turning the block in the direction that it would go into the wall. Detaching the ropes from the front of the sled, the crew exchanged the original lines for the latest set from the pulley straddling the trench. Because the piece of limestone hung over the sides, they had enough room to fasten a rope around each end, which would enable the pullers to drag the block down the trench-ramp and leave it next to the north wall.

Before the stone advanced toward its final destination, the builders had installed a set of wooden rails, approximately eight inches thick, on both doorjambs several inches away from the edge of the door. Climbing up to the opening above the doorframe (the slot where the last header was supposed to go), the tracks made a right-angled turn south and continued partway into the empty cavity.

The plan was to employ a proven process by making use of the 52-degree angle of the outer wall as a temporary ramp to help elevate the final casing stone before pushing it into the hole. Similar to the other four headers in that section of the wall, the eight-foot-long slab was designed to sit atop two small ledges formed by the blocks adjacent to the opening east and west. When workers slide the piece onto the ledges, the single remaining gap in the cladding would cease to exist.

To accomplish such a task, crews had to rearrange the lines again. Detaching the pull-ropes responsible for delivering the block to the bottom of the trench, they wrapped a couple of chokers around the slab at each end, approximately two feet in from the edges. The chokers were rendered near the back of the stone (the face cut at an angle) in anticipation of the lifting process. The position of a choker was important because wherever the loop ended up represented the side of the load that was going to rise up first.

After slicing through the lines tied around the block to separate it from the sled, the work gang prepared to raise the header by taking the ropes from the pulley overhead and connecting them to the chokers. Given the signal to pull, the two teams began walking north, causing the block to slowly stand before starting up the wooden rails scaling the side of the building.

As the header block ascended and reached the top of the door (the opening where the tracks made a turn), it tipped slightly forward so the base rested on the cavity's front edge. With the slot at the top of the doorframe only six feet above the bottom of the trench-ramp, the team had constructed scaffolding that had a small platform to help them maneuver the block into position. Using lever bars, the group jacked up the piece high enough off the rails to slip them out from underneath. Then, after removing the chokers, they eased the stone down to the ledges bordering the gap.

The final step was to push the block farther south until the face on that side was even with the back of the door. (The crew may have also spread a thin layer of Tafla clay or other type of slurry on the ledges flanking the hole to reduce friction and help the limestone slide in more easily.)

Since this block was part of the frame by which the door mechanism worked, stonecutters had precut a groove east to west on the underside of the header, a few inches back from the angled front edge. The concave channel provided a sufficient amount of room for the door to rotate to open and shut. Because the indentation ran across the bottom of the stone, it was invisible from the north side of the monument and did not spoil the look of the smooth exterior wall.

It was also true that like other locations inside the Great Pyramid where crews had inserted a block into a wall somewhat after the fact, the lintel stone had arrived from the quarry slanted on top to a certain degree, which made the north end of the block slightly taller than the south end. Moreover, the width of the block east to west had also diminished. The back end was shaved a fraction narrower than the front end. A perfect rectangle would have been too tight for the opening, requiring workers to force it into the slot. Refining the block's dimensions by a negligible amount meant that the "plug" would not only slip into its hole with ease but also lie flat against the surface of the wall.

Demolition

It is difficult to imagine how the ancient Egyptians must have felt on realizing that their pyramid was effectively complete. The entire structure was sealed up and for the moment, only a single door — six feet tall and six feet wide, and concealed within an outer wall that was 755 feet long end to end — permitted access to the building. But the celebrations were going to have to wait because the job would not really be finished until the platforms and ramps surrounding the Great Pyramid were dismantled, and when those structures were gone, people had a way to reach the secret doorway at Course 19 that was 70 feet above the ground.

It was all hands on deck when the builders began breaking down the ramps and platforms that had transferred people and supplies to and from the building site for more than a century. Since construction had ended at the northern platform, that was where work crews initiated the dismantling project. After getting rid of extraneous materials and equipment, the teams assigned to the platform and the lower deck associated with the trench would proceed to eliminate a massive volume of blocks encompassing a widespread area, and their efforts would not let up until they had worked their way down to ground level. Clearing out key parts of the infrastructure and related features that had made pyramid building possible unquestionably would take a long time.

For the most part, the deconstruction process consisted of prying up one block at a time — layer by layer. Employing shadoofs to lift the individual pieces of limestone by their chokers and drop them onto sleds, work gangs were poised to transport the discarded filler down the western ramp. The Egyptians probably held onto the dressed stones retrieved from the northern platform and the other structures they were breaking down. A ready supply of thousands of precut blocks would be a boon to future construction projects such as a *mastaba* or smaller pyramid.

The shadoof set up earlier on the south side of the platform to assist the work gang installing the door remained in place. Its arm was long enough to reach across the 10-foot-wide trench to transfer blocks brought over from the platform's east end to the other side of the gap and place them on sleds. Several more shadoofs assembled further north on top of the lower deck were picking up blocks unearthed from the work zone so crews could convey them to a storage area on the Giza Plateau.

The demolition process was not haphazard, and in many respects resembled a production line. The builders had to remain vigilant, since the routine they established would not work without taking a crucial factor into consideration: The only way the team would be able to keep extracting blocks was if the height of the entire surface on top were reduced with every layer they removed. For example, in the beginning, the crew posted east of the trench who were prying up the platform's upper layer and hooking the blocks onto the shadoof could not dig farther down because the machine's arm would have been too high, unable to reach the row below the top layer to catch another stone. As workers across the site handling the lever bars kept excavating blocks and lowering the floor, the height of every section of their work space — including the ramp on the building's west side — had to decrease in kind.

The challenge lay in trying to drop the floor and at the same time, keep it even. The restraint meant eliminating the stones from a single layer before moving on to the next level down to maintain a smooth, horizontal surface for transporting blocks and sleds over to the western ramp. Since the intersection where the floor met the ramp on the west side had to remain even and free of bumps or potholes, workers were also lowering that incline on a regular basis in concert with the progress made in tearing out the platforms. It was incumbent on every crew member to be aware of and work in unison with the other teams as they carted away filler stones. Otherwise, an irregular floor or blocks scattered around in disorganized piles might cause a delay in sending the materials down to the base of the pyramid. As a result, demolition across the site was highly coordinated in terms of its sequence and timing.

While a tremendous amount of work was occurring on the platforms at the top, a separate demolition team was attacking the primary ramp. Over the course of several years, the builders had removed and reused countless blocks from the steps running alongside the northern ramp as they narrowed down the two staircases. But its center section — at least 30 feet wide — had never been touched. Even excluding the portion at the top, which the builders had lowered and leveled out to accommodate the counterweight, the structure was still more than a third of a mile long. Rising from the riverbank, it stretched well beyond the edge of the Giza Plateau and up to the platform at the 25th course or almost 70 feet higher than the pyramid's base. There were thousands upon thousands of stones to carry away.

The crew tackling the ramp started at the top near the front edge of the lower deck and worked their way down. But instead of transporting the excavated blocks uphill to the west side of the pyramid, the ramp-team either pushed or used lengths of rope to pull the blocks of limestone toward the river. In general, the procedure mirrored the system employed in deconstructing the northern platform because workers were prying up individual pieces from the ramp and removing a single layer at a time. As they descended, the work gangs purposely retained an incline down the center — a slanted surface would allow them to continue to slide the upcoming stones toward the bottom. As soon as one layer was gone, crews using lever bars began to jimmy up blocks in the row beneath it. On and on they went, dismantling the main ramp leading to the pyramid until, after an enormous amount of time and effort, what had once been a long, protracted slope rising from the Nile would vanish altogether.

When the excavated blocks reached the water's edge, a couple of shadoofs on the riverbank loaded them onto small barges. One possibility has the ships sailing the castoff filler stones over to the docks near the Sphinx where they were unloaded and set on sleds and crews then transported them up the causeway to a storage area somewhere on the plateau. A good guess is that the builders stored the extra blocks near one of the quarries, since those facilities were already equipped to move heavy chunks of stone in and out.

It is impossible to pin down exactly how long it may have taken to demolish the giant platforms and ramps gracing the pyramid's north and west sides. Judging from what visitors see today, all we know for certain is that the ancient builders succeeded at their task. And while it may seem as if the construction era in the history of the Great Pyramid had come to an end, the Egyptians had other ideas. They were gearing up to fabricate a small but critical addition to their massive monument: a way to unlock the front door and go inside.

Portico

In the midst of stripping down the northern platform, work crews had treated one particular area as a discrete project. They wanted to transform the space below the hidden door in the north wall — between it and the base of the building — into a trim portico in the shape of a step-pyramid. The structure would be 70 feet high and extend out a good 30 feet on three sides. Since the porch-like addition was supposed to sit against the larger pyramid, it did not include a fourth, stepped wall at the back. The steps would be approximately two feet deep and 12 inches high, rising at a 52-degree angle, with the three staircases converging in a 10- to 12-foot-square platform at the top. Architects had sited the small pyramid to place the swinging door in the center on the landing's south side.

As the gangs of excavators were unearthing blocks in the northern platform, the team assigned to the area below the new door had not totally cleared out the area at the bottom by the north wall. Rather, they had added blocks in several places while also refilling part of the trench to delete the slope. Their job was to rework the stacks of blocks on the platform's interior and gradually turn them into something else. The tiered levels they fashioned, jutting out north, east, and west, would climb toward the 19th course and unite in a horizontal landing at the threshold of the hidden doorway.

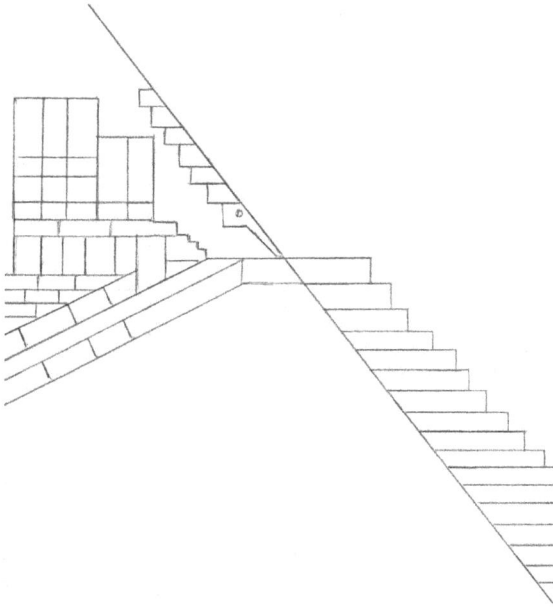

TURA DOOR IN SITU

This representation of the interior of the pyramid at Course 19 shows the hidden door and staircase associated with the portico on the right-hand side. The Descending Passage and short set of stairs leading to the area beneath the chevrons are depicted toward the left.

The finished portico consisted of ordinary filler blocks recycled from the demolition project under an outer shell of white Tura limestone. Based on the foresight and planning that the ancient Egyptians consistently demonstrated throughout the construction process, they probably stored the polished casing stones to sheath the portico's steps and summit on-site by building them into the northern platform early on. That way, when the time came to cover the addition with cladding, the raw materials would be readily at hand.

WAS-SCEPTER

Depicted on tomb and temple walls, the was-scepter symbolized power and dominion. An emblem of authority, this special staff was most often associated with the ancient Egyptians' gods. The Griffith theory suggests that in addition to its more metaphysical meaning, the was- scepter may have also served as a type of key. With that idea in mind, and recognizing that the shape at the top of the rod resembles a crowbar, a case could be made that the builders may have used this tool to help open the hidden door in the north wall of the Great Pyramid. Moreover, the length of the scepter would have allowed a priest, pharaoh, or other VIP to avoid having to bend over to slide the tip of the staff beneath the door's front edge.

As the rest of the northern platform and exterior ramps were fading away, the new step-pyramid — flush against the north wall — was slowly coming together. And the decision to clad it in pure white limestone, consistent with the Great Pyramid's façade, dispelled any notion that the portico was an afterthought. In fact, the structure was not merely an addition; it was central to fulfilling the project's core purpose. Priests, government officials, and other important members of the spiritual or social castes had to be able to get into the monument. The portico provided the only available route to that single point of entry.

A visitor who came up the steps to the platform atop the new step-pyramid would be able to take a blade or flat piece of metal and, using it like a crowbar, slip it underneath the door's front edge to pry it open. The perfectly balanced counterweight (a bulge of limestone at the back end) made the door open effortlessly, permitting entrants to crawl through the opening and let the mechanism shut it behind them. Once inside, they would be able to reopen the door and exit by simply pushing their hands against the bottom of the stone to make it swing out. Since the piece of limestone was only six feet tall in its frame, the bulkiest part of the block representing the counterweight did not leave enough room for anyone of normal height to walk through the entrance standing upright. Admittance into the Great Pyramid required a modicum of humility because it forced everyone to bend down.

• Into the Pyramid •

Archeologists have long suspected the existence of more than one entrance built into the sides of the Great Pyramid. Drawings of hypothetical porticos leading up to these potential doorways often include columns or other decorative features. According to the Griffith theory, there may indeed have been other ways to get inside the Great Pyramid at the time of its construction, but because those access points are not evident today, their existence is merely guesswork.

On the other hand, historical records have revealed the presence of at least one formal entryway on the north side. Whether it was a

step-pyramid that led up to the door or some other type of structure —
or whether the style of the addition was plain or elaborate — is largely
irrelevant to the primary issue. The problem the ancient Egyptians
successfully solved was getting the people inside.

PORTICO

Artist's rendering of the portico on the north side of the
Great Pyramid.

Timeless Monument

After a century-long effort, the Great Pyramid was finally complete. A byzantine mass of component parts had coalesced to produce an astonishing edifice whose presence shimmered in the blazing sun and would strike awe in the human heart. One more step awaited the Egyptians, though: performing the rites and rituals to formally consecrate a monument, which was built on sacred ground and would forever point toward the heavens.

This ancient culture must have been in touch with something profound — a state of consciousness unknown to most of humanity — to be able to develop such a structure, for even now, its beauty and mystery are mesmerizing. The Great Pyramid of Giza was the product of a people whose foresight, passion, and resolve led them to construct a tribute in stone to the potential of the human spirit — a silent witness to the creative forces at work in the Earth.

But perhaps the pyramid's most important legacy is what it can teach us about ourselves. Rising ever skyward and concealing secrets we can only imagine; its very presence seems to stir something deep within the soul. The Great Pyramid is a constant reminder to turn our gaze higher and remember that there is more to life than the here and now: what we see, hear, taste, touch, and smell ... even as it conveys the lesson of humility before the genius of those unnamed visionaries who bequeathed this ancient wonder to the ages.

While the riddle of how the Great Pyramid was constructed is not fully solved yet, the Griffith theory maintains that it is well within our reach to do so. The birth of the pyramid signified the birth of the best that the human race has to offer to the world. And we have the capacity to achieve that level of perfection again.

For countless centuries, the hypnotic pull of the Great Pyramid of Giza has challenged our preconceived notions and impelled us to reflect on its meaning and purpose. Is this architectural marvel merely a feature on the landscape to be investigated, measured, and analyzed? Or is it the timeless call to explore the great mystery that lives inside each of us?

RANDY L. GRIFFITH is a former ironworker who has spent more than 30 years researching the Great Pyramid. His new theory about its construction was developed in answer to a seminal question: If an ironworker were asked to build this edifice, how would he do it? Randy previously published *When Above Was Not Named Heaven* from the cuneiform script of the ancient Babylonian creation story, the Enūma Eliš.

M.K. WELSCH is an accomplished writer who spent the majority of her professional career in the not-for-profit world. She is the author of *Sacred Journey: Edgar Cayce, the Bible, and the Path to Enlightenment* published by A.R.E. Press. A lifelong student of metaphysics, M.K. is passionate about understanding the deeper questions of life, including unraveling the secrets behind one of the greatest mysteries of them all, the Great Pyramid of Giza.

www.ingramcontent.com/pod-product-compliance
Lightning Source LLC
Chambersburg PA
CBHW060304030426
42336CB00011B/924